**Evolutionary Dynamics
and Extensive Form Games**

Economic Learning and Social Evolution
General Editor
Ken Binmore, Director of the Economic Learning and Social Evolution Centre, University College London.

Evolutionary Dynamics and Extensive Form Games

Ross Cressman

The MIT Press
Cambridge, Massachusetts
London, England

This book was set in Palatino by Interactive Composition Corporation (in LATEX) and was printed and bound in the United States of America.

Library of Congress Cataloging-in-Publication Data

Cressman, Ross.
    Evolutionary dynamics and extensive form games / Ross Cressman.
       p.   cm. — (Economic learning and social evolution ; 5)
    Includes bibliographical references and index.
    ISBN 0-262-03305-4 (hc. : alk. paper)
    1. Game theory.   2. Evolution—Mathematical models.   I. Title.   II. MIT Press series on economic learning and social evolution ; 5.

QA269 .C69   2003
519.3—dc21   2002038682

Contents

Series Foreword

The MIT Press series on Economic Learning and Social Evolution reflects the continuing interest in the dynamics of human interaction. This issue has provided a broad community of economists, psychologists, biologists, anthropologists, mathematicians, philosophers, and others, with a sense of common purpose so strong that traditional interdisciplinary boundaries have melted away. We reject the outmoded notion that what happens away from equilibrium can safely be ignored, but think it no longer adequate to speak in vague terms of bounded rationality and spontaneous order. We believe the time has come to put some beef on the table.

The books in the series so far are:

- *Evolutionary Games and Equilibrium Selection*, by Larry Samuelson (1997). Traditional economic models have only one equilibrium, and so fail to come to grips with social norms whose function is to select an equilibrium when there are multiple alternatives. This book studies how such norms may evolve.

- *The Theory of Learning in Games*, by Drew Fudenberg and David Levine (1998). Von Neumann introduced "fictitious play" as a way of finding equilibria in zero-sum games. In this book the idea is reinterpreted as a learning procedure, and developed for use in general games.

- *Just Playing*, by Ken Binmore (1998). This book applies evolutionary game theory to moral philosophy. How and why do we make fairness judgments?

- *Social Dynamics*, edited by Steve Durlauf and Peyton Young (2001). The essays in this collection provide an overview of the field of social dynamics, in which some of the creators of the field discuss a variety of approaches, including theoretical model-building, empirical studies, statistical analyses, and philosophical reflections.

- *Evolutionary Dynamics and Extensive Form Games,* by Ross Cressman (2003). How is evolution affected by the timing structure of games? Does it generate backward induction? The answers show that orthodox thinking needs a lot of revision in some contexts.

Authors who share the ethos represented by these books, or who wish to extend it in empirical, experimental, or other directions, are cordially invited to submit outlines of their proposed books for consideration. Within our terms of reference, we hope that a thousand flowers will bloom.

Ken Binmore
ESRC Center for Economic Learning
and Social Evolution
University College London
Gower Street
London WC1E 6BT, UK
k.binmore@ucl.ac.uk

Preface

This book is a sequel to my earlier monograph, *The Stability Concept of Evolutionary Game Theory: A Dynamic Approach*, published some ten years ago in the series, Lecture Notes in Biomathematics. The final chapter of the monograph included material on the (dynamic) analysis of extensive form games meant to convince the reader of their untapped potential for models of behavioral evolution in biology. In retrospect, it is clear from research in the intervening years that the preliminary treatment there considerably underestimated this potential. Moreover, although the application of evolutionary game theory to biology has increased steadily during these years, it is fair to say its growth has been much more dramatic in other disciplines, notably, its explosion in models relevant for human behavior.

The approach I have pursued in this book is a result of these observations. In particular, there is no longer a need to justify the importance of studying evolutionary dynamics as this has been done by numerous authors (see references at the beginning of the Introduction). What has received much less attention is the analyses of these dynamics for games that are more naturally specified through their extensive form. This book then focuses on evolutionary dynamics that are adapted to extensive form games. It also emphasizes connections between the extensive form perspective and existing dynamic models that have traditionally been in applications to biology and economics. The book will be of particular interest to (evolutionary) game theorists but has also much to offer a broader readership interested in predicting how behaviors evolve in both human and other species.

The theory of evolutionary dynamics for extensive form games is not complete. The purpose of the book is to introduce this fascinating topic and develop an approach to it that I am confident will remain an essential method no matter where the theory eventually leads.

There are many colleagues who, perhaps unknowingly, have influenced my thinking about extensive form games and to whom I am indebted. Of these, Josef Hofbauer and Karl Schlag deserve special mention since I could not have written many parts of the text without their input. I would also like to thank Ken Binmore and Larry Samuelson for helpful suggestions concerning the content of the text and continual encouragement along the way.

Bernard Brooks produced the original files for all the diagrams; those graphing trajectories of the replicator dynamics are taken directly from numerical approximations of the differential equations using MAPLE. Bernie, Barbara Carroll, and Karen Cressman provided invaluable assistance with corrections and editing throughout, for which I am most grateful. Technical assistance on the final diagrams and the format of the text was provided by Pam Schaus and Mary Reilly. Many people at The MIT Press have been involved, especially Elizabeth Murry who, along with Ken Binmore, shares editorial responsibilities for this series on Economic Learning and Social Evolution. Also acknowledged is financial assistance from Wilfrid Laurier University and the Natural Sciences and Engineering Research Council of Canada.

Ross Cressman
Waterloo, Ontario
June 2002

Evolutionary Dynamics
and Extensive Form Games

1   Introduction

Extensive form games, with an explicit description of the sequential nature of the players' possible actions, played a central role in the initial development of classical game theory by von Neumann and Morgenstern (1944). On the other hand, most dynamic analyses of evolutionary games are based on their normal forms, as evidenced by standard books on the topic (e.g., Hofbauer and Sigmund 1988, 1998; Cressman 1992; Weibull 1995; Vega-Redondo 1996) as well as in other game theory books.[1] This is despite the fact that many interesting games are specified more naturally through their extensive forms.

The primary objective of this book is to generalize the techniques of dynamic evolutionary game theory to extensive form games. The ultimate goal is to gain as prominent a position for dynamic evolutionary game theory applied to extensive form games as the corresponding theory has deservedly attained for normal form games.

For many readers the formal proofs of the insights that the dynamic analyses of extensive form games provide for models of behavioral evolution will seem overly technical with unfamiliar mathematical manipulations. The more informal discussion in the following three sections of the Introduction is meant to be accessible to the non-game theorist, although even here some background knowledge is useful. Section 1.1 below makes a strong case for the importance of studying evolutionary dynamics based directly on the extensive form game structure. It gives a dynamic perspective to the classical game theory debate of how a game is best represented. Section 1.2 contrasts the reasons researchers interested in animal behavior as opposed to those interested in human

---

1. Interestingly many books on game theory published in the past decade include "evolutionary" sections (e.g., van Damme 1991; Binmore 1992; Mesterton-Gibbons 1992, 2000; Sigmund 1993; Owen 1995; Gintis 2000).

behavior were initially fascinated with evolutionary game theory. It also outlines new connections between these two groups that emerge from the extensive form perspective. Section 1.3 discusses behavioral evolution based on imitation, an area where the extensive form is indispensable for any nontrivial real-life applications.

In mathematical terms the book analyzes dynamical systems that model the evolution of behaviors (or strategies) in extensive form games. A great deal of time is devoted to the investigation of the convergence and stability properties of these dynamic trajectories. For example, as explained in section 1.2, the demonstration that behaviors converge to a unique rest point for a particular game has important implications for the practitioners of evolutionary game theory. Regrettably, it is well known that dynamic trajectories for many evolutionary games do not converge. This is especially true if there are a large number of pure strategies. In general, these high dimensional dynamical systems can exhibit all the complexities of arbitrary dynamical systems such as periodic orbits, limit cycles, bifurcations, and chaos. However, by the end of the book, I will have demonstrated that the extensive form structure of our evolutionary games imparts special properties on the evolutionary dynamic that makes its analysis more tractable than would otherwise be expected. This will be shown even when these games have a large number of pure strategies.

1.1   Extensive Form versus Normal Form

Every (finite) extensive form game has a normal form representation. Thus one way to analyze an extensive form game is simply to ignore the extensive form structure and study the game instead in its normal form representation. Many (evolutionary) game theorists share a common view (see section 1.5):

> [that a game's] extensive-form representation is an unnecessarily complex object to represent it. The alternative representation in normal (or strategic) form does not lose any essential information and it is a much more amenable object of analysis.

This book emphatically rejects the sentiments contained in this quotation taken from Vega-Redondo (1996). The following two elementary examples serve to illustrate that a game's normal form representation often does lose essential information from the perspective of dynamic evolutionary game theory.

The first example is based on the two-player Rock–Scissors–Paper Game whereby each player chooses one of the three strategies, R, S, or P, without knowing the opponent's choice (i.e., the players make simultaneous choices). In this game none of these strategies dominate both of the other two since R beats S, S beats P, and P beats R. No matter what specific payoffs are taken for interactions between pairs of strategies (as long as the payoffs reflect the cyclic dominance), it can be shown that there is a unique symmetric Nash equilibrium (NE) where each player uses the same mixed strategy. One interpretation of such a mixed strategy is that in repeated plays of the game (e.g., once a day), the player has a randomizing device whereby he/she uses R, S, and P on a particular day with fixed positive probabilities that give the frequency components of the mixed strategy. Dynamic evolutionary game theory then concerns whether the players' behavior evolves to this mixed NE. The extensive form and normal form analyses of this game are identical—a result that supports the contention that the extensive form is just an unnecessary complication. In fact, for many such payoff parameters, evolutionary game theory does predict both players evolve to play the NE.

Now consider the following seemingly inconsequential additional player information; namely both players know whether the game is played on an even numbered day or on an odd numbered day and that the payoffs between a given pair of strategies do not depend on which type of day it is. Now each player has nine strategies, each of which specify a choice of R, S, or P on even days and a possibly different choice on odd days. Intuitively, if payoff parameters are such that both players evolve to the NE of the base RSP Game without this additional information, we expect evolutionary game theory to predict play evolves to this same NE in the even numbered subgame (i.e., in the game corresponding to the even numbered days) and in the odd numbered subgame. However, as a normal form game, the subgame structure is hidden (see section 1.5). Moreover the predicted behavior does not always occur for the original standard dynamic of evolutionary game theory (i.e., the replicator dynamic). Mathematically the problem is that the evolution of strategy frequencies in the even subgame affects the evolution in the odd subgame. On the other hand, evolutionary dynamics based on the extensive form of this game, that respect its subgame structure, continue to agree with the intuitively expected behavior. Thus, for this example, knowledge of its extensive form is essential; without it

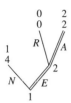

Figure 1.1.1
Extensive form of the Chain-Store Game.

the conclusions of dynamic evolutionary game theory are dramatically altered.[2]

The second example is the Chain-Store Game, a simplified caricature of the conflict between a potential entrant (player one) into a market controlled by a monopolist (player two). Its extensive form is given in figure 1.1.1, which indicates clearly the sequential nature of the players' actions.

Player one chooses first and decides whether to enter the market (E) or not (N). The monopolist does not want player one to enter since he/she then receives his/her highest payoff of 4 (to player one's payoff of 1). If player one does enter, then player two must decide whether to retaliate (R) or to acquiesce (A) and accept player one into the market. Retaliation leads to both players receiving payoff 0 (corresponding to a ruined market); otherwise, they share the market payoff of 4 equally and so each receives payoff 2.

The game has two Nash equilibrium outcomes. Either player one enters and player two acquiesces—this NE is labeled (E, A)—or player one does not enter. The outcome of player one not entering the market can only be maintained by a monopolist who is prepared to retaliate with a sufficiently high probability (specifically, he/she must be willing to retaliate at least half the time) if forced to make a decision. The question

---

2. (Generalized) RSP Games are introduced formally in chapter 2.6.1. The technical dynamic analysis for the nine-strategy normal form game is given in chapter 4.6.1. Explicit payoffs for the RSP Game are given for which all (interior) trajectories of the replicator dynamic converge to the unique mixed symmetric NE. It is shown that there are many interior replicator trajectories for the nine-strategy normal form game that have no single limiting behavior; rather, they evolve in a seemingly chaotic fashion. Details are provided as to how and when normal form evolutionary dynamics do not respect the subgame structure. The importance of the extensive form representation for this example, as a means to motivate evolutionary dynamics that respect the subgame structure (e.g., subgame monotone dynamics), is also discussed there as well as in chapters 9.2 and 9.4.

of which outcome (if either) predicts player behavior in this example has received much attention in the literature.[3]

For now, we concentrate on the game's normal form given by

$$
\begin{array}{c}
\quad\quad R \quad\quad A \\
\begin{array}{c} N \\ E \end{array}
\begin{bmatrix}
1,4 & 1,4 \\
0,0 & 2,2
\end{bmatrix}.
\end{array}
\tag{1.1.1}
$$

The prediction that players will use the NE (E, A) is easy to justify on dynamic grounds. Here each player's payoff decreases if his/her behavior unilaterally evolves away from (E, A) (e.g., player one's payoff decreases from 2 toward 1 in this case). (E, A) is called a strict NE. On the other hand, the Nash equilibrium outcome where player one does not enter is given by the set of strategies $\{(N, \lambda R + (1-\lambda)A) \mid \frac{1}{2} \leq \lambda \leq 1\}$ that indicates that the monopolist is prepared to retaliate with probability $\lambda \geq \frac{1}{2}$ if called upon. This set is called a NE component. No point in it is a strict NE since player two has no payoff incentive to maintain his/her current (mixed) strategy. Traditional evolutionary game theory for normal form games (see section 1.5) prefers behaviors converge to a unique NE, not to such a NE component that appears for (1.1.1) due to the payoff tie of 4 for player two if player one plays N. One approach to avoid such sets that is often taken for normal form games is that since payoff ties are not "generic" in this class of games, it suffices to consider games whose payoffs are slightly perturbed to break this tie. However, the normal form gives no indication which of player two's actions should be favored by this perturbation (i.e., whether R or A will have the higher payoff when player one chooses N). This knowledge is important since (N, R) becomes a strict NE if R is favored but no NE occurs with player one choosing N otherwise.

As the extensive form game in figure 1.1.1, the NE (E, A) is also easily distinguished from the other NE outcome; namely it is the only one

---

3. The question is considered more fully in chapter 3.3.2 as well as in chapter 8.1. The game is then referred to regularly in the remainder of chapter 8 and in chapter 9 where the extensive form version is emphasized.

It is no coincidence the Chain-Store Game is also discussed in the introductory chapters of Weibull (1995) and Samuelson (1997), since it is probably the most elementary example where (evolutionary) game theory does not give an unequivocal prediction of player behavior. The payoffs used in figure 1.1.1 are from Weibull (1995) where the game is also called the Entry Deterrence Game to emphasize the difference between it and the Chain-Store Game considered by Selten (1978) who initially raised the question of how a monopolist can maintain a credible threat to retaliate in order to continue his/her monopoly when this game is repeated against a chain of many potential entrants.

that specifies a NE action in the subgame following player one entering the market. This is called a subgame perfect NE. There are well-known arguments that NE which are not subgame perfect are unrealistic predictions of strategy behavior.[4] For example, from figure 1.1.1, it seems implausible that a monopolist would ever actually use R if called upon since he/she could do better by choosing A if player one enters the market. That is, there is a basic theoretical question of whether the outcome where player one does not enter is ever expected to occur. On the other hand, empirical evidence reported in Güth et al. (1982) (see also Gale et al. 1995), from experiments using human subjects playing the mathematically equivalent Ultimatum (Mini)Game in a laboratory setting, shows people often do play the outcome corresponding to player one not entering.

Of more immediate interest to us at this point is that the extensive form can also suggest what direction perturbations will favor. Gale et al. (1995) show that in certain perturbed dynamics (specifically, when the monopolist is much less concerned about the exact (mixed) strategy he/she uses than the potential entrant near the NE outcome where player one does not enter), this non–subgame perfect NE outcome can be predicted by the dynamic approach. The point worth making here is not whether an assumption stating which player is more careful when choosing his/her strategy is correct; rather, it is the fact that the reasonableness of such assumptions requires some knowledge of the sequential nature of the player decisions, an attribute of the game that is only clearly indicated through its extensive form.

The Chain-Store Game illustrates in an elementary fashion another important aspect of the extensive form that is lost in its normal form representation. The basic problem with justifying the non–subgame perfect NE outcome is that this outcome has an unreached decision point

---

4. Every extensive form game has at least one subgame perfect NE. The subgame perfect NEs can be found by applying the "backward induction" procedure of classical game theory (see section 6.1.2). For the elementary game in figure 1.1.1 (and also in figure 1.3.1 below assuming $a_1 > c_1, a_2 > b_2$, and $c_2 > d_2$), there is only one subgame perfect NE, and it is indicated by the double line in the game tree. This latter convention is used regularly throughout the book.

However, there is typically more than one extensive form game with a given normal form representation. In particular, it is easy to define an extensive form game, with normal form (1.1.1), that has no nontrivial subgames and so all NE are subgame perfect by default. Thus losing the extensive form structure has the perhaps unexpected consequence of losing a well-defined concept of subgame perfection as well. The question of whether non–subgame perfect NE can be justified on dynamic grounds is examined in chapters 7 and 8 for much longer extensive form games than the Chain-Store Game of figure 1.1.1.

(i.e., the monopolist's strategy is not revealed if the potential entrant chooses N). This automatically leads to insufficient evolutionary selection pressure in the unperturbed normal form dynamic to predict how player behavior will evolve when their strategies are near this NE outcome. Although the problem of unreached decision points at NE (i.e., that the "equilibrium path" does not specify "out-of-equilibrium" behavior) for extensive form games has received much attention in traditional (i.e., non evolutionary) game theory where philosophical arguments on the foundation of rational decision making are often invoked, it has been largely ignored by evolutionary game theorists. This is especially true for longer extensive form games in which player decision points follow earlier decisions by the same player where out-of-equilibrium behavior is almost guaranteed. For reasons similar to those discussed above for the RSP Game example, the standard evolutionary dynamics based on their normal form then rarely respect the extensive form structure of these longer games.

The approach I take in this book is to develop a dynamic theory of extensive form games that relies explicitly on the game tree. The examples analyzed throughout the book are, for the most part, relatively short extensive form games. It is my contention that one must thoroughly understand how the general theory applies to such elementary examples before arbitrarily long extensive form games can be satisfactorily handled. Moreover, with only the normal form (which will typically have a very large number of strategies), I believe it is a hopeless task to attempt to build a useful general evolutionary theory of extensive form games.

My own personal experience is that much of human behavior involves interactions between people who have a long sequence of encounters. It is inconceivable that current decisions do not depend in an intricate manner on choices made in previous encounters, a feature that is contained in the concept of a history (Osborne and Rubinstein 1994) of an extensive form game but is not explicitly revealed by the game's normal form. That is, the game's normal form is based implicitly on all strategies being played at essentially the same time between players who do not meet again. In fact the two examples discussed above are quite short extensive form games, and they satisfy the implicit assumptions that suggest a normal form analysis will be effective. However, as we have already seen, even here the normal form has serious shortcomings.

Let us now agree that the structure of extensive form games is important for the analysis of their evolutionary dynamics and concentrate instead on why this analysis is useful. To begin this process in the following two sections, I first return to the historical roots of evolutionary game theory in its applications to biology and economics.

1.2   Biology versus Economics

There are two main groups of practitioners of the concepts of evolutionary game theory, introduced in the order of when they first appeared. The first, who I call biological game theorists[5] after their founder (John Maynard Smith), consider the dynamical system as a model of behavioral evolution in a population where pure strategies (i.e., behaviors) that have higher payoff (i.e., fitness) increase in relative frequency due to their higher reproductive success. In particular, individuals in the population do not make conscious decisions on what strategy to use; rather, these are predetermined by nature. The evolutionary game theory models of interest to this group typically have an evolutionarily stable strategy (ESS). Such a rest point is then automatically dynamically stable and often unique given reasonable biological constraints. This group expects the ESS behavior to be observed in nature where evolutionary forces have had a long time to exert their influence. The obvious benefit to this predictive method is that it avoids the need to solve the underlying dynamical system. An ESS is especially appealing since it resists invasions by rare mutants that will appear over evolutionary time.

The later group, called economic game theorists after one of its early proponents (Reinhard Selten), takes the classical game theory perspective that individuals make rational decisions on their strategy choice. In biological terms, the difference between these groups becomes a question of nature versus nurture. Economic game theorists assume each individual chooses his[6] strategy based on his own circumstances or environment (nurture), while biologists assume nature predetermines strategy perhaps through the individual's genetic makeup. The interesting

---

5. Game theory also has interesting historical connections to biology before the advent of evolutionary game theory in the 1970s. In retrospect, Fisher's (1930) justification for the prevalence of 50 : 50 sex ratio in diploid species is an early example of strategic reasoning. That is, individuals in a population with a biased sex ratio do better by producing more offspring of the rarer sex and so shift the population toward producing males and females in equal numbers.

6. From now on, I will use "his" to represent "his/her" and "he" to represent "he/she," and the like. This is done for notational convenience and is not meant to suggest conscious decisions are the exclusive preserve of one gender.

games for economic game theorists tend to have many NE as possible solutions but often have no ESS. The problem then becomes which NE, if any, to consider the solution to the game. Elaborate rationality arguments are often needed (e.g., Harsanyi and Selten 1988; van Damme 1991) to select one. Restricting the choice to NE that are dynamically stable offers an especially appealing equilibrium selection technique for many economic game theorists (e.g., Samuelson 1997) since it typically assumes much less rationality on the part of the game's individual players.

The comparisons discussed above between the two groups were initially developed in models of two-player games where both players have the same set of possible strategies (as in the RSP Game considered in section 1.1).[7] The original ESS concept of Maynard Smith applies most directly to models in biology of a single species that reproduces asexually rather than to such economic models as monopolists and potential entrants where players clearly have totally different strategy sets. The concept has since been extended to the more realistic biological model of a sexually reproducing species (Cressman 1992; Hofbauer and Sigmund 1998) and to multi-species frequency-dependent evolution (Cressman et al. 2001). Special cases of these latter models include general n-player noncooperative games, a topic that has received much attention in standard economic game theorists' books (e.g., van Damme 1991; Binmore 1992).[8]

It is my contention that the spectacular growth of evolutionary game theory (for normal form games) over the past two decades is due in large part to an unusually strong bond between these two seemingly unrelated disciplines (biology and economics). During this time I have been continually surprised by unforeseen connections between biological and economic game theory in both their concepts and their techniques. In this regard consider the following two normal form connections: On the grand conceptual level, the general theory of natural selection at a single locus in a sexually reproducing species (originally developed without reference to game theory; see chapter 2.8) becomes a special class of dynamic evolutionary games where contestants split their payoffs equally—called partnership games in the economic literature (Hofbauer and Sigmund 1998). On the level of specific techniques, the perturbed

---

7. Technically these are called symmetric games (see chapter 2).
8. The well-known Buyer-Seller Game (Friedman 1991) is an elementary example of a two-player noncooperative game where the name already suggests different types of players.

payoff approach to break payoff ties in the Chain-Store Game discussed in section 1.1 has its biological counterpart in the Hawk-Dove-Retaliator Game of Maynard Smith (1982) who used the same technique to break the selective indifference in Dove-Retaliator contests.[9]

One means to justify the dynamic analysis of extensive form games as proposed in this book is then to demonstrate that it continues to build new connections between biology and economics. Here I mention briefly two instances. Coevolutionary models in population biology (i.e., the evolution of individual characteristics in ecological systems with multiple species) is a biological theory (e.g., Roughgarden 1979) that first matured without evolutionary game theory. Chapter 4.7 shows that the frequency component of these coevolutionary models is identical to the extensive form evolutionary dynamics of a class of asymmetric games developed by Balkenborg (1994) for economic game theorists. Chapter 5 on multilocus natural selection with additive fitness is another instance where the extensive form has unforeseen relevance for biological models through equating each decision point in a different class of asymmetric extensive form games with a particular locus. A by-product of this equivalence is that the concept of the Wright manifold from multilocus population genetics can be generalized to an arbitrary extensive form game (see chapter 6.3). In genetics, the Wright manifold is the set of genotypic frequencies that are in "linkage equilibrium" (i.e., allele frequencies at one locus are independent of those at the other loci). The re-interpretation in language more familiar to economic game theorists is that the Wright manifold is the set of mixed strategies where the behavior strategy in any subgame is independent of actions taken at decision points outside this subgame. This Wright manifold for general extensive form games plays a central role throughout the book, becoming equally useful for economic game theorists. For a specific application, the Wright manifold can be used to resolve the counterintuitive result for the example discussed in section 1.1 based on the RSP Game (see chapter 4.6.1). In particular, on the Wright manifold, the replicator dynamic predicts behaviors evolve to the unique NE in both even and odd numbered subgames, the intuitive result expected by economic game theorists.

---

9. The Chain-Store Game in section 1.1 is clearly presented in economic terms. With a few exceptions besides this section (notably chapters 2.8, 4.7, and all of chapter 5), the book describes player behavior as if it assumed conscious decisions, so the discussion may often seem more relevant for researchers whose primary interest is in modeling human behavior. In most cases the descriptions can be rephrased to be just as appealing to biological game theorists.

As may be already apparent by the preceding discussion, the line between these two groups has become increasingly blurred through interactions between them and the spread of evolutionary game theory to other disciplines. Biological game theorists (e.g., Maynard Smith 1982) implicitly give rational decision-making powers to their populations when they justify observed population behavior on arguments using strategic reasoning. On the other hand, the plethora of learning models analyzed by economic game theorists (e.g., Weibull 1995; Samuelson 1997; Fudenberg and Levine 1998) where individuals base their rational decisions on limited information (i.e., individuals are boundedly rational) lead naturally to population dynamics similar to those of interest to biological game theorists when applied to normal form games.

This book attempts to strike a middle ground between these two groups. Except for the development of dynamics based on explicit models of imitative behavior (see section 1.3 below), it ignores for the most part the nature versus nurture issue of which dynamic model is appropriate for a particular game (see section 1.5). Instead, it concentrates on the analyses of well-known dynamics, adapted for extensive form games, that have proved relevant for arbitrary evolutionary games—emphasizing their convergence and stability properties. The specific dynamics considered are monotone selection, best response, fictitious play and especially the various forms of the replicator dynamic—the initial dynamical system developed for (symmetric) normal form games from a biological perspective (Taylor and Jonker 1978). To appreciate this approach, it is important to understand the method as it applies to normal form games. The following paragraph begins this process which is then continued in chapter 2.

The emphasis on convergence and stability in this book is also apparent in the literature on the dynamics of normal form games. For instance, the *Folk Theorem of Evolutionary Game Theory* (Hofbauer and Sigmund 1998) forms the basis for evolutionary game theory as an equilibrium selection technique. It asserts the following three statements for all "reasonable" dynamics of a normal form evolutionary game:

   i. A stable rest point is a NE.

  ii. Any convergent trajectory evolves to a NE.

 iii. A strict NE is asymptotically stable.

Similarly the basic version of the *Fundamental Theorem of Natural Selection* (Weibull 1995) that asserts populations evolve so as to increase their mean fitness implies all limit points are NE (in fact, typically an ESS that is then asymptotically stable) of the corresponding normal form game.[10] Although neither "theorem" is universally true for all relevant dynamic models of behavioral evolution, their conclusions nonetheless provide an important benchmark for general techniques of dynamic evolutionary game theory.

1.3   Imitation

Imitation is clearly an important factor in explaining how humans adapt to their environments. Whether through formal learning processes (e.g., an education system) or through more informal means (e.g., our own observations), we become aware of how others behave in a given situation. We then decide on our own course of action, perhaps based on also knowing the consequences of these behaviors. "Imitative behavior" will mean that we either decide to adopt the known behavior of someone else or maintain our current behavior. Since similar processes occur in most animal species (e.g., parents nurturing their offspring), and especially in those species that have a societal structure, imitative behavior seems to be more important in realistic models of behavioral evolution relevant for biological game theorists than the following excerpt from Hofbauer and Sigmund (1998) might suggest:

The replicator dynamics mimics the effect of natural selection (although it blissfully disregards the complexities of sexual reproduction). In the context of games played by human societies, however, the spreading of successful strategies is more likely to occur through imitation than through inheritance. How should we model this imitation processes?

The extensive form is an effective tool for imitation models of real-life situations. In particular, as argued near the end of section 1.1, interactions

---

10. See chapter 2 for definitions and/or explanations of the technical terms from the theory of dynamical systems used in this paragraph (and elsewhere in the Introduction). In particular, convergence to NE often requires that all strategy types are initially present in the population. The Introduction also contains many technical terms from game theory (in particular, for extensive form games) that are not precisely explained here. Their formal definitions are found in various chapters of the book.

The difference between the first theorem being designated "folk" and the second "fundamental" seems to be based more on the discipline in which it originated (economics and biology respectively) than on its overall validity. It is interesting that the book I chose as a good reference for each of these theorems is written by researchers whose initial interest in dynamic evolutionary game theory places them in the opposite group of practitioners. This clearly illustrates how blurred the line separating these two groups has become.

among humans are often based on their past history. Such chains of interactions then translate into long extensive form games where earlier decisions can affect whether or not later decisions are ever encountered. Since we cannot imitate behaviors in eventualities that never occur, our imitation models must only imitate the known part of someone else's strategy (i.e., in the language of extensive form games, imitation cannot occur at unreached decision points).

Several sections in this book examine how such imitative behavior can be implemented in general extensive form games with a particular emphasis on the relationship of the resultant behavioral evolution to other standard evolutionary dynamics. The rigorous analysis of imitation is restricted to the subclass of "one-player extensive form games." Specifically, chapters 2.10, 4.6.2, and 8.4 develop models when the outcome of one other randomly chosen individual is observed in a one-player extensive form game. In these three chapters two aspects of the discussion above are considered; namely why an individual player uses imitative behavior and then how he uses it (i.e., when does he switch to the observed behavior and the mechanism for doing so). The discussion in the remainder of this section is limited to the latter aspect as it applies to the following elementary two-player extensive form game.

Take figure 1.3.1. First consider the decision facing player two.[11] He has four strategies, each of which specifies either ℓ or r in the left-hand subgame (i.e., when player one uses L) and either ℓ or r in the right-hand subgame. Suppose that his random observation is of a player using ℓ in the left-hand subgame together with the resulting payoff a_2. If he decides to imitate this behavior, he must still maintain his current behavior in the unreached right-hand subgame since no observation is available there. That is, player two cannot switch to the observed player's entire strategy (as might be expected if imitative behavior is applied to normal form games); rather, imitation can only affect subgame behavior along the observed outcome path.

---

11. When player one's strategy is fixed (in which case, this strategy can be replaced by a "move by nature"), figure 1.3.1 is an example from player two's perspective of a "parallel bandit" studied in chapter 4.6.2. This is a special class of one-player extensive form games (see chapter 8.4). Figure 1.3.1 is analyzed again in chapters 9.2 and 9.3 as a two-player game.

Notice that the orientation of the extensive form in figure 1.3.1 is opposite to that in figure 1.1.1. That is, there the sequential decisions that are taken later in the game tree are above the earlier ones, whereas here they are below. There seems to be no universally accepted orientation with sideways progressions also possible. Different orientations are used throughout the book but should not cause the reader undue difficulty.

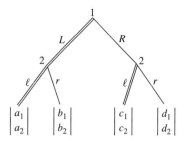

Figure 1.3.1
Extensive form example to illustrate imitative behavior.

As we will see (e.g., chapter 2.10), for both intuitive and technical reasons, the most important mechanisms for switching behavior use proportional imitation. For instance, suppose that a player only contemplates switching to the observed behavior if the resulting payoff is higher. Moreover, in this case, suppose the player switches with a probability proportional to the payoff difference. When these assumptions are applied to player two's decision in figure 1.3.1, an evolutionary dynamic emerges that respects the subgame structure.[12] Combined with a similar analysis in chapter 9.3 that assumes player one also uses proportional imitation, we find that the agenda outlined in the Folk Theorem of Evolutionary Game Theory is most easily accomplished by first applying convergence and stability concepts to the separate evolutionary dynamics in the two subgames. The resultant limiting behaviors are then used to shorten the extensive form game (technically, to "truncate" it) whose dynamic analysis becomes considerably easier. That is, we have a dynamic version of the backward induction procedure of classical game theory.

The example above, as well as others based on imitative behavior in this book, are admittedly oversimplified models of the complex phenomenon of imitation. However, they do serve several purposes. Their analyses illustrate how dynamical systems develop from underlying assumptions of player interactions. This forces us to deal carefully with the main issue already raised from other perspectives in the Introduction; namely how evolutionary game theory concepts that originated

---

12. Chapter 9.3 shows that this is essentially the replicator dynamic in each subgame. It is also interesting to note that the Wright manifold for the game in figure 1.3.1 appears automatically there as a natural feature of the evolutionary dynamics.

from applications to normal form games can be adapted to the extensive form.

One such concept, subgame monotonicity, is analyzed in chapter 9. The theory developed there shows that the Folk Theorem of Evolutionary Game Theory remains intact. Furthermore it shows how the dynamic analysis of a general extensive form game can be decomposed into that of shorter games before being recombined to give results for the more complicated original game. Although this process is nominally parallel to the backward induction procedure to find subgame perfect NE (see section 1.1), there are significant advantages to the dynamic approach. In particular, the influence of out-of-equilibrium behavior does not rely on assumptions of how rational players decide actions in situations they never encounter. Rather, the strength of selective pressures on such actions can be included explicitly in the dynamic model (see the discussion of the Chain-Store Game in section 1.1).

At the present time there is no universally accepted dynamic that evolutionary game theorists agree is important for general extensive form games. A case is implicitly made in this book that the replicator dynamic adapted to the extensive form structure may fulfill this role. However, whether or not this eventually happens, the theory and techniques developed here should be as important in any dynamic theory of extensive form games.

1.4 Organizational Matters

The reader may be surprised that the formal definition of an extensive form game does not appear until halfway through the book in chapter 6. This was done to avoid the complex formalism of extensive form games interfering with an intuitive understanding of the dynamic issues as they arise. For the most part the original dynamic analysis of each of the topics before chapter 6 is accomplished without specific reference to the associated game's extensive form. These include the symmetric and bimatrix games of chapters 2 and 3 respectively, the multi-locus model of natural selection in chapter 5, and, to a lesser extent, the general asymmetric games of chapter 4. In these chapters (beginning at the end of chapter 2), the book emphasizes how an informal appreciation of the extensive form assists in understanding the theory.

Chapter 6 summarizes the standard definition of general extensive form games needed for their dynamic analysis. Also emphasized here is the subgame structure and its relationship to the replicator dynamic. The dynamics of extensive form evolutionary games are not well understood for complex game trees without many subgames. Instead, chapters 7 and 8 consider two important particular classes of extensive form games (simultaneity games and perfect information games) where there is a great deal of subgame decomposition. Since much of the material here is new, there is a greater emphasis on examples to illustrate the techniques. Chapter 9 on subgame monotonicity returns to a more general perspective as a means to connect the concepts introduced in chapters 6 to 8. These four chapters leave many open problems for general extensive form games that suggest directions for future research.

The first time technical terms appear, they are indicated by a different *font* than that of the surrounding text. Each chapter concludes with a Notes section that discusses some of the primary references. These references should not be regarded as a complete list of the related literature. I have used the convention that the phrases "see Notes" and "see Appendix" in a particular chapter refers to the corresponding section at the end of that chapter. Another convention used throughout is that the third section of chapter 3, for instance, is referred to as section 3.3 in chapter 3 and as chapter 3.3 elsewhere. Theorems, figures, displayed equations, and the like, are numbered consecutively starting at the beginning of each section.

1.5   Notes

There is a considerable literature that argues all extensive form games with the same (reduced-strategy) normal form are strategically equivalent when played by rational players (e.g., Kolberg and Mertens 1986). These arguments are usually based on transformations of extensive form games similar to those introduced by Thompson (1952) and Dalkey (1953). In particular, Elmes and Reny (1994) show all extensive form games with the same (reduced) normal form can be transformed into one another. Moreover Mailath et al. (1993) construct normal form counterparts for many concepts that seem initially to rely in an essential way on the extensive form structure. For instance, they recover "normal form subgames" corresponding to subgames of the extensive form. Thus, technically speaking, the nine-strategy normal form of the first example (based on the RSP Game) does not hide its subgame structure. Similarly the subgame perfect NE can be retrieved from the normal form of the Chain-Store Game. However, in these cases, the normal form

constructions of elementary extensive form concepts are themselves un-
necessarily complex objects that are certainly no easier to analyze than
in their original extensive form. In fact standard dynamic analyses of
normal form games do not take into account these constructions.

Setwise solution concepts based on the dynamics of normal form
games have also been considered in the literature. These include sets
that may contain nonequilibrium strategies—such as ES* (evolutionarily stable*) sets (Weibull 1995) and sets closed under (weakly) better
replies (Ritzberger and Weibull 1995)—as well as sets of NE—such as
EES (equilibrium evolutionarily stable) sets (Swinkels 1992). Every normal form game contains sets of the first type but not necessarily of the
second type. Of particular interest in this book are the ESSets (evolutionarily stable sets) and the SESets (strict equilibrium sets) introduced
by Thomas (1985) and Balkenborg (1994) respectively. These are finite
unions of NE components with desirable dynamic stability properties
for the symmetric and bimatrix normal form games of chapters 2 and
3 respectively. For the general extensive form games of chapters 7 and
8, the stability of NE components containing a subgame perfect NE
receives special attention.

The issue of which evolutionary dynamic is appropriate to model a
particular game is beyond the scope of this book. As well as the dynamics analyzed here, biological game theorists model population behavior where individual fitness is a function of aggregate population
strategy (rather than pairwise interactions), the so-called playing the
field method (Maynard Smith 1982). Extensive form reasoning through
sequential effects of such aggregate interactions has recently been recognized as an important factor for realistic models of biological systems
(e.g., Hammerstein 2001; McNamara and Houston 1999). Other (normal form) dynamics based on aggregate behavior are also prevalent
among both groups of practitioners, such as payoff positive dynamics
(Weibull 1995) and adaptive dynamics (Hofbauer and Sigmund 1998).
There is also considerable research by economic game theorists on another means to select NE by evolutionary methods; namely the stochastic models introduced by Foster and Young (1990) and Kandori et al.
(1993) that examine the effect of infrequent mutation. They emphasize
the long-run stationary distribution as the mutation rate approaches
zero rather than the evolutionary dynamic. It is interesting to note that
mutation was also central to the earlier development of the ESS concept (e.g., Maynard Smith 1982) as a strategy that is uninvadable by rare
mutants.

2

Symmetric Normal Form Games

Although this book emphasizes extensive form games, we begin with a review of dynamic evolutionary game theory for symmetric normal form games.[1] This is partly for historical reasons as the theory of dynamic evolutionary games first developed in the biological literature where extensive form games were initially of little interest. Moreover many of the techniques used to analyze the dynamics of extensive form games are based on those for symmetric normal form games, and so a good understanding of dynamic evolutionary game theory for symmetric normal form games is essential background knowledge. The proofs for many of the results included in this chapter are omitted as they are contained in standard books on the subject (see Notes). The proofs given here either have, as yet, appeared only in research articles or illustrate techniques that are required in subsequent chapters.

2.1 The Replicator Dynamic

In a *symmetric normal form game*, G, there are n possible *pure strategies* denoted $e_1, \ldots, e_n$. $S = \{e_1, \ldots, e_n\}$ is then the *set of pure strategies*. G is a *two-player game* where a contest involving players using strategies e_i and e_j results in a *payoff* $\pi(e_i, e_j)$ for (the player using) strategy e_i. Mixed strategies are also important in evolutionary game theory. Each $p \in \Delta^n \equiv \{(p_1, \ldots, p_n) \mid p_i \geq 0, \sum p_i = 1\}$ represents a *mixed strategy* and Δ^n (also denoted $\Delta(S)$) is called the *mixed-strategy space* (or *strategy simplex*). It is the $n - 1$ dimensional simplex of frequency vectors in R^n with vertices at the unit coordinate vectors. The vector $(0, \ldots, 0, 1, 0, \ldots, 0)$, which has 1 in the ith component and 0 everywhere else, represents e_i.

---

1. Normal form games are also known as *strategic form games*, a phrase that will not be used again in this book.

There are two interpretations of a mixed strategy p. One is as a strategy played by an individual player. In this case, the ith component p_i represents the probability this individual player uses pure strategy e_i in a particular contest. The *expected payoff* to a player using p in a contest with a player using $\hat{p}$ is then

$$\pi(p, \hat{p}) = \sum_{i,j=1}^{n} p_i \pi(e_i, e_j) \hat{p}_j.$$

For symmetric normal form games, we will usually write this payoff in matrix form as

$$\pi(p, \hat{p}) = p \cdot A\hat{p} = \sum_{i,j=1}^{n} p_i a_{ij} \hat{p}_j,$$

where $A = [a_{ij}]$ is the $n \times n$ *payoff matrix* with entries $a_{ij} = \pi(e_i, e_j)$.[2]

The second interpretation is the one used most often in dynamic evolutionary game theory. Here it is assumed that there is a large population of individuals who each use some pure strategy. The population is in *state* $p \in \Delta^n$ if its ith component, p_i, is the current proportion of individuals in the population (i.e., *frequency*) using pure strategy e_i. If contests[3] occur through random pairwise interactions and population size is effectively infinite (or if random pairs also include the possibility an individual plays against himself), then the expected payoff of someone using pure strategy e_i is $\pi(e_i, p) = e_i \cdot Ap$. The dynamic evolutionary game theory considered in this book assumes that the frequency vector p evolves over time through some mechanism that translates expected payoffs into a deterministic dynamic on Δ^n.

The original dynamic for evolutionary games interpreted payoff as the *reproductive success* or *fitness* of each individual in the population. When offspring are assumed to inherit the identical strategy of their single parent in this biological model,[4] the standard replicator dynamic emerges in either its continuous-time overlapping generation version or in its

---

2. In this notation, p and $\hat{p}$ are actually column vectors and $p \cdot A\hat{p}$ is the dot product of vectors in R^n.

3. A contest in a two-player game is a play of the game where each player chooses one of his possible pure or mixed strategies. From a population perspective, such a contest is often called an interaction between two individuals. In particular, the evolutionary model developed here assumes payoffs result through pairwise interactions rather than through a playing the field mechanism mentioned in chapter 1.5.

4. Technically the population is a haploid species or else reproduction is parthenogenetic.

discrete-time nonoverlapping generation version. Let us briefly out-
line derivations of these dynamics from first principles (see section 2.10
below for another derivation based on imitative behavior that yields
slightly different versions of the replicator dynamics).

For the discrete generation model, each individual in the population
lives for one generation during which time it interacts with exactly one
randomly chosen opponent. This individual's payoff is the number of
offspring it produces in the next generation and so must be nonnegative.
Thus, if n_i is the number of individuals using strategy e_i at generation
t, then the expected number at generation $t + 1$ is $n_i' = n_i(e_i \cdot Ap)$.[5] Evolutionary game theory is traditionally concerned with the evolution of
strategy frequency $p_i = n_i / \sum_j n_j$. Here $p_i' = n_i e_i \cdot Ap / \sum_j n_j e_j \cdot Ap =$
$(\sum_j n_j) p_i e_i \cdot Ap / (\sum_j n_j) \sum_j p_j e_j \cdot Ap = p_i(e_i \cdot Ap / p \cdot Ap)$, where, to
avoid the possibility of division by zero, we will assume that all en-
tries a_{ij} are positive. Thus the standard *discrete-time replicator dynamic* is

$$p_i' = p_i \frac{e_i \cdot Ap}{p \cdot Ap}. \tag{2.1.1}$$

There are several ways to develop the continuous-time replicator dynamic. Perhaps the simplest is to assume that expected individual fitness is the net growth rate (i.e., birth rate − death rate). Notice that
payoffs can be negative in this scenario. Then $\dot{n}_i = n_i e_i \cdot Ap$, where
$\dot{n}_i$ is the time derivative of n_i. From calculus, $\dot{p}_i = d(n_i / \sum_j n_j)/dt =$
$(n_i e_i \cdot Ap \sum_j n_j - n_i \sum_j n_j e_j \cdot Ap)/(\sum_j n_j)^2 = p_i(e_i - p) \cdot Ap$. The standard continuous-time *replicator dynamic*[6] is

$$\dot{p}_i = p_i(e_i - p) \cdot Ap. \tag{2.1.2}$$

An alternative derivation using the discrete-time replicator dynamic
leads to the *payoff-adjusted* continuous-time replicator dynamic. If we
take the approximation $\dot{p}_i = \lim_{\Delta t \to 0}[p_i(t + \Delta t) - p_i(t)/\Delta t] \cong p_i(t + 1)$
$- p_i(t)$ as exact, then (2.1.1) implies that

$$\dot{p}_i = p_i \left(\frac{(e_i - p) \cdot Ap}{p \cdot Ap} \right).$$

---

5. Notice that the explicit dependence of $n_i(t)$ and $p(t)$ on time t is usually notationally
suppressed.
6. Unless otherwise stated, "replicator dynamic" for a symmetric normal form game
refers to this standard continuous-time version. In later chapters we call this the *symmetric
replicator dynamic* to avoid ambiguities.

Since $p \cdot Ap$ is positive and bounded away from 0 for all $p \in \Delta^n$, the trajectories of this are identical to those of (2.1.2) except for a rescaling of time.[7]

Some notation is needed here to summarize well-known properties of the replicator dynamics in (2.1.1) and (2.1.2). Both of these are *autonomous* deterministic dynamics that leave Δ^n *forward invariant*. That is, for every initial state p at $t = 0$, there is a unique trajectory $p(t) \in \Delta^n$ for all $t \geq 0$ (for all $t \in \mathbf{N}$) that satisfies (2.1.2) (respectively (2.1.1)). Autonomous implies that $\hat{p}(t)$ given by $\hat{p}(t) = p(t + \varepsilon)$ is a trajectory for the dynamic for every relevant ε (i.e., $\varepsilon > 0$ or $\varepsilon \in \mathbf{N}$ respectively) whenever $p(t)$ is a trajectory. Furthermore the interior of Δ^n denoted by $\overset{\circ}{\Delta}(S) \equiv \{p \in \Delta^n \mid p_i > 0 \text{ for all } i\}$ is also forward invariant as is each face $\Delta(\hat{S}) = \{p \in \Delta^n \mid p_i = 0 \text{ for any } e_i \notin \hat{S}\}$, where $\hat{S}$ is any nonempty subset of S. $\overset{\circ}{\Delta}(S)$ is also called the set of *completely mixed strategies* or set of *polymorphic states*. The *support* of p is $\mathrm{supp}(p) \equiv \{e_i \mid p_i > 0\}$. Thus $p \in \overset{\circ}{\Delta}(\mathrm{supp}(p))$. The *rest points* of an autonomous dynamic on Δ^n are those frequency vectors p that satisfy $\dot{p}_i = 0$ (respectively $p_i' = p_i$) for all $1 \leq i \leq n$. The rest points of (2.1.1) and (2.1.2) are exactly those $p \in \Delta^n$ for which $e_i \cdot Ap = p \cdot Ap$ for all $e_i \in \mathrm{supp}(p)$.

A crucial property for us is that both dynamics satisfy the Folk Theorem of Evolutionary Game Theory (see chapter 1 and theorem 2.5.3 below) when convergence of trajectories is only examined for interior trajectories. Specifically, a limit point of a convergent interior trajectory or a stable rest point p^* must be a *symmetric Nash equilibrium* (i.e., p^* is a best reply against itself as defined in section 2.5 below). On the other hand, although all symmetric NE are rest points, only some are either stable or the unique limit point of an interior trajectory. Thus, by restricting attention to these latter two classes of symmetric NE, we have an initial equilibrium selection technique based on dynamic evolutionary game theory.

There are other deterministic dynamics that share the properties of the replicator dynamic discussed above. Of particular interest to economic game theorists are the general class of monotone selection dynamics (of which the replicator dynamic is a special case) and the continuous-time best response dynamic with its discrete-time counterpart fictitious

---

7. The exact form of (2.1.2) can also be produced in this manner by an "overlapping" generation model where it is assumed that a fraction $\tau > 0$ of the total population reproduces each time interval of length τ and then let $\tau \to 0$.

play, both of which rely on the players having more information as to the current state of the population than monotone selection dynamics require. Convergence and/or stability are also important to biologists because these properties allow them to predict the observed behavior of the population without an explicit solution of the dynamical system (see chapter 1). Biological game theorists are more interested in the replicator dynamic (for it does not assume individuals make conscious decisions) and in its generalizations to evolutionary models of diploid populations (e.g., section 2.8 below).

The alternative dynamics for economic game theorists are introduced in sections 2.3 and 2.4 after the dynamic classification of symmetric normal form games with two strategies is completed in section 2.2. These games provide an elementary illustration of the concepts introduced so far in a setting where all deterministic evolutionary dynamics are essentially equivalent.

2.2 Dynamics for Two-Strategy Games

When $S = \{e_1, e_2\}$, let the 2×2 payoff matrix be denoted by $A = \begin{bmatrix} a & b \\ c & d \end{bmatrix}$. Since $p_2 = 1 - p_1$, the mixed strategy space Δ^2 is the one-dimensional line in figure 2.2.1. The qualitative behavior of a one-dimensional autonomous dynamic can be understood to a large extent by its phase portrait (see figure 2.2.1) which shows the direction of the vector field at each point of Δ^2. For instance, the replicator dynamic (2.1.2) is

$$\dot{p}_1 = p_1(e_1 \cdot Ap - p \cdot Ap)$$

$$= p_1 p_2(e_1 \cdot Ap - e_2 \cdot Ap)$$

$$= p_1 p_2(ap_1 + bp_2 - (cp_1 + dp_2))$$

$$= p_1(1 - p_1)((a - c + d - b)p_1 + b - d). \tag{2.2.1}$$

The rest points of this dynamic (i.e., those $0 \leq p_1 \leq 1$ for which $\dot{p}_1 = 0$) are $p_1 = 0$, $p_1 = 1$, and any solutions of $(a - c + d - b)p_1 = d - b$ satisfying $0 < p_1 < 1$. These latter are called *interior rest points*. The three possible phase portraits can be classified by the signs of $a - c$ and $d - b$.[8]

---

8. It is clear from (2.2.1) that the actual trajectories for (2.1.2) only depend on the payoff differences $a - c$ and $b - d$. Thus the payoff matrix can be taken as $\begin{bmatrix} a-c & 0 \\ 0 & d-b \end{bmatrix}$ for these games.

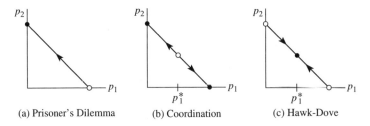

(a) Prisoner's Dilemma   (b) Coordination   (c) Hawk-Dove

Figure 2.2.1
Phase portrait of the replicator dynamic for two-strategy games. Trajectories lie on the line $p_1 + p_2 = 1$. Circles indicate rest points of the dynamic (solid are stable and empty unstable) while arrows indicate increasing t.

We label these three classes by a particularly well-known game that is an example of each.

Prisoner's Dilemma Class   (Payoffs satisfy $(a - c)(d - b) \leq 0)^9$ We can assume, by reordering the strategies if necessary, that $a \leq c$ and $d \geq b$. From (2.2.1), there are no interior rest points since

$$(a - c + d - b)p_1 + b - d \leq \min\{(d - b)(p_1 - 1), (a - c)p_1\} < 0$$

for all $0 < p_1 < 1$. The phase portrait is given in figure 2.2.1a where every initial interior point evolves monotonically to $p_1 = 0$ as $\dot{p}_1$ is always negative. This is called the Prisoner's Dilemma Class since it includes the payoff structure for the Prisoner's Dilemma Game that has

$$A = \begin{array}{c} \\ C \\ D \end{array} \begin{array}{c} C \quad D \\ \left[\begin{array}{cc} R & S \\ T & P \end{array} \right] \end{array}$$

with $T > R > P > S$. In this game players either Cooperate (C) or Defect (D) and receive payoffs that are known as Temptation (T), Reward (R), Punishment (P), and Sucker (S). In dynamical terms, the dilemma is that the population evolves to mutual defection (i.e., everyone receives P) even though individuals are better off if they mutually cooperate and receive R. We call the case $(a - c)(d - b) = 0$ the Degenerate Prisoner's Dilemma.

---

9. We discard the case $d = b$ and $a = c$ since every point $0 \leq p_1 \leq 1$ is then a rest point and so the dynamic is uninteresting.

Coordination Class   (Payoffs satisfy $a > c$ and $d > b$)   Since $(a-c)(d-b) > 0$, the dynamic (2.2.1) can be rewritten as $\dot{p}_1 = (a - c + d - b)p_1(1 - p_1)(p_1 - p_1^*)$, which has

$$p_1^* = (d - b)/(a - c + d - b) \tag{2.2.2}$$

as the unique interior rest point. Then $\dot{p}_1 > 0$ if and only if $p_1 > p_1^*$. Thus any initial point $p_1(0) > p_1^*$ evolves monotonically to $p_1 = 1$, whereas $p_1(0) < p_1^*$ implies p_1 evolves to 0 (see figure 2.2.1b). The typical Coordination Game that has payoff matrix $A = \begin{bmatrix} a & 0 \\ 0 & d \end{bmatrix}$ where a and d are both positive is in this class. The replicator dynamic demonstrates that different convergent trajectories may have different stable limit points (i.e., one population may eventually coordinate itself on one of the two pure strategies in figure 2.2.1b, while another evolves to the other pure strategy). In particular, the replicator dynamic does not initially suggest a means for all individuals to coordinate mutual play on the first pure strategy in the Coordination Game that has $a > d$.

Hawk-Dove Class   (Payoffs satisfy $a < c$ and $d < b$)   As shown in figure 2.2.1c, every interior point $p_1(0)$ now evolves monotonically under (2.2.1) to the interior rest point p_1^* given by (2.2.2). This is called the Hawk-Dove class after the Hawk-Dove Game with payoff matrix

$$A = \begin{matrix} H \\ D \end{matrix} \begin{matrix} H & D \\ \begin{bmatrix} \dfrac{V}{2} - C & V \\ 0 & \dfrac{V}{2} \end{bmatrix} \end{matrix},$$

where $C > V/2 > 0$. The Hawk-Dove Game is one of the earliest games considered by biological game theorists who used it as a model of pairwise animal conflict over a resource of value V. Hawks (H) fight over the resource at a cost of C, whereas Doves (D) simply split the resource and Hawk-Dove contests are won at no cost by H. The dynamic in figure 2.2.1c illustrates the intuitive idea that a polymorphic population should emerge if strategies do well (i.e., have the higher payoff) whenever they are rare.

The three qualitatively different dynamic behaviors exhibited in figure 2.2.1 can all be described by a comparison of payoffs to the two pure strategies (i.e., $e_1 \cdot Ap$ compared to $e_2 \cdot Ap$). Specifically, p_1 is

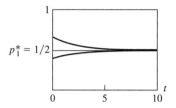

Figure 2.2.2
Typical trajectories for the Hawk-Dove Game. Two trajectories of (2.2.1) for the Hawk-Dove Game with $C = V = 2$. The trajectory above $p_1^* = \frac{1}{2}$ has initial point $p_1 = \frac{2}{3}$, and the one below has $p_1 = \frac{2}{5}$.

strictly increasing (i.e., $\dot{p}_1 > 0$) at an interior point if and only if $e_1 \cdot Ap > p \cdot Ap$ if and only if $e_1 \cdot Ap > e_2 \cdot Ap$. Analogously, for the discrete-time replicator dynamic, p_1 is strictly increasing (i.e., $p_1' > p_1$) if and only if $e_1 \cdot Ap > e_2 \cdot Ap$. Thus the qualitative dynamics for the Prisoner's Dilemma Class are the same for both the continuous-time and discrete-time replicator dynamics. The same is true for the Coordination Class.

The Hawk-Dove Class must be treated more carefully since it is possible that p_1' is on the opposite side of p_1^* than p_1 (i.e., evolution may not occur monotonically). A priori p_1' could even be farther away from the rest point than p_1 which would then suggest that the discrete-time dynamic may not converge to p_1^*. The details given in the partial proof of the following theorem show these possibilities cannot occur for the discrete-time replicator dynamic (but see example 2.3.3 in section 2.3 below). The remainder of the straightforward proof of theorem 2.2.1 is omitted. Figure 2.2.2 shows some sample trajectories for the replicator dynamic (2.2.1) of the Hawk-Dove Game with $C = V = 2$ which clearly indicate convergence takes infinite time as p_1 approaches $p_1^* = \frac{1}{2}$ asymptotically as $t \to \infty$.

Theorem 2.2.1   *For symmetric normal form games with two strategies, every interior trajectory of (2.1.1) or (2.1.2) evolves monotonically toward a rest point of the dynamic that is a symmetric NE. If not initially at rest, this convergence takes infinite time.*

Proof   Consider (2.1.1) for the Hawk-Dove Class (i.e., $0 < a < c$ and $0 < d < b$). Without loss of generality, assume $0 < p_1 < p_1^*$. To show p_1 evolves monotonically to p_1^* in infinite time, it is sufficient to prove that $p_1' < p_1^*$ since $e_1 \cdot Ap > e_2 \cdot Ap$ implies $p_1 < p_1'$ in this case. To show $p_1' < p_1^*$, notice that this inequality is equivalent to each of the following four conditions:

i. $p_1(e_1 \cdot Ap / p \cdot Ap) < (b - d)/[b + c - (a + d)]$

ii. $(c - a)p_1 e_1 \cdot Ap < (b - d)p_2 e_2 \cdot Ap$

iii. $(c-a)p_1 < cp_1 + dp_2$, since $(b-d)p_2 - (c-a)p_1 = e_1 \cdot Ap - e_2 \cdot Ap > 0$ for $p_1 < p_1^*$

iv. $(d - a)p_1 < d$

Clearly, if $a \geq d$, then $p_1' < p_1^*$. On the other hand, if $a < d$, then $p_1' < p_1^*$ if and only if $p_1 < d/(d - a)$. But $d/(d - a) > (b - d)/[b + c - (a + d)] = p_1^*$, since $dc + ab > ad + ad$ and so $p_1 < d/(d - a).$[10]   ∎

2.3 Monotone Selection Dynamics

This section and the following introduce other deterministic dynamics for general symmetric normal form games and compare the properties of these dynamics to those of the replicator dynamic when there are two strategies. One such class of dynamics is the monotone selection dynamics. These are autonomous dynamical systems that, in continuous time, have the form

$$\dot{p}_i = f_i(p) \tag{2.3.1}$$

and in discrete time,

$$p_i' = p_i + f_i(p), \tag{2.3.2}$$

where the vector field $f(p) = (f_1(p), \ldots, f_n(p))$ satisfies the relevant conditions in the following two definitions:

Definition 2.3.1 *The continuous-time dynamic (2.3.1) is a (regular) selection dynamic if, for all $1 \leq i \leq n$,*

i. *$f_i(p)$ is Lipschitz continuous on some open neighborhood in $\mathbf{R}^n$ of Δ^n.*

ii. *$\sum_{i=1}^{n} f_i(p) = 0$ for all $p \in \Delta^n$.*

iii. *$f_i(p)/p_i$ extends to a continuous real-valued function on Δ^n.*

---

10. Note that $p_1' = b/(b + c) = p_1^*$ after one generation if $a = d = 0$. Otherwise (e.g., if $a > 0$ and $d > 0$ as we assume for the discrete dynamics), the trajectory does not reach p_1^* in finite time.

The discrete-time dynamic (2.3.2) is a (regular) *selection dynamic if, in addition to these three conditions,* Δ^n *is forward invariant[11] along with each of its faces and their interiors. Condition iii is the regularity condition and will always be assumed for our selection dynamics. If* $f_i(p)/p_i$ *is continuously differentiable on some open neighborhood in* $\mathbf{R}^n$ *of* Δ^n, *the selection dynamic will be called* smooth.

Some technical remarks are in order here, especially for the continuous-time dynamic (2.3.1). Lipschitz continuity means there is some positive k such that $|f_i(p) - f_i(\hat{p})| < k|p - \hat{p}|$ for all p and $\hat{p}$ in the given neighborhood. It is a standard assumption in dynamical systems theory to ensure that for any $p(0) \in \Delta^n$, there is a unique trajectory $p(t)$ satisfying (2.3.1) that is defined for all $0 \leq t \leq t_0$ for some $t_0 > 0$. By condition ii, $(\sum \dot{p}_i) = 0$, so $\sum p_i$ is constant. By condition iii, $\dot{p}_i = f_i(p) = 0$ whenever $p_i = 0$. Together these imply that $p(t)$ is defined for all $t \geq 0$ and $\mathrm{supp}(p(t)) = \mathrm{supp}(p(0))$. In particular, Δ^n is forward invariant.

Although there are other selection dynamics considered in the literature, we concentrate on those that are monotone according to the following definition (i.e., strategies with higher expected payoffs increase in relative frequency). Since $d(p_i/p_j)/dt = (\dot{p}_i p_j - p_i \dot{p}_j)/(p_j)^2 = (p_i/p_j)[(f_i(p)/p_i) - (f_j(p)/p_j)]$ whenever $p_i p_j > 0$, p_i increases relative to p_j if $f_i(p)/p_i > f_j(p)/p_j$. Monotonicity then connects the growth rates $f_i(p)/p_i$ from equations (2.3.1) and (2.3.2) to the expected payoffs $e_i \cdot Ap$ as follows:

Definition 2.3.2   *A selection dynamic is* monotone *if, for all* $p \in \Delta^n$, $f_i(p)/p_i > f_j(p)/p_j$ *if and only if* $e_i \cdot Ap > e_j \cdot Ap$. *It is* aggregate monotone *if, for all* $p, r, s \in \Delta^n$, $\sum_{i=1}^{n}(r_i - s_i)(f_i(p)/p_i) > 0$ *if and only if* $r \cdot Ap > s \cdot Ap$. *A monotone selection dynamic is* uniformly monotone *if, for some* $K \geq 1$, $K|e_i \cdot Ap - e_j \cdot Ap| \geq |(f_i(p)/p_i) - (f_j(p)/p_j)| \geq (1/K)|e_i \cdot Ap - e_j \cdot Ap|$ *for all* $p \in \Delta^n$.

Every aggregate monotone selection dynamic is monotone (take r and s to be the pure strategies e_i and e_j respectively), but not conversely unless we have a two-strategy game. Aggregate monotonicity is especially relevant in population models where individuals can play

---

11. Forward invariance for the discrete-time dynamic does not follow from these three conditions since it is possible p_i' may be negative when p_i is positive. Thus we add forward invariance as a separate condition. Although Lipschitz continuity is no longer required on theoretical grounds, we maintain it here since these vector fields typically arise through their continuous-time analogues.

mixed strategies such as r or s in Δ^n since it then implies the relative frequency of mixed strategists with higher expected payoffs increases. Uniform monotonicity requires a positive linear correlation between relative growth rates and payoff differences.

The replicator dynamic is then the special monotone selection dynamic that has $f_i(p) = p_i(e_i \cdot Ap - p \cdot Ap)$ for continuous time and $f_i(p) = p_i(e_i \cdot Ap - p \cdot Ap)/(p \cdot Ap)$ for discrete time. It is straightforward to verify the replicator dynamic is uniformly aggregate monotone. Conversely, the vector field for any aggregate monotone selection dynamic is a positive multiple of that for the replicator dynamic at each point $p \in \Delta^n$ which implies that their continuous-time trajectories are identical up to a rescaling of time (see Notes). In fact theorem 2.2.1 for two-strategy games remains valid for any continuous-time monotone selection dynamic, not only those that are aggregate monotone (see theorem 2.4.1 below). On the other hand, for general discrete-time monotone selection dynamics, the theorem only applies to games of the Prisoner's Dilemma or the Coordination Classes. In all these cases the phase portrait is the appropriate diagram in figure 2.2.1. The following example shows theorem 2.2.1 is not correct for all discrete-time monotone selection dynamics and Hawk-Dove games:

Example 2.3.3 Let $A = \begin{bmatrix} 1 & 2 \\ 2 & 1 \end{bmatrix}$ with $p_1^* = \frac{1}{2}$. Consider the discrete dynamic $p_1' = p_1 + rp_1(1 - p_1)(\frac{1}{2} - p_1)$, where $0 < r < 16$ is a fixed parameter that regulates the rate at which evolution acts (i.e., larger r imply evolutionary changes occur faster). From the graphs of p_1' versus p_1 for various values of r in figure 2.3.1, it is apparent this is a discrete-time monotone selection dynamic that leaves Δ^2 and its interior forward invariant. In fact, since $f_i(p) = rp_i(1 - p_i)(\frac{1}{2} - p_i)$, the calculation $(f_1(p)/p_1) - (f_2(p)/p_2) = r(\frac{1}{2} - p_1) = \frac{1}{2}r(e_1 \cdot Ap - e_2 \cdot Ap)$ implies that the dynamic is a smooth aggregate uniformly monotone selection dynamic.

Thus $p_1' > p_1$ if and only if $0 < p_1 < p_1^* = \frac{1}{2}$. For $0 < r \leq 4$, convergence of any initial interior $p_1(0)$ to p_1^* is monotone.[12] For $4 < r \leq 8$, all interior trajectories converge to p_1^* but not necessarily monotonically. In fact, if $p_1(0)$ is sufficiently close to p_1^*, the trajectories oscillate from one side to the other of p_1^*. For almost all $p_1(0)$ there is eventually this oscillation (except on a countable set of measure zero that reaches p_1^* in finite

---

12. This follows from figure 2.3.1a since p_1' is an increasing function of p_1 that is concave down for $p_1 < p_1^* = \frac{1}{2}$ and concave up for $p_1 > p_1^*$.

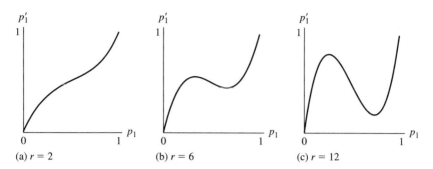

(a) r = 2   (b) r = 6   (c) r = 12

Figure 2.3.1
Graph of p_1' versus p_1 for example 2.3.3.

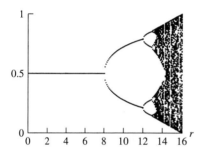

Figure 2.3.2
Bifurcation diagram for example 2.3.3. This diagram indicates the limit points of almost all interior trajectories. For $0 < r \leq 8$, all interior trajectories converge to $p_1^* = \frac{1}{2}$. As r increases beyond 8, first a stable limit cycle of period two appears and then a period four cycle at $r = 12$, and so on, until finally chaos sets in.

time). Finally, for $8 < r < 16$, complex dynamic behavior emerges as $r = 8$ is a critical value for a period-doubling bifurcation of the dynamic (since $dp_1'/dp_1|_{p_1=1/2} = -1$ when $r = 8$). From the bifurcation diagram of figure 2.3.2, we see chaotic behavior occurs before r reaches 14.

Example 2.3.3 illustrates that complex dynamic behavior can result from elementary discrete-time evolutionary processes. This is one of the main reasons dynamic evolutionary game theory deals primarily with continuous-time dynamics. Somewhat surprisingly, the discrete-time monotone selection dynamics still satisfy the Folk Theorem of Evolutionary Game Theory (see theorem 2.5.3 below). In this book we will continue to consider discrete-time evolutionary processes from time to time, especially the following fictitious play process that often behaves better than a general discrete-time monotone selection dynamic (see also sections 2.8.1 and 2.10 below for other discrete-time evolutionary processes).

2.4 Fictitious Play and Best Response Dynamic

As an individual adjustment process in a two-player normal form game, fictitious play assumes each player has an *initial belief* as to the initial strategy, $p(1)$, that his opponent will use. In the fictitious play each player would play a best reply to his *current belief*, and this causes his opponent to adjust his belief to a weighted average of this best reply and his current belief. Specifically, for symmetric normal form games where both players are assumed to have the same initial belief, the *fictitious play* process is

$$p(m+1) = \frac{m}{m+1}p(m) + \frac{1}{m+1}BR(p(m)), \qquad (2.4.1)$$

where $BR(p(m)) \equiv \{\hat{p} \in \Delta^n \mid \hat{p} \cdot Ap(m) \geq p \cdot Ap(m) \text{ for all } p \in \Delta^n\}$ is the *set of best replies* to $p(m)$.[13] Thus $p(2) = \frac{1}{2}p(1) + \frac{1}{2}BR(p(1))$, $p(3) = \frac{2}{3}p(2) + \frac{1}{3}BR(p(2)) = \frac{1}{3}(p(1) + BR(p(1)) + BR(p(2)))$, and so on. Clearly, if $p \in BR(p)$ (i.e., p is a symmetric NE), then the constant solution $p(m) = p$ for all m satisfies (2.4.1).

For symmetric normal form games, fictitious play also emerges as the following population adjustment process: At generation 1, there is only one player in the population, and this player uses some strategy $p(1) \in \Delta^n$. At generation 2, a second player enters who chooses a strategy to maximize his expected payoff in a random contest (i.e., he chooses a best reply to $p(1)$). If one new player enters each generation and plays a best reply to the existing average population strategy (and no previous player ever leaves or changes his strategy), then the average population strategy at generation k, $p(k)$, satisfies (2.4.1).

Let us consider fictitious play for two-strategy symmetric normal form games. By a careful examination of all possible cases, it can be shown that every fictitious play trajectory converges to some symmetric NE if a particular $b \in BR(p)$ is chosen for every $p \in \Delta^2$. For the nondegenerate Prisoner's Dilemma Class (i.e., $a < c$ and $b < d$), $BR(p) = e_2$ for all $p \in \Delta^2$ since e_2 is the *strictly dominant strategy* (i.e., $e_1 \cdot Ap < e_2 \cdot Ap$ for

---

13. If $BR(p)$ is single valued for all $p \in \Delta^n$, then $p(m+1)$ is well defined in (2.4.1). Otherwise, it would be more notationally correct to write (2.4.1) as $(m+1)p(m+1) - mp(m) \in BR(p(m))$ even though the given formula is more common.

all $p \in \Delta^2$). Thus $p(m) = p(1)/m + e_2 m/(m+1)$ for every initial $p(1)$, and so $p(m)$ converges to e_2 monotonically in infinite time.

For the Coordination Class it is clear that $p(m)$ converges monotonically to e_2 if $p_1(1) < p_1^*$ and to e_1 if $p_1(1) > p_1^*$ in infinite time where p_1^* is the equilibrium value given in (2.2.2). On the other hand, Coordination games already illustrate a new complication for fictitious play processes; namely there is more than one fictitious play trajectory through some initial points. Specifically, if $p_1(1) = p_1^*$, then $BR(p(1)) = \Delta^2$. In order to define a deterministic dynamic, a single strategy in Δ^2 must be chosen[14] in $BR(p^*)$. This choice is called a *tie-breaking rule*. Then, if $p_1(1) = p_1^*$, $p(m)$ converges monotonically to e_2 if the choice $b = (b_1, b_2)$ in $BR(p^*)$ has $b_1 < p_1^*$, to e_1 if $b_1 > p_1^*$ and $p(m) = p^*$ for all m if $b_1 = p_1^*$.

The most interesting two-strategy dynamic for fictitious play is again the Hawk-Dove Class. Suppose that $p_1^* = \frac{1}{2}$ as in example 2.3.3. If $p(1) \notin \{e_1, e_2, p^*\}$, fictitious play oscillates on either side of p^* as it converges to it. Notice that the sequence of best replies does not converge but the fictitious play sequence (i.e., the sequence of current beliefs) does. If $p(1) \in \{e_1, e_2\}$, then $p(2) = p^*$, which is a rest point if $p^* \in BR(p^*)$ is chosen as the tie-breaking rule. On the other hand, if e_1 or e_2 is chosen in $BR(p^*)$, then there is no rest point, although $p(m)$ converges to p^* at the same time that $p(m) = p^*$ for each even m.

The *best response dynamic* for symmetric normal form games is the following continuous-time analogue of fictitious play: From (2.4.1), $p(m+1) - p(m) = (BR(p(m)) - p(m))/(m+1)$. If we equate this difference to $\dot{p}(m)$, we obtain a nonautonomous system due to the positive factor $1/(m+1)$. The best response dynamic ignores this factor (just as the replicator dynamic (2.1.2) ignores the positive denominator $p \cdot Ap$ in (2.1.1)) to become

$$\dot{p} = BR(p) - p. \tag{2.4.2}$$

This dynamic[15] can also be developed from first principles as an overlapping generation population model where a fraction $\tau > 0$ of the total population revise their strategy in each time interval of length τ by

14. Common choices are some pure strategy in $BR(p)$ or p itself if $p \in BR(p)$. We will see another important choice for the best response dynamic later this section.
15. Technically (2.4.2) is a *differential inclusion* rather than a dynamical system since $BR(p)$ is a set-valued function (see appendix B, chapter 7.7). In general, $BR(p)$ is only upper semicontinuous in p (specifically, $BR(p) \subset BR(p_0)$ for every p in some neighborhood of p_0). At those $p \in \Delta^n$ where $BR(p)$ is not single valued, we can only expect $p(t)$ to have a right-hand derivative that satisfies (2.4.2).

choosing a current best reply. The dynamic (2.4.2) results when we let $\tau \to 0$.

Trajectories for (2.4.2) are again not unique for a given initial point $p(0)$ since the vector field $BR(p) - p$ is not single valued. The general trajectories can be quite complicated, especially when there is a large number n of pure strategies. However, we will restrict attention to piecewise linear trajectories of (2.4.2) that are defined for all $t \geq 0$ for a given initial point $p(0)$. To construct these, note that $b \in BR(p)$ is a best response to all $(1 - \varepsilon)p + \varepsilon b$ $(0 \leq \varepsilon \leq \varepsilon_0)$ for some $\varepsilon_0 > 0$ if and only if $b \in BR(p)$ and b is a best reply to itself among all $BR(p)$. Such a b exists since this is the same as asserting that b is a NE of the game whose strategies have support contained in $BR(p)$. Thus the best response trajectory can travel in the straight line from p toward b for a positive amount of time (if $p \in BR(p)$, then p can be chosen as b in which case the line becomes constant thereafter) until b must be altered, and then this process is iterated.[16]

For two-strategy games the phase portraits are identical to figure 2.2.1 except that the unstable rest points shown there (indicated by empty circles) are not necessarily rest points of the best response dynamic. In particular, we have the following generalization of theorem 2.2.1 to the dynamics of sections 2.3 and 2.4:

Theorem 2.4.1 *For every symmetric normal form game[17] with two strategies, every trajectory of the continuous-time monotone selection and best response dynamics as well as the fictitious play process converges to a rest point of the replicator dynamic. Every interior trajectory converges to a symmetric NE.*

There are several interesting differences between the deterministic dynamics of sections 2.3 and 2.4. The most significant is that the vector fields for (2.4.1) and (2.4.2) in section 2.4 are not continuous. There are abrupt changes at those $p \in \Delta^n$ with at least two pure strategies in $BR(p)$. That is, these dynamics are not (regular) selection dynamics (in fact fictitious play is not even autonomous). Although it is still true that Δ^n is forward invariant for these dynamics, its faces are not. In general, the support of $p(t)$ increases in t (i.e., $\text{supp}(p(t)) \subseteq \text{supp}(p(\hat{t}))$ whenever $t \leq \hat{t}$). In particular, $\overset{\circ}{\Delta}(S)$ remains forward invariant.

---

16. There is a potential difficulty with this construction if the total length of this countably infinite number of time intervals is finite. In this case there will be a unique "accumulation" point for this finite time from which the process can be restarted.

17. In the degenerate case where $a = c$ and $b = d$, the statement is still true, although of little interest since every $p \in \Delta^2$ is a rest point of (2.1.2).

One other difference of note is that best response trajectories that converge to an interior NE, p^*, typically do so in finite time (cf. theorem 2.2.1). For instance, for the Hawk-Dove Class with interior rest point p^*, the unique best response trajectory with initial point $p_1(0) > p_1^*$ consists of the single line segment

$$
p(t) = \begin{cases}
(1 - \exp(-t))e_2 + \exp(-t)p(0) & \text{if } 0 \leq t \leq \ln\left(\dfrac{p_1(0)}{p_1^*}\right), \\[3mm]
p^* & \text{if } t > \ln\left(\dfrac{p_1(0)}{p_1^*}\right),
\end{cases}
$$

that reaches p^* at time $\ln(p_1(0)/p_1^*)$ (there is a similar formula for $p(t)$ when $p_1(0) < p_1^*$).

2.5   Convergence and Stability: NE and ESS

All of the dynamics for symmetric normal form games considered in the previous sections satisfy the Folk Theorem of Evolutionary Game Theory as stated in theorem 2.5.3 below. To make the statement rigorous, we first provide formal definitions of the equilibrium and stability concepts that have only been introduced informally to this point.

Definition 2.5.1   *For a symmetric normal form game, p^* is a symmetric NE if it is a best reply against itself and it is a strict symmetric NE if it is the unique best reply against itself. In terms of the $n \times n$ payoff matrix A, p^* is a symmetric NE if $p \cdot Ap^* \leq p^* \cdot Ap^*$ for all $p \in \Delta^n$ which is strict if $p \cdot Ap^* < p^* \cdot Ap^*$ whenever $p \neq p^*$.*
    $p^* \in \Delta^n$ is an evolutionarily stable strategy (ESS) *if it is a symmetric NE and $p^* \cdot Ap > p \cdot Ap$ for all $p \in \Delta^n$ for which $p \neq p^*$ and $p \cdot Ap^* = p^* \cdot Ap^*$. $p^* \in \Delta^n$ is a* neutrally stable strategy (NSS) *if it is a symmetric NE and $p^* \cdot Ap \geq p \cdot Ap$ whenever $p \cdot Ap^* = p^* \cdot Ap^*$.[18] Clearly, every strict symmetric NE is an ESS and every ESS is an NSS.*

Definition 2.5.2   *$p^* \in \Delta^n$ is* stable *for an autonomous dynamic on Δ^n if, for all open neighborhoods U of p^*, there is another open neighborhood O of p^* such that any dynamic trajectory with initial point in $O \cap \Delta^n$ remains inside $U \cap \Delta^n$. $p^* \in \Delta^n$ is* unstable *if it is not stable. $p^* \in \Delta^n$ is* attracting *if there is some open neighborhood U of p^* such that all trajectories that are initially in $U \cap \Delta^n$ converge to p^* in which case $U \cap \Delta^n$ is called a* basin of attraction *of p^*. $p^* \in \Delta^n$ is* asymptotically stable *if it is stable and attracting. $p^* \in \Delta^n$*

---

18. An NSS is also known as a *weak ESS*.

is globally asymptotically stable *if it is asymptotically stable and all interior trajectories converge to* p^* *(i.e.,* $\overset{\circ}{\Delta}(S)$ *is contained in a basin of attraction of* p^**).*

It is implicitly understood in definition 2.5.2 that the autonomous dynamic is forward invariant on the compact set Δ^n. It is then sometimes useful to rephrase stability concepts in terms of the ω-limits of dynamic trajectories.[19] For instance, $p^* \in \Delta^n$ is attracting if, for some open neighborhood U of p^*, all trajectories initially in $U \cap \Delta^n$ have p^* as their only ω-limit point. A point $p^* \in \Delta^n$ is called an ω-*limit point* of the trajectory $p(t) \in \Delta^n$ if there is a sequence $t_m \to \infty$ such that $\lim_{m \to \infty} p(t_m) = p^*$. The ω-*limit set*, Ω, of a trajectory is the set of all its ω-limit points. Ω is nonempty by the compactness of Δ^n.

Although definition 2.5.2 is formally restricted to dynamical systems that are autonomous such as a monotone selection dynamic, it is also applicable to the differential inclusion given by the best response dynamic. In fact we will apply the same definition to the nonautonomous fictitious play process as well with the understanding that stability only refers to the "tail end" of a fictitious play trajectory (e.g., p^* is stable if, for some positive integer m, $p(m) \in O \cap \Delta^n$ implies that $p(m + k) \in U \cap \Delta^n$ for all positive integers k, etc.).

Theorem 2.5.3 *Every evolutionary dynamic considered to this point satisfies the Folk Theorem of Evolutionary Game Theory. These are the continuous-time and discrete-time monotone selection dynamics (including the replicator dynamics) as well as fictitious play and the best response dynamic. Specifically, we have the following:*

  i. *If* $p^* \in \Delta^n$ *is stable, it is a symmetric NE.*

 ii. *If an interior trajectory converges to* p^**, it is a symmetric NE.*

iii. *A strict symmetric NE is asymptotically stable.*

Proof Most of the details of the proof are omitted. Parts i and ii follow from the fact $p^* \notin BR(p^*)$ if p^* is not a symmetric NE. Also $\{\sum p_i \mid e_i \in BR(p^*)\}$ is strictly increasing along any interior trajectory in some neighborhood of p^* under any of these evolutionary dynamics. Conversely, for part iii, if p^* is a strict symmetric NE, then p^* is a pure strategy e_i that is the unique best reply in $BR(p)$ for all p in some neighborhood of p^*. Thus p_i monotonically increases to 1 for all p initially sufficiently close to p^*. ∎

---

19. This perspective is particularly important in chapter 9.

It is well-known that every symmetric normal form game has at least one symmetric NE and that some games do not have a strict symmetric NE. From theorem 2.5.3 we see that the concept of dynamic stability of a strategy p^* is somewhere between that of symmetric and strict symmetric NE. That is, all strict symmetric NE are stable strategies and all stable strategies are symmetric NE. None of these sets are equal. For instance, the interior equilibrium of the two-strategy Coordination Class is a symmetric NE that is not stable, whereas it is stable but not a strict symmetric NE for the Hawk-Dove Class. However, dynamic stability is actually equivalent to the ESS concept for two-strategy games by the following result:

Theorem 2.5.4   *Consider two-strategy games[20] and any of the dynamics specified in theorem 2.5.3 with the exception of the discrete-time monotone selection dynamics. Then every interior trajectory that is not initially at rest converges to an ESS. Furthermore, for all these dynamics, the following three statements are equivalent:*

  i. $p^* \in \Delta^n$ is stable.

 ii. p^* is asymptotically stable.

iii. p^* is an ESS.

Theorem 2.5.4 exemplifies the original appeal to biological game theorists of the dynamic approach. In general, biologists who model species behavior through game theory expect to observe an ESS strategy for natural populations that are no longer evolving. From their perspective, if a stable population is not at an ESS, individuals will have already appeared who use a behavior p for which $p^* \cdot Ap \leq p \cdot Ap$.[21] Such a population would then continue to evolve since there is no selection against this *mutant* behavior p. Thus a determination of the ESSs of the model is their primary interest from the game theory method.

The ideal situation for economic game theorists who use dynamic evolutionary game theory as an equilibrium selection technique is that there is a unique ESS and no other strategy is dynamically stable. The problem of multiple ESSs arises already for two-strategy Coordination Games. Here additional dynamic techniques (e.g., spatial and/or stochastic effects) can be used to select one (typically the one with the larger basin

---

20. Here we ignore the degenerate case noted in theorem 2.4.1.
21. An important equivalence here (see theorem 2.7.1 below) is that p^* is an ESS if and only if $p^* \cdot Ap > p \cdot Ap$ for all $p \in \Delta^n$ that are sufficiently close (but not equal) to p^*.

of attraction for the replicator dynamic which happens to be the risk dominant strategy[22] in this case). Such considerations are beyond the scope of this book. Unfortunately, for symmetric normal form games with more than two strategies, the correspondence between dynamic stability and the ESS concept is much more tenuous as will become clear in the following section.

2.6 Three-Strategy Game Dynamics

We do not give a complete classification of all possible phase portraits for three-strategy games[23] as we did in figure 2.2.1 for the three classes of two-strategy games. Rather we focus on a few particular classes of three-strategy games whose analysis will be important for our treatment of extensive form games or that illustrate many of the added complexities that can arise when there are more than two pure strategies. In this section we concentrate on the graphs of the dynamic trajectories. Since these trajectories are curves in the two-dimensional triangle $\Delta(\{e_1, e_2, e_3\})$ with vertices at the three pure strategies $\{e_1, e_2, e_3\}$, convergence and stability can be pictured geometrically. However, the formal proofs for the statements concerning these trajectories rely on the analytic techniques introduced in section 2.7 below.

2.6.1 Rock–Scissors–Paper Games

An important class of three-strategy games are the Rock–Scissors–Paper Games (RSP) where best replies to pure strategies cycle (here R beats S beats P beats R). This cyclic dominance occurs for payoff matrices of the form

$$
\begin{array}{c@{\quad}c@{\quad}c@{\quad}c}
 & R & S & P \\
\begin{array}{c} R \\ S \\ P \end{array} &
\multicolumn{3}{l}{
\left[\begin{array}{ccc}
\varepsilon & 1 & -1 \\
-1 & \varepsilon & 1 \\
1 & -1 & \varepsilon
\end{array} \right]
}
\end{array}
\tag{2.6.1}
$$

whenever $|\varepsilon| < 1$ is a parameter that is usually considered to be close to 0. When $\varepsilon = 0$, we have the classic zero-sum RSP Game. For all $|\varepsilon| < 1$,

---

22. The risk dominant strategy for the Coordination Class Game with payoff matrix $\begin{bmatrix} a & b \\ c & d \end{bmatrix}$ is the pure strategy whose column corresponds to $\max\{a - c, d - b\}$.
23. For instance, there are approximately fifty different possible phase portraits for the replicator dynamic (see Notes).

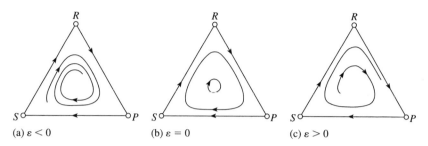

Figure 2.6.1
Replicator dynamic for RSP Games.

$p^* = (\frac{1}{3}, \frac{1}{3}, \frac{1}{3})$ is the unique symmetric NE, which is an ESS if and only if $\varepsilon < 0$ and an NSS if and only if $\varepsilon \leq 0$.[24] Of particular interest to us is the relationship between this NE and the dynamic trajectories. Let us first consider continuous-time dynamics.

The results for the replicator dynamic are most easily understood by calculating the time derivative of the function $V(p) \equiv p_1 p_2 p_3$ which has a unique maximum value on Δ^3 at p^*. Since

$$\frac{d}{dt} p_1 p_2 p_3 = -\varepsilon p_1 p_2 p_3 \left[\left(p_1 - \frac{1}{3} \right)^2 + \left(p_2 - \frac{1}{3} \right)^2 + \left(p_3 - \frac{1}{3} \right)^2 \right]$$

$$= -\varepsilon p_1 p_2 p_3 \left[p_1^2 + p_2^2 + p_3^2 - \frac{1}{3} \right],$$

$\dot{V}(p)$ does not change sign for any trajectory of (2.1.2) in the interior of Δ^3 (this is related to the concept of a Lyapunov function discussed in section 2.7 below). For instance, when $\varepsilon < 0$, $V(p)$ is strictly increasing unless $\dot{V}(p) = 0$ (i.e., unless $p = p^*$ or p is on the boundary of Δ^3). Similarly, since $\dot{V}(p) = 0$ for all p when $\varepsilon = 0$, every level curve of V in the interior of Δ^3 (these are the simple closed curves around p^* in figure 2.6.1b) is forward invariant.

Thus p^* is globally asymptotically stable if and only if p^* is an ESS. In this case (i.e., if $\varepsilon < 0$), the interior trajectories spiral around p^* as they converge to it. Typical trajectories are shown in figure 2.6.1a. Figure 2.6.1b illustrates that p^* is stable when it is an NSS for $\varepsilon = 0$. Finally figure 2.6.1c shows p^* is unstable for $\varepsilon > 0$ since the trajectories then spiral outward to the boundary of Δ^3 for any initial interior state except p^*.

---

24. To verify these results, it is easy to show that $p \cdot Ap^* = p^* \cdot Ap^*$ for all $p \in \Delta^3$ and that $p^* \cdot Ap - p \cdot Ap = -\varepsilon(p_1^2 + p_2^2 + p_3^2 - \frac{1}{3})$. Furthermore $p_1^2 + p_2^2 + p_3^2 > \frac{1}{3}$ for all $p \in \Delta^3$ with $p \neq p^*$.

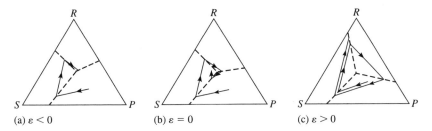

Figure 2.6.2
Best response dynamic for RSP Games.

The best response dynamic, drawn in figure 2.6.2 for $\varepsilon = 0$ and $\varepsilon = \pm\frac{1}{2}$, has p^* globally asymptotically stable for $\varepsilon \leq 0$ and unstable for $\varepsilon > 0$ in which case a unique limit cycle emerges that attracts all initial points. Notice that for $\varepsilon \leq 0$, the piecewise linear segments of the best response trajectory become increasingly short and that p^* is reached in finite time even though there are infinitely many such segments. From section 2.7 below, the relevant function to prove these results is now

$$V(p) = p \cdot Ap - \max_i \{e_i \cdot Ap\}.$$

In summary, equilibrium selection via dynamic evolutionary game theory for the continuous-time replicator and best response dynamics is closely related to the ESS analysis in RSP games. Specifically, p^* is stable if and only if it is an NSS. It is globally asymptotically stable for the replicator dynamic if and only if it is an ESS and for the best response dynamic if and only if it is an NSS. However, it is also clear that these dynamics do not always converge to a single limit point (e.g., for $\varepsilon > 0$) in which case no equilibrium solution can be selected by this method.[25]

General continuous-time monotone selection dynamics display more complicated phenomena for all $|\varepsilon| < 1$. For instance, with $\varepsilon = 0$, it can be shown that (2.3.1) with

$$f_i(p) = p_i \left(p_{i-1} \left(p_{i+1} - \frac{1}{3} \right) F_{i+1} - p_{i+1} \left(p_{i-1} - \frac{1}{3} \right) F_{i-1} \right)$$

is a smooth uniformly monotone selection dynamic[26] for any choice of

---

25. However, it is true that the average strategy over one cycle along an interior periodic trajectory is p^* for either the replicator or the best response dynamic.
26. The subscripts used to define this vector field are cyclic in $\{1, 2, 3\}$. That is, if $i = 3$, then $i + 1 = 1$, and so on. The replicator dynamic has $F_i(p) = 1$ for $i = 1, 2, 3$.

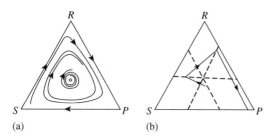

Figure 2.6.3
(a) Monotone selection dynamic for the zero-sum RSP Game (i.e., $\varepsilon = 0$) with a stable limit cycle. (b) The "never worst response" dynamic for the zero-sum RSP Game.

smooth positive-valued functions $F_i(p)$ that satisfy

$$\left(p_1 - \frac{1}{3}\right)F_1 + \left(p_2 - \frac{1}{3}\right)F_2 + \left(p_3 - \frac{1}{3}\right)F_3 = 0.$$

Now $d\,p_1 p_2 p_3/dt = 3 p_1 p_2 p_3 (p_1 - \frac{1}{3})(p_3 - \frac{1}{3})(F_3 - F_1)$ can be positive or negative, so an appropriate choice of F_i (see Notes) can lead to trajectories shown in figure 2.6.3a where p^* is unstable and is surrounded by stable and unstable limit cycles.

In fact p^* may be unstable even when it is an ESS. To see this, consider the trajectories in figure 2.6.3b when $\varepsilon = 0$ for the "never worst response" dynamic

$$\dot{p} = p - WR(p),$$

where $WR(p) \equiv \{\hat{p} \mid \hat{p} \cdot Ap \leq \tilde{p} \cdot Ap \text{ for all } \tilde{p} \in \Delta^n\}$. It is apparent these interior trajectories diverge from p^*. It is also apparent that trajectories of a monotone selection dynamic can be drawn arbitrarily close to these at least until we approach the boundary of Δ^n. Although p^* is not an ESS when $\varepsilon = 0$, the same approach shows p^* is unstable whenever ε is sufficiently close to zero. This includes cases with $\varepsilon < 0$ for which p^* is an ESS. On the other hand, theorem 2.7.4 in section 2.7 below shows that any smooth continuous-time uniformly monotone selection dynamic has p^* asymptotically stable if $\varepsilon < 0$ and unstable if $\varepsilon > 0$. That is, the instability of an ESS based on the trajectories in figure 2.6.3b rely on the vector field of a monotone selection dynamic near p^* having no linear dependence on payoff comparisons (i.e., the vector field cannot be uniformly monotone).

The discrete-time replicator dynamic is not defined for RSP games since some entries in the payoff matrix (2.6.1) are negative. Instead, let

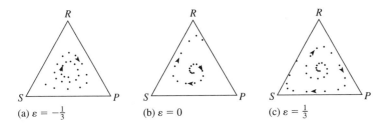

Figure 2.6.4
Discrete-time replicator dynamic for RSP Games.

us consider the discrete-time replicator dynamic for payoff matrices of the form

$$\begin{bmatrix} 1+\varepsilon & 2 & 0 \\ 0 & 1+\varepsilon & 2 \\ 2 & 0 & 1+\varepsilon \end{bmatrix}, \tag{2.6.2}$$

where $\varepsilon > -1$. Since these add the same constant, 1, to every entry of the RSP payoff matrix, their continuous-time replicator and best response dynamics are identical to the corresponding RSP Game (2.6.1). On the other hand, from figure 2.6.4 it is clear the discrete-time dynamics are unstable at p^* for $\varepsilon = 0$ and $\varepsilon = \pm\frac{1}{3}$ with trajectories spiraling toward the boundary.[27] In particular, there are ESSs that are unstable for the discrete-time replicator dynamic.

From the preceding analysis of RSP games, it seems the best chance we have to generalize our result for two-strategy games that ESSs correspond to dynamically stable equilibria is to restrict attention to continuous-time uniformly monotone and best response dynamics. The following example, which is also used in chapter 4.6.1, demonstrates further complications already arise in this correspondence for the replicator dynamic applied to three-strategy games.

Example 2.6.1 (A one-parameter family of generalized RSP Games) Consider the class of three-strategy games with payoff matrices of the form

$$\begin{bmatrix} 0 & 2-\alpha & 4 \\ 6 & 0 & -4 \\ -2 & 8-\alpha & 0 \end{bmatrix}. \tag{2.6.3}$$

---

27. The local instability of p^* is shown analytically at the end of section 2.7 below by calculating the eigenvalues of the linearized dynamic.

For $2 < \alpha < 8$ this is a generalized RSP Game with the required cyclic dominance. These form part of the parameter range, $-16 < \alpha < 14$, for which there is a unique interior symmetric NE $p^* = (28 - 2\alpha, 20, 16+\alpha)/(64-\alpha)$. For the replicator dynamic, p^* is globally asymptotically stable if and only if $-16 < \alpha < 6.5$, whereas it is an ESS if and only if $-16 < \alpha < 3.5$ and an NSS if and only if $-16 < \alpha \leq 3.5$.[28] Thus there are asymptotically stable rest points of the replicator dynamic that are neither an ESS nor an NSS.

2.6.2   ESSets and NE Components

One added complexity for extensive form games is that sets of NE will naturally appear. These can also arise for three-strategy games as the examples in section 2.6.3 show. Important sets of NE are the *NE components,* which are connected sets of NE that are maximal with respect to set inclusion (i.e., a NE component is not properly contained in another connected set of NE). Every NE component is closed. Furthermore no point in a NE component E with at least two elements can be asymptotically stable for a monotone selection dynamic since every $p \in E$ is a rest point. We are then often interested in the dynamic stability of E as a set according to the following generalization of definition 2.5.2.

Definition 2.6.2   *A closed set $E \subset \Delta^n$ is stable for a dynamic on Δ^n if, for all open neighborhoods U of E, there is another open neighborhood O of E such that any dynamic trajectory with initial point in $O \cap \Delta^n$ remains inside $U \cap \Delta^n$. $E \subset \Delta^n$ is attracting if there is some open neighborhood U of E such that all trajectories that are initially in $U \cap \Delta^n$ converge to E.[29] $E \subset \Delta^n$ is asymptotically stable if it is stable and attracting. $E \subset \Delta^n$ is globally asymptotically stable if it is asymptotically stable and all interior trajectories converge to E.*

Other important sets of NE for us are the ESSets of definition 2.6.3 due to their special dynamic properties. For instance, every ESSet is asymptotically stable for the replicator dynamic (theorem 2.7.4 below).

Definition 2.6.3   *A set E of symmetric NE is an* evolutionarily stable set *(ESSet) if, for all $p^* \in E$, $p^* \cdot Ap > p \cdot Ap$ whenever $p \cdot Ap^* = p^* \cdot Ap^*$ and $p \notin E$.*

---

28. For the best response dynamic, p^* is asymptotically stable if and only if $-16 < \alpha \leq 6.5$.
29. That is, the ω-limit set of all these trajectories is contained in E.

Every ESSet is a disjoint union of connected NE components, each of which must then be a connected ESSet. In particular, any ESS is a single-ton ESSet. Furthermore every p^* in an ESSet is an NSS by theorem 2.7.1 below.

2.6.3 More Three-Strategy Games

In this section we briefly summarize examples of three-strategy games that contain interesting ESSets.

Example 2.6.4 (An ESSet for a symmetric payoff matrix) A nontrivial example of a three-strategy game with an ESSet that is also relevant for models of natural selection (see section 2.8 below) has symmetric payoff matrix

$$\begin{bmatrix} 1 & 1 & 0 \\ 1 & 1 & 1 \\ 0 & 1 & 1 \end{bmatrix}. \tag{2.6.4}$$

From figure 2.6.5 the set E consisting of the two edges of Δ^3 that meet at e_2 is globally asymptotically stable for the replicator and best response dynamics (and for our other evolutionary dynamics as well).

Let us show $E = \{p \in \Delta^3 \mid p_1 p_3 = 0\}$ is an ESSet for this game. If $p^* = e_2$, then $p \cdot Ap^* = 1$ for all $p \in \Delta^3$ and $p^* \cdot Ap = 1 \geq 1 - 2p_1 p_3 = p \cdot Ap$ with equality if and only if $p \in E$. Similarly, if $p_3^* = 0$ and $p_1^* > 0$, then $1 - p_1^* p_3 = p \cdot Ap^* \leq p^* \cdot Ap^* = 1$ with equality if and only if $p_3 = 0$. In particular, $p \cdot Ap^* = p^* \cdot Ap^*$ implies $p \in E$, and so E is an ESSet. Furthermore E is the unique NE component of this game.

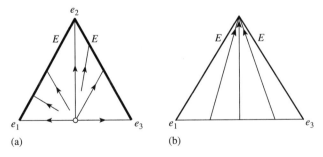

Figure 2.6.5
Phase portraits of example 2.6.4 for (a) replicator dynamic and (b) best-response dynamic.

Example 2.6.5 (Mixed-Strategy Games)   ESSets also arise naturally when individual players may use mixed strategies. For example, suppose that the three possible individual behaviors for a two-strategy game with payoff matrix $\begin{bmatrix} a & b \\ c & d \end{bmatrix}$ are, in order, $\{e_1, \frac{1}{2}(e_1+e_2), e_2\}$. Then the payoff matrix for the three-strategy game is

$$\begin{bmatrix} a & \dfrac{a+b}{2} & b \\[2mm] \dfrac{a+c}{2} & \dfrac{a+b+c+d}{4} & \dfrac{b+d}{2} \\[2mm] c & \dfrac{c+d}{2} & d \end{bmatrix}. \tag{2.6.5}$$

Trajectories of the replicator dynamic on Δ^3 lie on curves of the form $p_2^2 = p_1 p_3$ as shown in figure 2.6.6a. If there is a rest point $(p_1^*, 0, p_3^*)$ with $p_1^* p_3^* > 0$ (i.e., the two-strategy game has an interior rest point), then the line segment $E = \{p \in \Delta^3 \mid p_1 + \frac{1}{2}p_2 = p_1^*\}$ is a NE component of (2.6.5). Furthermore E is an ESSet if and only if the two-strategy game is of the Hawk-Dove Class. Trajectories of the best response dynamic in this case (figure 2.6.6b) are clear from the fact $\frac{1}{2}(e_1 + e_2) \notin BR(p)$ unless $p \in E$.

Examples 2.6.4 and 2.6.5 illustrate the general result that an ESSet must be the intersection of Δ^n with a finite union of linear subspaces of $\mathbf{R}^n$. Moreover, if an ESSet E contains two strategies with the same support, then the intersection of Δ^n with the line through these points must be a subset of E. In particular, if an interior strategy belongs to an ESSet E, then E is the only ESSet and consists of a single linear subspace of $\mathbf{R}^n$ intersected with Δ^n.

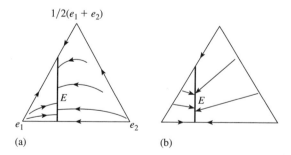

(a)   (b)

Figure 2.6.6
Phase portrait for the mixed-strategy Hawk-Dove Game of example 2.6.5. The right- and left-hand portraits are the replicator and best-response dynamic respectively.

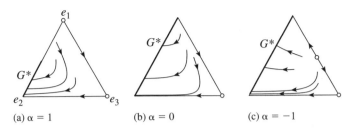

Figure 2.6.7
Phase portraits of the replicator dynamic for example 2.6.6.

Example 2.6.6 (Boundary NE Components)   Our last class of three-strategy games with payoff matrix of the form

$$\begin{bmatrix} 0 & 0 & -1 \\ 0 & 0 & 0 \\ \alpha & -1 & 0 \end{bmatrix} \tag{2.6.6}$$

shows the existence of other types of NE components. There are no interior NE since e_2 weakly dominates e_1 (i.e., $e_2 \cdot Ap \geq e_1 \cdot Ap$ for all $p \in \Delta^3$ with strict inequality if p is in the interior of Δ^3). The pure strategies e_2 and e_3 are NE for all values of α. Neither is an ESS. In fact, although e_3 is an isolated NE, it is unstable. On the other hand, e_2 is not isolated but belongs to a NE component G^* that contains all other NE. This NE component is the line segment on the boundary of Δ^3 with endpoints $\{e_1, e_2\}$ if $\alpha < 0$ (i.e., $G^* = \{p \in \Delta^3 \mid p_3 = 0\}$ which is then an ESSet) and the non-ESSet $G^* = \{p \in \Delta^3 \mid p_3 = 0, p_1 \leq 1/(1+\alpha)\}$ if $\alpha \geq 0$.

The preceding static results correspond remarkably well with the stability for the replicator dynamic as shown in figure 2.6.7 for $\alpha = 0$ and $\alpha = \pm 1$. Every point on the edge $\{e_1, e_2\}$ is a rest point, and so none is asymptotically stable. For $\alpha < 0$, every point on this edge is stable, and the edge as a whole is asymptotically stable since it is an ESSet. For $\alpha > 0$, only those p in the NE component G^* are stable. G^* itself is not asymptotically stable, although it is *globally interior attracting*.[30] The case $\alpha = 0$ is also interesting in that G^* is interior attracting but not asymptotically stable since e_1 is not stable. The vertices in all three phase diagrams in figure 2.6.7 (and also figure 2.6.8) are in the same order.

---

30. That is, G^* attracts all interior trajectories (see definition 8.2.1 in chapter 8).

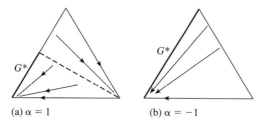

(a) $\alpha = 1$ (b) $\alpha = -1$

Figure 2.6.8
Phase portraits of the best response dynamic for example 2.6.6.

The best response dynamic of figure 2.6.8 is clear from the fact that $e_3 \in BR(p)$ if and only if $\alpha p_1 \geq p_2$. Thus every trajectory converges to the set of NE with interior ones evolving to either e_2 or e_3. In particular, G^* is neither asymptotically stable nor interior attracting for $\alpha > 0$ but is asymptotically stable for $\alpha < 0$.

2.7   Dynamic Stability for General Games

Dynamic stability has mostly been examined in the previous sections through geometric arguments for two- and three-strategy games. When there are more than three strategies, this geometric intuition breaks down and other techniques are needed to prove dynamic stability. The two most common are Lyapunov functions and linearization. A well-known illustration of both for continuous-time dynamics in evolutionary game theory is the demonstration following theorem 2.7.1 that an interior ESS $p^* \in \Delta^n$ of a symmetric normal form game is asymptotically stable for the replicator dynamic. The application of these methods to ESSs and ESSets rely on the properties summarized in the following theorem.

Theorem 2.7.1   *E is an ESSet if and only if each $p^* \in E$ has a neighborhood for which $p^* \cdot Ap \geq p \cdot Ap$ for all p in this neighborhood with equality if and only if $p \in E$. If an ESSet E contains an interior NE, then this inequality condition holds for all $p \in \Delta^n$. In particular, p^* is an ESS if and only if $p^* \cdot Ap > p \cdot Ap$ for all p that are sufficiently close (but not equal) to p^* and an interior ESS if and only if $p^* \cdot Ap > p \cdot Ap$ for all $p \neq p^*$. If p and q are elements of an ESSet for a symmetric normal form game with payoff matrix A and $p \cdot Aq = q \cdot Aq$, then $q \cdot Ap = p \cdot Ap$.*

Proof   Only the last statement will be proved since the other results are either well known or their proofs are straightforward. Suppose that p and q are elements of an ESSet E and $p \cdot Aq = q \cdot Aq$. Since $[(p+q)/2] \cdot Aq = \frac{1}{2}(p \cdot Aq + q \cdot Aq) = q \cdot Aq$ and $q \cdot A[(p+q)/2] - [(p+q)/2] \cdot A[(p+q)/2] = \frac{1}{4}[q \cdot Ap - p \cdot Ap + q \cdot Aq - p \cdot Aq] \leq 0$, $[(p+q)/2] \in E$. Therefore

$$0 \geq p \cdot A\frac{p+q}{2} - \frac{p+q}{2} \cdot A\frac{p+q}{2}$$

$$= \frac{p-q}{2} \cdot A\frac{p+q}{2}$$

$$= \frac{1}{4}[p \cdot Ap + p \cdot Aq - q \cdot Ap - q \cdot Aq]$$

$$= \frac{1}{4}[p \cdot Ap - q \cdot Ap]$$

$$\geq 0$$

since $p \in E$. Thus $q \cdot Ap = p \cdot Ap$. ∎

Suppose that p^* is an interior ESS and consider the function $V : \Delta^n \to \mathbf{R}^{\geq 0}$ given by[31]

$$V(p) = \prod_{i=1}^{n}(p_i)^{p_i^*}. \tag{2.7.1}$$

This is a nonnegative real-valued function that is positive in the interior of Δ^n and takes on its unique maximum at $p = p^*$. Furthermore, from the replicator dynamic (2.1.2),

$$\dot{V}(p) = \sum_{j=1}^{n} p_j^*(p_j)^{p_j^*-1} p_j(e_j - p) \cdot Ap \prod_{i \neq j}(p_i)^{p_i^*}$$

$$= V(p) \sum_{j=1}^{n} p_j^*(e_j - p) \cdot Ap$$

$$= V(p)(p^* - p) \cdot Ap.$$

Thus, by theorem 2.7.1, $\dot{V}(p) \geq 0$ with equality if and only if $p = p^*$ or p is on the boundary of Δ^n. That is, $V(p)$ is a strict Lyapunov function according to definition 2.7.2.

---

31. This same formula is also a Lyapunov function for a boundary ESS p^* when we adopt the convention that $(p_i)^{p_i^*} = 1$ if $p_i^* = 0$. In this case $V(p)$ still takes its unique maximum at p^* and its derivative is positive in a neighborhood of p^*.

For the linearization technique, let $p_i = p_i^* + x_i$ for each $p \in \Delta^n$. Then $x \equiv (x_1, \ldots, x_n) \in X^n \equiv \{(x_1, \ldots, x_n) \in \mathbf{R}^n \mid \sum x_i = 0\}$, and from (2.1.2),

$$\dot{x}_i = \dot{p}_i = (p_i^* + x_i)(e_i - (p^* + x)) \cdot A(p^* + x)$$

$$= p_i^*(e_i - p^*) \cdot Ax + x_i(e_i - p^*) \cdot Ax - (p_i^* + x_i)x \cdot Ax$$

$$= \sum_j L_{ij} x_j + \text{higher-order terms,}$$

where L is the $n \times n$ matrix with entries

$$L_{ij} = p_i^*(a_{ij} - p^* \cdot Ae_j). \tag{2.7.2}$$

Then $L : X^n \to X^n$ and $\langle x, Lx \rangle = \sum_{ij} x_i a_{ij} x_j - \sum_i x_i \sum_j p^* \cdot Ae_j = x \cdot Ax = (p - p^*) \cdot A(p - p^*) = p \cdot Ap - p^* \cdot Ap < 0$ for all nonzero $x \in X^n$ where $\langle x, y \rangle \equiv \sum_i x_i y_i / p_i^*$ is the Shahshahani inner product on X^n (see Notes). Thus L is a negative definite matrix on X^n, and so all its eigenvalues have negative real part. By theorem 2.7.3, either method shows p^* is asymptotically stable.

Definition 2.7.2   *Consider an autonomous dynamical system, $\dot{x}_i = f_i(x)$, on $\mathbf{R}^k$ with a rest point at x^*.*

i. A real-valued function $V(x)$ is a local Lyapunov function *if, for some neighborhood U of x^*, $V(x)$ is continuously differentiable and*

$$V(x) < V(x^*) \qquad \text{for all } x \in U$$

$$\dot{V}(x) = \sum_{j=1}^{k} \frac{\partial V(x)}{\partial x_j} f_j(x) \geq 0 \qquad \text{for all } x \in U.$$

$V(x)$ is a strict Lyapunov function *if it is a local Lyapunov function that satisfies $\dot{V}(x) > 0$ for all $x \in U$ with $x \neq x^*$.*

ii. If $f_i(x)$ is continuously differentiable at x^* for $i = 1, \ldots, k$, the linearized dynamic *about x^* is*

$$\dot{x}_i = \sum_{j=1}^{k} L_{ij} x_j,$$

where $L_{ij} = \partial f_i(x)/\partial x_j|_{x=x^*}$ is the $k \times k$ Jacobian matrix.

Theorem 2.7.3   *Suppose that the dynamical system, $\dot{x}_i = f_i(x)$, on $\mathbf{R}^k$ has a rest point at x^*. Then x^* is stable if there exists a local Lyapunov function $V(x)$ (in this case the ω-limit set of every nearby trajectory is contained in*

$\{x \mid \dot{V}(x) = 0\}$). *It is asymptotically stable if the Lyapunov function is strict or if the eigenvalues of the Jacobian all have negative real part. It is unstable if some eigenvalue of the Jacobian has positive real part (or if $-V$ is a strict Lyapunov function).*

Definition 2.7.2 and theorem 2.7.3 give the basic theory for these two fundamental linearization and Lyapunov techniques that are sufficient to prove the stability results summarized in theorem 2.7.4. The most direct proof of these stability results (see section 2.11, the appendix, for details) for the replicator and best response dynamics rely on the Lyapunov functions (2.7.1) and

$$V(p) = p \cdot Ap - \max_i \{e_i \cdot Ap\} \tag{2.7.3}$$

respectively. On the other hand, the linearization technique is most appropriate for the final two statements of theorem 2.7.4.

Theorem 2.7.4 *Suppose that E is an ESSet. Then E is asymptotically stable for the replicator dynamic and forward invariant for the best response dynamic.*[32] *If E contains a NE p^* such that $p^* \cdot Ap \geq p \cdot Ap$ for all $p \in \Delta^n$, it is globally asymptotically stable for the replicator dynamic. If E contains an interior NE, it is globally asymptotically stable for the replicator, best response, and fictitious play dynamics.*

Every NSS (in particular, every p^* in an ESSet) is stable for the replicator dynamic.[33] *If there is a $p^* \in \Delta^n$ such that $p^* \cdot Ap > p \cdot Ap$ for all $p \neq p^*$ (in particular, if p^* is an interior ESS), then p^* is an ESS that is globally asymptotically stable for the replicator, best response, and fictitious play dynamics. A regular*[34] *ESS (in particular, any interior ESS) is asymptotically stable for all smooth uniformly monotone selection dynamics. Furthermore a hyperbolic*[35] *rest point of the replicator dynamic is asymptotically stable if and only if it is asymptotically stable for all smooth uniformly monotone selection dynamics.*

---

32. A strategy that is forward invariant for all piecewise linear best response trajectories (e.g., an ESS) is also called a *socially stable strategy*. An analogous concept for sets is that of a *cyclically stable set*. A connected ESSet is cyclically stable. Asymptotic stability of an arbitrary ESSet under the best response dynamic remains an open problem, although it has been shown that any ESS is asymptotically stable.

33. This is not true for the best response dynamic as can be seen from example 2.6.6. Here the only NSS that is stable (for interior trajectories) is the pure strategy e_2.

34. A *regular* ESS is an ESS that is also a quasi-strict NE. A NE p^* is *quasi-strict* if $BR(p^*) = \Delta(\text{supp}(p^*))$.

35. A rest point of a smooth continuous-time dynamical system is *hyperbolic* if no eigenvalue of the Jacobian has zero real part.

Remark 2.7.5 The details provided in the appendix actually prove stronger statements than those given in theorem 2.7.4. For instance, it is shown that every trajectory of the replicator dynamic that is initially sufficiently close to an ESSet actually converges to a single point in E. Theorem 2.7.4 can be used to classify the stability of rest points for entire classes of dynamics. In particular, the interior symmetric NE p^* of example 2.6.1 is hyperbolic for the replicator dynamic if $\alpha \neq 6.5$ since the two eigenvalues from (2.7.2) of L restricted to X^3 are

$$\frac{8(\alpha - 6.5)}{64 - \alpha} \pm \frac{4\sqrt{(3\alpha - 7)^2 - 1000}}{64 - \alpha}.$$

Thus, if $-16 < \alpha < 6.5$, p^* is asymptotically stable for any smooth uniformly monotone selection dynamic and unstable for $6.5 < \alpha < 14$.

Each of the two techniques has its own advantages and disadvantages. A Lyapunov function is often difficult to find. This is the main reason the proof in the appendix of asymptotic stability of an ESS for a general uniformly monotone selection dynamic uses linearization techniques. On the other hand, if a Lyapunov function is found, it usually conveys a more complete global description of the dynamic such as the global asymptotic stability of an ESSet containing an interior point under the replicator or best response dynamics. In fact the Lyapunov approach can sometimes be used to find asymptotically stable limit cycles.[36] For instance, when $\varepsilon > 0$ in the RSP game (2.6.1) of section 2.6.1, trajectories of the best response dynamic converge to the limit cycle $\{p \in \Delta^3 \mid V(p) = 0\}$ as shown in figure 2.6.2c where $V(p) \equiv \max_i \{e_i \cdot Ap\} - \varepsilon$ since this function satisfies $\dot{V}(p) = -V(p)$.

Linearization is of little use for the best response dynamic since this vector field is not usually continuous (let alone differentiable) at a NE (i.e., best replies typically change abruptly in any neighborhood of a NE). For smooth vector fields such as the replicator dynamic, linearization directly provides information on the local nature of the dynamic if and only if the rest point is hyperbolic. However, nonhyperbolic rest points are present in extensive form games whenever different pure strategies produce the same NE outcome. As we will see, in this case, there will automatically be a zero eigenvalue.

---

36. An *asymptotically stable limit cycle* is a periodic trajectory of the dynamical system such that any nearby trajectory approaches it asymptotically.

Zero eigenvalues already arise in normal form games whenever the NE component is not a singleton set (e.g., all three examples in section 2.6.3) or for any boundary NE that is not quasi-strict. For instance, the linearization method applied to the replicator dynamic at a boundary rest point becomes

$$L_{ij} = \begin{cases} \delta_{ij}(e_i - p^*) \cdot Ap^* & \text{if } p_i^* = 0, \\ p_i^*(a_{ij} - p^* \cdot Ae_j) & \text{if } p_i^* \neq 0, \end{cases} \qquad (2.7.4)$$

where δ_{ij} is the *Kronecker delta* that is 1 when $i = j$ and 0 otherwise. The diagonal entries, $(e_i - p^*) \cdot Ap^*$ for those $p_i^* = 0$, are then eigenvalues of L. If p^* is not quasi-strict, then $(e_i - p^*) \cdot Ap^* = 0$ for some $p_i^* = 0$. In particular, every eigenvalue of the linearization L at an ESS p^* on the boundary has negative real part if and only if p^* is a regular ESS.

Stability of quasi-strict NE in a NE component that is not a singleton set can often be determined by extending the linearization method, even though zero eigenvalues are unavoidable in this case. The technique is called *center manifold theory* and relies on the fact that through each rest point of a smooth continuous-time dynamical system, there exists an invariant manifold that is tangent to the eigenspace corresponding to all eigenvalues of zero real part. The general theory asserts that if all other eigenvalues have negative real part, then every trajectory that is initially sufficiently close to the rest point asymptotically approaches a nearby trajectory that lies in the center manifold. Since, in many relevant situations this center manifold is in fact the NE component, the original trajectory approaches a unique limit in the NE component (i.e., the rest point is stable although not asymptotically so). For instance, this method shows every quasi-strict NE in an ESSet E is stable for any smooth uniformly monotone selection dynamic. Furthermore nearby trajectories converge to a unique limit point in E (see remark 2.7.5).

Center manifold theory also establishes the results concerning example 2.6.6 in section 2.6.3 when there is no ESSet (i.e., $\alpha \geq 0$ in the payoff matrix (2.6.6)). In this case the linearization of the replicator dynamic at the rest point $(p_1^*, p_2^*, 0)$ is

$$L = \begin{bmatrix} 0 & 0 & 0 \\ 0 & 0 & 0 \\ 0 & 0 & \alpha p_1^* - p_2^* \end{bmatrix}.$$

If $\alpha p_1^* > p_2^*$, the rest point is unstable (in fact, it is not a NE). If $\alpha p_1^* < p_2^*$, it is a quasi-strict NE that has a one-dimensional zero eigenspace. The center manifold is the invariant edge with endpoints $\{e_1, e_2\}$ that consists entirely of rest points. Since the other relevant eigenvalue is negative, $(p_1^*, p_2^*, 0)$ is stable. This shows every point in the NE component $G^* = \{p \in \Delta^3 \mid p_3 = 0, p_1 \leq 1/(1+\alpha)\}$ is stable except the endpoint where $\alpha p_1^* = p_2^*$.[37]

Both fundamental techniques have counterparts for discrete dynamical systems. Lyapunov functions $V(p)$ have a local isolated maximum at p^* and now satisfy $V(p') \geq V(p)$ in a neighborhood of p^* (see section 2.8.1 below). It is strict if $V(p') > V(p)$ whenever $p \neq p^*$ in this neighborhood. Entries in the Jacobian of the linearization are again partial derivatives in the Taylor expansion of the vector field about the rest point. In particular, the linearized replicator dynamic (2.1.1) about p^* is $x_i' = \sum_{j=1}^{n} L_{ij} x_j$ where

$$L_{ij} = \begin{cases} \delta_{ij} e_i \cdot Ap^*/p^* \cdot Ap^* & \text{if } p_i^* = 0, \\[2mm] \delta_{ij} + \dfrac{p_i^*(a_{ij} - p^* \cdot Ae_j)}{p^* \cdot Ap^*} & \text{if } p_i^* \neq 0. \end{cases}$$

The condition for stability now becomes that the eigenvalues of L have modulus less than 1. With these modifications, the statements in theorem 2.7.3 remain valid.

For instance, the linearization about $p^* = (\frac{1}{3}, \frac{1}{3}, \frac{1}{3})$ of the RSP game (2.6.2) of section 2.6.1 for $\varepsilon > -1$ is

$$L = \begin{bmatrix} 1 + \dfrac{2\varepsilon}{3(3+\varepsilon)} & \dfrac{3-\varepsilon}{3(3+\varepsilon)} & -\dfrac{1}{3} \\[4mm] -\dfrac{1}{3} & 1 + \dfrac{2\varepsilon}{3(3+\varepsilon)} & \dfrac{3-\varepsilon}{3(3+\varepsilon)} \\[4mm] \dfrac{3-\varepsilon}{3(3+\varepsilon)} & -\dfrac{1}{3} & 1 + \dfrac{2\varepsilon}{3(3+\varepsilon)} \end{bmatrix}.$$

Its relevant eigenvalues (i.e., those of L restricted to X^3) are $1 + \varepsilon/(3+\varepsilon) \pm \sqrt{3}i/(3+\varepsilon)$ which have modulus $2\sqrt{\varepsilon^2 + 3\varepsilon + 3}/(3+\varepsilon) > 1$ for all $\varepsilon > -1$. That is, for $-1 < \varepsilon < 0$, the ESS $p^* = \frac{1}{3}(1, 1, 1)$ is unstable for the discrete replicator dynamic.

---

37. At this endpoint the linearization is the zero matrix that has two relevant zero eigenvalues and so the center manifold is all of Δ^3. Although its stability when $\alpha > 0$ can still be shown by extending the linearization technique, the method will not be described here since it is not used elsewhere in the book.

2.8   Natural Selection at a Single Locus

One of the early breakthroughs for dynamic evolutionary game theory was the realization that the classical models of natural selection are special cases of the replicator dynamics. There are numerous biological assumptions behind the description of natural selection as an evolutionary game. These are most clear when generations are discrete, and there are n possible alleles $A_1, \ldots, A_n$ at a single autosomal locus that determines individual *viability* (i.e., survival to maturity) in a diploid population. That is, viability depends only on the *genotype* $A_i A_j$ of the individual.

2.8.1   Discrete-Time Viability Selection

Suppose that there is random mating at the adult (mature) stage of the previous generation, adult genotypic frequencies of males and of females are equal, and all mating couples produce the same number of offspring through Mendelian segregation.[38] Thus, if p_i is the frequency of allele A_i among the offspring of this generation (which is equal to the frequency of allele A_i among the adults of the previous generation), then the immature zygotes $A_i A_j$ are in Hardy-Weinberg proportions (i.e., the frequency of ordered genotype $A_i A_j$ is $p_i p_j$). If w_{ij} is the viability of an individual of genotype $A_i A_j$ for both males and females,[39] the proportion of adults of genotype $A_i A_j$ in the current generation is $w_{ij} p_i p_j / \sum_{k,\ell} w_{k\ell} p_k p_\ell$. Thus $p_i' = \sum_j w_{ij} p_i p_j / \sum_{k,\ell} w_{k\ell} p_k p_\ell$ which is given in matrix form using the symmetric $n \times n$ *viability matrix* W by

$$p_i' = p_i \frac{e_i \cdot Wp}{p \cdot Wp}. \tag{2.8.1}$$

This is the classical *discrete-time viability selection equation* for natural selection at a single diploid locus. It is none other than the discrete-time replicator dynamic (2.1.1) with viabilities interpreted as payoffs for interactions among the alleles.

We have already seen in section 2.6 that the discrete-time replicator dynamic can be quite complex when there are three (or more) strategies.

---

38. In particular, all couples have the same number of sons, which also equals their number of daughters.

39. We also assume there is no *position effect* as to which allele is on which chromosome at the "diploid" locus. This means that $w_{ij} = w_{ji}$.

Furthermore, unless the trajectories converge, the ES structure often bears little resemblance to the evolutionary process. However, for natural selection, the symmetry of the matrix W has a considerable number of implications. The most important consequence, part of the Fundamental Theorem of Natural Selection for a single locus, states that the population mean viability, $p \cdot Wp$, is a Lyapunov function. This, in turn, implies that every trajectory of (2.8.1) converges.

The symmetry of W also imparts special properties onto the ES structure. A connected set E is an ESSet if and only if $p \cdot Wp$ takes on a strict local maximum value on E (i.e., $p \cdot Wp = w$ for all $p \in E$ and, for all $p \in \Delta^n$ in some neighborhood of E, $p \cdot Wp < w$ if and only if $p \notin E$). There is at least one ESSet; namely $\{p \in \Delta^n \mid p \cdot Wp = w^*\}$ is an ESSet where $w^* \equiv \max\{p \cdot Wp \mid p \in \Delta^n\}$. For most viability matrices[40] every ESSet is a finite union of ESSs and p^* is an ESS if and only if p^* is an isolated local maximum of $p \cdot Wp$.

The following theorem summarizes well-known classical results from population genetics that are presented here in a form that emphasizes their connection with evolutionary game theory.

Theorem 2.8.1   *Every trajectory of the discrete-time viability selection equation (2.8.1) converges to some NE of the game restricted to those alleles that are initially present. Almost all (i.e., up to a set of measure zero) initial $p(0)$ evolve to an ESSet. A NE p^* is stable if and only if it is in an ESSet. If some interior p^* is in an ESSet, this is the only ESSet and every interior trajectory converges to it. A set of rest points is asymptotically stable if and only if it is an ESSet. p^* is asymptotically stable if and only if it is an ESS.*

2.8.2   Continuous-Time Natural Selection

The *continuous-time selection equation* at a single locus,

$$\dot{p}_i = p_i(e_i - p) \cdot Mp, \tag{2.8.2}$$

corresponds to the replicator dynamic (2.1.2) with symmetric payoff

---

40. For instance, this statement is true if every principal submatrix of W (i.e., every square matrix formed by taking k rows and the corresponding k columns of W for some $1 \le k \le n$) has nonzero determinant. This is a *generic* property in the sense that the set of W that satisfies it is an open dense set (in fact its complement is a set of measure zero) of all possible viability matrices. Notice that the symmetric payoff matrix in example 2.6.4 does not satisfy this property.

matrix M.[41] All the statements of theorem 2.8.1 remain true for the dynamic (2.8.2). However, compared to (2.8.1), the continuous-time selection equation is not universally accepted by all biologists as a correct model of natural selection. This is due to the fact that the derivation of (2.8.2) from an overlapping generations model with continuous random mating and reproduction assumes the population is always in Hardy-Weinberg proportions. This will not be true unless the genotypic birth rates and death rates that underlie selection satisfy certain restrictive conditions.

The simplest assumptions on these nonnegative fertility and mortality rates that fully justify (2.8.2) are additive effects on fertility (i.e., a couple consisting of an $A_i A_j$ male and an $A_k A_\ell$ female have $F_{ij,k\ell} = F_{ij} + F_{k\ell}$ offspring in equal sex ratio per unit time) and on mortality (i.e., an $A_i A_j$ individual has a probability $D_{ij} = D_i + D_j$ of dying per unit time). If N_{ij} is the number of ordered genotype $A_i A_j$ and couples form at random, then $N_{ij} N_{k\ell}/2N$ is the expected number of couples with an $A_i A_j$ male and an $A_k A_\ell$ female where N is the total population size. Thus with Mendelian segregation we obtain

$$\dot{N}_{ij} = \sum_{k\ell} \frac{(F_{ik,j\ell} + F_{j\ell,ik}) N_{ik} N_{j\ell}}{2N} - D_{ij} N_{ij}.$$

With sex independent fertility and no position effects (i.e., $F_{ik,j\ell} = F_{ki,j\ell} = F_{ki,\ell j} = F_{ik,\ell j} = F_{ik} + F_{j\ell}$), we find that

$$\dot{p}_{ij} = p_i \sum_k F_{j\ell} p_{j\ell} + p_j \sum_k F_{ik} p_{ik} - (D_i + D_j) p_{ij}$$

$$- 2p_{ij} \left(\sum_{k\ell} F_{k\ell} p_{k\ell} - \sum_k D_k p_k \right),$$

where $p_{ij} = N_{ij}/N$ is the frequency of genotype $A_i A_j$ and $p_i = \sum_j p_{ij}$ is the frequency of allele A_i in the population. This latter frequency satisfies

$$\dot{p}_i = \sum_k F_{ik} p_{ik} - D_i p_i - \sum_k D_k p_{ik} - p_i \left(\sum_{k\ell} F_{k\ell} p_{k\ell} - 2 \sum_k D_k p_k \right).$$

$$(2.8.3)$$

---

41. Traditionally the discrete-time viability matrix has been denoted by W and its continuous-time analogue by M with entries m_{ij} (which can now be negative) called the *Malthusian fitness* of genotype $A_i A_j$.

The population maintains Hardy-Weinberg proportions, $p_{ij} = p_i p_j$, if $d(p_{ij} - p_i p_j)/dt = 0$ when $p_{ij} = p_i p_j$. From the calculations above

$$\frac{d}{dt}(p_{ij} - p_i p_j) = -2(p_{ij} - p_i p_j)\sum_{k\ell} F_{k\ell}\, p_{k\ell} - (p_{ij} - p_i p_j)(D_i + D_j)$$

$$+ p_j \sum_k D_k\, p_{ik} + p_i \sum_k D_k\, p_{kj} - 2p_i p_j \sum_k D_k\, p_k$$

$$= -2(p_{ij} - p_i p_j)\sum_{k\ell} F_{k\ell}\, p_{k\ell} - (p_{ij} - p_i p_j)(D_i + D_j)$$

$$+ p_j \sum_k D_k(p_{ik} - p_i p_k) + p_i \sum_k D_k(p_{kj} - p_k p_j).$$

Thus a population that is initially in Hardy-Weinberg proportions remains there. Furthermore, if all mortality rates are equal to $D > 0$, every population asymptotically approaches these proportions.

With additive fertility and mortality effects the allele frequency dynamic (2.8.3), assuming Hardy-Weinberg proportions, becomes

$$\dot{p}_i = p_i\left(\sum_k (F_{ik} - D_i)p_k - \sum_{k\ell} p_k(F_{k\ell} - D_k)p_\ell\right).$$

This is the continuous-time selection equation (2.8.2) at a single locus with Malthusian fitness parameter $m_{ij} = F_{ij} - D_i$ interpreted as the net payoff to allele A_i in an $A_i A_j$ individual.[42]

2.9   One-Stage Simultaneity Games

So far evolutionary games have been analyzed through their normal form which, for symmetric normal form games, means through their payoff matrix. Since this book progressively places more emphasis on the extensive form in the following chapters, it is important to realize every m-player normal form game can be represented in an essentially unique way as an extensive form game where each player has exactly one *information set*, each *path* to an *endpoint* $z \in Z$ in the *game tree* intersects all m information sets, and there are no *moves by nature*. For two-player symmetric normal form games, this representation assumes that each player in the contest has a set of possible actions (i.e., the n pure

---

42. In fact we can instead take m_{ij} as the symmetric Malthusian fitness parameter $F_{ij} - D_i - D_j$ without affecting the continuous-time dynamic.

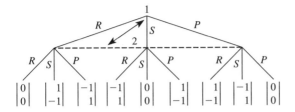

Figure 2.9.1
Extensive form of the zero-sum RSP Game.

strategies of the game) and must choose one of these without knowing the opponent's choice. Let us adopt the usual convention that player one chooses first.

For instance, the *symmetric extensive form* of the classical zero-sum RSP Game of section 2.6.1 becomes the *one-stage (symmetric) simultaneity game* given in figure 2.9.1. There is exactly one information set for each player (the information set for player two joins all his possible actions by a dashed line in figure 2.9.1). The *symmetry* between these information sets is indicated by the double arrow, $\leftrightarrow$, in figure 2.9.1 and implies both players have the same possible actions (R, S, or P) at all their *decision points*. There is also a symmetry in the payoffs $\begin{vmatrix} a \\ b \end{vmatrix}$ at the endpoints $z_1, z_2, \ldots, z_9$ in Z. For instance, the payoffs $\begin{vmatrix} 1 \\ -1 \end{vmatrix}$ along the path to z_2 (i.e., the path corresponding to actions R and S by players one and two respectively that yield payoffs of 1 and -1 respectively) are symmetric with payoffs $\begin{vmatrix} -1 \\ 1 \end{vmatrix}$ along the path to z_4 (where players one and two take actions S and R respectively).

We will postpone the formal definitions of the phrases above given in italics until we introduce general extensive form games in chapters 6 and 7. For now it suffices to appreciate that the one-stage simultaneity game representation of a normal form game is most appropriate when no player can base the action he chooses at one decision point on the actions at other decision points. There is then a one-to-one correspondence between these extensive form representations and the normal form game. When a game is most intuitively described as a sequence of actions, some of which can depend on previous choices, a more general extensive form seems more appropriate. To a large extent, the remainder of this book (especially starting in chapter 3.4) can be thought of as exploring the dynamic consequences of knowing the game comes from an extensive form other than a one-stage simultaneity game.

2.10 Multi-armed Bandits

The continuous- and discrete-time replicator dynamics were derived in section 2.1 as a model of reproduction in a biological population. In that model individuals did not consciously make decisions. Instead, good strategies proliferated through higher reproductive success.[43] On the other hand, the population interpretation of the fictitious play process (and the best response dynamic) in section 2.4 assumes players make a rational decision to play a best reply to the current population state. However, such rational choice depends on a great deal of information, namely the current mean population strategy as well as the current expected payoffs of all possible actions in this situation.

This section, as well as chapters 4.6.2 and 8.4, examine alternative means to derive evolutionary dynamics. We assume that players still make rational decisions but that these are based on a much more limited amount of available information. To simplify the analysis further, we also avoid complications due to strategic interactions among the players by considering only one-player games against nature in these three sections. However, the complexity of these games does increase, ending in chapter 8.4 examining arbitrary one-player extensive form games.

Here we treat very elementary one-player games against nature. Specifically, suppose that this player is faced with a decision problem known as an *n-armed bandit* with $n \geq 2$ (see Notes).[44] In extensive form this consists of a single decision point with n possible actions (i.e., pure strategies), each of which leads to one of the endpoints $z_1, z_2, \ldots, z_n$ (figure 2.10.1 is the extensive form of a 3-armed bandit). Thus in this section we identify the set S of pure strategies with the endpoints z in Z. At each endpoint $z \in Z$, a probability distribution P^z of realized payoffs (i.e., a *lottery*) is specified. That is, an *n-armed bandit* models an elementary

---

43. The same intuitive justification based on individual reproduction can also be made for the general monotone selection dynamics of section 2.3 if fitness is only assumed to be an increasing function of expected payoffs instead of a direct correspondence existing between payoff and number of offspring.

44. The phrase "*n*-armed bandit" comes from the alternative description of a *slot machine* as a single or 1-armed bandit. In our bandits, the player must choose one of the arms. In order to model a slot machine where one choice is not to choose the single arm, we could introduce a fictitious second arm for which the realized payoff is always equal to 0. It is then debatable for "real-life" slot machines whether players want to choose the best action.

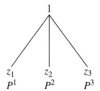

Figure 2.10.1
Extensive form of the Three-Armed Bandit.

decision problem under uncertainty (see Notes). If the expected value of P^z is given by π_z, the player wants to choose the *best* action (i.e., the one that leads to the highest π_z) but cannot be sure which action this is.

In the discrete-time model the player instead makes his choice using a behavioral rule that is based solely on the following limited information: the pure strategy z that he used and its realized payoff x in the previous time interval together with the same information (w and y respectively) for one other randomly sampled individual in the population.[45]

A *behavioral rule* F for an n-armed bandit is then a map $F(z, x, w, y)_e$ that specifies the probability of choosing pure strategy e in the next time interval given the information (z, x, w, y). That is, F is a formula to precisely describe how players enact their rational behavior (i.e., an explicit mechanism to translate what is often referred to as a *rule of thumb*). When all players use the same behavioral rule, an evolutionary dynamic results (e.g., (2.10.1) below).

The basic questions we consider in this section are the properties that characterize behavioral rules under which a large population with everyone using the same rule (and some individuals initially playing each pure strategy) is guaranteed to converge to a state where each individual makes the best choice. These are called *good behavioral rules*. In dynamical terms, the pure strategy (or set of mixed strategies) with the highest payoff is globally asymptotically stable if and only if F is a good behavioral rule. It is shown in theorem 2.10.1 below (and the discussion following it) that the replicator dynamic is the only standard

---

45. Each individual in the population must choose a pure strategy in a given time interval but may make this choice using a randomizing device. For general extensive form bandits, only the endpoint reached (rather than the strategy) and its realized payoff are observed for the randomly sampled individual (see chapters 4.6.2 and 8.4). For the multi-armed bandits of this section, observing the endpoint reached reveals the player's strategy.

evolutionary dynamic induced by some good behavioral rule. In fact the arguments there suggest why such behavioral rules are the ones most likely to be used by rational players in an n-armed bandit. This then provides one justification for the replicator dynamic (see Notes) based on rational behavior of individuals rather than on aggregate population behavior, the original approach taken in section 2.1.

To begin our analysis of behavioral rules for multi-armed bandits, consider the following elementary example. Let F be the behavioral rule for the bandit in figure 2.10.1 given by

$$F(z, x, w, y)_e = \begin{cases} 1 & \text{if } e = z_1, \\ 0 & \text{otherwise.} \end{cases}$$

This F that always chooses z_1 is not a good behavioral rule unless, by luck, z_1 happens to be the best action.

To avoid such degenerate situations, we insist the information in a given time interval is never sufficient to infer the best action in the n-armed bandit. Thus a 2-armed bandit where realized payoffs equal expected payoffs (i.e., each P^z is a delta distribution) is not allowed since the best action is automatically known if own and sampled strategy differ. On the other hand, 3-armed bandits with delta payoff distributions are potentially admissible if the information (z, x, w, y) does not reveal the ordering of the expected payoffs for the (other) pure strategies. This requires that we seek behavioral rules that are simultaneously good for a collection of bandits. It is surprisingly difficult to give a priori minimal conditions for such a collection of multi-armed bandits. Instead, as we develop the properties of our rules, the conditions needed for each property will be made explicit. In particular, the conditions are all met for the collection of all n-armed bandits whose realized payoffs are arbitrary distributions on a finite interval $[\alpha, \omega]$ with $\alpha < \omega$. Denote this set by $MAB(n, [\alpha, \omega])$.

Our first property is that good behavioral rules must be *imitative* in that $F(z, x, w, y)_e$ must be 0 if e is not a pure strategy corresponding to endpoint z or w. If this were not the case, there would be a bandit in our collection for which $\{z, w\}$ was the set of best pure actions (and payoffs x and y are possible). Then the set of strategies (both pure and mixed) with expected payoff $\pi_z = \pi_w$ is not asymptotically stable under F since this set is not forward invariant. An immediate consequence is that a good behavioral rule for an n-armed bandit will also be a good behavioral rule for bandits with less than n arms since F is imitative.

For any imitative rule the induced discrete-time deterministic population dynamic becomes

$$p'_z = p_z + p_z \sum_{w \in Z} p_w (F(w, z) - F(z, w)), \qquad (2.10.1)$$

where $F(w, z)$ is the *switching rate* from pure strategy w to z.[46] One interpretation of this switching rate is to assume players form random pairs who sample each other. Then the change $p'_z - p_z$ in the proportion of players using pure strategy z between consecutive time intervals due to encounters with w is the encounter rate (i.e., $p_z p_w$) times the net switching rate $F(w, z) - F(z, w)$ from strategy w to z.

An intuitive imitative rule is Imitate if Better, F^{IB}, which switches to the sampled strategy if and only if its realized payoff is higher. That is, if $w \neq z$,

$$F^{IB}(z, x, w, y)_w = \begin{cases} 1 & \text{if } y > x, \\ 0 & \text{otherwise.} \end{cases}$$

This rule does well for any bandit with delta payoff distributions. Then, from (2.10.1), if z is the unique best action,

$$p'_z = p_z + p_z \sum_{w \neq z} p_w$$

$$= p_z + p_z(1 - p_z),$$

so p_z increases monotonically to 1 if it is initially positive. It is also clear that this is the fastest p_z can converge to 1 under any imitative rule.

However, F^{IB} does not do well in all circumstances. As an elementary example, consider a 2-armed bandit where P^z is the delta distribution with $\pi_z = 1$ and P^w is the distribution with $\pi_w = 2$ given by $P^w(0) = \frac{3}{4}$ and $P^w(8) = \frac{1}{4}$. Then $p'_z = p_z + \frac{1}{2} p_z p_w$ since $F^{IB}(w, z) = \frac{3}{4}$ and $F^{IB}(z, w) = \frac{1}{4}$. Thus the population evolves to $p_z = 1$, even though w is the best action. For this reason F^{IB} is not a good behavioral rule.

In fact it can be shown (see Notes) that for fixed z and w, $F(z, x, w, y)_w - F(w, y, z, x)_z$ must be linear in the payoff difference $y - x$ (i.e., of the form $\sigma_{zw}(y - x)$ for some $\sigma_{zw} > 0$) if F is a good behavioral rule. Otherwise, there will be an elementary 2-armed bandit similar to the previous

---

46. That is, $F(w, z)$ is the probability an individual imitates sampled strategy z if current strategy is w. For instance, if P^z and P^w are discrete payoff distributions in a given bandit, this is the expected value $F(w, z) = \sum_{x,y} F(w, x, z, y)_z P^w(x) P^z(y)$. Notice that the value of $F(z, z)$ is immaterial in (2.10.1). For convenience, we set $F(z, z) = 0$.

example with three possible realized payoffs for which the population evolves to the worst action. In particular, the set of realized payoffs must be contained in a compact interval since $F(z, x, w, y)_w$ is a probability between 0 and 1. If $[\alpha, \omega]$ is the smallest such interval, then we have the second property of good behavioral rules; namely for every pair of distinct endpoints in Z,

$$F(z, x, w, y)_w - F(w, y, z, x)_z = \sigma_{zw}(y - x) \qquad (2.10.2)$$

for some constant $0 < \sigma_{zw} = \sigma_{wz} \leq 1/(\omega - \alpha)$. It is not difficult to show that the net switching rate for such F is σ_{zw} times the expected value of $P^z - P^w$ (i.e., $F(w, z) - F(z, w) = \sigma_{zw}(\pi_z - \pi_w)$). From (2.10.1) the population dynamic becomes

$$p'_z = p_z + p_z \sum_{w \in Z} p_w \sigma_{zw}(\pi_z - \pi_w), \qquad (2.10.3)$$

from which it is clear that p_z is a Lyapunov function for any best action z that is initially present. That is, the set of best strategies is globally asymptotically stable if F satisfies (2.10.2).

An important class of good behavioral rules (see theorem 2.10.1 below for its connection to the replicator dynamic) is the set of those F for which all σ_{zw} are equal (to $\sigma > 0$). For all such F the dynamic becomes

$$p'_z = p_z + \sigma p_z(\pi_z - \pi(p)), \qquad (2.10.4)$$

where $\pi(p)$ is the average payoff $\sum_z p_z \pi_z$ when the population is in state p. To compare this to the replicator dynamic, consider the symmetric normal form game where the payoff π_z to pure strategy z does not depend on his opponent (i.e., each entry in this row of the payoff matrix is π_z). The replicator dynamic (2.1.2) is then

$$\dot{p}_z = p_z(\pi_z - \pi(p)).$$

That is, the continuous-time approximation $\dot{p}_z \cong (p'_z - p_z)$ for the dynamic induced by F is none other than (2.1.2) (up to the positive constant σ).

The following theorem summarizes the two properties characterizing a good behavioral rule and the special connection to the replicator dynamic discussed above:[47]

---

47. The theorem is stated for convenience with respect to the collection $MAB(n, [\alpha, \omega])$ of n-armed bandits. It is clear from the discussion above that the result remains true for much smaller collections of bandits.

Theorem 2.10.1 *F is a good behavioral rule for $MAB(n, [\alpha, \omega])$ if and only if F is imitative and satisfies (2.10.2). A behavioral rule induces a discrete version of the replicator dynamic if and only if F is a good behavioral rule with all $\sigma_{zw} = \sigma > 0$.*

There are in fact arguments based on dynamic considerations to assert that all σ_{zw} should be equal (to σ) and that σ should be $1/(\omega - \alpha)$. To justify the first property, suppose that there are at least three actions and $\sigma_{12} > \sigma_{13}$ (here σ_{12} has the obvious meaning $\sigma_{z_1 z_2}$, etc.) for F. Consider a bandit where z_3 is the unique best action but π_{z_3} is almost equal to π_{z_2} which in turn is much larger than π_{z_1}. It is then straightforward to provide population states for which p_2 is initially increasing more than p_3 and others for which $p_2'/p_2 > p_3'/p_3$. Thus such F cannot generate discrete versions of the best response or monotone selection dynamics. In other words, the replicator dynamic is the only standard evolutionary dynamic that is induced by a good behavioral rule and this occurs only when all σ_{zw} are equal.

The second property is based on the rate of convergence to the best action. Suppose that F is a good behavioral rule with all $\sigma_{zw}^F = 1/(\omega - \alpha)$. If p is an interior initial point and H is another good behavioral rule with $\sigma_{zw}^H < \sigma_{zw}^F$ for some $\pi_z \neq \pi_w$, then it can be shown from (2.10.3) and (2.10.4) that $\pi^F(p) > \pi^H(p)$ at any subsequent time. Thus the population evolves in such a way that it is always closer under F to the set of best actions than under any other good behavioral rule.

There are three intuitive good behavioral rules with all $\sigma_{zw} = 1/(\omega - \alpha)$ given in the following definition that play a central role in the more general extensive form bandits of chapters 4.6.2 and 8.4.

Definition 2.10.2 *The imitative behavioral rules PIR, PRR, and POR (with $\sigma = 1/(\omega - \alpha)$) are defined as follows:*

i. The proportional imitation rule (PIR) imitates the sampled strategy if it realizes a higher payoff and does this with probability $(y - x)/(\omega - \alpha)$. That is, whenever $z \neq w$,

$$F^{PIR}(z, x, w, y)_w = \begin{cases} \dfrac{1}{\omega - \alpha}(y - x) & \text{if } y > x, \\ 0 & \text{if } y \leq x. \end{cases}$$

ii. The proportional reviewing rule (PRR) imitates the sampled strategy with probability $F^{PRR}(z, x, w, y)_w = (\omega - x)/(\omega - \alpha)$ if own last payoff was x.

iii. The proportional observation rule *(POR) imitates the sampled strategy that has payoff y with probability* $F^{POR}(z, x, w, y)_w = (y - \alpha)/(\omega - \alpha)$.

Although PIR is similar to Imitate if Better in that it only switches strategies if the sampled payoff is higher than own realized payoff, the probability of such switches now depends linearly on the payoff difference. PRR and POR are based on less information than PIR; namely on own and on sampled payoffs respectively. Heuristically, switching under PRR indicates dissatisfaction with one's own payoff whereas switching under POR anticipates a high expected payoff for the sampled strategy. Of course, any convex linear combination of these three rules induces the identical population dynamic (2.10.4).[48]

2.11　Appendix

Proof of Theorem 2.7.4

The results for fictitious play (recall that asymptotic stability here only refers to the tail end of fictitious play trajectories) follow from those of the best response dynamic together with the general theory connecting these two processes (in particular, see proposition 7.7.2 in appendix B of chapter 7). The proofs provided here for the statements concerning the other dynamics are given in the three stages: (1) the replicator dynamic, (2) the best response dynamic, and (3) smooth uniformly monotone selection dynamics.

1. Most of these well-known results concerning the replicator dynamic follow from the function $V(p)$ given in (2.7.1) and the comparisons of $p^* \cdot Ap$ and $p \cdot Ap$ in theorem 2.7.1. Only a few details are provided here. For instance, $\dot{V}(p) \geq 0$ for all p sufficiently close to an NSS p^*, and so p^* is stable by theorem 2.7.3. It is also interesting to note that every trajectory $p(t)$ that is initially close to an ESSet E converges to a unique ω-limit point in E. To see this, note that $\{p(t) \mid \dot{V}(p(t)) = 0\} \subset E$, and so the trajectory has some limit point p^* in E. If we now take $V(p)$ in (2.7.1) as the Lyapunov function given by p^*, then $V(p)$ increases monotonically to $V(p^*)$ for this trajectory, and so $p(t)$ converges to p^*.

2. For the statements concerning the best response dynamic, recall that we have restricted attention to piecewise linear best response

---

48. In this regard PIR is an extreme point of the convex set of all good behavioral rules that induce (2.10.4), whereas PRR and POR are not.

trajectories. Let us first show E is forward invariant. Suppose that the initial point of the trajectory p^* is in E and the trajectory evolves toward b along the line segment $(1 - \varepsilon)p^* + \varepsilon b$, where $b \in BR((1 - \varepsilon)p^* + \varepsilon b)$, for all $0 \le \varepsilon \le \varepsilon_0$ with $0 < \varepsilon_0 < 1$. If $b \notin E$, then $b \cdot Ap^* = p^* \cdot Ap^*$ and $p^* \cdot Ab > b \cdot Ab$. In this case $p^* \cdot A((1 - \varepsilon)p^* + \varepsilon b) > b \cdot A((1 - \varepsilon)p^* + \varepsilon b)$, which is a contradiction. Thus $b \in E$, $b \cdot Ap^* = p^* \cdot Ap^*$ and $p^* \cdot Ab = b \cdot Ab$ by theorem 2.7.1. It is now straightforward to show $(1 - \lambda)p^* + \lambda b \in E$ for all $0 \le \lambda \le 1$. In particular, this linear piece of the best response trajectory lies completely in E.

Now suppose that E contains an interior NE. Then E is the only connected NE component. For a linear piece of the best response trajectory that is evolving toward the best reply b, consider the function

$$V(p) = p \cdot Ap - b \cdot Ap.$$

Then $V(p) \le 0$ with equality if and only if p is a NE if and only if $p \in E$. Since $\dot{p} = b - p$ and $(p - b) \cdot A(b - p) \ge 0$, $\dot{V}(p) = (b - p) \cdot Ap + (p - b) \cdot A(b - p) \ge 0$ with equality if and only if $p \in E$. Thus $V(p)$ is a Lyapunov function for all of Δ^n, and so E is globally asymptotically stable.

If $p^* \cdot Ap > p \cdot Ap$ for all $p \ne p^*$, consider $V(p) = p^* \cdot Ap - b \cdot Ap$. Then $V(p) \le 0$ with equality if and only if $p^* \in BR(p)$. Furthermore $\dot{V}(p) = (p^* - b) \cdot A(b - p) > 0$ unless $b = p^*$. Thus every piecewise linear best response trajectory converges to the set of strategies for which the only choice for a linear piece of the trajectory is toward p^* and so p^* is globally asymptotically stable.

3. The final statement of the theorem concerning monotone selection dynamics is proved using the linearization technique. We first show that the linearization of any smooth monotone selection dynamic is a nonnegative scalar multiple of L given in (2.7.2) when we restrict to the invariant subspace $X^k \equiv \{(x_1, \ldots, x_n) \mid x_i = 0 \text{ if } p_i^* = 0 \text{ and } \sum x_i = 0\}$ of X^n. From (2.3.1) the linearization about p^* is

$$\dot{x}_i = \sum_j J_{ij} x_j,$$

where J is the $n \times n$ Jacobian matrix with entries $J_{ij} = \partial f_i(p^*)/\partial x_j$. Then $f_i(p^* + x) \cong f_i(p^*) + e_i \cdot Jx$. Order the pure strategies so that $p_i^* \ne 0$ for $1 \le i \le k$ and $p_i^* = 0$ for $k + 1 \le i \le n$. From definition 2.3.2, for $1 \le i, j \le k$ and $x \in X^k$, $(e_i \cdot Jx)/p_i^* = (e_j \cdot Jx)/p_j^*$ if and only if $e_i \cdot Ax = e_j \cdot Ax$ since $f_i(p^*) = f_j(p^*) = 0$ at the rest point p^*.

Thus, for $1 \leq i, j \leq k$ and $x \in X^k$, $(e_i \cdot Jx)/p_i^* = (e_j \cdot Jx)/p_j^*$ if and only if $(e_i \cdot Lx)/p_i^* = (e_j \cdot Lx)/p_j^*$ from (2.7.2). Thus the orthogonal projections v_{ij} and v_{ij}' of $(e_i/p_i^* - e_j/p_j^*)J$ and $(e_i/p_i^* - e_j/p_j^*)L$ respectively onto X^k are linearly dependent for all $1 \leq i, j \leq k$. That is, $v_{ij} = c_{ij} v_{ij}'$ where, by monotonicity, $c_{ij} \geq 0$. Furthermore, since p^* is an isolated rest point of the replicator dynamic, the projections of $\{(e_i/p_i^* - e_k/p_k^*)L \mid 1 \leq i < k\} = \{(e_i - e_k)A \mid 1 \leq i < k\}$ onto X^k is a linearly independent subset of X^k and so form a basis. Moreover v_{ij}' is the projection of $(e_i - e_j)A = (e_i - e_k)A - (e_j - e_k)A$, and so $v_{ij}' = v_{ik}' - v_{jk}'$. Similarly $v_{ij} = v_{ik} - v_{jk}$. Since $\{v_{ik}', v_{jk}'\}$ are linearly independent for all $1 \leq i < j < k$, the triangle with nonparallel sides $\{v_{ik}', v_{jk}', v_{ij}'\}$ is similar to the triangle with sides $\{v_{ik}, v_{jk}, v_{ij}\}$, and so $c \equiv c_{ij} = c_{ik} = c_{jk} \geq 0$ for all $1 \leq i < j < k$. Thus, if $x \in X^k$, $(e_i/p_i^* - e_j/p_j^*) \cdot Jx = c(e_i/p_i^* - e_j/p_j^*) \cdot Lx$, and so $J = cL$ on the invariant set X^k since $\{(e_i/p_i^* - e_k/p_k^*) \mid 1 \leq i < k\}$ is a basis of X^k. By uniform monotonicity, $c > 0$.

If $k < n$, the linearization of the replicator dynamic as given by (2.7.4) equals

$$
L_{ij} = \begin{cases} p_i^*(a_{ij} - p^* \cdot Ae_j) & \text{if } p_i^* \neq 0, \\ \delta_{ij}(e_i - p^*) \cdot Ap^* & \text{if } p_i^* = 0. \end{cases}
$$

At a regular ESS, $(e_i - p^*) \cdot Ap^* < 0$ if $p_i^* = 0$, and so the only possible nonzero entry in the ith row of L is the negative diagonal entry of $(e_i - p^*) \cdot Ap^*$. A similar linearization for a monotone selection dynamic shows $J_{ij} = \delta_{ij}(f_i(p^*)/p_i^*)$ if $p_i^* = 0$ and, by definition 2.3.2, $f_i(p^*)/p_i^*$ is negative if $(e_i - p^*) \cdot Ap^* < 0$. Thus the linearized stability of p^* under the uniformly monotone selection dynamic reduces to the eigenvalues of J restricted to X^k. Since L is negative definite on X^k and $J = cL$ with $c > 0$, all eigenvalues of J have negative real part. By theorem 2.7.3, p^* is asymptotically stable.   ∎

2.12   Notes

Evolutionary game theory and the ESS solution concept originated in the biological literature with Maynard Smith and Price (1973) and Maynard Smith (1974). Taylor and Jonker (1978) introduced the replicator dynamic for a biological population with interactions given through a symmetric normal form game. Maynard Smith (1982), Hofbauer and Sigmund (1988, 1998), and Cressman (1992) are good reference books that emphasize this biological perspective (most of the results concerning the replicator dynamic mentioned in this chapter are in at least one of these books). The connection of the above-mentioned aspects of evolutionary game theory with classical game theory solution concepts (i.e., with the literature on NE refinements) are summarized in van Damme (1991) (see also Bomze and Pötscher 1989).

Monotone selection dynamics, defined by Samuelson and Zhang (1992) but studied earlier under different names by Nachbar (1990) and Friedman (1991), were the first major contribution to dynamic evolutionary game theory from economic game theorists. This is despite the fact the fictitious play process was introduced much earlier by Brown (1950) and Robinson (1951) but was not a mainstream part of dynamic evolutionary game theory until Matsui (1992) introduced the best response dynamic and Hofbauer (1995a) applied dynamical systems techniques to study its stability. Weibull (1995) and Samuelson (1997) give excellent accounts of the uses of dynamic evolutionary game theory (especially monotone selection dynamics) from the perspective of economic game theorists. In particular, both include the proof that the vector field of an aggregate monotone selection dynamic is essentially that of the replicator dynamic. Smooth uniformly monotone dynamics were introduced in Cressman (1997a) where they were called "nondegenerate."

Bomze (1983, 1995) classifies the possible phase portraits for replicator dynamics of three-strategy games and ESSets are defined by Thomas (1985; see also Cressman 1992). Weibull (1995) summarizes an extension of setwise stability to ES^* sets that need not only contain rest points of the dynamic. Another setwise concept (Swinkels 1992) for the best response dynamic is that of an EES (equilibrium evolutionarily stable) set. Every ESSet is an EES set but not conversely. The class of (generalized) RSP games that includes those in example 2.6.1 has been used extensively by many researchers (e.g., Weissing 1991; Hofbauer and Sigmund 1998) for illustrative purposes. Cressman (1997a) explicitly constructs the family of uniformly monotone selection dynamics considered in section 2.6.1 for the classical RSP game and proves the asymptotic stability of a regular ESS. Friedman (1991) provides an example of a nonuniform monotone selection dynamic for which a regular ESS is not stable. The "never worst response" dynamic was considered in Hofbauer (1995b).

The partial proof of theorem 2.7.1 given in the text is from Bomze (1995). The Shahshahani inner product was introduced in Shahshahani (1979; see also Hofbauer and Sigmund 1998). Socially stable strategies and cyclically stable sets are analyzed in Matsui (1992). Linearization and Lyapunov function techniques for evolutionary games are used extensively in Cressman (1992; where further applications of center manifold theory are given) and Hofbauer and Sigmund (1998) respectively. Lyapunov functions for the best response dynamic were introduced by Hofbauer (1995a). A good reference for the mathematical theory of center manifolds is Wiggins (1990).

The Fundamental Theorem of Natural Selection has a long history beginning with Fisher (1930). The results quoted in section 2.8 can be found in Lyubich (1992), Nagylaki (1992), and Bürger (2000) (see also Cressman 1999 for the game-theoretic emphasis adopted here). The close connection between game theory and natural selection was recognized almost as soon as dynamic evolutionary game theory developed (e.g., Akin 1982; Lessard 1984; Hines 1987).

Bandit problems considered in section 2.10 and elsewhere in the book are all cases of decision problems under uncertainty. Other researchers (e.g., Rothschild 1974; Fudenberg and Levine 1998) have analyzed more complex methods to update choices that rely on more player information than considered here. Our imitation model is based on Schlag (1998) where other justifications of PIR, PRR, and POR are given (see also Helbing 1992; Cressman and Schlag 1998b) as well as the proofs of claims not provided in the text. The replicator dynamic has also been developed using other rationality assumptions (e.g., Weibull 1995; Samuelson 1997).

3   Bimatrix Games

Bimatrix games are two-player games where each player has a finite set of possible pure strategies. However, unlike symmetric normal form games, there is no a priori assumption that the strategy sets of the two players are the same. Thus a general two-player game in normal form, G, has strategy sets $S = \{e_1, \ldots, e_n\}$ and $T = \{f_1, \ldots, f_m\}$ for players one and two respectively.

Payoffs to player k (where $k = 1$ or 2) when player one uses e_i and player two f_j are denoted by $\pi_k(e_i, f_j)$. When these are considered as entries a_{ij} for $k = 1$ and b_{ji} for $k = 2$ of the pair of payoff matrices (A, B), we have the *bimatrix normal form of G*. That is, $A = [a_{ij}]$ is an $n \times m$ matrix and $B = [b_{ji}]$ an $m \times n$ matrix with $a_{ij} = \pi_1(e_i, f_j)$ and $b_{ji} = \pi_2(e_i, f_j)$. For a contest involving mixed strategies $p \in \Delta^n$ and $q \in \Delta^m$ of players one and two respectively, the expected payoffs are conveniently denoted by $p \cdot Aq$ and $q \cdot Bp$ for players one and two respectively (the dot product here is the same as in chapter 2).

The one-stage extensive form of a bimatrix game is given in figure 3.0.1 where each player again has one information set, but unlike chapter 2.8, there is no symmetry connecting these sets. A special case arises if the two strategy sets S and T can be identified with each other through a one-to-one correspondence (i.e., e_i corresponds to f_i for $1 \leq i \leq n$) in such a way that the payoffs satisfy $\pi_1(e_i, f_j) = \pi_2(e_j, f_i)$. A symmetry can then be added to figure 3.0.1 and $A = B$ are both $n \times n$ matrices. In this case we have the *bimatrix normal form of a symmetric normal form game* or simply a *symmetric bimatrix game*. An elementary example is the Owner-Intruder Game of section 3.2.1 below.

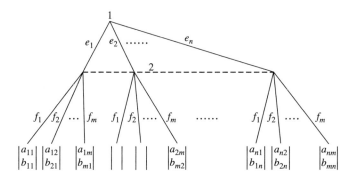

Figure 3.0.1
One-stage extensive form of a bimatrix game.

3.1   Nash Equilibria and Strict Equilibrium Sets

To extend the static equilibrium conditions of chapter 2.5 to bimatrix games, we must consider a mixed strategy for each of the two players. Suppose that $(p, q) \in \Delta^n \times \Delta^m$ is such a *strategy pair*. The intuitive definition of a NE is that neither player has a unilateral incentive to choose a different strategy if the other player is using his NE mixed strategy. The related concept, an ESSet, consists of NE whose strategy pairs include any unilateral shift by one of the players to a strategy for which he is payoff indifferent. Their formal definitions follow (see also definition 4.3.1 for the corresponding concepts in an n-player game).

Definition 3.1.1   *(i) A strategy pair $(p^*, q^*) \in \Delta^n \times \Delta^m$ is a* Nash equilibrium (NE) *for the bimatrix game (A, B) if $p \cdot Aq^* \le p^* \cdot Aq^*$ and $q \cdot Bp^* \le q^* \cdot Bp^*$ for all $(p, q) \in \Delta^n \times \Delta^m$. A NE (p^*, q^*) is* strict *if both inequalities are strict whenever $p \ne p^*$ and $q \ne q^*$.*

   (ii) A set $F \subseteq \Delta^n \times \Delta^m$ is a strict equilibrium set (SESet) *if it is a set of NE and $(p, q^*) \in F$ whenever $p \cdot Aq^* = p^* \cdot Aq^*$ and $(p^*, q) \in F$ whenever $q \cdot Bp^* = q^* \cdot Bp^*$ for some $(p^*, q^*) \in F$.*

The class of SESets is a natural extension to bimatrix games of the ESSets for a symmetric normal form game (the comparison to definition 2.6.3 in chapter 2 is more clear if we restate definition 3.1.1 (ii) as $p^* \cdot Aq^* > p \cdot Aq^*$ whenever $(p, q^*) \notin F$ and $(p^*, q^*) \in F$, etc.). For instance, a strict NE (p^*, q^*) is the bimatrix counterpart of an ESS as characterized in theorem 2.7.1 of chapter 2 in that $p^* \cdot Aq > p \cdot Aq$

for all (p, q) sufficiently close (but not equal) to (p^*, q^*) if and only if $p \cdot Aq^* < p^* \cdot Aq^*$. There are also many similarities between the structures of these two types of sets. From the static perspective[1] every strict NE is a singleton SESet as is every finite union of strict NE. Furthermore there are SESets that are not of this form. However, by the following result there can be no interior points in an SESet except in the degenerate situation where all strategies have equivalent payoffs (i.e., all points of $\Delta^n \times \Delta^m$ are NE and so this is the only SESet):

Theorem 3.1.2 *Every SESet F is a finite union of cartesian products of faces of $\Delta^n \times \Delta^m$. That is, $F = \bigcup_{k=1}^{N} \Delta(S_k) \times \Delta(T_k)$ for some subsets $S_1, \ldots, S_N$ and $T_1, \ldots, T_N$ of S and T respectively. In particular, any strict NE must be a pure strategy.*

This result follows from theorem 4.3.2 in chapter 4, so its proof will not be given here. For an example of a connected SESet that is not a single face of $\Delta^n \times \Delta^m$, see case 7 of the two-strategy bimatrix games of section 3.3.2 below. Since no completely mixed strategy pair is in an SESet, an interior ESS p^* of a symmetric normal form game cannot generate an SESet $\{(p^*, p^*)\}$ of the corresponding symmetric bimatrix game. On the other hand, we do have the following result:

Theorem 3.1.3 *If G is a symmetric bimatrix game (A, A) and F is an SESet, then $E \equiv \{p^* \in \Delta^n \mid (p^*, p^*) \in F\}$ is an ESSet of A if it is nonempty.*

Proof Suppose $p^* \in E$. Then $p \cdot Ap^* \leq p^* \cdot Ap^*$ for all $p \in \Delta^n$ since $(p^*, p^*) \in F$ is a NE. Thus p^* is a symmetric NE of A. Now suppose $p^* \in E$, $p \notin E$ and $p \cdot Ap^* = p^* \cdot Ap^*$. We must show that $p^* \cdot Ap > p \cdot Ap$. Since F is an SESet, $(p, p^*) \in F$ and so is a NE. Thus $p^* \cdot Ap \geq p \cdot Ap$. Furthermore, if $p^* \cdot Ap = p \cdot Ap$, then $(p, p) \in F$ which contradicts the assumption that $p \notin E$. Thus $p^* \cdot Ap > p \cdot Ap$. ∎

3.2 Bimatrix Replicator and Best Response Dynamics

In analogy to the population model used in chapter 2 to motivate the symmetric replicator dynamic, assume that we have two large populations, the first (respectively, second) consisting of individuals who use pure strategies from the strategy set of player one (respectively, player

---

1. Similarities between their dynamic properties are developed in the remainder of the chapter.

two). If both population sizes are always equal and all individuals are paired (i.e., one from each population) at random at an average rate of once per unit time, the continuous-time *bimatrix replicator dynamic* (3.2.1) emerges:[2]

$$\dot{p}_i = p_i(e_i - p) \cdot Aq,$$

(3.2.1)

$$\dot{q}_j = q_j(f_j - q) \cdot Bp.$$

As in chapter 2, this dynamic assumes that the expected individual payoff is the net growth rate (i.e., birth rate $-$ death rate) of strategy use attributed to this individual. This dynamic on $\Delta^n \times \Delta^m$ leaves its interior as well as each of its faces forward invariant.

An unexpected result, especially given the intricacies between dynamic stability and static equilibrium concepts developed in chapter 2, is the equivalence given in theorem 3.2.1. Its proof is again postponed since it is part of theorem 4.5.3ii in chapter 4 (see also theorem 3.4.2 below). Thus the SESet concept is an equilibrium selection criterion with a dynamic justification.[3]

Theorem 3.2.1   *A set F of rest points of the bimatrix replicator dynamic (3.2.1) is asymptotically stable if and only if F is an SESet. In particular, a rest point of (3.2.1) is asymptotically stable if and only if it is a strict NE.*

Combined with Theorem 3.1.3, we have the somewhat surprising fact that an ESS p^* of a symmetric normal form game, A, cannot correspond to an asymptotically stable equilibrium (p^*, p^*) for the corresponding symmetric bimatrix game unless p^* is a pure strategy. To see this more clearly, we analyze the dynamic in detail for the Hawk-Dove Game with $A = \begin{bmatrix} a & b \\ c & d \end{bmatrix}, a < c, b > d$ in section 3.2.1 below. Recall that this is the only two-strategy symmetric normal form game with an interior ESS. In the biological literature the corresponding symmetric bimatrix game is usually called the Owner-Intruder Game with player one identified

---

2. This dynamic forms the basis of two-species frequency-dependent dynamics with only interspecific interactions when the species are both haploid. See chapter 4.7.2 for the corresponding model with both inter- and intraspecific interactions.

3. Of course, a given bimatrix game may have no SESet, just as many symmetric normal form games in chapter 2 have no ESS or ESSet (or, for that matter, any asymptotically stable equilibrium). Theorem 3.2.1 has recently been generalized to other evolutionary dynamics (see Notes) that include all monotone selection dynamics for bimatrix games. Specifically, if F is a connected set of rest points that contains a pure strategy pair, then F is asymptotically stable for any such dynamic if and only if F is an SESet.

as the owner and player two as the intruder.[4] It is also clear from the phase portraits for this game (figure 3.2.1 below) that the interior ESS corresponds to an unstable rest point for the bimatrix replicator dynamic as well as for the bimatrix best response dynamic which is developed as follows:

As a two-species population model, the bimatrix best response dynamic approximates the discrete-time adaptive process whereby the same fraction $\tau > 0$ of each population revise their strategy by choosing a current best reply in each small time interval of length τ. In analogy to chapter 2.4, as $\tau \to 0$, the continuous-time *bimatrix best response dynamic* given by

$$\dot{p} = BR(q) - p,$$
$$\dot{q} = BR(p) - q.$$

(3.2.2)

emerges where $BR(q) \equiv \{\hat{p} \in \Delta^n \mid \hat{p} \cdot Aq \geq p \cdot Aq \text{ for all } p \in \Delta^n\}$ and $BR(p)$ is defined similarly. There are again piecewise linear solutions defined for all $t \geq 0$ through any initial point $(p(0), q(0)) \in \Delta^n \times \Delta^m$. For instance, if $b_1 \in BR((1-\varepsilon)q(0)+\varepsilon b_2)$ and $b_2 \in BR((1-\varepsilon)p(0)+\varepsilon b_1)$ whenever $0 \leq \varepsilon \leq \varepsilon_0$, then $(p(t), q(t)) \equiv (b_1+(p(0)-b_1)e^{-t}, b_2+(q(0)-b_2)e^{-t})$ is a linear solution of (3.2.2) for all $0 \leq t \leq -\ln(1-\varepsilon_0)$.

Asymptotic stability of sets of rest points under the best response dynamic (3.2.2) is no longer equivalent to the SESet concept as in theorem 3.2.1. For instance, the only NE of the Buyer-Seller Game (case 2 of section 3.3.1 below) is in the interior (and so not strict) but is asymptotically stable for the bimatrix best response dynamic (see figure 3.3.2). It is unknown whether every SESet F is asymptotically stable. Those F that are connected and *closed under simultaneous best responses* (i.e., $(b_1, b_2) \in F$ whenever $b_1 \in BR(p^*)$ and $b_2 \in BR(q^*)$ for some $(p^*, q^*) \in F$) are asymptotically stable since they are precisely the SESets that consist of a single face of $\Delta^n \times \Delta^m$ and so every nearby best response trajectory evolves closer (in euclidean distance) to this face. In particular, a strict NE is asymptotically stable. Furthermore, by considering the projection of the symmetrized best response dynamic (3.4.3) as discussed in section 3.4.2 below, if every ESSet is asymptotically stable under the symmetric best response dynamic (2.4.2), then every SESet is asymptotically stable (see also the first footnote of theorem 2.7.4 in chapter 2).

---

4. Since the players can condition their strategy choice on their role as owner or as intruder, bimatrix games are also special cases of asymmetric games that are considered in general in chapter 4.

3.2.1   The Owner-Intruder Game

From the discussion following theorem 3.2.1, the bimatrix normal form of this game is

$$
\begin{array}{c}
 & \text{Intruder} \\
 & \begin{array}{cc} H & D \end{array} \\
\text{Owner} \begin{array}{c} H \\ D \end{array} &
\begin{bmatrix} a, a & b, c \\ c, b & d, d \end{bmatrix},
\end{array}
$$

where $a < c$ and $b > d$. Each entry in the bimatrix is an ordered pair of payoffs whose first component is the owner's payoff and second the intruder's.

Since $p_2 = 1 - p_1$ and $q_2 = 1 - q_1$, strategy pairs correspond to points in the unit square $[0, 1]^2 \equiv \{(p_1, q_1) \,|\, 0 \le p_1 \le 1, 0 \le q_1 \le 1\}$. Clearly, $(1, 0)$ and $(0, 1)$ are the only strict NE, and they correspond to the pure strategies "Owners play H and Intruders play D" and "Owners play D and Intruders play H" respectively. The only other NE is unstable (see figure 3.2.1 below) and is given by (p_1^*, q_1^*) where

$$
p_1^* = q_1^* = (b - d)/(b - d + c - a).
$$

That is, the interior ESS $(p_1^*, 1 - p_1^*)$ of the Hawk-Dove Game with payoff matrix $\begin{bmatrix} a & b \\ c & d \end{bmatrix}$ corresponds to an unstable NE of the Owner-Intruder Game.

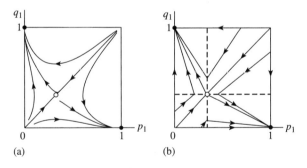

(a)   (b)

Figure 3.2.1
Phase portraits for the Owner-Intruder Game under (a) the replicator dynamic and (b) the best response dynamic. The phase portraits are given in horizontal pairs here and in the nine cases of sections 3.3.1 and 3.3.2. The phase portrait at the left is that of the replicator dynamic while that at the right is the best response dynamic.

The bimatrix replicator dynamic is also on the unit square. From (3.2.1) and the payoff matrix,

$$\dot{p}_1 = p_1(1 - p_1)[b - d + (a + d - b - c)q_1],$$

$$\dot{q}_1 = q_1(1 - q_1)[b - d + (a + d - b - c)p_1].$$

Since $\dot{p}_1 = \dot{q}_1$ when $p_1 = q_1$, the line $p_1 = q_1$ is invariant[5] for (3.2.1), and on this line every interior trajectory converges to (p_1^*, q_1^*).

Now suppose $0 < p_1 < q_1$ initially. Then $(d/dt) \ln(p_1/q_1) = (\dot{p}_1/p_1) - (\dot{q}_1/q_1)$ is given by $(1 - p_1)[b - d + (a + d - b - c)q_1] - (1 - q_1)[b - d + (a + d - b - c)p_1]$ which equals $(q_1 - p_1)(a - c)$. Similarly $(d/dt) \ln((1 - p_1)/(1 - q_1)) = (q_1 - p_1)(b - d)$. Thus p_1/q_1 and $(1 - q_1)/(1 - p_1)$ are both decreasing from which it follows easily that $q_1 - p_1$ is increasing.[6] Therefore any initial point with $p_1 < q_1$ evolves to $(0, 1)$. Similarly initial points with $p_1 > q_1$ evolve to $(1, 0)$. The phase portrait (figure 3.2.1) has two asymptotically stable rest points $(0, 1)$ and $(1, 0)$ whose basins of attraction are bounded by the diagonal *separatrix* $p_1 = q_1$.

Heuristically, if owners are more likely to play Hawk initially than intruders (i.e., $p_1 > q_1$), this bias will increase until all owners are Hawks and all intruders are Doves. The NE at (p_1^*, q_1^*) is an unstable saddle point for (3.2.1) while the two strict NE points are the only asymptotically stable points as predicted by theorem 3.2.1 since the only SESets are the nonempty subsets of $\{(0, 1), (1, 0)\}$. The same conclusions arise for the best response dynamic (3.2.2).

3.3 Dynamics for Two-Strategy Bimatrix Games

In this section we classify the bimatrix replicator and best response dynamics for all bimatrix games where both players have two possible pure strategies. The following techniques simplify the classification: First, since these dynamics depend only on relative payoffs,

$$\begin{bmatrix} a, \alpha & b, \gamma \\ c, \beta & d, \delta \end{bmatrix} \quad \text{and} \quad \begin{bmatrix} a - c, \alpha - \gamma & 0, 0 \\ 0, 0 & d - b, \delta - \beta \end{bmatrix}$$

---

5. The invariance of the diagonal for the Owner-Intruder Game generalizes to all symmetric bimatrix games. That is, for any bimatrix game of the form (A, A), $\{(p, q) \mid p = q \in \Delta^m\}$ is invariant under (3.2.1). Furthermore, on this set, the dynamic restricts to the replicator dynamic for the symmetric normal form game A.

6. That is, $q_1 - p_1$ is a strict Lyapunov function for interior trajectories with $p_1 < q_1$ initially, and so these trajectories converge to the unique maximum of $q_1 - p_1$, which occurs at $(0, 1)$.

are equivalent (i.e., they have the same dynamic trajectories). Thus, by relabeling the payoffs, we may assume the bimatrix has the form

$$\begin{bmatrix} a, \alpha & 0, 0 \\ 0, 0 & d, \delta \end{bmatrix}. \tag{3.3.1}$$

Furthermore all these games with the same sign structure of the four payoff parameters $\{a, d, \alpha, \delta\}$ in (3.3.1) have qualitatively the same trajectories and so can be classified according to the signs of the four parameters.

Finally, by interchanging strategies f_1 and f_2 of player two and then considering relative payoffs, bimatrices

$$\begin{bmatrix} a, \alpha & 0, 0 \\ 0, 0 & d, \delta \end{bmatrix} \quad \text{and} \quad \begin{bmatrix} -d, -\alpha & 0, 0 \\ 0, 0 & -a, -\delta \end{bmatrix}$$

are equivalent. For instance, the Owner-Intruder Game that has all these parameters negative is equivalent to the symmetric bimatrix game based on the Coordination Game of chapter 2.2 that has all these parameters positive.

The classification is divided into three cases where all four payoff parameters in (3.3.1) are nonzero (a situation we will say is nondegenerate in section 3.3.1) followed by six degenerate cases in section 3.3.2. A complete analysis of the bimatrix replicator dynamic is given in each case along with the phase portrait. The analogous analysis of the bimatrix best response dynamic is, for the most part, left to the reader although all the phase portraits are provided.

3.3.1   Nondegenerate Bimatrix Games

If all four payoff parameters in (3.3.1) are nonzero, there is an interior NE if and only if ad and $\alpha\delta$ are both positive. This NE is

$$(p_1^*, q_1^*) = \left(\frac{\delta}{\alpha + \delta}, \frac{d}{a + d} \right). \tag{3.3.2}$$

By the simplification above, there are only two qualitatively different possibilities, either all four parameters are positive or a and d are both positive and α and δ are both negative. These first two cases are the most interesting, as evidenced by their repeated use for illustrative purposes in what follows, and so are given names (the Two-Player Coordination Game and the Buyer-Seller Game respectively). Case 3 assumes $ad < 0$.

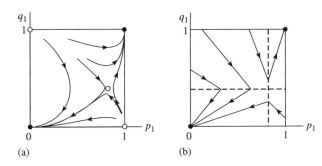

Figure 3.3.1
Phase portraits for the Two-Player Coordination Game.

Case 1 The Two-Player Coordination Game (all parameters positive)
These include the Owner-Intruder Games and the symmetric bimatrix
game based on the Coordination Game. However, to emphasize that
there are games in this class that are not symmetric bimatrix games,
let us consider the specific Two-Player Coordination Game with payoff
bimatrix

$$\begin{bmatrix} 3,1 & 0,0 \\ 0,0 & 2,4 \end{bmatrix}.$$

To classical game theorists, this is known as a Battle-of-the-Sexes Game[7]
in which, as a male-female contest, it is typically assumed the male prefers one form of entertainment and the female prefers another but both
prefer to be together at the same entertainment event rather than apart.

The problem then is how to coordinate on one of the two strict NE
(i.e., on (e_1, f_1) or on (e_2, f_2)). Although dynamic evolutionary game
theory as studied in this text does not predict a priori which sex will go
to his/her preferred event, it does show clearly that a substantial initial
advantage in favor of one sex will only increase over time until this sex
"wins" every contest. By an argument similar to that used in section 3.2.1
for the Owner-Intruder Game, it can be shown the replicator dynamic
has dynamic trajectories as in figure 3.3.1a.

Notice the similarity between the trajectories of the replicator dynamics in figures 3.2.1a and 3.3.1a. The interior NE given for both by (3.3.2)
(which is $(p_1^*, q_1^*) = (0.8, 0.4)$ for the specific Two-Player Coordination

---

7. I prefer not to use this name for case 1 since, in the biological literature, "Battle-of-the-
Sexes" refers to a bimatrix game with the same dynamics as case 2 (i.e., as a Buyer-Seller
Game).

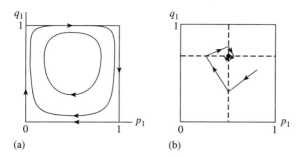

Figure 3.3.2
Phase portraits for the Buyer-Seller Game.

Game) is a saddle point[8] whose stable manifold is a separatrix bounding the domains of attraction for the two strict NE at diagonally opposite vertices of the unit square. However, for the Two-Player Coordination Game, this separatrix is no longer expected to be the diagonal of the unit square joining the other two vertices.

Case 2   The Buyer-Seller Game (a and d positive, α and δ negative) The only NE is (p_1^*, q_1^*) given in (3.3.2) and there are no SESets. On the boundary of the unit square, trajectories of (3.2.1) form a heteroclinic cycle (figure 3.3.2a). Interior trajectories form periodic closed curves that cycle around (p_1^*, q_1^*) since

$$H(p_1, q_1) = \frac{q_1^d (1 - q_1)^a}{p_1^\delta (1 - p_1)^\alpha}$$

is a constant of motion (i.e., $dH/dt = 0$) and $H(p_1, q_1)$ attains its maximum at (p_1^*, q_1^*). We will see that this is the only two-strategy bimatrix game for which the interior trajectories of the bimatrix replicator dynamic (3.2.1) do not all converge to a NE. On the other hand, from figure 3.3.2b it is clear all best response trajectories do converge to (p_1^*, q_1^*) as they spiral around this point in a piecewise linear fashion.

---

8. The formal definition of saddle point, stable manifold, heteroclinic cycle, etc. can be found in standard texts on dynamical systems. For these two-dimensional systems, a *saddle point* is a hyperbolic rest point that has one positive and one negative eigenvalue. The *stable manifold* is an invariant curve through the rest point corresponding to its negative eigenvalue. A *heteroclinic cycle*, as referred to in case 2, is a finite sequence of complete trajectories (i.e., defined for all $t \in \mathbf{R}$), each of which joins different rest points that together form a cycle of rest points.

This is called the Buyer-Seller Game since it has the same sign structure as a bimatrix game such as

$$
\begin{array}{c}
\qquad\qquad \text{Seller} \\
\qquad\qquad H \qquad C \\
\text{Buyer} \;
\begin{array}{c} T \\ I \end{array}
\left[
\begin{array}{cc}
5,4 & 1,6 \\
4,0 & 3,-2
\end{array}
\right],
\end{array}
$$

which can be used as an elementary model for the exchange of a good between a buyer and a seller. In this game a seller either gives an accurate appraisal of the good in question (i.e., is Honest (H)) or over represents its worth (i.e., Cheats (C)). Buyers, in turn, can either Trust (T) the seller's representation or Inspect (I) to determine the good's worth. The payoffs in the bimatrix reflect the intuition that if a seller is honest, it is better to trust (to save the cost of inspection), and if he cheats, it is better to inspect. Similarly, for sellers, it is best to be honest if the buyer inspects and to cheat if the buyer trusts. The cyclic nature of these best replies suggests general evolutionary trajectories in the unit square either cycle or spiral around the NE $(p_1^*, q_1^*) = (\frac{1}{2}, \frac{2}{3})$ as in figure 3.3.2 for this game. However, the exact forms of the trajectories shown in figure 3.3.2ab depend on the specific evolutionary dynamic.

Case 3 ($a < 0 < d$ and $\delta > 0$)[9] This class includes the symmetric bimatrix game based on the Prisoner's Dilemma Game of chapter 2.2 (in which case α is also negative). Since all interior trajectories converge to the unique SESet $\{(e_2, f_2)\}$ no matter what the sign of α (figure 3.3.3), we have combined all these into a single class. The general sign structure is

$$
\left[
\begin{array}{cc}
-,\alpha & 0,0 \\
0,0 & +,+
\end{array}
\right],
$$

where $\alpha \neq 0$.

3.3.2   Degenerate Bimatrix Games

Every parameter that is zero in the parameter set $\{a, d, \alpha, \delta\}$ of (3.3.1) corresponds to an edge of the unit square consisting entirely of rest points

---

9. Note that if $\delta < 0$, we obtain the same sign structure by interchanging f_1 and f_2, and so we can assume $\delta > 0$.

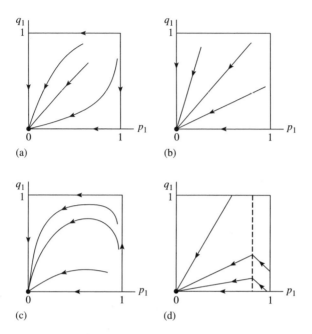

Figure 3.3.3
Four phase portraits for case 3. The top two are for $\alpha < 0$ and the bottom two for $\alpha > 0$.

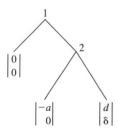

Figure 3.3.4
Extensive form for degenerate bimatrix games with two strategies.

of (3.2.1). Without loss of generality, we assume that $\alpha = 0$ through-out this section. Each degenerate bimatrix game is then equivalent to the bimatrix normal form of the extensive form game with game tree shown in figure 3.3.4. This particular extensive form becomes important in chapter 8 as an elementary example of a perfect information game (see chapter 8.1). For each of the following six degenerate cases, we briefly describe the NE and SESet structure, discuss the replicator dynamic for all of them and best response dynamic for some.

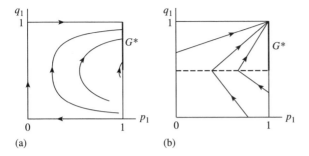

Figure 3.3.5
Phase portraits for the Centipede Game of Length Two.

Our first cases (cases 4, 5, and 6) are those where α is the only parameter that is zero. By interchanging f_1 and f_2 if necessary, we can assume $\delta < 0$. Then $\dot{q}_1 > 0$ for all interior trajectories and $p_1 = 1$ is an edge that consists entirely of rest points for (3.2.1). Again, it is the first two cases (the Centipede Game of Length Two and the Chain-Store Game) that are the most interesting as we will see in chapter 8 where the reasons for their names will also be clarified (see also chapter 1.1). All three cases have a single distinguished pure strategy NE (called subgame perfect in chapter 8) whose NE component is denoted here by G^*.

When exactly two payoff parameters are zero, these can be either one for each player (case 7) or both for the same player (case 8). Both of these include subcases that depend on the sign of the remaining two parameters. The last possibility (case 9) is when three parameters are zero.[10]

Case 4 The Centipede Game of Length Two ($\alpha = 0$, a and d positive, $\delta < 0$) There is a single NE component $G^* = \{(e_1, (\lambda, 1 - \lambda)) \mid 1 \geq \lambda \geq d/(a + d)\}$ that is globally interior asymptotically stable (i.e., all interior trajectories converge to G^* and those that are initially close to G^* stay close) for the bimatrix replicator and best response dynamics (figure 3.3.5). There is no SESet.

Case 5 The Chain Store Game ($\alpha = 0$, a and d negative, $\delta < 0$) There is a single SESet $G^* = \{(e_2, f_1)\}$ and one other NE component $G = \{(e_1, (\lambda, 1 - \lambda)) \mid 0 \leq \lambda \leq d/(a + d)\}$. G^* is asymptotically stable

---

10. The case where all four are zero is completely uninteresting for both the bimatrix replicator dynamic (here all points are rest points) and the bimatrix best response dynamic (here all curves are best response trajectories).

and every point in the interior of the line segment G is neutrally stable (see figure 3.3.6) for the bimatrix replicator dynamic.

Case 6 $(\alpha = 0, ad < 0, \delta < 0)$ If $a < 0$, $G^* = \{(e_2, f_1)\}$ is a globally asymptotically stable strict NE. If $a > 0$, the line $p_1 = 1$ (i.e., $G^* = \{(e_1, (\lambda, 1 - \lambda)) \mid 0 \leq \lambda \leq 1\}$) is a globally asymptotically stable SESet (figure 3.3.7).

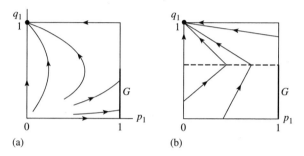

Figure 3.3.6
Phase portraits for the Chain-Store Game.

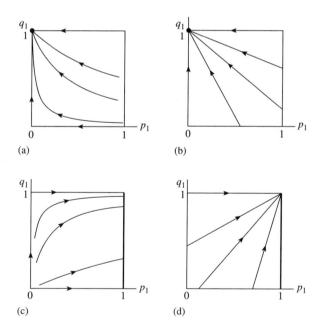

Figure 3.3.7
Phase portraits for case 6. The top two diagrams have $\alpha < 0$ and the bottom two $\alpha > 0$.

Case 7 $(a = \alpha = 0, d\delta \neq 0)$ If two payoff parameters are zero, one for each player, we can assume that $a = \alpha = 0$ by interchanging f_1 and f_2 if necessary. Then $p_1 = 1$ and $q_1 = 1$ are adjacent edges consisting entirely of rest points of (3.2.1). If $d > 0$ and $\delta > 0$, $(0, 0)$ is a globally asymptotically stable strict NE. If $d < 0$ and $\delta < 0$, the two edges are all NE and form a globally asymptotically stable SESet. If $d < 0$ and $\delta > 0$, $p_1 = 1$ is interior asymptotically stable but not asymptotically stable nor an SESet (figure 3.3.8).

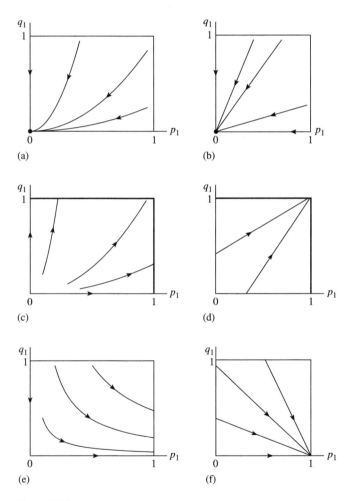

Figure 3.3.8
Phase portraits for case 7. The top two diagrams have $d > 0$ and $\delta > 0$, the middle two have $d < 0$ and $\delta < 0$, and the bottom two $d < 0$ and $\delta > 0$.

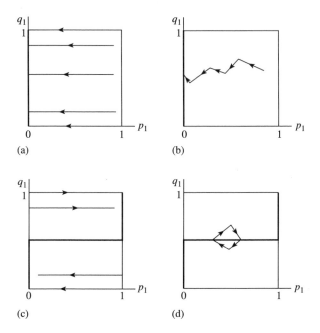

Figure 3.3.9
Phase portraits for case 8. The top two diagrams have $a < 0$ and $d > 0$, and the bottom two have $a > 0$ and $d > 0$.

Case 8 $(\alpha = \delta = 0, ad \neq 0)$ Now suppose that two payoff parameters are zero, both for player two (i.e., $\alpha = \delta = 0$). Then $\dot{q}_1 = 0$ for (3.2.1), and we essentially have the replicator dynamic for player one with the two vertical edges $p_1 = 0$ and $p_1 = 1$ consisting entirely of rest points. The most interesting possibility is when there is a line of interior NE (i.e., $ad > 0$). Here trajectories of the bimatrix best-response dynamic may be identical to those of the bimatrix replicator dynamic (if the best reply for player two is taken to be its current state) but can also cycle as in the bottom right-hand diagram in figure 3.3.9 for certain other choices of best replies. In fact this is the only two-strategy bimatrix game where the ω-limit points of bimatrix best response trajectories are not necessarily NE.

Case 9 $(a = \alpha = d = 0, \delta < 0)$ Here $\dot{p}_1 = 0$ and $\dot{q}_1 > 0$ for all interior trajectories. Three edges (i.e., all except $p_1 = 0$) are rest points of (3.2.1). Although there is no SESet, the edge $q_1 = 1$ is interior asymptotically stable for the bimatrix replicator and best response dynamics (figure 3.3.10).

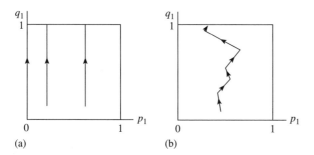

Figure 3.3.10
Phase portraits for case 9.

Remark 3.3.1 A quick glance at the phase portraits of two-strategy bimatrix games reveals that all interior trajectories of (3.2.1) converge to a NE except for the Buyer-Seller Game. However, unlike two-strategy symmetric games where every case has at least one ESSet (see theorem 2.5.4 of chapter 2), many two-strategy bimatrix games have no SESet. On the other hand, there are stable NE and stable NE components in every case. Phase portraits of a continuous-time monotone selection dynamic are qualitatively similar to those of (3.2.1) except for the Buyer-Seller Game (these latter are analyzed in example 3.5.2 below). Thus any such dynamic can be used as an equilibrium selection technique by eliminating those NE (components) that are not dynamically stable.

Each trajectory of the best response dynamic also converges to a single NE except in figures 3.3.9 and 3.3.10. Moreover, if tie-breaking rules are used for which the best reply of a player can only depend on the strategy of the other and not on his own strategy, trajectories as shown in these two figures are not possible and all best response trajectories converge to a NE.

3.4   Symmetrized Bimatrix Games

The bimatrix replicator and best response dynamics, (3.2.1) and (3.2.2), are two-species models of the evolution of pairs of strategy frequencies in $\Delta^n \times \Delta^m$, whereas dynamic evolutionary game theory was initially developed as a single-species model where the underlying dynamic is based on a symmetric normal form game. We will see that these models are closely connected through the *symmetrization of the bimatrix game.*[11] To this end, suppose that every individual has two possible roles in a random contest; namely he may find himself in the role of player one in some contests and in the role of player two in others. Thus, in a symmetrized bimatrix game, a pure strategy consists of a pair of choices $[e_i, f_j]$ in $S \times T$ that specifies which choice an individual will use in each of his roles. There are nm such strategies.

Furthermore we assume that the role assignment is random. Thus, in a given contest, either contestant is as likely to be in the role of player one as in the role of player two. The expected payoff to $[e_i, f_j]$ in a contest against $[e_k, f_\ell]$ is then

$$m_{ij,k\ell} \equiv \tfrac{1}{2}(e_i \cdot Af_\ell + f_j \cdot Be_k).$$

That is, the symmetrized bimatrix game consists of the strategy set $S \times T$ and the $nm \times nm$ payoff matrix M with entries $m_{ij,k\ell}$. For example, the Symmetrized Buyer-Seller Game has four pure strategies $\{[T, H], [T, C], [I, H], [I, C]\}$, where $[T, H]$ means "Trust if buyer and Honest if seller," and so on. From the payoffs given in case 2 of section 3.3.1, the 4×4 payoff matrix is (with pure strategies given this order)

$$\frac{1}{2}\begin{bmatrix} 5+4 & 1+4 & 5+0 & 1+0 \\ 5+6 & 1+6 & 5-2 & 1-2 \\ 4+4 & 3+4 & 4+0 & 3+0 \\ 4+6 & 3+6 & 4-2 & 3-2 \end{bmatrix}.$$

The extensive form representation of a symmetrized bimatrix game is particularly useful. An initial move by nature (player 0) assigns the roles of player one and player two to the two contestants at random. This splits the game tree into left- and right-hand *subgames.*[12] In figure 3.4.1 player one is the buyer in the left-hand subgame and the seller in the right-hand subgame.

Symmetry interconnects the information sets in these subgames and is indicated by double arrows, $\leftrightarrow$, in the extensive form. For instance, one such connection in figure 3.4.1 joins the information set where player one is the buyer to that where player two is the buyer.

---

11. Symmetrized bimatrix games are also known as *role games.*
12. See chapter 6 for the formal definition of the subgame concept. In chapter 4.5 these are called *truly asymmetric subgames.*

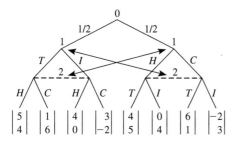

Figure 3.4.1
Symmetrized Buyer-Seller Game in extensive form.

Mixed strategies in these symmetrized games are also important. They are elements $p \in \Delta^{nm}$ with components p_{ij} giving the frequency of strategy $[e_i, f_j]$. The expected payoff to p against $\hat{p}$ is

$$p \cdot M\hat{p} = \tfrac{1}{2}(p^1 \cdot A\hat{p}^2 + p^2 \cdot B\hat{p}^1). \tag{3.4.1}$$

Here $p^1 \in \Delta^n$ and $p^2 \in \Delta^m$ are the *role-conditioned strategies* with components $p_i^1 = \sum_j p_{ij}$ and $p_j^2 = \sum_i p_{ij}$ respectively.

There is a close connection between a bimatrix game and its symmetrization from both the static and dynamic perspectives of evolutionary game theory as we will see in the remainder of this section. The following result summarizes the static connection. Sections 3.4.1 and 3.4.2 develop the dynamic perspective.

Theorem 3.4.1 *$E \subseteq \Delta^{nm}$ is an ESSet of the symmetrized bimatrix game (A, B) if and only if $F \equiv \{(p^1, p^2) \mid p \in E\} \subseteq \Delta^n \times \Delta^m$ is an SESet of the bimatrix game (A, B) and $E = \{p \in \Delta^{nm} \mid (p^1, p^2) \in F\}$. In particular, every ESS of the symmetrized bimatrix game (A, B) is a pure strategy $[e_i, f_j] \in \Delta^{nm}$ that corresponds to a strict NE (e_i, f_j) of the bimatrix (A, B).*

Proof (a) Suppose that E is an ESSet of the symmetrized bimatrix game and $(p^{1*}, p^{2*}) \in F$. That is, (p^{1*}, p^{2*}) are the conditional frequencies for some $p^* \in E$. For $p^1 \in \Delta^n$, define $p \in \Delta^{nm}$ by $p_{ij} = p_i^1 p_j^{2*}$. Then

$$p^1 \cdot Ap^{2*} + p^{2*} \cdot Bp^{1*} = 2p \cdot Mp^* \leq 2p^* \cdot Mp^* = p^{1*} \cdot Ap^{2*} + p^{2*} \cdot Bp^{1*}$$

Thus $p^1 \cdot Ap^{2*} \leq p^{1*} \cdot Ap^{2*}$ for all $p^1 \in \Delta^n$. By the same argument applied to $p^2 \in \Delta^m$, we see that (p^{1*}, p^{2*}) is a NE of the bimatrix game. Now assume $p^1 \cdot Ap^{2*} = p^{1*} \cdot Ap^{2*}$ for some $(p^{1*}, p^{2*}) \in F$. By the calculation above, $p \cdot Mp^* = p^* \cdot Mp^*$. Since E is an ESSet, either $p^{1*} \cdot Ap^{2*} + p^{2*} \cdot Bp^1 = 2p^* \cdot Mp > 2p \cdot Mp = p^1 \cdot Ap^{2*} + p^{2*} \cdot Bp^1$ or $p \in E$.

Since $p^1 \cdot Ap^{2*} = p^{1*} \cdot Ap^{2*}$, $p \in E$ and so $(p^1, p^{2*}) \in F$. Thus F is an SESet.

Finally, if $(p^1, p^2) \in F$, then $(p^1, p^2) = (p^{*1}, p^{*2})$ for some $p^* \in E$. Therefore

$$p \cdot Mp^* = p^* \cdot Mp^* = p^* \cdot Mp = p \cdot Mp,$$

and so $p \in E$ for all $p \in \Delta^{nm}$ with conditional frequencies (p^1, p^2) since E is an ESSet. That is, $E = \{p \in \Delta^{nm} \mid (p^1, p^2) \in F\}$.

(b) Conversely, suppose that F is an SESet and $p^* \in E \equiv \{p \in \Delta^{nm} \mid (p^1, p^2) \in F\}$. If $p \cdot Mp^* = p^* \cdot Mp^*$, then $p^1 \cdot Ap^{*2} = p^{*1} \cdot Ap^{*2}$ and $p^2 \cdot Bp^{*1} = p^{*2} \cdot Bp^{*1}$ since (p^{*1}, p^{*2}) is a NE. Thus (p^{*1}, p^2) and (p^1, p^{*2}) are both in the SESet F. In particular, $p^{*1} \cdot Ap^2 \geq p^1 \cdot Ap^2$ and $p^{*2} \cdot Bp^1 \geq p^2 \cdot Bp^1$. That is, $p^* \cdot Mp \geq p \cdot Mp$. If there is an equality, then $p^{*1} \cdot Ap^2 = p^1 \cdot Ap^2$, and so $(p^1, p^2) \in F$ since F is an SESet. In other words, E is an ESSet since either $p^* \cdot Mp > p \cdot Mp$ or $p \in E$.   ∎

Thus theorem 3.4.1 shows the ES structure of the symmetrization corresponds to the SESet structure of the original bimatrix game. It combines with the classification of two-strategy bimatrix games in section 3.3 to yield all the ESSets of their symmetrizations. For instance, the Symmetrized Buyer-Seller Game has no ESSet.

3.4.1   The Symmetrized Bimatrix Replicator Dynamic

The *symmetrized replicator dynamic* of a bimatrix game (A, B) is the symmetric replicator dynamic applied to a symmetrized bimatrix game. By (3.4.1), this dynamic on Δ^{nm} is given by

$$\dot{p}_{ij} = p_{ij}([e_i, f_j] - p) \cdot Mp. \tag{3.4.2}$$

The following theorem gives a fundamental connection between the bimatrix and symmetrized replicator dynamics. Most of the proof is postponed to chapter 4.5 (see theorem 4.5.3ii there). The statement of theorem 3.2.1 is repeated in theorem 3.4.2 for the sake of completeness.

Theorem 3.4.2   *Let (A, B) be a bimatrix game. $E \subset \Delta^{nm}$ is an asymptotically stable set of rest points of the symmetrized replicator dynamic (3.4.2) for the symmetrization of (A, B) if and only if E is an ESSet if and only if $E = \{p \in \Delta^{nm} \mid (p^1, p^2) \in F\}$ for some SESet F of (A, B). $F \subset \Delta^n \times \Delta^m$ is an asymptotically stable set of rest points of the bimatrix replicator dynamic (3.2.1)* *for (A, B) if and only if F is an SESet if and only if $F = \{(p^1, p^2) \mid p \in E\}$ for some ESSet E of the symmetrization of (A, B).*

Proof The only part of the proof provided here is that an asymptotically stable set of rest points F of the bimatrix replicator dynamic (3.2.1) is an SESet. Suppose that F is connected and that $(p^*, q^*) \in F$ is not a pure strategy pair. We first show by induction on the size of the supports of p^* and q^* that F contains the face of $\Delta(S) \times \Delta(T)$ on which (p^*, q^*) is interior. By lemma 4.5.2 of chapter 4, there is a path in F from (p^*, q^*) to a pure strategy pair. Without loss of generality, there is a $\hat{p} \neq p^*$ along this path with the same support as p^*. Then every point p in $\Delta(S)$ on the line through $\hat{p}$ and p^* is a rest point, and so (p, q^*) is in F. The line segment from p^* to $\hat{p}$ extends to a point, say $\tilde{p}$, on the boundary of $\Delta(S)$. Thus, by induction, $(p, q) \in F$ for all supp$(p) \subset$ supp$(\tilde{p})$ and supp$(q) \subset$ supp(q^*). Since each $(p, q) \in F$ is a NE, if supp$(p) \subset$ supp$(\tilde{p})$ and supp$(q) \subset$ supp(q^*), then $\pi_1(p, q) = \pi_1(p^*, q)$ and $\pi_2(p, q) = \pi_2(p, q^*)$.[13] By extending the line segment from p^* to $\hat{p}$ in the other direction to the boundary of supp(p^*), we have $\pi_1(p, q) = \pi_1(p^*, q)$ and $\pi_2(p, q) = \pi_2(p, q^*)$ for all supp$(p) \subset$ supp(p^*) and supp$(q) \subset$ supp(q^*). Thus all points in supp$(p^*) \times$ supp(q^*) are rest points and so in F. In particular, F is a finite union of faces of $\Delta(S) \times \Delta(T)$.

Finally, to show that F is an SESet, suppose that $(p^*, q^*) \in F$ and that $\pi_1(p, q^*) = \pi_1(p^*, q^*)$. For any pure strategy f in the support of q^*, $(p^*, f) \in F$. Then all points on the face $(\hat{p}, f)$, where supp$(\hat{p}) \subset$ supp$(p) \cup$ supp(p^*), are rest points of the bimatrix replicator dynamic, and so in F. Since this is true for all such f, (supp$(p) \cup$ supp$(p^*)) \times$ supp(q^*) is also a set of rest points. In particular, $(p, q^*) \in F$.   ∎

The elegance of the statement of theorem 3.4.2 on asymptotic behavior hides the complicated relationship between general trajectories for a symmetrized bimatrix game in the $(nm - 1)$-dimensional simplex Δ^{nm} and those of (3.2.1) for the original bimatrix game in its $(n + m - 2)$-dimensional strategy space $\Delta^n \times \Delta^m$. However, the proof of theorem 3.4.2 relies heavily on the existence of an invariant $(n + m - 2)$-dimensional manifold of the symmetrized replicator dynamic where the trajectories of the symmetrized replicator dynamic (3.4.2) induce those of (3.2.1). This is called the *Wright manifold* due to its relevance for two-locus

---

13. If, for instance, $\pi_1(p^*, q) < \pi_1(p, q)$, then $\pi_1(p^*, (1 - \varepsilon)q^* + \varepsilon q) \leq \pi_1(p, (1 - \varepsilon)q^* + \varepsilon q)$ for all $|\varepsilon|$ sufficiently small. This is clearly impossible by considering $\pm\varepsilon$.

genetic models (see chapter 5). Specifically, define the Wright manifold[14] W as

$$W = \{p \in \Delta^{nm} \mid p_{ij} = p_i^1 p_j^2\}.$$

The most direct way to show W is invariant is to give another characterization of it. To this end, notice that $p_{ij} p_{k\ell} = p_i^1 p_j^2 p_k^1 p_\ell^2 = p_{i\ell} p_{kj}$ for all $1 \le i, k \le n$ and $1 \le j, \ell \le m$ if $p \in W$. Conversely, if $p_{ij} p_{k\ell} = p_{i\ell} p_{kj}$ for all $1 \le i, k \le n$ and $1 \le j, \ell \le m$, then $p_i^1 p_j^2 = \sum_\ell p_{i\ell} \sum_k p_{kj} = \sum_k \sum_\ell p_{i\ell} p_{kj} = \sum_k \sum_\ell p_{ij} p_{k\ell} = p_{ij}$ and so $p \in W$. Thus

$$W = \{p \in \Delta^{nm} \mid p_{ij} p_{k\ell} = p_{i\ell} p_{kj} \text{ for all } 1 \le i, k \le n \text{ and } 1 \le j, \ell \le m\}.$$

Furthermore, from (3.4.1) and (3.4.2), $d(p_{ij} p_{k\ell} - p_{i\ell} p_{kj})/dt = 0$ if $p \in W$ and so W is invariant for (3.4.2).

On the Wright manifold W, $\dot{p}_i^1 = \sum_j \dot{p}_{ij} = \sum_j p_{ij}([e_i, f_j] - p) \cdot Mp = \frac{1}{2}(\sum_j p_i^1 p_j^2((e_i - p^1) \cdot Ap^2 + (f_j - p^2) \cdot Bp^1))$. Since $\sum_j p_j^2 f_j = p^2$, we have

$$\dot{p}_i^1 = \frac{1}{2} p_i^1 (e_i - p^1) \cdot Ap^2,$$

$$\dot{p}_j^2 = \frac{1}{2} p_j^2 (f_j - p^2) \cdot Bp^1,$$

which is the bimatrix replicator dynamic (up to the irrelevant factor $\frac{1}{2}$) on $\Delta^n \times \Delta^m$. Thus the trajectories of (3.4.2) project onto trajectories of (3.2.1). That is, if $p(t)$ is a trajectory in W of the symmetrized replicator dynamic, then $(p^1(t), p^2(t))$ is a trajectory of (3.2.1). A crucial part of the proof of theorem 3.4.2 is then based on the fact that this implies that any asymptotically stable set E of rest points of (3.4.2) must project onto an asymptotically stable set F of rest points of (3.2.1).

The calculation above to show W is invariant under the symmetrized replicator dynamic also shows the invariance of all *generalized Wright*

---

14. Elements in W are also called the *mixed-strategy representatives* of the behavior strategies (see chapter 6) at the two information sets of player one in the extensive form of a symmetrized bimatrix game such as figure 3.4.1. There is a technical issue with calling W a manifold since points on the boundary of W do not have neighborhoods that are diffeomorphic to an open subset of euclidean space of dimension $n + m - 2$. The same issue occurs in chapter 4.4, whereas the term is used in its correct mathematical sense in the formal definition of the Wright manifold of an extensive form game (definition 6.3.1) by restricting attention to interior strategies. Any possible harm done by these minor mathematical inconsistencies is more than outweighed by its general acceptance as an important concept in population genetics.

manifolds for the symmetrization of (A, B). These are sets of the form

$$W_K \equiv \{p \in \Delta^{nm} \mid p_{ij} p_{k\ell} = K_{ij,k\ell} p_{i\ell} p_{kj}\}$$

for some set of positive constants $K = \{K_{ij,k\ell}\}$ for which this set contains some element in the interior of Δ^{nm}. The projection map $p \in \Delta^{nm} \rightarrow (p^1, p^2) \in \Delta^n \times \Delta^m$ restricts to a bijection of each W_K onto $\Delta^n \times \Delta^m$.[15] Since the trajectories on these manifolds may be qualitatively different than those on W, there is in general a complicated relationship between trajectories of the symmetrized and bimatrix replicator dynamics.

These complications are already apparent for two-strategy bimatrix games where each generalized Wright manifold is now indexed by a single positive constant K as

$$W_K = \{p \in \Delta^4 \mid p_{11} p_{22} = K p_{12} p_{21}\}.$$

The most startling difference occurs for case 2 (the Buyer-Seller Game) where the symmetrized replicator dynamic has no asymptotically stable set of rest points by theorem 3.4.2. With the payoffs given in section 3.3.1 as

$$\begin{bmatrix} 5,4 & 1,6 \\ 4,0 & 3,-2 \end{bmatrix},$$

the symmetrized replicator dynamic on W (i.e., when $K = 1$) induces the bimatrix replicator dynamic and so trajectories form periodic orbits around $(\frac{1}{3}, \frac{1}{6}, \frac{1}{3}, \frac{1}{6})$. The only NE component of the symmetrized game is $E = \{p \in \Delta^4 \mid p^1 = (\frac{1}{2}, \frac{1}{2}), p^2 = (\frac{2}{3}, \frac{1}{3})\}$, and it intersects each generalized Wright manifold in exactly one point. By a careful analysis (see Notes) of the trajectories on each generalized Wright manifold, it can be shown that this point is globally asymptotically stable if $K > 1$. Moreover, if $K < 1$, the only point in $E \cap W_K$ is unstable and all nonstationary trajectories evolve to the boundary of W_K.

The differences are not as pronounced for symmetric bimatrix games (A, A)—especially when there are only two strategies. All symmetrizations of symmetric bimatrix games have another important invariant manifold besides the generalized Wright manifolds; namely $L = \{p \in \Delta(S \times S) \mid p^1 = p^2\}$. This linear manifold of dimension $n(n - 1)$

---

15. This bijection of W_K onto $\Delta^n \times \Delta^m$ is a homeomorphism (i.e., continuous with continuous inverse) and also a diffeomorphism between their interiors. These facts are not needed for what follows, so their proofs are omitted.

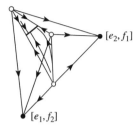

Figure 3.4.2
Replicator dynamic for the Symmetrized Owner-Intruder Game. The triangle L (with vertices the empty circles) separates the basins of attraction of $[e_1, f_2]$ and $[e_2, f_1]$.

is of intuitive interest since it is where the population as a whole does not condition its strategy on the role of its individual members.[16] It also exhibits several properties that make it interesting for the dynamic analysis. One is that the intersection of L with the Wright manifold projects onto the invariant diagonal $\{(p, q) \in \Delta^n \times \Delta^n \mid p = q\}$ discussed in section 3.2.1. Another is that the symmetrized replicator dynamic on L is automatically a mixed strategy dynamic as discussed in example 2.6.5 of chapter 2.

To gain a better appreciation of the general points in the preceding paragraph, consider the Symmetrized Owner-Intruder Game. Here $L = \{p \in \Delta^4 \mid p_{12} = p_{21}\}$ is the triangle with vertices $\{[e_1, f_1], \frac{1}{2}([e_1, f_2] + [e_2, f_1]), [e_2, f_2]\}$ in figure 3.4.2. The triangle separates the basins of attraction of the strict NE $[e_1, f_2]$ and $[e_2, f_1]$ in this figure. The trajectories of (3.4.2) restricted to L are those of the replicator dynamic for the symmetric normal form game with payoff matrix

$$
\begin{bmatrix}
a & \frac{1}{2}(a+b) & b \\
\frac{1}{2}(a+c) & \frac{1}{4}(a+b+c+d) & \frac{1}{2}(b+d) \\
c & \frac{1}{2}(c+d) & d
\end{bmatrix}.
$$

Since $a < c$ and $b > d$ for the Owner-Intruder Game of section 3.2.1, the set of interior NE for its symmetrization is the line $E = \{p \in \Delta^4 \mid p_{12} = p_{21}, p_{11} + p_{12} = (b-d)/(b-d+c-a)\}$ that is contained in L. The Wright manifold intersects L in the parabola through $(\frac{1}{4}, \frac{1}{2}, \frac{1}{4})$

---

16. The corresponding intuitive concept of the Wright manifold is as those points in Δ^{nm} where the average population strategy in the first role is independent of the average population strategy in the second role.

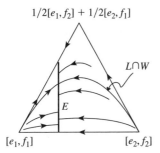

$1/2[e_1,f_2] + 1/2[e_2,f_1]$

$L \cap W$

E

$[e_1,f_1]$ $[e_2,f_2]$

Figure 3.4.3
Invariant triangle L and the trajectories of (3.4.2) on it for the Symmetrized Owner-Intruder
Game. Here $b + c - (a + d)$ is negative.

in figure 3.4.3. The other curves in this figure are intersections with a
generalized Wright manifold. All trajectories in the interior of L flow
along these curves to a unique point in E.

3.4.2 The Symmetrized Best Response Dynamic

We will consider two methods to symmetrize the best response dynamic
for a bimatrix game. As we will see, there is an even closer relationship
between trajectories of the bimatrix best response dynamic (3.2.2) for
the bimatrix game and those of both these symmetrizations. The fundamental reason for this is that for $p \in \Delta^{nm}$, $[e_i, f_j] \in BR(p)$ if and only
if $e_i \in BR(p^2)$ and $f_j \in BR(p^1)$. This carries over to mixed strategy best
responses as well; namely $b \in \Delta^{nm}$ is in $BR(p)$ if and only if $b^1 \in BR(p^2)$
and $b^2 \in BR(p^1)$.

The first method to symmetrize the best response dynamic is to simply
take the symmetric best response dynamic of chapter 2 applied to the
symmetric normal form of the symmetrization of (A, B). That is, from
chapter 2.4,

$$\dot{p}_{ij} = (BR_{ij}(p) - p_{ij}). \tag{3.4.3}$$

For this dynamic, $\dot{p}_i^1 = \sum_{j=1}^{m} \dot{p}_{ij} = \sum_{j=1}^{m}(BR_{ij}(p) - p_{ij}) = BR_i(p^2) - p_i^1$
where $BR_{ij}(p)$ is the ijth component of $BR(p) \subset \Delta^{nm}$ and $BR_i(p^2)$ is the
ith component of $BR(p^2) \subset \Delta^n$. Thus the dynamic (3.4.3) projects onto
$\Delta^n \times \Delta^m$ as

$$\dot{p}_i^1 = BR_i(p^2) - p_i^1,$$
$$\dot{p}_j^2 = BR_j(p^1) - p_j^2.$$

This is well defined if we assume (an assumption we will use hereafter) that the tie-breaking rule is the same for all $p \in \Delta^{nm}$ with the same p^1 and p^2. Since this is then the bimatrix best response dynamic on $\Delta^n \times \Delta^m$, the trajectories of (3.4.3) project onto trajectories of (3.2.2). That is, if $p(t)$ is a trajectory under (3.4.3), then $(p^1(t), p^2(t))$ is a trajectory under (3.2.2). Recall that the same projection technique applied to the replicator dynamic is valid for (3.4.2) only on the invariant Wright manifold. Although the Wright manifold is no longer invariant for (3.4.3), it will still play an important role in the analysis as we will see below.

The preceding result answers the most important questions concerning (3.4.3) but does leave open some of the finer details. For example, suppose that a projected trajectory of (3.4.3) converges (necessarily to some NE $(p^*, q^*) \in \Delta^n \times \Delta^m$ of the bimatrix game (A, B)). Then the trajectory itself must converge to the NE set $\{p \in \Delta^{nm} \mid p^1 = p^*, p^2 = q^*\}$. However, this does not mean a priori that the trajectory converges to a single NE point unless either p^* or q^* is a pure strategy. These issues become clear by considering the Symmetrized Buyer-Seller and Owner-Intruder games. For the Buyer-Seller Game, each trajectory of (3.2.2) converges to the unique NE that is completely mixed. It can be shown (see Notes) that every trajectory of (3.4.3) that is not initially a NE converges to the unique NE that is on the Wright manifold of this game.

On the other hand, for the Symmetrized Owner-Intruder Game, the strict NE $[e_1, f_2]$ and $[e_2, f_1]$ are again asymptotically stable with basins of attraction separated by the triangle with vertices $\{[e_1, f_1], \frac{1}{2}([e_1, f_2] + [e_2, f_1]), [e_2, f_2]\}$. For each initial point on this triangle, the trajectory of (3.4.3) converges either to one of these two strict NE or else to some point in $E = \{p \in \Delta^4 \mid p_1^1 = p_1^2 = p_1^*\}$ as shown in figure 3.4.4. In particular, the limit points need not be on the Wright manifold for this example.

The second method to symmetrize the best response dynamic is to assume that adjustments are only made in actions chosen for the current role.[17] Recall that for our symmetrized bimatrix games, it is assumed a player is as likely to be in the role of player one as in the role of player two. If individuals adjust by adopting a best reply to the current population in the opposite role and by leaving their choice in that role unchanged,

---

17. The first best response dynamic (3.4.3) for symmetrized bimatrix games assumes that each individual adjusts his strategy in each role simultaneously.

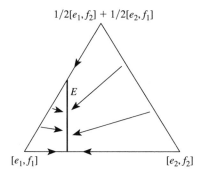

Figure 3.4.4
Trajectories of (3.4.3) on the triangle L.

then $\frac{1}{2}[\sum_k p_{kj} BR_i(p^2) - p_{ij}] = \frac{1}{2}[p_j^2 BR_i(p^2) - p_{ij}]$ accounts for the net rate of change to strategy $[e_i, f_j]$ of players who are now in the role of player one. Combined with the analogous term for players who are now in the role of player two, we have

$$\dot{p}_{ij} = \frac{1}{2}[p_j^2 BR_i(p^2) - p_{ij}] + \frac{1}{2}[p_i^1 BR_j(p^1) - p_{ij}]. \tag{3.4.4}$$

We call this the *symmetrized best response dynamic* since we feel this interpretation of role identification is more realistic.

Since $\dot{p}_i^1 = \sum_j \dot{p}_{ij} = \frac{1}{2}[BR_i(p^2) - p_i^1] + \frac{1}{2}[p_i^1 - p_i^1]$, the dynamic induces (3.2.2) up to the irrelevant factor $\frac{1}{2}$. That is,

$$\dot{p}^1 = \frac{1}{2}[BR(p^2) - p^1],$$
$$\dot{p}^2 = \frac{1}{2}[BR(p^1) - p^2].$$

Furthermore the Wright manifold is globally attracting for the dynamic (3.4.4) on Δ^{nm}. To see this, consider

$$\frac{d}{dt}(p_i^1 p_j^2 - p_{ij}) = \frac{1}{2}[BR_i(p^2) - p_i^1]p_j^2 + p_i^1 \frac{1}{2}[BR_j(p^1) - p_j^2]$$

$$- \frac{1}{2}[p_j^2 BR_i(p^2) - p_{ij}] - \frac{1}{2}[p_i^1 BR_j(p^1) - p_{ij}] \tag{3.4.5}$$

$$= -(p_i^1 p_j^2 - p_{ij}).$$

Thus, along any trajectory of (3.4.4), $p_i^1 p_j^2 - p_{ij}$ is exponentially decreasing to zero for all i, j. The result follows from the characterization of the Wright manifold as $W = \{p \in \Delta^{nm} \mid p_{ij} = p_i^1 p_j^2 \text{ for all } i, j\}$.

One consequence of this analysis is that NE of the symmetrized game are not rest points of (3.4.4) unless they are also points on the Wright manifold. This result can also be seen directly from (3.4.4) by taking $BR(p^2) = p^1 = p^*$ and $BR(p^1) = p^2 = q^*$ at a NE. Then $p_j^2 BR_i(p^2) - p_{ij} = 0$ if and only if $p_{ij} = p_i^1 p_j^2$, and so on. For instance, every trajectory of (3.4.4) for the Symmetrized Buyer-Seller Game converges to the unique NE on the Wright manifold. Those trajectories that are initially at another NE evolve along the one-dimensional NE set $E = \{p \in \Delta^{nm} \mid p^1 = p^*, p^2 = q^*\}$ toward this NE on the Wright manifold.

For the Symmetrized Owner-Intruder Game, every trajectory converges to a NE. All those on one side of L converge to the corresponding strict NE. Those on L either converge to one of these or to the unique NE point $(p_1^{1*} p_1^{2*}, p_1^{1*} p_2^{2*}, p_2^{1*} p_1^{2*}, p_2^{1*} p_2^{2*})$ in the interior of the Wright manifold.

3.5   Bimatrix Monotone Selection Dynamics

Monotone selection dynamics for a bimatrix game can be developed indirectly by applying the theory of chapters 2.3 and 2.7 to the game's symmetrization. However, the induced trajectories then are not expected to correspond to monotone dynamics, as defined below, for the two population evolutionary system (3.5.1). In particular, the Wright manifold need no longer be invariant. Thus in this section we directly generalize to bimatrix games the concept of monotone selection dynamics introduced in chapter 2.3 for symmetric normal form games. We restrict attention to continuous-time dynamics. Of special interest is the relationship between the stability of the bimatrix replicator dynamic to that of other bimatrix monotone selection dynamics (cf. the last statement of theorem 2.7.4 in chapter 2, which involves uniformly monotone selection dynamics for symmetric normal form games).

By remark 3.3.1, all interior trajectories of (3.2.1) for two-strategy bimatrix games in section 3.3 converge to a NE (except for the Buyer-Seller Game), and so this dynamic can be used as an equilibrium selection technique. In fact, with this one exception which is analyzed more fully in example 3.5.2 below, phase portraits of any continuous-time bimatrix monotone selection dynamic for all two-strategy bimatrix games are qualitatively similar to those of (3.2.1).

Analogous to chapter 2.3, a (smooth) *bimatrix monotone selection dynamic* on $\Delta^n \times \Delta^m$ can be written in the form

$$\dot{p}_i = g_i(p, q),$$
$$\dot{q}_j = h_j(p, q),$$

(3.5.1)

where the vector fields $g(p, q) = (g_1(p, q), \ldots, g_n(p, q))$ and $h(p, q) = (h_1(p, q), \ldots, h_m(p, q))$ satisfy the following five conditions.

i. $g_i(p, q)$ and $h_j(p, q)$ are Lipschitz continuous real-valued functions defined on some neighborhood of $\Delta^n \times \Delta^m$ for all i and j.

ii. $\sum_{i=1}^{n} g_i(p, q) = 0 = \sum_{j=1}^{m} h_j(p, q)$ for all $(p, q) \in \Delta^n \times \Delta^m$.

iii. $g_i(p, q)/p_i$ and $h_j(p, q)/q_j$ extend to continuously differentiable functions defined on some neighborhood of $\Delta^n \times \Delta^m$ for all i and j.

iv. $e_i \cdot Aq > e_k \cdot Aq$ if and only if $g_i(p, q)/p_i > g_k(p, q)/p_k$.

v. $f_j \cdot Bp > f_\ell \cdot Bp$ if and only if $h_j(p, q)/q_j > h_\ell(p, q)/q_\ell$.

The concepts of *aggregate monotone* and *uniformly monotone* are also straightforward extensions of definition 2.3.2 in chapter 2 to bimatrix games.

The bimatrix replicator dynamic (3.2.1) (which has $g_i(p, q) = p_i(e_i - p) \cdot Aq$ and $h_j(p, q) = q_j(f_j - q) \cdot Bp$) is clearly a bimatrix uniformly aggregate monotone selection dynamic. All bimatrix monotone selection dynamics have the same set of rest points. The comparison of a rest point's stability under the bimatrix replicator dynamic to the stability under other bimatrix monotone selection dynamics is initially investigated through their linearizations.

Following the method of part 3 in the appendix of chapter 2, to linearize (3.5.1) about a rest point (p^*, q^*), let $p_i = p_i^* + x_i$ and $q_j = q_j^* + y_j$ where $x \in X^n$ and $y \in X^m$. Then

$$\dot{x}_i = \sum_k J_{ik}^{11} x_k + \sum_\ell J_{i\ell}^{12} y_\ell,$$
$$\dot{y}_j = \sum_k J_{jk}^{21} x_k + \sum_\ell J_{j\ell}^{22} y_\ell,$$

where, for instance, J^{11} is the $n \times n$ matrix with entries $J_{ik}^{11} = \partial g_i(p^*, q^*)/\partial x_k$ that forms the part of the Jacobian that reflects how perturbations from equilibrium in population one affect this same population.

The linearization method applied to the bimatrix replicator dynamic (3.2.1) yields

$$
J_{ik}^{11} = \begin{cases} 0 & \text{if } p_i^* \neq 0, \\ \delta_{ik}(e_i - p^*) \cdot Aq^* & \text{if } p_i^* = 0, \end{cases}
$$

$$
J_{i\ell}^{12} = \begin{cases} p_i^*(e_i - p^*) \cdot Af_j & \text{if } p_i^* \neq 0, \\ 0 & \text{if } p_i^* = 0, \end{cases}
$$

and analogous expressions for the entries of J_{jk}^{21} and $J_{j\ell}^{22}$ involving the $m \times n$ matrix B. In particular, if $p_i^* = 0$, the only possible nonzero entry in the ith row of the linearization is the diagonal entry $(e_i - p^*) \cdot Aq^*$. These real eigenvalues must all be negative if linearization alone is to imply asymptotic stability of (p^*, q^*) (i.e., (p^*, q^*) must be a quasi-strict NE). In fact the same conclusion is true for any bimatrix monotone selection dynamic by conditions iv and v above,[18] and so we will assume for the remainder of the section (except for theorem 3.5.4) that $(e_i - p^*) \cdot Aq^* < 0$ and $(f_j - q^*) \cdot Bp^* < 0$ whenever $p_i^* = 0$ and $q_j^* = 0$ respectively. Thus we can restrict attention to the face $\Delta^{\hat{n}} \times \Delta^{\hat{m}}$ of $\Delta^n \times \Delta^m$ for which (p^*, q^*) is interior. On this face the linearization of (3.5.1) in block form (e.g., the upper left-hand 0 is the $\hat{n} \times \hat{n}$ zero matrix) is

$$
\begin{pmatrix} \dot{x} \\ \dot{y} \end{pmatrix} = \begin{pmatrix} 0 & J^{12} \\ J^{21} & 0 \end{pmatrix} \begin{pmatrix} x \\ y \end{pmatrix}. \tag{3.5.2}
$$

The method of part 3 in the appendix of chapter 2 combined with the above results yields the following theorem:

Theorem 3.5.1   *Suppose that (p^*, q^*) is a quasi-strict NE. Then (p^*, q^*) is asymptotically stable for any bimatrix monotone selection dynamic if and only if it is asymptotically stable on the face of $\Delta^n \times \Delta^m$ for which (p^*, q^*) is interior. On this invariant face, there are nonnegative constants c and d for any bimatrix monotone selection dynamic such that the matrices J^{12} and J^{21} in (3.5.2) are c and d times the respective matrices in the linearization of the bimatrix replicator dynamic (3.2.1). Moreover c and d are both positive for any bimatrix uniformly monotone selection dynamic. Conversely, any rest point (p^*, q^*) that can be shown to be asymptotically stable under some bimatrix uniformly monotone selection dynamic by the linearization technique is a quasi-strict NE.*

---

18. For instance, the linearized dynamic has diagonal eigenvalue $g_i(p^*, q^*)/p_i^*$ if $p_i^* = 0$, which is negative if (p^*, q^*) is a quasi-strict NE by condition iv since $g_i(p^*, q^*)/p_i^* < g_k(p^*, q^*)/p_k^* = 0$ for any k with $p_k^* \neq 0$.

Unfortunately, theorem 3.5.1 is a rather negative result if one wants to analyze asymptotic stability through linearization as shown by the following example (see also theorem 3.5.3 below).

Example 3.5.2 Linearization of the Buyer-Seller Game   For specific bimatrix payoffs,[19] take

$$
\begin{array}{c}
\qquad \text{Seller} \\
\qquad H \quad\ C \\
\text{Buyer} \begin{array}{c} T \\ I \end{array} \begin{bmatrix} 8,7 & 4,9 \\ 7,3 & 6,1 \end{bmatrix}.
\end{array}
$$

The only (quasi-strict) NE of a Buyer-Seller Game is the interior one given by (3.3.2). Here $(p_1^*, q_1^*) = (\frac{1}{2}, \frac{2}{3})$. From (3.5.2) the linearization of (3.2.1) on the unit square is

$$
\begin{pmatrix} \dot{x} \\ \dot{y} \end{pmatrix} = \begin{pmatrix} 0 & \frac{3}{4} \\ -\frac{8}{9} & 0 \end{pmatrix} \begin{pmatrix} x \\ y \end{pmatrix}, \tag{3.5.3}
$$

where x and y are $p_1 - p_1^*$ and $q_1 - q_1^*$ respectively. The purely imaginary eigenvalues, $\pm\sqrt{(2/3)}i$, are consistent with the neutral stability of (p_1^*, q_1^*) for (3.2.1) exhibited by the periodic trajectories in figure 3.3.2. Analogous to the RSP Game of chapter 2.6.1, (p_1^*, q_1^*) can be made either asymptotically stable or unstable with nearby stable limit cycles by carefully redefining the vector field to obtain other bimatrix uniformly monotone selection dynamics.

One such perturbation is the *payoff-adjusted bimatrix replicator dynamic*[20]

$$
\dot{p}_i = \frac{p_i(e_i - p) \cdot Aq}{p \cdot Aq},
$$

$$
\dot{q}_j = \frac{q_j(f_j - q) \cdot Bp}{q \cdot Bp}.
$$

---

19. This is the same bimatrix game as case 2 in section 3.3.1 except that a payoff of 3 was added to each entry to ensure that all payoffs are positive. This change, which has no effect on monotone trajectories, was done to consider the payoff-adjusted bimatrix replicator dynamic.

20. This is the continuous-time approximation of the discrete-time evolutionary process $p_i' = p_i e_i \cdot Aq/p \cdot Aq$, $q_j' = q_j f_j \cdot Bp/q \cdot Bp$ that translates payoffs as the (nonnegative) expected number of offspring in the next generation. A similar dynamic (2.1.1) was considered in chapter 2.1 where the positive denominator was discarded for the continuous-time approximation since it has no effect on the evolutionary trajectories.

It is straightforward to verify that this is a bimatrix uniformly monotone selection dynamic for any bimatrix game with positive payoffs. Furthermore, its linearization about an interior NE (p^*, q^*) has $c = 1/p^* \cdot Aq^*$ and $d = 1/q^* \cdot Bp^*$ respectively.

Thus, linearization of our Buyer-Seller Game about (p_1^*, q_1^*) still leads to purely imaginary eigenvalues. However, it can be shown that (p_1^*, q_1^*) is globally asymptotically stable for the payoff-adjusted bimatrix replicator dynamic since a positive multiple of this vector field is volume decreasing (see Notes).

The emergence of purely imaginary eigenvalues in the above example is no coincidence. In general, the characteristic polynomial $P(\lambda)$ for the Jacobian matrix in (3.5.2) has the form $\lambda^{|\hat{n}-\hat{m}|} Q(\lambda^2)$ for some polynomial Q. Thus either all eigenvalues associated with $\Delta^{\hat{n}} \times \Delta^{\hat{m}}$ have zero real part or there are eigenvalues of positive and of negative real part (specifically, if λ is an eigenvalue, so is $-\lambda$). In particular, no hyperbolic rest point of any bimatrix uniformly monotone selection dynamic (3.5.1) is asymptotically stable unless it is a pure strategy pair. Such a pure strategy pair must be quasi-strict by theorem 3.5.1 and so must be a strict NE. In summary, we have

Theorem 3.5.3 (p^*, q^*) *is a hyperbolic rest point of the bimatrix replicator dynamic if and only if it is a hyperbolic rest point of every bimatrix uniformly monotone selection dynamic. For any such hyperbolic rest point (p^*, q^*), the following statements are equivalent:*

   i. (p^*, q^*) *is asymptotically stable for (3.2.1).*

   ii. (p^*, q^*) *is asymptotically stable for (3.5.1).*

   iii. (p^*, q^*) *is a strict NE pair.*

   iv. (p^*, q^*) *is a two-species ESS.*[21]

Theorem 3.5.3 is the analogue of theorem 3.2.1 for isolated NE and general uniformly monotone selection dynamics whenever the linearization technique alone determines asymptotic stability (i.e., asymptotic stability is equivalent to strict NE). The following result for sets of rest points is a consequence of center manifold theory. Specifically, the center manifold of the linearized dynamic at each point of such an SESet is the SESet itself.

---

21. See chapter 4.7.2 for the concept of a two-species ESS.

Theorem 3.5.4 *Suppose that F is an SESet that consists of a single face. Then F is asymptotically stable and every point (p*, q*) in F is Lyapunov stable for any bimatrix uniformly monotone selection dynamic.*

Remark 3.5.5 The guiding principle of our treatment of monotone selection dynamics in this section (and in chapter 2) where linearization techniques are emphasized is that the replicator dynamic, in either its symmetric or bimatrix normal form setting, is the basis for an evolutionary analysis of all these smooth adjustment processes that many economic game theorists feel better reflect their assumption that players make rational decisions. Stated in terms of dynamical systems, the results point to the fact that the replicator dynamic is to these monotone selection dynamics as the linearized dynamic is to a general dynamical system. That is, we need only consider higher-order (nonlinear) terms of the adjustment process if dynamic stability is not established one way or the other by the replicator dynamic. As we have already seen, quite a lot can be said without examining higher-order terms. On the other hand, interested readers can gain a better appreciation of the complexities that arise when such higher-order terms must be included in the analysis of dynamical systems relevant for evolutionary game theory by referring to literature cited in the Notes.

3.6 Notes

SESets for bimatrix games were defined and characterized by Balkenborg (1994). The bimatrix replicator dynamic was introduced by Taylor (1979) and theorem 3.2.1 for strict NE was proved by Selten (1980). The generalization of theorem 3.2.1 to other dynamics is from Balkenborg and Schlag (2001). The dynamic classification of nondegenerate two-strategy bimatrix games for the bimatrix replicator dynamic is contained in Hofbauer and Sigmund (1988, 1998). Sets that are closed under either best or better responses but do not necessarily consist entirely of rest points were considered by Weibull (1995) and by Ritzberger and Weibull (1995).

The symmetrized replicator dynamic in section 3.4 for two-strategy games such as the Buyer-Seller Game was analyzed in Gaunersdorfer et al. (1991). The cyclic nature of trajectories in the Buyer-Seller Game are also used in models of crime deterrence (e.g., Cressman et al. 1998). Theorem 3.4.1 is contained in Balkenborg (1994). The Wright manifold for bimatrix games was formally introduced by Cressman (2000),

although it has much earlier precedents starting with the mixed strategy representatives of Kuhn (1953; see also Selten 1983). Berger (2001)
proved convergence to the Wright manifold for the best response dynamic (3.4.3) applied to the Buyer-Seller Game. The global attraction
of the Wright manifold for the symmetrized best response dynamic is
similar to the extensive form interpretation of recombination given in
Cressman (1999) and also in chapter 5.2.

Hofbauer and Sigmund (1988) showed the NE of the Buyer-Seller
Game is globally asymptotically stable for the payoff-adjusted bimatrix
replicator dynamic (example 3.5.2). Weibull (1995) established results
similar to theorems 3.5.1 to 3.5.4 for NE and/or faces of the strategy
space with respect to other bimatrix selection dynamics. Higher-order
nonlinear terms in the evolutionary dynamics of bimatrix games (see
remark 3.5.5) were considered in Cressman (1992) and Hofbauer (1996).

An *asymmetric (two-player) game* has a finite set $\{u_1, u_2, \ldots, u_N\}$ of N *roles* or *information situations*. In a given contest, players one and two are assigned roles u_k and u_ℓ respectively with probability $\rho(u_k, u_\ell)$. For each role u_k there is a finite set S_k of choices available to a player assigned this role. We assume that $\rho(u_k, u_\ell) = \rho(u_\ell, u_k)$ (i.e., role assignment is independent of player designation), and we are only interested in pairs of information situations (u_k, u_ℓ) for which this probability is positive. Two classes of asymmetric games that have special properties (sections 4.5 and 4.6 respectively) are the *truly asymmetric games* that satisfy $\rho(u_k, u_k) = 0$ for all k and the *truly symmetric games* where $\rho(u_k, u_\ell) = 0$ for all $k \neq \ell$.

When $u_k = u_\ell$ and $|S_k| = n$, payoffs are assumed to be those of a symmetric normal form game with $n \times n$ payoff matrix A_{kk}. When $u_k \neq u_\ell$, payoffs are given by a bimatrix game[1] $(A_{k\ell}, A_{\ell k})$. Thus, if $N = 1$, we have a truly symmetric game (since $\rho(u_1, u_1) = 1$) that is simply the symmetric normal form game A_{11}. On the other hand, if $N = 2$ and $\rho(u_1, u_2) = \frac{1}{2}$, this truly asymmetric game is the symmetrization of the bimatrix game (A_{12}, A_{21}). That is, asymmetric two-player games include the symmetrized bimatrix games of chapter 3 and the symmetric normal form games of chapter 2. We will refer to these two special cases from time to time throughout the chapter as we develop the general theory of asymmetric games.

An added feature of general asymmetric games that can often be exploited to great advantage in their analysis is their subgame structure.

---

1. For notational convenience, we use $A_{k\ell}$ and $A_{\ell k}$ in place of A and B respectively as were used in chapter 3 for this bimatrix game. $A_{k\ell}$ is then of size $n \times m$ and $A_{\ell k}$ of size $m \times n$ when $|S_k| = n$ and $|S_\ell| = m$.

A *subgame* of an asymmetric game is a subset of the N roles that satisfies $\rho(u_k, u_\ell) = 0$ whenever u_k is in this subset and u_ℓ is not.[2]

General asymmetric games have received much less attention in the literature than either symmetric normal form games or bimatrix games. For this reason this chapter devotes considerably more space than chapters 2 and 3 to the description of their theoretical structure (e.g., NE, ESSet, Wright manifold) and to the development of several relevant examples (e.g., age-structured games, parallel bandits, two-species games, hierarchical games) to illustrate the importance of this general class. Proportionally less space is allotted to the dynamic analysis where only the properties of the replicator dynamic are investigated.[3]

4.1   The Normal Form

A pure strategy of the asymmetric game specifies a choice in S_k for each role u_k. It is an element of the cartesian product $S \equiv \times_{k=1}^N S_k = S_1 \times \cdots \times S_N$ and so can be denoted as e_i where $i = (i_1, \ldots, i_N)$ is a multi-index with N components.[4] There are $\Pi_{k=1}^N |S_k|$ pure strategies with payoffs to e_i in a contest against e_j given by

$$\pi(e_i, e_j) = \sum_{k,\ell=1}^N \rho(u_k, u_\ell) e_{i_k} \cdot A_{k\ell} e_{j_\ell}. \qquad (4.1.1)$$

This formula can be extended to mixed strategies $p, \hat{p} \in \Delta(S)$ in the usual manner by

$$\pi(p, \hat{p}) = \sum_{k,\ell=1}^N \rho(u_k, u_\ell) p^k \cdot A_{k\ell} \hat{p}^\ell. \qquad (4.1.2)$$

Here, for example, $p^k \in \Delta(S_k)$ is the role-conditioned strategy in role k given by $(p_1^k, \ldots, p_{|S_k|}^k)$ whose component p_r^k is the conditional

---

2. The formal definition of a subgame of an extensive form game (chapter 6.1.2) when applied to the extensive form of an asymmetric game as defined in section 4.2 below is slightly different than this. However, it is straightforward to adjust the definition of the extensive form of an asymmetric game so that the two concepts coincide (see remark 4.4.1).
3. The only exception is a brief consideration of the best response dynamic in section 4.4.2 which emphasizes the relevance of the Wright manifold (see theorem 4.4.2 below) in analogy to the symmetrized best response dynamic in chapter 3.4.2.
4. If the multi-index i is understood, the pure strategy is denoted by e and then e_k denotes the choice in role u_k.

frequency

$$p_r^k = \sum_{i_k = r} p_i \tag{4.1.3}$$

that mixed strategy p specifies the rth choice in S_k.

Thus, as a normal form game with S the set of pure strategies and entries in the payoff matrix given by (4.1.1), we have the somewhat paradoxical conclusion that an asymmetric game is in fact a symmetric normal form game. As such, the usual static and dynamic concepts of chapter 2 (NE, ESS, symmetric replicator dynamic, etc.) apply. Since we know from chapter 2 that the general dynamic analysis of symmetric normal form games with a large number of pure strategies is often formidable, our initial impression may be that there is little hope in analyzing asymmetric games from the evolutionary game theory perspective. However, as we will see in the remainder of this chapter, there are substantial consequences that the asymmetric structure and the subgame structure impart to this analysis. A firm conceptual understanding of the extensive form provides a first step in this direction.

Remark 4.1.1   There are several ways to define the extensive form of an asymmetric game, all with the same normal form. The formal approach for this book given in the following section does not emphasize the subgame structure as defined in chapter 6.1.2. An alternative method to construct an extensive form for an asymmetric game that has a subgame consisting of a proper subset of the N roles is as follows: Let nature take the initial move with two alternatives, each leading to another move by nature. The probability nature chooses the first alternative is the sum of all the $\rho(u_k, u_\ell)$ for u_k and u_ℓ in this subset while that for the other alternative is this sum for the complementary subset (which is also a subgame). From both secondary moves by nature, an extensive form for the corresponding subgame can be constructed as in the following section (or the method above can be continued for subgames of these subgames). Then both subgames are in fact subgames of the extensive form game as defined in chapter 6.1.2.

These alternative constructions again illustrate the point made in chapter 1.1 that the extensive form is much better suited than the normal form to emphasize possible sequential features of how decisions are taken. The approach taken in the following section suggests the roles interact with each other simultaneously.

4.2 The Extensive Form: NE and ESSets

In the extensive form game tree of an asymmetric game, there is an initial move by nature, where the possible edges are in one-to-one correspondence with ordered pairs of assigned roles (u_k, u_ℓ) that occur with positive probability $\rho(u_k, u_\ell)$. Each of these edges is labeled by its corresponding probability and leads to a decision point of player one. Player one has $|S_k|$ choices at the decision point following the edge labeled $\rho(u_k, u_\ell)$. Each such choice leads to a decision point of player two who then has $|S_\ell|$ choices, all of which lead to an endpoint with the appropriate payoffs to the two players (see figure 4.2.1 below for a concrete illustration of such a game tree).[5] Each of the N information sets of player one encloses all those decision points of player one where this player has a particular role u_k, which is then used to label this set. The analogous information sets of player two are also labeled $u_1, \ldots, u_N$. Finally, the symmetry is a one-to-one correspondence between the information sets of player one with the information sets of player two that have the same label.

A mixed strategy $p \in \Delta(S)$ for an asymmetric game induces a *local behavior strategy* $p^k \in \Delta(S_k)$, whose components are given by (4.1.3), at the two player information sets labeled u_k. These local behavior strategies combine to yield the surjective projection map

$$\text{proj} : \Delta(S) \to \Delta(S_1) \times \cdots \times \Delta(S_N)$$

$$p \mapsto (p^1, \ldots, p^N).$$

(4.2.1)

For each $p \in \Delta(S)$, proj(p) is called a *behavior strategy*. Of central importance is the fact that $\pi(p, \hat{p})$ can be expanded as a sum of local role specific payoff functions π_k; namely, $\pi(p, \hat{p}) = \sum_{k=1}^{N} \pi_k(p^k, \text{proj}(\hat{p}))$ where

$$\pi_k(p^k, \text{proj}(\hat{p})) \equiv \sum_{\ell=1}^{N} \rho(u_k, u_\ell) p^k \cdot A_{k\ell} \hat{p}^\ell.$$

(4.2.2)

---

5. As another illustration, consider figure 3.4.1 in chapter 3.4. This symmetrization of the bimatrix Buyer-Seller Game is the extensive form of an asymmetric game with $N = 2$ and $\rho(u_1, u_2) = \frac{1}{2}$.

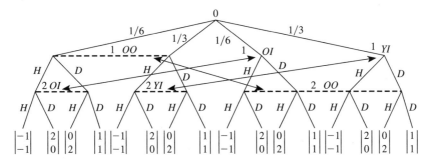

Figure 4.2.1
Extensive form of the Three-Role Age-Structured Owner-Intruder Game of section 4.2.1.

The NE structure of the asymmetric game is then easily described in terms of the local behavior strategies. Specifically, $p^* \in \Delta(S)$ is a symmetric NE (i.e., $\pi(p, p^*) \leq \pi(p^*, p^*)$ for all $p \in \Delta(S)$) if and only if, for all k, $\pi_k(p^k, \mathrm{proj}(p^*)) \leq \pi_k(p^{*k}, \mathrm{proj}(p^*))$ for all $p^k \in \Delta(S_k)$. In other words, for each role u_k, p^{*k} is a NE for the local symmetric game induced by p^* at u_k by the projection map.[6] The following definition and theorem extend these ideas to the ES structure of the asymmetric game:

Definition 4.2.1 *E is a* local ESSet *for an asymmetric game with N roles if, for each role u_k, the ESSet conditions of definition 2.6.3 in chapter 2 hold for the local symmetric game induced at role u_k by the projection map applied to each element of E. Specifically, for each $p^* \in E$, the following two conditions must hold for all k where $\mathrm{proj}(p^*)\backslash p^k$ replaces the kth component of $\mathrm{proj}(p^*)$ with p^k:*

i. $\pi_k(p^k, \mathrm{proj}(p^*)) \leq \pi_k(p^{*k}, \mathrm{proj}(p^*))$ for all $p^k \in \Delta(S_k)$.

ii. if $\pi_k(p^k, \mathrm{proj}(p^*)) = \pi_k(p^{*k}, \mathrm{proj}(p^*))$ for some $p^*\backslash p^k \notin E$,[7] then $\pi_k(p^k, \mathrm{proj}(p^*)\backslash p^k) < \pi_k(p^{*k}, \mathrm{proj}(p^*)\backslash p^k)$.

In particular, p^* is a local ESS *if $\{p^*\}$ is a local ESSet.*

---

6. The payoffs of this induced game at role u_k are more correctly given by multiplying (4.2.2) by the factor $1/\sum_{\ell=1}^{N} \rho(u_k, u_\ell)$. However, since this positive factor does not affect the static analysis, we ignore it.

7. Here $p^*\backslash p^k$ denotes any strategy $p \in \Delta(S)$ for which $\mathrm{proj}(p) = \mathrm{proj}(p^*)\backslash p^k$. By (4.2.2), this choice of $p^*\backslash p^k$ is immaterial in $\pi(p^*\backslash p^k, p^*)$, and so any local ESSet must satisfy $E = \mathrm{proj}^{-1}[\mathrm{proj}[E]]$ (i.e., $E = \{p \mid \mathrm{proj}(p) = \mathrm{proj}(p^*)$ for some $p^* \in E\}$).

Theorem 4.2.2   *If E is an ESSet of an asymmetric game, then E is a local ESSet. In particular, if $p^* \in \Delta(S)$ is an ESS, then p^* is a local ESS.*

Proof   By chapter 2.6.2, E is a disjoint union of connected NE components. In particular, from (4.2.2), if $p^* \in E$, then $\pi(p^*\backslash p^k, p^*) - \pi(p^*, p^*) = \pi_k(p^k, \mathrm{proj}(p^*)) - \pi_k(p^{*k}, \mathrm{proj}(p^*)) \leq 0$ for all $p^k \in \Delta(S_k)$. Now suppose that $\pi_k(p^k, \mathrm{proj}(p^*)) = \pi_k(p^{*k}, \mathrm{proj}(p^*))$ and $p^*\backslash p^k \notin E^k$. Then $\pi(p^*\backslash p^k, p^*) = \pi(p^*, p^*)$ and $\pi(p^*, p^*\backslash p^k) > \pi(p^*\backslash p^k, p^*\backslash p^k)$ since E is an ESSet. Thus, by (4.2.2), $\pi_k(p^{*k}, \mathrm{proj}(p^*)\backslash p^k) > \pi_k(p^k, \mathrm{proj}(p^*)\backslash p^k)$.   ∎

Theorem 4.2.2 provides a procedure (illustrated by the example in section 4.2.1) to determine the ES structure of an asymmetric game by considering the easier to analyze induced games. However, it must be emphasized that the converse of theorem 4.2.2 is not true in general. That is, there are local ESSets that are not ESSets of the asymmetric game (see section 4.7.1). On the other hand, the converse is true for the truly asymmetric games of section 4.5 (theorem 4.5.3i) and for the truly symmetric games of section 4.6 (theorem 4.6.1). In fact, for truly asymmetric games, p^* is a local ESS if and only if p^* is a strict NE.

4.2.1   An Age-Structured Owner-Intruder Game

Consider the Owner-Intruder Game where individuals can also condition their strategy on their relative age. If individuals are either "young" or "old" and all owners are old, then there are three possible role assignments {Old Owner OO, Old Intruder OI, Young Intruder YI}. Figure 4.2.1 gives the extensive form of a game where Old Owners are twice as likely to meet Young Intruders as Old Intruders. That is, $\rho(u_1, u_2) = \frac{1}{6}$ and $\rho(u_1, u_3) = \frac{1}{3}$. The payoffs given there assume each bimatrix game is the Owner-Intruder Game of chapter 3.2.1 with an explicit payoff matrix of $\begin{bmatrix} -1, -1 & 2, 0 \\ 0, & 2 & 1, 1 \end{bmatrix}$.

Let us apply theorem 4.2.2 to find the possible ESSets of this truly asymmetric game. By theorems 4.3.2 and 4.5.3i below, we will see that an ESSet E of this game must contain a pure strategy. For notational convenience, a pure strategy e_i which plays H in the first role of OO will be denoted $H**$, where the two asterisks hold places for the choices of e_i in the second role of OI and in the third role of YI. Similarly $*H*$ is a pure strategy that plays H in the second role of OI, and so on.

First, suppose that HHH or DHH is in E. The game induced for the OO role by either HHH or DHH has payoff matrix (for the row player)

$$
\begin{array}{cc}
 & \begin{array}{cc} HHH & DHH \end{array} \\
\begin{array}{c} \text{Old} \\ \text{Owners} \end{array} \begin{array}{c} H \\ D \end{array} & \left[\begin{array}{cc} -3 & -3 \\ 0 & 0 \end{array} \right].
\end{array}
$$

For instance, H and D both receive a payoff of $\frac{1}{6}(-1) + \frac{1}{3}(-1) = \frac{1}{6}(-3)$ against HHH.[8] Since $-3 < 0$, $HHH \notin E$. By a similar argument applied to the payoff matrix,

$$
\begin{array}{cc}
 & \begin{array}{cccc} *HH & *HD & *DH & *DD \end{array} \\
\begin{array}{c} \text{Old} \\ \text{Owners} \end{array} \begin{array}{c} H \\ D \end{array} & \left[\begin{array}{cccc} -3 & 3 & 0 & 6 \\ 0 & 2 & 1 & 3 \end{array} \right],
\end{array}
$$

the columns give the game induced at the OO role by each pure strategy. Thus we see that DHH, HHD, DDH, and HDD are the only possible pure strategies in a local ESSet. That is, by theorem 4.2.2, the pure strategies in E are contained in $\{DHH, HHD, DDH, HDD\}$.

The same technique applied to the OI role yields payoff matrix

$$
\begin{array}{cc}
 & \begin{array}{cc} H** & D** \end{array} \\
\begin{array}{c} \text{Old} \\ \text{Intruders} \end{array} \begin{array}{c} H \\ D \end{array} & \left[\begin{array}{cc} -1 & 2 \\ 0 & 1 \end{array} \right],
\end{array}
$$

and shows that the only possible pure strategies in E are $DH*$ and $HD*$. It is the same matrix (up to the factor 2) in the YI role implying pure strategies in E have the form $H * D$ or $D * H$. That is, by theorem 4.2.2 applied to the induced game with respect to each of the three roles the only possible pure strategies in E are HDD and DHH.

It is not difficult to verify that HDD and DHH are in fact ESSs. The general theory of truly asymmetric games in section 4.5 then guarantees that the only connected ESSets of this game are the singletons DHH and HDD. Our conclusion for this example is that the age structure can be ignored for the game's static ES analysis as these answers are the same as those for the Owner-Intruder Game of chapter 3.2.1 without age structure (i.e., the ESSs are still "play H if owner and D if intruder" and "play D if owner and H if intruder"). In section 4.5.1 below we will examine how these static results relate to the game's dynamic analysis.

---

8. From (4.2.2), the payoff matrix is actually $\frac{1}{6}$ of the one displayed. The factor $\frac{1}{6}$ is deleted for convenience throughout this section.

An alternative method to obtain the ES structure of this game and, in particular, to find these two pure strategy ESSs is to calculate its 8×8 payoff matrix as a symmetric normal form game; namely

$$
\begin{array}{l}
HHH \\
HHD \\
HDH \\
HDD \\
DHH \\
DHD \\
DDH \\
DDD
\end{array}
\begin{bmatrix}
-6 & 0 & -3 & 3 & 3 & 9 & 6 & 12 \\
-4 & 2 & -1 & 5 & 1 & 7 & 4 & 10 \\
-5 & 1 & -2 & 4 & 2 & 8 & 5 & 11 \\
-3 & 3 & 0 & 6 & 0 & 6 & 3 & 9 \\
-3 & -1 & -2 & 0 & 6 & 8 & 7 & 9 \\
-1 & 1 & 0 & 2 & 4 & 6 & 5 & 7 \\
-2 & 0 & -1 & 1 & 5 & 7 & 6 & 8 \\
0 & 2 & 1 & 3 & 3 & 5 & 4 & 6
\end{bmatrix} .
$$

Clearly, HDD and DHH are the only strict symmetric NE as they are the only diagonal entries that have the largest payoff in their corresponding column. There are several reasons the local ESSet method is preferred to this alternative. First, the payoff matrix method is much more time-consuming—especially as the number of pure strategies increases. A more important reason is that an ESSet is difficult to recognize from a payoff matrix if it does not consist of strict NE.

4.3   SESets and Agent Normal Forms

Much of the dynamic theory for bimatrix games developed in chapter 3 generalizes to asymmetric games. These generalizations rely heavily on the projection map (4.2.1) and two methods to assign agents to player information sets. In this section we develop the familiar agent normal form and relate it in theorem 4.3.3 to the SESet concept of the following definition. The second method, called the symmetric agent normal form, is only applicable to the truly asymmetric games of section 4.5, and so its introduction is postponed until then.

Definition 4.3.1   Let G be an n-player normal form game with pure strategy set $T = T_1 \times \cdots \times T_n$ where T_k is the pure strategy set of player k. The payoff functions $\hat{\pi}_k : (T_1 \times \cdots \times T_n) \to \mathbf{R}$ specify the payoff $\hat{\pi}_k(e_{i_1}, \ldots, e_{i_n})$ to player k when player ℓ ($1 \le \ell \le n$) is using strategy $e_{i_\ell} \in T_\ell$. These can be extended in the usual fashion to mixed strategies $p = (p^1, \ldots, p^n)$ in $\Delta(T_1) \times \cdots \times \Delta(T_n)$.[9]

---

9. Here and in theorem 4.3.2 we denote elements of $\Delta(T_1) \times \cdots \times \Delta(T_n)$ as p opposed to the notation proj(p) that is used for asymmetric games in the rest of the chapter.

For a strategy $p \in \Delta(T_1) \times \cdots \times \Delta(T_n)$ and a $\hat{p}^k \in \Delta(T_k)$, $p \backslash \hat{p}^k$ is the strategy that replaces the kth component of p with $\hat{p}^k$ (e.g., $p \backslash \hat{p}^2 = (p^1, \hat{p}^2, p^3, \ldots, p^n)$). A set $F \subset \Delta(T_1) \times \cdots \times \Delta(T_n)$ is a strict equilibrium set (SESet) *if it is a set of NE (i.e., for all k, $\hat{\pi}_k(p \backslash \hat{p}^k) \le \hat{\pi}_k(p)$ whenever $p \in F$ and $\hat{p}^k \in \Delta(T_k)$) that is closed under mixed-strategy best replies by each player k.[10] In particular, a singleton SESet is a strict NE.*

When $n = 2$, payoffs can be given in matrix form, and so every two player normal form game is a bimatrix game.[11] The SESet of definition 3.1.1 in chapter 3 is then a special case of definition 4.3.1. Similarly the following result generalizes theorem 3.1.2 of chapter 3 to n-player normal form games.

Theorem 4.3.2 *If F is an SESet of an n-player normal form game, then F is a finite union of faces of $\Delta(T_1) \times \cdots \times \Delta(T_n)$. In particular, F is closed and contains at least one pure strategy $(e_{i_1}, \ldots, e_{i_n})$.*

Proof Suppose that $p = (p^1, \ldots, p^n)$ belongs to an SESet F and $\hat{p}^k \in T_k$ with $\operatorname{supp}(\hat{p}^k) \subset \operatorname{supp}(p^k)$. Then, for every pure strategy $e_{r'} \in T_k$ of player k, $\hat{\pi}_k(p \backslash e_{r'}) \le \hat{\pi}_k(p) = \sum_{e_r \in T_k} p_r^k \hat{\pi}_k(p \backslash e_r)$ since p is a NE. Thus $\hat{\pi}_k(p \backslash e_r) = \hat{\pi}_k(p)$ for all $e_r \in \operatorname{supp}(p^k)$. Furthermore $\hat{\pi}_k(p \backslash \hat{p}^k) = \sum_{r=1}^{|T_k|} \hat{p}_r^k \hat{\pi}_k(p \backslash e_r) = \hat{\pi}_k(p)$. Thus $p \backslash \hat{p}^k \in F$.

Now suppose that $\operatorname{supp}(\hat{p}^k) \subset \operatorname{supp}(p^k)$ for all k. The argument above shows that $p \backslash \hat{p}^1 \in F$ and, with p replaced by $p \backslash \hat{p}^1$, that $p \backslash \hat{p}^1 \backslash \hat{p}^2 \equiv (p \backslash \hat{p}^1) \backslash \hat{p}^2 \in F$ since $\operatorname{supp}(\hat{p}^2) \subset \operatorname{supp}(p^2)$, and so on. Thus $\hat{p} \in F$, and so the face $\operatorname{supp}(p^1) \times \cdots \times \operatorname{supp}(p^n)$ is a subset of F. Since there are only a finite number of possible faces, F can be written as a finite union of faces, each of which is closed. Since each face of F contains a pure strategy, F contains at least one pure strategy. ∎

The *agent normal form of an asymmetric game* with N roles is the $2N$-player game that introduces a separate player (i.e., an agent) at each of the $2N$ player information sets of the extensive form. The pure strategy space is the set of $2N$-tuples in $S \times S$ where $S = S_1 \times \cdots \times S_N$ and

---

10. A set of NE F is *closed under mixed-strategy best reply* by player k if $p \backslash \hat{p}^k \in F$ whenever $\hat{p}^k \in \Delta(T_k)$ and $\hat{\pi}_k(p \backslash \hat{p}^k) = \hat{\pi}_k(p)$ for some $p \in F$. A closely related concept, defined in terms of pure strategy combinations but not restricted to sets of NE, is that of *closed under (weakly) better reply* (see Notes).

11. A symmetric normal form game is then a two-player normal form game where $T_1 = T_2$ and $\pi(e_i, e_j) = \hat{\pi}_1(e_i, e_j) = \hat{\pi}_2(e_j, e_i)$.

the mixed-strategy payoff functions for $\text{proj}(p)$, $\text{proj}(\hat{p}) \in \Delta(S_1) \times \cdots \times \Delta(S_N)$ are given by

$$\hat{\pi}_k(\text{proj}(p), \text{proj}(\hat{p})) = \pi_k(p^k, \text{proj}(\hat{p})),$$

$$\hat{\pi}_{N+k}(\text{proj}(p), \text{proj}(\hat{p})) = \pi_k(\hat{p}^k, \text{proj}(p)),$$

for $1 \le k \le N$.[12]

As an elementary example, the agent normal form of an asymmetric game with one role (i.e., $N = 1$) is the symmetric bimatrix game (A_{11}, A_{11}). In this special case the following result repeats theorem 3.1.3 of chapter 3.1 since the asymmetric game is then the symmetric normal form game with payoff matrix A_{11}.

Theorem 4.3.3 *If F is an SESet of the 2N-player agent normal form of an asymmetric game with N roles, then $E = \{p^* \in \Delta(S) \mid (\text{proj}(p^*), \text{proj}(p^*)) \in F\}$ is an ESSet of the asymmetric game if it is nonempty.*

Proof Suppose that $p^* \in E$ and that $\pi(\hat{p}, p^*) = \pi(p^*, p^*)$ with $\hat{p} \notin E$. Then, for all $1 \le k \le N$, $\pi_k(\hat{p}^k, \text{proj}(p^*)) = \pi_k(p^{*k}, \text{proj}(p^*))$. In particular, $\hat{\pi}_1(\text{proj}(p^*)\backslash\hat{p}^1, \text{proj}(p^*)) = \hat{\pi}_1(\text{proj}(p^*), \text{proj}(p^*))$. Since F is an SESet, $(\text{proj}(p^*)\backslash\hat{p}^1, \text{proj}(p^*)) \in F$. Similarly $\hat{\pi}_2(\text{proj}(p^*)\backslash\hat{p}^1\backslash\hat{p}^2, \text{proj}(p^*)) = \hat{\pi}_2(\text{proj}(p^*)\backslash\hat{p}^1, \text{proj}(p))$, and so we have $(\text{proj}(p^*)\backslash\hat{p}^1\backslash\hat{p}^2, \text{proj}(p^*)) \in F$, and so on. Thus $(\text{proj}(\hat{p}), \text{proj}(p^*)) \in F$.

Similarly $(\text{proj}(p^*), \text{proj}(\hat{p})) \in F$ and so is a NE. Thus, for all $1 \le k \le N$, $\hat{\pi}_k(\text{proj}(p^*)\backslash\hat{p}^k, \text{proj}(\hat{p})) \le \hat{\pi}_k(\text{proj}(p^*), \text{proj}(\hat{p}))$. That is, $\pi_k(\hat{p}^k, \text{proj}(\hat{p})) \le \pi_k(p^{*k}, \text{proj}(\hat{p}))$ for all $1 \le k \le N$. In particular, $\pi(\hat{p}, \hat{p}) \le \pi(p^*, \hat{p})$. If $\pi(\hat{p}, \hat{p}) = \pi(p^*, \hat{p})$, then $\pi_k(\hat{p}^k, \text{proj}(\hat{p})) = \pi_k(p^{*k}, \text{proj}(\hat{p}))$ for all $1 \le k \le N$. By the same argument as above applied to $\hat{\pi}_{N+k}$ we see that $(\text{proj}(\hat{p}), \text{proj}(\hat{p})) \in F$ and so $\hat{p} \in E$. Thus either $\pi(\hat{p}, \hat{p}) < \pi(p^*, \hat{p})$ or $\hat{p} \in E$. That is, E is an ESSet. ∎

Remark 4.3.4 The consequences of a subgame structure on the static results of sections 4.2 and 4.3 have been deliberately omitted in order to emphasize the parallels between the bimatrix games of chapter 3 (which have no subgames) and the asymmetric games of this chapter. Interested readers can readily develop intuitive results such as that E is an ESSet of an asymmetric game if and only if it induces an ESSet in each

---

12. In particular, the payoff of agent k for player one only depends on the strategies of the agents for player two, and vice versa. We have reverted to using $\text{proj}(p)$ as a generic element of $\Delta(S_1) \times \cdots \times \Delta(S_N)$ for these agent normal form games to emphasize its difference from $p \in \Delta(S)$ for asymmetric games.

subgame, and so on. For this reason most of the explicit examples in this chapter have no subgames (e.g., figure 4.2.1) with the notable exceptions of sections 4.6.1 and 4.6.2 (see figures 4.6.1 and 4.6.2). However, the subgame structure will play an increasingly important theoretical role for the dynamic analysis in the following sections.

4.4 Dynamics and the Wright Manifold

The *asymmetric replicator dynamic* on $\Delta(S)$,

$$\dot{p}_i = p_i(\pi(e_i, p) - \pi(p, p)) \tag{4.4.1}$$

is the symmetric replicator dynamic applied to the symmetric normal form of an asymmetric game. This generalizes the replicator dynamics introduced in chapters 2 and 3. Specifically, when $N = 1$, (4.4.1) is the symmetric replicator dynamic (2.1.2) of chapter 2. Furthermore, when $N = 2$ and $\rho(u_1, u_2) = \frac{1}{2}$, (4.4.1) is the symmetrized replicator dynamic (3.4.2) of chapter 3.

In special cases, such as the truly asymmetric games of section 4.5, we are able to characterize all asymptotically stable sets of rest points of (4.4.1). However, its general analysis is extremely complicated (see section 4.6.1 for an elementary example with a complicated asymmetric replicator dynamic). For this reason, we restrict our analysis to the *Wright manifold of the asymmetric game* for the most part. In analogy to chapter 3.4.1, this submanifold of $\Delta(S)$ is given by

$$W = \{p \in \Delta(S) \mid p_i = p_{i_1}^1 p_{i_2}^2 \cdots p_{i_N}^N \text{ for every } i = (i_1, \ldots, i_N)\}. \tag{4.4.2}$$

The following alternative characterization of W that parallels chapter 3.4.1 is also important. Let I be a subset of $\{1, \ldots, N\}$ and $p_{i\backslash j}^I$ be the frequency of pure strategy $e_{i\backslash j}^I$ whose kth component is i_k if $k \in I$ and j_k if $k \notin I$. By (4.4.2), if $p \in W$, then clearly, $p_i p_j = p_{i\backslash j}^I p_{j\backslash i}^I$ for all $I \subset \{1, \ldots, N\}$. Conversely, if $p_i p_j = p_{i\backslash j}^I p_{j\backslash i}^I$ for all i, j where $I = \{1\}$, then

$$p_{i_1}^1 \sum_{j_1} p_{(j_1, i_2, \ldots, i_N)} = \sum_{j_2} \cdots \sum_{j_N} p_{(i_1, j_2, \ldots, j_N)} \sum_{j_1} p_{(j_1, i_2, \ldots, i_N)}$$

$$= \sum_{j_1} \cdots \sum_{j_N} p_{i\backslash j}^{\{1\}} p_{j\backslash i}^{\{1\}} = \sum_j p_i p_j = p_i.$$

A straightforward extension of this calculation shows that $p_i = p_{i_1}^1 \sum_{j_1} p_{(j_1, i_2, \ldots, i_N)} = p_{i_1}^1 \sum_{j_1} p_{i_2}^2 \sum_{j_2} p_{(j_1, j_2, i_3, \ldots, i_N)} = \cdots = p_{i_1}^1 p_{i_2}^2 \cdots$

$p_{i_N}^N \sum_j p_j = p_{i_1}^1 p_{i_2}^2 \dots p_{i_N}^N$ if $p_i p_j = p_{i\backslash j}^I p_{j\backslash i}^I$ for all i, j and all $I \subset \{1, \dots, N\}$. That is,

$$W = \{p \in \Delta(S) \mid p_i p_j = p_{i\backslash j}^I p_{j\backslash i}^I \text{ for all } i, j \text{ and } I \subset \{1, \dots, N\}\}. \quad (4.4.3)$$

As we will see, the Wright manifold has special significance for both the replicator dynamic (section 4.4.1) and the best response dynamic (section 4.4.2).

4.4.1   The Replicator Dynamic and Subgames

In chapter 3.4 we showed that the Wright manifold of a symmetrized bimatrix game is invariant under (4.4.1) where it induces the bimatrix replicator dynamic. To see that the Wright manifold of a general asymmetric game continues to be invariant under (4.4.1), consider

$$\frac{d}{dt}\left(p_i p_j - p_{i\backslash j}^I p_{j\backslash i}^I\right) = p_i p_j (\pi(e_i, p) + \pi(e_j, p) - 2\pi(p, p))$$

$$- p_{i\backslash j}^I p_{j\backslash i}^I \left(\pi\left(e_{i\backslash j}^I, p\right) + \pi\left(e_{j\backslash i}^I, p\right) - 2\pi(p, p)\right).$$

From (4.2.2), $\pi(e_i, p) + \pi(e_j, p) = \sum_k (\pi_k(e_{i_k}, \text{proj}(p) + \pi_k(e_{j_k}, \text{proj}(p)) = \pi(e_{i\backslash j}^I, p) + \pi(e_{j\backslash i}^I, p)$. Thus, by (4.4.3), $d(p_i p_j - p_{i\backslash j}^I p_{j\backslash i}^I)/dt = 0$ whenever $p \in W$ and so W is invariant.

Let us consider the dynamic (4.4.1) restricted to W. From (4.4.2), it is clear the projection map (4.2.1) restricted to W is a bijection onto $\Delta(S_1) \times \cdots \times \Delta(S_N)$. Furthermore, from (4.1.2), (4.2.2), and (4.4.2), the induced dynamic on $\Delta(S_1) \times \cdots \times \Delta(S_N)$ is given by

$$\dot{p}_{i_k}^k = \sum_{\{j \mid j_k = i_k\}} \dot{p}_j = \sum_{\{j \mid j_k = i_k\}} p_j (\pi(e_j, p) - \pi(p, p))$$

$$= \sum_{\{j \mid j_k = i_k\}} \sum_\ell p_{j_1}^1 \cdots p_{j_N}^N (\pi_\ell(e_{j_\ell}, \text{proj}(p)) - \pi_\ell(p^\ell, \text{proj}(p)))$$

$$\hspace{9cm} (4.4.4)$$

$$= p_{i_k}^k (\pi_k(e_{i_k}, \text{proj}(p)) - \pi_k(p^k, \text{proj}(p)))$$

$$= p_{i_k}^k \sum_{\ell=1}^N \rho(u_k, u_\ell)(e_{i_k} - p^k) \cdot A_{k\ell} p^\ell.$$

If there are no interactions between players in the same role (i.e., $\rho(u_k, u_k) = 0$ for all k and so we have a truly asymmetric game), this is the N-player replicator dynamic considered in section 4.5 below. However, in general, there will be some such interactions, and so we call the dynamic (4.4.4) the *N-species replicator dynamic* for an asymmetric game with N roles.[13] As a population game, this dynamic models the frequency evolution of an N-species system with pairwise intraspecific interactions for species k if $\rho(u_k, u_k) \neq 0$ and interspecific interactions between species k and ℓ when $\rho(u_k, u_\ell) \neq 0$ for $k \neq \ell$ (see section 4.7.2 below for the $N = 2$ case).

It is also clear from (4.4.4) that the Wright manifold has another important dynamic property compared to the asymmetric replicator dynamic (4.4.1); namely it restricts to a replicator dynamic on any subgames of the extensive form. Specifically, if the information situations of an asymmetric game can be partitioned into subsets where $\rho(u_k, u_\ell) = 0$ whenever u_k and u_ℓ are in different subsets, then the N-species replicator dynamic (4.4.4) on the Wright manifold becomes the M-species replicator dynamic on any such subset that contains M information situations. Thus an understanding of these lower-dimensional dynamics for the subgames leads to a complete understanding of (4.4.4). However, as we will see in the example of section 4.6.1, one cannot generalize this intuition to arbitrary trajectories of (4.4.1) that are not on the Wright manifold.

Remark 4.4.1   An alternative development of the N-species replicator dynamic is as follows: Consider the symmetric bimatrix game of an asymmetric game. $W \times W$ is then invariant for the bimatrix replicator dynamic on which the projection map induces the dynamic

$$\dot{p}_{i_k}^k = p_{i_k}^k \sum_{\ell=1}^{N} \rho(u_k, u_\ell)(e_{i_k} - p^k) \cdot A_{k\ell} q^\ell,$$

$$\dot{q}_{i_\ell}^\ell = q_{i_\ell}^\ell \sum_{k=1}^{N} \rho(u_k, u_\ell)(e_{i_\ell} - q^\ell) \cdot A_{\ell k} p^k,$$

on $\Delta(S_1) \times \cdots \times \Delta(S_N) \times \Delta(S_1) \times \cdots \times \Delta(S_N)$. This is a $2N$-player replicator dynamic for which the diagonal $\{(\text{proj}(p), \text{proj}(q)) \in \Delta(S_1) \times \cdots \times \Delta(S_N) \times \Delta(S_1) \times \cdots \times \Delta(S_N) \mid \text{proj}(p) = \text{proj}(q)\}$ is invariant. Clearly, on this diagonal, the dynamic is (4.4.4). We developed the N-species replicator dynamic directly from first principles since we will have no further use of the above $2N$-player replicator dynamic.

---

13. The usual N-species replicator dynamic is $\dot{p}_{i_k}^k = p_{i_k}^k \sum_{\ell=1}^{N}(e_{i_k} - p^k) \cdot A_{k\ell} p^\ell$. The extra factors $\rho(u_k, u_\ell)$ in (4.4.4) can be included in the payoff matrices $A_{k\ell}$.

4.4.2   Best Response Dynamics

Best response dynamics for asymmetric games can be analyzed in analogy to the treatment of symmetrized bimatrix games in chapter 3.4.2. Again, $e_i \in BR(p)$ if and only if $e_{i_k} \in BR^k(p)$ for all k where $BR^k(p)$ is the set of best responses in role u_k (i.e., a set in $\Delta(S_k)$) to the population state $p \in \Delta(S)$. Again, we assume the tie-breaking rule only depends on the behavior strategy $\text{proj}(p)$ of the population state.

One best response dynamic for an asymmetric game is the best response dynamic applied to its symmetric normal form (i.e., $\dot{p}_i = BR(p) - p_i$). The trajectories then project to trajectories of an N-species best response dynamic

$$\dot{p}_r^k = BR_r^k(p) - p_r^k,$$

where $(BR_1^k(p), \dots, BR_{|S_k|}^k(p)) \in BR^k(p)$. This is an N-player best response dynamic if there are no intraspecific payoff effects.

We are more interested in the situation where individuals only adjust choices in their current role, as in the development of the symmetrized best response dynamic of chapter 3.4.2. The resultant analogue of (3.4.4) is the *asymmetric best response dynamic*

$$\dot{p}_i = \sum_{\ell=1}^{N} \rho(u_1, u_\ell) \left[\sum_{j_1=1}^{|S_1|} p_{j_1 i_2 \dots i_N} BR_{i_1}^1(p) - p_i \right] + \cdots$$

$$+ \sum_{\ell=1}^{N} \rho(u_N, u_\ell) \left[\sum_{j_N=1}^{|S_N|} p_{i_1 \dots i_{N-1} j_N} BR_{i_N}^N(p) - p_i \right]. \tag{4.4.5}$$

Trajectories now project to the weighted N-species best response dynamic

$$\dot{p}_r^k = \sum_{\ell=1}^{N} \rho(u_k, u_\ell) \left[BR_r^k(p) - p_r^k \right]. \tag{4.4.6}$$

This is shown in appendix A as part of the proof of the following theorem that emphasizes again the importance of the Wright manifold:

Theorem 4.4.2   *For any asymmetric game the Wright manifold is globally asymptotically stable for the asymmetric best response dynamic (4.4.5). In fact this convergence is exponential in the sense that* $|p_i - p_{i_1}^1 p_{i_2}^2 \cdots p_{i_N}^N| \le B e^{-ct}$ *for some positive constants B and c independent of the multi-index i.*

4.5 Truly Asymmetric Two-Player Games

An asymmetric (two-player) game is called *truly asymmetric* if $\rho(u_k, u_k) = 0$ for all $k = 1, \ldots, N$. Thus a symmetrized bimatrix game corresponds to a truly asymmetric game with $N = 2$. Much of the theory for symmetrized bimatrix games developed in chapter 3.4 generalizes to all truly asymmetric games.

For these games we can assign one agent to the two information sets (one for each player) with the same label. The *symmetric agent normal form of a truly asymmetric game*[14] with N roles is then an N-player game with strategy set S_k for player k whose payoff functions are given by[15]

$$\pi_k(p^k, \text{proj}(\hat{p})) = \sum_{\substack{\ell=1 \\ \ell \neq k}}^{N} \rho(u_k, u_\ell) p^k \cdot A_{k\ell} \hat{p}^\ell. \tag{4.5.1}$$

The essential point here is that there are no self-interactions among any of the N players. In contrast, information sets in an asymmetric game with N roles and $\rho(u_k, u_k) \neq 0$ for some k cannot be assigned agents in such a way as to produce an N-player game.

Remark 4.5.1 Symmetric agent normal form games are examples of the class of N-player *linear incentive games* (see Notes). These are N-player games that satisfy the condition that the difference between the payoffs for any two pure strategies of a player depend linearly on the probabilities in the mixed strategies of the other $N - 1$ players. In fact, from the dynamic perspective of this book where evolutionary game theory depends only on payoff differences, the class of symmetric agent normal form games is identical to the class of N-player linear incentive games. That is, every N-player linear incentive game is dynamically equivalent (i.e., the trajectories are identical) to a symmetric agent normal form of a truly asymmetric game with N roles.

As an N-player normal form game, the usual concepts of NE and SESet from section 4.3 apply to the symmetric agent normal form. The following theorem summarizes the static and dynamic properties of the ES structure for truly asymmetric games and their relationship to their

---

14. This is also called the *agent representation* of a truly asymmetric game.
15. This is a slight abuse of the notation used in definition 4.3.1 since there the domain of the payoff function π_k should be S. A more rigorous notation in (4.5.1) would be $\hat{\pi}_k(\text{proj}(\hat{p}) \backslash p^k)$, but we will continue using the symbol π_k.

symmetric agent normal forms. It contains many previous results from chapters 3 and 4. In particular, theorems 3.4.1 and 3.4.2 in chapter 3 are parts i and ii respectively of theorem 4.5.3. The following lemma needed for theorem 4.5.3 is proved in appendix B.

Lemma 4.5.2   *Every closed asymptotically stable set of the N-player replicator dynamic of a truly asymmetric game with N roles contains a pure strategy. In particular, no closed set contained in the interior of the strategy space* $\Delta(S_1) \times \cdots \times \Delta(S_N)$ *is asymptotically stable.*

Theorem 4.5.3   *Suppose that G is a truly asymmetric game with N roles and pure strategy set* $S = S_1 \times \cdots \times S_N$.

i. $E \subseteq \Delta(S)$ *is a local ESSet as given in definition 4.2.1 of section 4.2 if and only if E is an ESSet of G if and only if E corresponds*[16] *under the projection map (4.2.1) to an SESet F of the symmetric agent normal form of G. In particular,* p^* *is an ESS if and only if it is a strict NE.*

ii. *The following four statements are also equivalent.*

   $E \subseteq \Delta(S)$ *is an asymptotically stable set of rest points of the asymmetric replicator dynamic (4.4.1) for G.*

   E is an ESSet of G.

   E corresponds to an SESet F of the symmetric agent normal form of G.

   F is an asymptotically stable set of rest points of the N-player replicator dynamic (4.4.4).

Proof (i) By theorem 4.2.2, any ESSet is a local ESSet. Now show proj[E] is an SESet if E is a local ESSet. Suppose that $p^* \in E$ and that $\pi_k(p^k, \text{proj}(p^*)) = \pi_k(p^{*k}, \text{proj}(p^*))$. Then $\pi_k(p^k, \text{proj}(p^*) \backslash p^k) = \pi_k(p^k, \text{proj}(p^*)) = \pi_k(p^{*k}, \text{proj}(p^*)) = \pi_k(p^{*k}, \text{proj}(p^*) \backslash p^k)$ since G is truly asymmetric. Thus, by definition 4.2.1, any $p^* \backslash p^k \in E$ and so is a NE. This implies that $\text{proj}(p^*) \backslash p^k$ is an element of $F = \text{proj}[E]$, and so F is closed under best replies by player k. That is, F is an SESet.

Finally, suppose that F is an SESet of the symmetric agent normal form of G. To show that $E \equiv \{p \in \Delta(S) \,|\, \text{proj}(p) \in F\}$ is an ESSet, let $p^* \in E$. Clearly, p^* is a NE. It is sufficient to show that, for any $p \in \Delta(S)$ with $\pi(p, p^*) = \pi(p^*, p^*)$, either $\pi(p^*, p) > \pi(p, p)$ or $\pi(p^*, p) = \pi(p, p)$ and $p \in E$. Since $\pi(p, p^*) = \pi(p^*, p^*)$, $\pi_k(p^k, \text{proj}(p^*)) =$

---

16. E corresponds to F if and only if $F = \text{proj}[E]$ and $E = \text{proj}^{-1}[F]$.

$\pi_k(p^{*k}, \text{proj}(p^*))$ for all k. Thus $\text{proj}(p^*) \backslash p^k \in F$. In particular,

$$\pi_1(p^{*1}, \text{proj}(p^*) \backslash p^k) \geq \pi_k(p^1, \text{proj}(p^*) \backslash p^k) \qquad \text{for all } k, \text{ and}$$

$$\pi_1(p^1, \text{proj}(p^*) \backslash p^1) \geq \pi_1(p^{*1}, \text{proj}(p^*) \backslash p^1).$$

Since G is truly asymmetric, $\pi_1(p^1, \text{proj}(p^*) \backslash p^1) = \pi_1(p^1, \text{proj}(p^*))$. Thus from (4.2.2),

$$\pi_1(p^{*1}, \text{proj}(p)) + (N - 2)\pi_1(p^{*1}, \text{proj}(p^*))$$

$$= \sum_{\ell=1}^{N} \rho(u_1, u_\ell) \left(\sum_{k=2}^{N} p^{*1} \cdot A_{1\ell} p^\ell + (N - 2) \sum_{k=2}^{N} p^{*1} \cdot A_{1\ell} p^{*\ell} \right)$$

$$= \sum_{k=2}^{N} \pi_1(p^{*1}, \text{proj}(p^*) \backslash p^k)$$

$$\geq \sum_{k=2}^{N} \pi_1(p^1, \text{proj}(p^*) \backslash p^k)$$

$$= \pi_1(p^1, \text{proj}(p)) + (N - 2)\pi_1(p^1, \text{proj}(p^*))$$

$$\geq \pi_1(p^1, \text{proj}(p)) + (N - 2)\pi_1(p^{*1}, \text{proj}(p^*)).$$

That is, $\pi_1(p^{*1}, \text{proj}(p)) \geq \pi_1(p^1, \text{proj}(p))$. Since this holds for each k in place of player one, $\pi(p^*, p) = \sum_k \pi_k(p^{*k}, \text{proj}(p)) \geq \sum_k \pi_k(p^k, \text{proj}(p)) = \pi(p, p)$.

Furthermore, if $\pi(p^*, p) = \pi(p, p)$, then $\pi_\ell(p^{*\ell}, \text{proj}(p^*) \backslash p^k) = \pi_\ell(p^\ell, \text{proj}(p^*) \backslash p^k)$ for all k, ℓ. Since F is an SESet, $\text{proj}(p^*) \backslash p^k \backslash p^\ell \in F$ for all k, ℓ.[17] If $N > 2$, then $\sum_{2 \leq k < \ell \leq N} \pi_1(p^{*1}, \text{proj}(p^*) \backslash p^k \backslash p^\ell) \geq \sum_{2 \leq k < \ell \leq N} \pi_1(p^1, \text{proj}(p^*) \backslash p^k \backslash p^\ell)$. Rearranging terms, we conclude that

$$\binom{N-1}{1}\pi_1(p^{*1}, \text{proj}(p)) + \binom{N-2}{2}\pi_1(p^{*1}, \text{proj}(p^*))$$

$$\geq \binom{N-1}{1}\pi_1(p^1, \text{proj}(p)) + \binom{N-2}{2}\pi_1(p^1, \text{proj}(p^*)),$$

where $\binom{n}{m} = n!/(m!(n - m)!)$. But $\pi_1(p^{*1}, \text{proj}(p)) = \pi_1(p^1, \text{proj}(p))$ and $\pi_1(p^{*1}, \text{proj}(p^*)) = \pi_1(p^1, \text{proj}(p^*))$. Thus, for example, $\pi_1(p^{*1}, \text{proj}(p^*) \backslash p^2 \backslash p^3) = \pi_1(p^1, \text{proj}(p^*) \backslash p^2 \backslash p^3)$, and then $\text{proj}(p^*) \backslash p^1 \backslash p^2 \backslash p^3 \in F$, and so on. By induction on N, $\text{proj}(p) \in F$, and so $p \in E$.

(ii) Suppose that $E \subseteq \Delta(S)$ is an asymptotically stable set of rest points of the asymmetric replicator dynamic (4.4.1) for G. Clearly, E

---

17. This completes the proof that E is an ESSet if $N = 2$.

is a closed set. For each $p^* \in E$, $\{p \in E \mid \text{proj}(p) = \text{proj}(p^*)\}$ contains a single point in W and is also a connected set of rest points and so a subset of E. Since the Wright manifold W is invariant under (4.4.1), $E \cap W$ is a nonempty asymptotically stable set of rest points of the asymmetric replicator dynamic. Since $\text{proj}[E] = \text{proj}[E \cap W]$ and the projection map on W induces the N-player replicator dynamic (4.4.4), E corresponds to an asymptotically stable set of rest points of (4.4.4).

The next step in the proof is to show that an asymptotically stable set F of rest points of the N-player replicator dynamic (4.4.4) is an SESet. The proof when $N = 2$ is given in chapter 3. The details provided here for the case $N = 3$ include all the added complexities that arise in the general proof. We will first show by induction on the size of the support that, if $p^* \in F$, then any $\{p \mid \text{supp}(p) \subset \text{supp}(p^*)\}$ is a subset of F, and that if every edge in $\text{supp}(p^*)$ is in F, then $\{p \mid \text{supp}(p) \subset \text{supp}(p^*)\}$ is a subset of F. This is clearly true if p^* is a pure strategy. If p^* is not a pure strategy, then by lemma 4.5.2, there is a path in F from p^* to a pure strategy and so a straight line to a point $\tilde{p}$ in F whose support is a proper subset of $\text{supp}(p^*)$. Extend this line in the other direction to get another $\tilde{p}$ whose support is a proper subset of $\text{supp}(p^*)$. By induction, the supports of these endpoints are both subsets of F. Let $S' \equiv \{e \mid e \text{ is in the support of either endpoint}\}$. Then $\pi_k(p^k, e) = \pi_k(e_k, e)$ for all k and all p with $\text{supp}(p) \subset \text{supp}(p^*)$ whenever $e \in S'$.[18] Thus, any edge in $\text{supp}(p^*)$ connected to an $e \in S'$ is a set of rest points, and since F is asymptotically stable, this edge is in F. For $N = 3$, every $e' \in \text{supp}(p^*)$ is either in S' or is on an edge connected to S'. Thus every $e' \in \text{supp}(p^*)$ is in F. Since every edge is invariant under (4.4.4) and every edge in $\text{supp}(p^*)$ has its vertices in F, the asymptotic stability of F implies that these latter edges are contained in F. By induction, every lower-dimensional face in $\text{supp}(p^*)$ is in F. Now suppose that $\text{supp}(\tilde{p}) = \text{supp}(p^*)$. If each such $\tilde{p}$ is a rest point of (4.4.4), then $\text{supp}(p^*)$ is contained in the asymptotically stable set F. Thus all we need to show is that $\pi_k(p^k, \tilde{p}) = \pi_k(\tilde{p}^k, \tilde{p})$ for all p with support in $\text{supp}(p^*)$. If $e \in \text{supp}(p^*)$, then $\pi_k(p^k, p^* \backslash e_\ell) = \pi_k(p^{*k}, p^* \backslash e_\ell)$ since $p^* \backslash e_\ell$ is a NE (and if $\pi_k(p^k, p^* \backslash e_\ell) < \pi_k(p^{*k}, p^* \backslash e_\ell)$ for some p^k, then $\pi_k(p^k, p^* \backslash e_\ell) > \pi_k(p^{*k}, p^* \backslash e_\ell)$ for some other p^k). Similarly $\pi_k(p^k, \tilde{p} \backslash e_\ell) = \pi_k(\tilde{p}^k, \tilde{p} \backslash e_\ell)$ since $\tilde{p} \backslash e_\ell$ is a NE in a lower dimensional

---

18. This is clearly true if we replace e by any (mixed) strategy in the support of $\tilde{p}$ and sufficiently close to $\tilde{p}$ or else we could show some points on the face containing this endpoint were not NE by looking on both sides. The extension to the entire support of the endpoint is straightforward.

face of supp(p^*). $\pi_k(p^k, \tilde{p}) = \pi_k(p^k, \tilde{p}\backslash e_k) = \pi_k(\tilde{p}^k, \tilde{p}\backslash e_k) = \pi_k(\tilde{p}^k, \tilde{p})$ since the game is truly asymmetric. Thus F is a finite union of faces, and we only need to show that it is closed under best replies by each of the N players. If $\pi_1(\tilde{p}^1, p^*) = \pi_1(p^{*1}, p^*)$, then $\pi_1(\tilde{e}_1, e) = \pi_1(e_1, e)$ for all $e \in$ supp(p^*) and $\tilde{e}_1 \in$ supp($\tilde{p}^1$). Then the edge from e to $e\backslash\tilde{e}_1$ is entirely in F. Similarly the edge from $e\backslash\tilde{e}_1$ to $e\backslash\tilde{e}_1'$ is also in F. Thus every edge in supp($p^*\backslash\tilde{p}^1$) is in F. By induction, supp($p^*\backslash\tilde{p}^1$) $\subset F$. In particular, $p^*\backslash\tilde{p}^1 \in F$.

Finally, suppose that F is an SESet of the symmetric agent normal form of G. Then, by part i, $E \equiv \text{proj}^{-1}[F]$ is an ESSet of the truly asymmetric game G and so an asymptotically stable set of rest points of the asymmetric replicator dynamic by chapter 2. ∎

4.5.1 The Age-Structured Owner-Intruder Game Dynamic

In this section we consider briefly the replicator dynamic on the Wright manifold for the Age-Structured Owner-Intruder Game of section 4.2.1 where we previously showed that its only ESSets are nonempty subsets of $\{HDD, DHH\}$. This is a truly asymmetric game with three roles. From (4.4.4), the corresponding 3-species replicator dynamic on the unit cube $[0, 1]^3$ with coordinates ($p_H^{OO}, p_H^{OI}, p_H^{YI}$) is

$$\dot{p}_H^{OO} = p_H^{OO} p_D^{OO} \left[\frac{1}{6}(p_D^{OI} - p_H^{OI}) + \frac{1}{3}(p_D^{YI} - p_H^{YI}) \right],$$

$$\dot{p}_H^{OI} = \frac{1}{6} p_H^{OI} p_D^{OI} (p_D^{OO} - p_H^{OO}),$$

$$\dot{p}_H^{YI} = \frac{1}{3} p_H^{YI} p_D^{YI} (p_D^{OO} - p_H^{OO}).$$

The phase portrait is given in figure 4.5.1 where the interior NE form a line (through the interior of the cube) that joins ($\frac{1}{2}, 0, \frac{3}{4}$) to ($\frac{1}{2}, 1, \frac{1}{4}$) and includes the obvious equilibrium ($\frac{1}{2}, \frac{1}{2}, \frac{1}{2}$).

On the front and back faces with $p_H^{OO} = 1$ and $p_H^{OO} = 0$ respectively, we have a bimatrix game between Old Intruders and Young Intruders. On the front face, the payoff matrix

$$
\begin{array}{cc}
 & \text{Young Intruders} \\
 & \begin{array}{cc} H & \quad D \end{array}
\end{array}
$$

$$
\begin{array}{cc}
\text{Old} \quad\quad H \\
\text{Intruders} \quad D
\end{array}
\begin{bmatrix}
-\frac{1}{6}, -\frac{1}{3} & -\frac{1}{6}, \frac{2}{3} \\
\frac{1}{3}, -\frac{1}{3} & \frac{1}{3}, \frac{2}{3}
\end{bmatrix}
$$

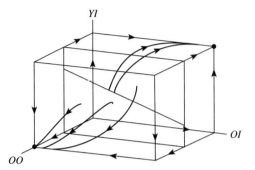

Figure 4.5.1
Replicator dynamic on the Wright manifold for the Age-Structured Owner-Intruder Game.

reflects the fact there are no direct interactions between players in these two roles. This is a Prisoner's Dilemma type bimatrix game (see case 3 in chapter 3.3.1) where every interior trajectory converges to $(1, 0, 0)$ (i.e., to HDD). The ruled surface generated by each of these (complete) trajectories and lines parallel to the OO-axis is invariant under the dynamic.

Both side faces are Owner-Intruder type bimatrix games (see case 1 in chapter 3.3.1) with a separatrix dividing the basins of attraction of the two stable corners. There is another important invariant surface $\sum$ through the interior of the unit cube that intersects the faces in these two separatrices together with the top front and bottom back edges. $\sum$ includes the line of interior NE that attracts all interior initial points lying on this surface. Furthermore a careful analysis[19] shows that all initial interior points above $\sum$ evolve to $(0, 1, 1)$ (i.e., to DHH) and all those below to HDD.

Qualitatively, the replicator dynamic on the Wright manifold of the Age-Structured Owner-Intruder Game is the same as the Owner-Intruder Game without age-structure from chapter 3.[20] In both cases an initial sufficient bias of owners playing a different strategy than intruders guarantees the population will evolve to all owners playing their initial predominant strategy and all intruders the other. Furthermore the phase portraits of all these dynamics (see figures 3.2.1, 3.4.2, and 4.5.1)

---

19. Parts of this are easy to show. For instance, p_H^{OO} strictly increases to 1 if we are initially in the region where $p_H^{OO} > \frac{1}{2}$, $p_H^{OI} < \frac{1}{2}$ and $p_H^{YI} < \frac{1}{2}$ which implies convergence to HDD.
20. This is true whether we consider the bimatrix replicator dynamic of chapter 3.2.1 or the symmetrized replicator dynamic of chapter 3.4.1.

contain a curve or surface that divides the strategy space into the respective domains of attraction of the two strict NEs.

4.6   Truly Symmetric Two-Player Games

An asymmetric (two-player) game is called *truly symmetric* if $\rho(u_k, u_\ell) = 0$ whenever $k \neq \ell$.[21] In particular, a symmetric normal form game is truly symmetric with $N = 1$. The information sets of every truly symmetric game can be partitioned into those of N symmetric subgames (or, more correctly, truly symmetric subgames). Perhaps because of this, truly symmetric games have received little attention in the literature since it seems intuitively clear that a separate analysis of each subgame can lead to a complete understanding of these extensive form games. Theorems 4.6.1 and 4.6.2 below, on the ES structure and their dynamic stability properties, support this intuition. These are the analogues of our results for truly asymmetric games given in parts i and ii of theorem 4.5.3 respectively. However, sections 4.6.1 and 4.6.2 demonstrate important differences between an analysis of the separate subgames and of the complete truly symmetric extensive form game. These differences (especially those of section 4.6.1) are essential to appreciate the complexities that arise in sections 4.7 and 4.8 when the asymmetric games are neither truly symmetric nor truly asymmetric.

Theorem 4.6.1 $E \subseteq \Delta(S)$ *is an ESSet of a truly symmetric game with N roles if and only if E is a local ESSet. In particular, $E^k \equiv \{p^k \mid p \in E\}$ is an ESSet for the truly symmetric subgame formed by the two information sets (one each for players one and two) that are labeled u_k and $E = \text{proj}^{-1}[\text{proj}[E]]$.*

Proof   By theorem 4.2.2, all we need to show is that $E \equiv \text{proj}^{-1}[E^1 \times \cdots \times E^N]$ is an ESSet if, for all k, E^k is an ESSet of the kth subgame with payoff matrix A_{kk}. Suppose that p^* is in E. Since p^{*k} is a NE for all k, $\pi(p, p^*) = \sum_k \rho(u_k, u_k) p^k \cdot A_{kk} p^{*k} \leq \sum_k \rho(u_k, u_k) p^{*k} \cdot A_{kk} p^{*k} = \pi(p^*, p^*)$, and so p^* is a NE.

To complete the proof that E is an ESSet, it is enough to show that $\pi(p^*, p) > \pi(p, p)$ whenever $p^* \in E$, $p \notin E$, and $\pi(p, p^*) = \pi(p^*, p^*)$. Since p^* is a NE and $\pi(p, p^*) = \pi(p^*, p^*)$, $p^k \cdot A_{kk} p^{*k} = p^{*k} \cdot A_{kk} p^{*k}$ for all k. If $\pi(p^*, p) \leq \pi(p, p)$, then $p^{*k} \cdot A_{kk} p^k \leq p^k \cdot A_{kk} p^k$ for some k, say $k = 1$. Since E^1 is an ESSet, $p^1 \in E^1$, and so, by theorem 2.7.1 in

---

21. To avoid degeneracies, we assume $\rho(u_k, u_k) > 0$ for $k = 1, \ldots, N$ and that each player information set has at least two choices.

chapter 2, $p^{*1} \cdot A_{11} p^1 = p^1 \cdot A_{11} p^1$. Thus $p^{*k} \cdot A_{kk} p^k \leq p^k \cdot A_{kk} p^k$ for some $k > 1$, say $k = 2$. The argument above can now be applied recursively to yield $p^k \in E^k$ for all k. This contradicts our assumption that $p \notin E$. ∎

Notice that the concept of an SESet (for the agent normal form) of a truly symmetric game no longer characterizes ESSets. In particular, an ESS is not necessarily a strict NE. Furthermore, we know from chapter 2 that unlike truly asymmetric games, there are asymptotically stable sets of rest points of the symmetric replicator dynamic that are not ESSets for symmetric normal form games with more than two strategies. However, if all subgames have exactly two strategies (i.e., if $|S_k| = 2$ for all k), we have the following intuitive result relating dynamic stability of the extensive form game to that of its subgames:

Theorem 4.6.2   *Suppose that G is a truly symmetric game such that each information situation has two strategies. A set of rest points E is asymptotically stable for the asymmetric replicator dynamic (4.4.1) if and only if E is an ESSet if and only if E corresponds under the projection map to $E^1 \times \cdots \times E^N$ where, for all k, E^k is an asymptotically stable set of rest points of the symmetric replicator dynamic for the two-strategy truly symmetric subgame with information sets labeled u_k. In particular, if E is connected, then E^k is a singleton ESS whenever its corresponding subgame does not consist entirely of rest points of the replicator dynamic.*

Proof   If E is an asymptotically stable set of rest points, then it is asymptotically stable when restricted to the Wright manifold. Since, for each k, this is the symmetric replicator dynamic for the two-strategy game A_{kk}, E^k is asymptotically stable if and only if it is an ESSet of A_{kk}. Since E is asymptotically stable, it must contain $\{p \mid \text{proj}(p) = \text{proj}(p^*)$ for some $p^* \in E\}$, and so E is a local ESSet. By theorem 4.6.1, E is an ESSet of the truly symmetric game. By chapter 2, an ESSet is an asymptotically stable set of rest points. ∎

Theorems 4.6.1 and 4.6.2 show that the asymptotic stability of sets of rest points of a truly symmetric game can be characterized completely in terms of the dynamics of its subgames when there are two strategies in each. The results are important given that many examples in the evolutionary game theory literature satisfy these conditions. However, the following section shows that one must exercise caution extending the intuition behind theorems 4.6.1 and 4.6.2 as the number of strategies increases.

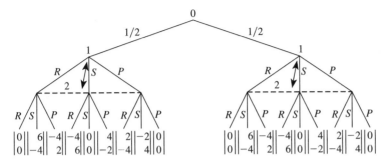

Figure 4.6.1
Extensive form game for section 4.6.1.

4.6.1   A Truly Symmetric Game Dynamic Counterexample

Consider the truly symmetric game of figure 4.6.1 with two information situations that are reached equally often (i.e., $\rho(u_1, u_1) = \frac{1}{2} = \rho(u_2, u_2)$). The two symmetric subgames, A_{11} and A_{22}, are both given by the same three-strategy (generalized) Rock–Scissors–Paper[22] symmetric normal form game with payoff matrix

$$A = \begin{array}{c} R \\ S \\ P \end{array} \begin{bmatrix} 0 & 6 & -4 \\ -4 & 0 & 4 \\ 2 & -2 & 0 \end{bmatrix}.$$

One interpretation[23] of figure 4.6.1 is as a model of an exogenous shock, called a *sunspot*, that has no effect on payoff. That is, players may condition their play on whether or not there is a sunspot on a particular day, but payoffs between two given local behavior strategies do not depend on the presence of the sunspot. If the random sunspot appears half the time on average, the game's extensive form is given by figure 4.6.1.

The evolutionary analysis of each Rock–Scissors–Paper subgame is straightforward from chapter 2.6. There is a unique symmetric NE $p_0^* = (10, 8, 11)/29$ that is globally asymptotically stable under the symmetric replicator dynamic (and the best response dynamic). Although p_0^* is not an ESS (e.g., since $p_0^* \cdot Ap < p \cdot Ap$ for $p = (\frac{1}{2}, \frac{1}{2}, 0) \in \Delta^3$), standard

---

22. This is example 2.6.1 in chapter 2 with $\alpha = 6$ (and with e_1 and e_2 interchanged).
23. Another interpretation is that of indistinguishable firms competing simultaneously in two identical but separate markets (perhaps the separation is by geography). Again, strategies can be chosen that depend on the market, but a given pair of local behavior strategies in one market yields the same payoff as it does in the other market.

evolutionary processes do evolve to p_0^*. Intuitively we also expect the evolutionary analysis of the truly symmetric game of figure 4.6.1 to predict that the evolutionary system will evolve to p_0^* in each subgame. The essential message of the following technical analysis is the surprising result that this is not always the case.

The set E of symmetric NE for this truly symmetric extensive form example with 9 pure strategies is the four-dimensional hyperplane of strategies that project to p_0^* in both subgames. That is, $E = \{p \in \Delta^9 \mid p^1 = p_0^* = p^2\}$. Intuition suggests that E will be asymptotically stable under the asymmetric replicator dynamic (4.4.1). For our counterexample (i.e., a $p^* \in E$ that is unstable), notice that E contains $\{p \in \Delta^9 \mid p_i = p_{0i_1}^* p_{0i_2}^* + x_{i_1} y_{i_2}$ with $x, y \in X^3\}$, where $X^3 = \{x = (x_1, x_2, x_3) \mid x_1 + x_2 + x_3 = 0\}$. Consider the line segment of NE p^r of the form $p_i^r = p_{0i_1}^* p_{0i_2}^* + r x_{i_1} y_{i_2}$ with $x = (-4, 1, 3)$ and $y = (-2, -1, 3)$. Then $p^r \in \Delta^9$ for all $0 \leq r \leq 110/12(29)^2 \cong 0.0109$ with one endpoint ($r = 0$) on the Wright manifold. At the upper limit for r, the line segment meets the boundary of Δ^9 on the face where the third component of p^r is zero when the entries are given in the order $(p_{11}, p_{12}, p_{13}, p_{21}, p_{22}, p_{23}, p_{31}, p_{32}, p_{33})$.

The linearization of the asymmetric replicator dynamic (4.4.1) is the 9×9 matrix with entries $L_{ij} = p_i^r (\pi(e_i, e_j) - \pi(p^r, e_j))$. Its ninth-order characteristic polynomial[24] is

$$\lambda^9 + \frac{8}{29}\lambda^8 + \left(\frac{7056}{841} - 220r^2\right)\lambda^7 + \left(\frac{28160}{24389} + \frac{193536}{29}r^2\right)\lambda^6$$

$$+ \left(\frac{12390400}{707281} - \frac{42325056}{841}r^2\right)\lambda^5.$$

There are five zero eigenvalues, four of which are due to the dimension of E and the fifth to the invariance of Δ^9 for the replicator dynamic.

When $r = 0.01$, the four nonzero eigenvalues correct to four decimal places are $\lambda = 0.0054 \pm 2.5355i$ and $\lambda = -0.1433 \pm 1.3862i$. Since two eigenvalues have positive real part, $p^* = p^{0.01}$ is unstable. That is, almost all trajectories that start arbitrarily close (but not equal) to p^* do not stay close. This result initially leaves open the possibility that these unstable trajectories stay close to E. However, p^* is the unique point of intersection of E with a four-dimensional generalized Wright manifold

---

24. This characteristic polynomial is exact as can be verified by a tedious hand calculation or by using a computer algebra program such as MAPLE. Since determination of the eigenvalues reduces to factoring a fourth-order polynomial, these can be given algebraically by MAPLE again. They are reported here to four decimal places.

$W_K(p^*)$ that is invariant under (4.4.1) (see chapter 3.4.1). Furthermore $W_K(p^*)$ intersects E transversely at p^* (i.e., the tangent space to $W_K(p^*)$ at p^* also intersects the hyperplane E only at p^*). Thus trajectories that diverge from p^* also diverge from E and so E is unstable. In fact computer simulations indicate these trajectories never return to p^* but get very close to the boundary of Δ^9 and remain there.

As r increases from 0 to 0.0109, the asymmetric replicator dynamic (4.4.1) restricted to the four-dimensional invariant generalized Wright manifold $W_K(p^r)$ undergoes a *Hopf bifurcation* as a pair of nonzero eigenvalues crosses the imaginary axis at approximately $r^* = 0.0096$. That is, for $0 \leq r < r^*$, p^r is asymptotically stable on $W_K(p^r)$ and unstable for $r^* < r \leq 0.0109$. The simulations referred to above suggest the bifurcation is subcritical since no limit cycles are apparent.[25] It would be mathematically interesting to see if other parametric curves in E or other payoff matrices A lead to supercritical Hopf bifurcations.

Also interesting is the fact that the parameter range for r when p^r is unstable is very restricted, occurring far from the unique NE $p^0 \in \Delta^9$ on the Wright manifold (given by $p_i^0 = p_{0i_1}^* p_{0i_2}^*$) and close to the boundary of Δ^9 where the asymmetric replicator dynamic is least related to the replicator dynamic on the subgames. Of course, on the Wright manifold, the dynamic restricts to the replicator dynamic (up to the positive factor $\rho(u_i, u_i) = \frac{1}{2}$) on each subgame and so all trajectories in the interior of W converge to p^0. Thus the counterintuitive possibility of dynamic instability caused by a sunspot phenomenon can be avoided by assuming that the only replicator dynamics that are relevant for evolutionary processes are those on the Wright manifold. This appeals to the intuition that an individual should choose a local behavior strategy in each subgame that is independent of his choice in the other subgame (and so the initial population state will be a point in W). However, since all individuals are pure strategists in the standard dynamic model used in evolutionary game theory, it is hard to imagine how the initial population could coordinate itself to be given by a state in W.

A second alternative to avoid such counterexamples is to insist that ESSs (or perhaps ESSets) are the only NE that predict the eventual outcome of evolutionary processes. That is, by theorem 4.6.1, the ES structure of a truly symmetric game is completely given by the ES structure

---

25. Hopf bifurcations (along with their classification as subcritical or supercritical) are defined formally in standard texts on dynamical systems. Details are not provided here since these concepts will not be used again.

of its subgames. However, many interesting symmetric games have no ESSs (e.g., the extensive form game of figure 4.6.1 and both of its subgames), and so a theory of equilibrium selection based on ESSets rather than dynamic stability has serious limitations.

A final alternative relies on the observation that, at some points of Δ^9, the asymmetric replicator dynamic (or, for that matter, any monotone selection dynamic with respect to the normal form) for our counterexample increases the conditional frequency p_1^1 of the pure strategy that chooses R in the left-hand subgame Γ_{u_1} in cases where R has the lowest payoff in Γ_{u_1}. Such points cannot be on the Wright manifold. In the terminology of chapter 9, where these issues will be revisited, the asymmetric replicator dynamic is not *subgame monotone*.[26] If the asymmetric replicator dynamic (4.4.1) is justified through imitative behavior based on observed payoffs and strategies (see chapter 2.10), one could argue that consistency between dynamic stability of the extensive form game and that of its subgames should not be expected when individuals do not base their behavioral decisions on information concerning payoffs in the subgames. From this perspective the consistency between their static structures (theorem 4.6.1) could be viewed as the more surprising result.

It is also interesting to note that the best-response dynamic applied to our truly symmetric extensive form example does not have this inconsistency problem since a best reply to the current state must induce a best reply to each subgame state. Thus, E is globally asymptotically stable under the best response dynamic (in fact, under the asymmetric best response dynamic (4.4.5), the point $p^0 \in E \cap W$ is globally asymptotically stable).

4.6.2   Parallel Bandits
Coauthor: Karl H. Schlag[27]

A *parallel bandit* is a one-player game against nature where the only move nature makes is the initial one. Specifically, at the initial move,

---

26. The concept of dynamics on the subgames is also central in the following section on parallel bandits.
27. This section and chapter 8.4 on extensive form bandits were written jointly by myself and Karl H. Schlag, Economics Department, European University Institute, 50016 San Domenico di Fiesole, Italy. Along with chapter 2.10, these three sections examine evolutionary dynamics that result from imitative behavior based on a single observed outcome in the corresponding one-player extensive form game.

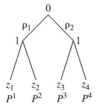

Figure 4.6.2
Extensive form for a Parallel Bandit with $N = 2$.

nature selects decision k (where $1 \leq k \leq N$) with probability $\rho_k > 0$ (see figure 4.6.2 above for the extensive form of a parallel bandit in the special case when $N = 2$).[28] The player then faces the selected decision. Each decision k is an n_k-armed bandit as in chapter 2.10 with a fixed finite number n_k of possible actions S_k (where $n_k \geq 2$ for at least one k). Thus an individual's plan of action in each of the N multi-armed bandits (i.e., his *strategy*) is described by an $e \in \times S_k \equiv S$, where e_k denotes the action chosen at decision k for all $1 \leq k \leq N$. The realized payoff from the choice at decision k that leads to endpoint z continues to be drawn independently and at random from a probability distribution P^z. The parallel bandit is then the tuple $\langle (\rho_k)_{k=1,...,N}, S_k, (z, P^z)_{z \in Z} \rangle$. To ease technical complications, we will assume P^z is a discrete probability distribution on the same finite interval $[\alpha, \omega]$ for all endpoints z. The set of parallel bandits that have the extensive form described above is denoted by $PB((S_k, [\alpha, \omega])_{k=1,...,N})$.[29]

Each $z \in Z$ corresponds to a unique decision k and action $e_k \in S_k$. If nature selects decision k and $z = e_k$, then $\pi_z \equiv \sum_{x \in [\alpha, \omega]} x P^z(x)$ is the expected payoff of choosing action e_k. Let $\gamma(z, e)$ be the probability

---

28. Alternatively, the extensive form of a parallel bandit with N decision points is a truly symmetric extensive form game with N roles where, in each subgame, the player's payoff depends only on his own actions there. In particular, the decisions selected by nature have unrelated consequences. The "bandit" terminology is used since the observations are of realized rather than expected payoffs (i.e., at each endpoint z, there is a lottery given by the distribution P^z). The case $N = 1$ is the multi-armed bandit of chapter 2.10. One justification for the terminology "parallel" is that the player's decisions are connected in parallel in the bandit's extensive form.

29. Other sets of parallel bandits can be used in place of $PB((S_k, [\alpha, \omega])_{k=1,...,N})$ without altering the results of this section. In analogy to chapter 2.10, we may again assume that individuals have partial information about the parallel bandits they are facing as long as uncertainty remains about the set of best actions at each decision. It is also possible to have $\rho_k = 0$ for some decision k. The finite interval $[\alpha_k, \omega_k]$ containing the support of the payoff distribution P^z can depend on the decision k that z follows.

endpoint z is reached if strategy e is used. That is,

$$\gamma(z, e) \equiv \begin{cases} \rho_k & \text{if } z = e_k \text{ for some } k, \\ 0 & \text{otherwise.} \end{cases}$$

Then the expected payoff $\pi(e)$ of pure strategy e for this one-player game against nature is given by $\pi(e) \equiv \sum_{z \in Z} \gamma(z, e)\pi_z$. A mixed strategy or *state* p is an element of $\Delta(\times S_k)$ and $\pi(p) = \sum_{e \in S} p_e \pi(e) = \sum_i p_i \pi(e_i)$ is the expected payoff in state p where $p_i = p_{e_i}$ is the frequency of pure strategy e_i. This payoff can also be expressed as $\pi(p) = \sum_{k=1}^{N} \rho_k \sum_{z \in Z_k} p_z \pi_z$ where Z_k is the set of endpoints that follow decision k and $p_z \equiv \sum_{e_k=z} p_e$ is the frequency that endpoint z is reached if nature chooses decision k. The set of best strategies, denoted $\Delta\{\arg \max\{\pi(e) \mid e \in \times S_k\}\}$, consists of those states p for which $z = e_k$ is a best action at each decision k whenever $p_z > 0$. *Play* in a given round consists of the decision k faced and the action e_k chosen and so can also be denoted by the corresponding endpoint z.[30]

As in our analysis of multi-armed bandits in chapter 2.10, each individual makes an observation of the play of another individual before facing a new decision. We are particularly interested in the existence and characterization of *good behavioral rules* (i.e., what rules make the set of best strategies asymptotically stable) and their relationship to the standard dynamics of evolutionary game theory applied to these games against nature. In our discrete-time model the player's behavioral rule is based solely on the following limited information: the pure strategy e he used in the previous time interval together with its play z and realized payoff x as well as the play w and realized payoff y of one other randomly sampled individual in the population.

A *behavioral rule* for a parallel bandit is then a map $F(e, z, x, w, y)_{e'}$ that specifies the probability an individual adopts pure strategy e' in the next round if his own last strategy is e with experienced play z and payoff x and the sampled play (i.e., the play of the sampled individual) is w with payoff y. When experienced and sampled decisions coincide we speak of *within-decision learning*, when they differ we speak of *cross-decision learning*.

Imitation continues to be important for good behavioral rules (see theorem 4.6.3 below). However, for parallel bandits, playwise imitation is the natural generalization of imitative behavior introduced in

---

30. When the meaning of z is ambiguous, we will use "play z" or "endpoint z" to clarify its use.

chapter 2.10. An individual who changes his strategy adopts (or pastes) the sampled action at the sampled decision and keeps his previous plan of action at all other decisions. Formally, a behavioral rule F is *playwise imitative* if $F(e, z, x, w, y)_{e'} = 0$ whenever $\gamma(z, e)\gamma(w, e\backslash w)P^z(x)P^w(y) > 0$ and $e' \notin \{e, e\backslash w\}$. For general extensive form bandits, $e\backslash w$ is the same strategy as e except that at any decision point on the path to w it prescribes the action leading to w (see chapter 8.4). For parallel bandits, this means that if $w = e_k$, then $e\backslash w = e\backslash e_k$.

In analogy to the dynamic (2.10.1) of chapter 2, when each individual in the population adopts the same playwise imitative behavioral rule F, the discrete-time deterministic dynamic on $\Delta(\times S_k)$ becomes

$$p'_e = p_e + \sum_{e', e'' \in S} p_{e'} p_{e''} F(e', e'', e) - \sum_{e' \in S} p_e p_{e'} F(e, e'). \qquad (4.6.1)$$

Here $F(e', e'', e) \equiv \sum_{z, w \in Z} \gamma(z, e')\gamma(w, e'') \sum_{x, y \in [\alpha, \omega]} P^z(x)P^w(y)F(e', z, x, w, y)_e$ is the expected probability a player switches to strategy e if his own last strategy is e' and the sampled individual is using strategy e''. Also $F(e, e') \equiv \sum_{\{e'' \in S \mid e'' \neq e\}} F(e, e', e'')$ is the expected probability of switching to some other strategy from own strategy e if sampled strategy is e'.

Theorem 4.6.3   *If F is a good behavioral rule for $PB((S_k, [\alpha, \omega])_{k=1,..,N})$, then F is playwise imitative and satisfies*

$$F(e\backslash w, e) > F(e, e\backslash w) \qquad (4.6.2)$$

whenever $\pi(e) > \pi(e\backslash w)$. Conversely, if F is playwise imitative and satisfies (4.6.2), then the best strategy is asymptotically stable in any parallel bandit for which this strategy is unique.

Proof   Suppose that F is a good behavioral rule. Then $\Delta(\arg\max\{\pi(e) \mid e \in \times S_k\})$ is asymptotically stable for all bandits B in $PB((S_k, [\alpha, \omega])_{k=1,...,N})$. If F is not playwise imitating, there are payoffs $x, y \in [\alpha, \omega]$ such that $F(e, z, x, w, y)_{e'} > 0, \gamma(z, e) > 0$ and $P^z(x)P^w(y) > 0$ for some strategy $e' \notin \{e, e\backslash w\}$. Consider a bandit B in $PB((S_k, [\alpha, \omega])_{k=1,..,N})$ satisfying the conditions above for which $\pi(e) = \pi(e\backslash w) > \pi(e')$ for all strategies $e' \notin \{e, e\backslash w\}$. Then the set of best strategies for B, $\Delta\{e, e\backslash w\}$, is not invariant under F, and hence it is not asymptotically stable. By contradiction, F is playwise imitative.

If F does not satisfy (4.6.2), then $F(e\backslash w, e) \leq F(e, e\backslash w)$ for some B with $\pi(e) > \pi(e\backslash w)$. Consider a new bandit B' that has the same distribution as B at each endpoint z where $\gamma(z, e)$ or $\gamma(z, e\backslash w)$ is positive and has P^z the delta distribution at α otherwise (i.e., all realized payoffs at these z are the minimum possible payoff α). Then e is the unique best strategy. Since F is playwise imitative, $\Delta(\{e, e\backslash w\})$ is invariant from (4.6.1). Furthermore the one-dimensional dynamic on $\Delta(\{e, e\backslash w\})$ is

$$p'_e = p_e + p_e p_{e/w} \left(F(e\backslash w, e) - F(e, e\backslash w) \right).$$

Since $F(e\backslash w, e) \leq F(e, e\backslash w)$ is also true for B', e is not asymptotically stable. Thus F satisfies (4.6.2).

Conversely, suppose that F is playwise imitative and that (4.6.2) holds for some parallel bandit B which has a unique best strategy. This must be a pure strategy e^*. We will prove e^* is asymptotically stable through the linearization of (4.6.1) about $p_{e^*} = 1$.

For any other pure strategy e, the only relevant interaction terms in this linearization are those that involve e^*. If e differs from e^* in two or more decisions, then no individuals switch to e through these relevant interactions, and from (4.6.1) we can instead linearize

$$p'_e = p_e - p_e p_{e^*} F(e, e^*).$$

On the other hand, if $e = e^*\backslash w$ where $w \in Z_k$ (i.e., e differs from e^* exactly at decision k), we can consider

$$p'_e = p_e + p_e p_{e^*}(F(e^*, e) - F(e, e^*))$$
$$+ \sum_{e' \notin \{e^*, e\}} p_{e'} p_{e^*}(F(e^*, e', e) + F(e', e^*, e)).$$

Now order these pure strategies e so that those that differ from e^* at exactly one decision are before those that differ from e^* in two or more decisions. For these latter strategies, the only possible nonzero term in the corresponding row of the linearization is the diagonal entry $1 - F(e, e^*)$. For the former strategies, $\sum_{e' \notin \{e^*, e\}} p_{e'} p_{e^*}(F(e^*, e', e) + F(e', e^*, e))$ only involves strategies e' that differ from e^* in exactly two decisions. Furthermore the only possible nonzero entry that involves interactions of e^* with strategies that differ from e^* at exactly one decision is the diagonal entry $1 + F(e^*, e) - F(e, e^*)$.

Thus the Jacobian of the linearization is an upper triangular matrix, and so e^* is asymptotically stable if all its diagonal entries have modulus less than 1 (see the analysis at the end of chapter 2.7). By (4.6.2),

$$0 \leq 1 + F(e^*, e) - F(e, e^*) < 1$$

when e differs from e^* at exactly one decision. Similarly, for the remaining e (all of which differ from e^* in at least two decisions), clearly

$$0 \le 1 - F(e, e^*) < 1$$

if we can show that $F(e, e^*) > 0$ for all $e \ne e^*$. To verify this, choose a $w \in Z$ such that $\gamma(w, e^*) > \gamma(w, e) = 0$. Then, from the notation following (4.6.1),

$$F(e, e^*) \ge \gamma(w, e^*) \sum_{z \in Z} \gamma(z, e) \sum_{x, y \in [\alpha, \omega]} F(e, z, x, w, y)_{e/w} P^z(x) P^w(y)$$
$$= F(e, e \backslash w).$$

But $\pi(e \backslash w) > \pi(e)$, and so by (4.6.2), $F(e, e \backslash w) > F(e \backslash w, e) \ge 0$.

The eigenvalue analysis above shows e^* is asymptotically stable. ∎

Corollary 4.6.4 *If F makes the set of best strategies asymptotically stable in $PB((S_k, [\alpha, \omega])_{k=1,...,N})$, then the induced dynamic is never best reply monotone[31] for any bandit in $PB((S_k, [\alpha, \omega])_{k=1,...,N})$ that has at least two decision points $\{k, \ell\}$ and at least two actions at both of these with different expected payoffs.[32]*

Proof Consider a parallel bandit that has at least two decision points $\{k, \ell\}$ and at least two actions at each that have different expected payoffs. Let e be the strategy that leads to a best action at all decisions and e' be the same strategy as e except at k and ℓ where it leads to the worst action. Since e and e' differ at two decision points and F is playwise imitative, if $p \in \Delta(\{e, e'\})$ and $p_e p_{e'} > 0$, then $p'_e \le p_e$ by (4.6.1) since players using strategy e' cannot switch to strategy e in one time period. Thus F is not best-reply monotone. ∎

By corollary 4.6.4, none of the traditional best-reply monotone dynamics of evolutionary game theory (i.e., the replicator, best-reply or monotone selection dynamics) can be induced by behavioral rules based on

---

31. In a one-player game against nature, a *best reply monotone dynamic* is one that strictly increases the total frequency of the set of best pure strategies $\Delta\{\arg\max\{\pi(e) \mid e \in \times S_k\}\}$ if this frequency is not 0 or 1. These dynamics make the set of best strategies asymptotically stable in all parallel bandits. Furthermore all of the standard evolutionary dynamics are best reply monotone.

32. A parallel bandit that has at most one decision point with actions that have different expected payoffs can be treated as a single multi-armed bandit. As we will see, many of the behavioral rules from section 2.10 then easily generalize to induce a best reply monotone dynamic; namely the discrete replicator dynamic on these "degenerate" parallel bandits. This special circumstance is of little interest in the remainder of this section.

observed play of parallel bandits. However, there still are many good behavioral rules. For instance, consider the playwise imitative rule F that switches only after within-decision learning where switching rates are given by one of the imitative rules PIR, POR, and PRR of definition 2.10.2 in chapter 2—recall, for example, that the proportional imitation rule (PIR) imitates the sampled play (if its realized payoff is higher than that of one's own play) with probability proportional to the payoff difference. Then $F(e, z, x, w, y)_{e'} = 0$ if endpoints z and w follow different decision points, and from (2.10.2), $F(e\backslash z, z, x, w, y)_{e\backslash w} - F(e\backslash w, w, y, z, x)_{e\backslash z} = (y - x)/(\omega - \alpha)$ if $z, w \in Z_k$. Thus, for these latter z and w, $F(e\backslash z, e\backslash w) - F(e\backslash w, e\backslash z)$ is given by

$$(\rho_k)^2 \sum_{x, y \in [\alpha, \omega]} [F(e\backslash z, z, x, w, y)_{e\backslash w} - F(e\backslash w, w, y, z, x)_{e\backslash z}] P^z(x) P^w(y)$$

$$= (\rho_k)^2 \sum_{x, y \in [\alpha, \omega]} \frac{y - x}{\omega - \alpha} P^z(x) P^w(y)$$

$$= (\rho_k)^2 \frac{\pi_w - \pi_z}{\omega - \alpha} \tag{4.6.3}$$

$$= \rho_k \frac{\pi(e\backslash w) - \pi(e\backslash z)}{\omega - \alpha}.$$

This clearly satisfies (4.6.2), and by theorem 4.6.3, F is a good behavioral rule in any parallel bandit that contains a unique best strategy. In fact, for $z \in Z_k$, a similar calculation to (4.6.3) yields the following dynamic at decision k:

$$p'_z = p_z + (\rho_k)^2 p_z \sum_{w \in Z_k} p_w \left[\frac{\pi_z - \pi_w}{\omega - \alpha} \right]$$

$$= p_z + \frac{(\rho_k)^2}{\omega - \alpha} p_z \left(\pi_z - \sum_{w \in Z_k} p_w \pi_w \right).$$

This is a discrete version of the standard replicator dynamic. Thus we say F is a *subbandit monotone rule* at each of the N decision points since each induced dynamic in these multi-armed subbandits is a monotone selection dynamic.[33]

An important property of any subbandit monotone rule for a parallel bandit is that the frequency of the best action(s) at each decision increases

---

33. That is, if $z, w \in Z_k$ and $p_z p_w > 0$, then $p'_z/p'_w > p_z/p_w$ if and only if $\pi_z > \pi_w$. In analogy to chapter 2.10, it can be shown that the only traditional dynamic of evolutionary game theory that can be induced in a subbandit is the standard replicator dynamic.

(the increase is strict unless this frequency is either 0 or 1), and so the set of best strategies is globally asymptotically stable whether or not there is a unique best strategy. That is, any subbandit monotone rule is a good behavioral rule.

Rules that involve cross-decision learning (especially those based on PIR, POR, and PRR) can also be subbandit monotone. One, in particular, the playwise imitative rule F^{POR} that uses POR to determine switching probabilities whether or not the experienced and sampled endpoints follow the same decision (i.e., $F^{POR}(e, z, x, w, y)_{e \setminus w} = (y - \alpha)/(\omega - \alpha)$ whenever $w \in Z_k$ and $e_k \neq w$) deserves special attention. It satisfies a similar identity as (4.6.3); namely

$$F^{POR}(e \setminus z, e \setminus w) - F^{POR}(e \setminus w, e \setminus z) = \rho_k \frac{\pi_w - \pi_z}{\omega - \alpha} = \frac{\pi(e \setminus w) - \pi(e \setminus z)}{\omega - \alpha}$$

if $z, w \in Z_k$. The extra ρ_k factor in (4.6.3) reflects the fact that the F^{POR} rule can learn at decision k without experienced payoff occurring at this decision. The induced dynamic under F^{POR} at decision k is for any $z \in Z_k$,

$$p'_z = p_z + \frac{\rho_k}{\omega - \alpha} p_z \left(\pi_z - \sum_{w \in Z_k} p_w \pi_w \right). \tag{4.6.4}$$

In particular, F^{POR} is subbandit monotone and so is a good behavioral rule. We consider F^{POR} better than the rules that only involve within-decision learning since this dynamic evolves to the set of best strategies faster.[34]

These nice properties of F^{POR} are not surprising for the following heuristic reasons. An individual using the proportional observation rule (POR) ignores his own payoff and thus can treat each decision separately. Specifically, applying F^{POR} is as if the individual has N separate copies of the single decision rule POR, one for each decision. In each round the individual applies the copy of POR associated to the sampled decision. Of course, any other rule F^f (e.g., PRR or PIR) that satisfies $F^f(e, z, x, w, y) = f(x, y)$ if $z, w \in Z_k$ where

$$f(x, y) - f(y, x) = \frac{y - x}{\omega - \alpha} \tag{4.6.5}$$

---

34. The difference in speed of convergence is related to the difference between the factors ρ_k and $(\rho_k)^2$.

can be used instead for within-decision learning without changing the dynamic, since the experienced and sampled decision need not be separated in these circumstances. The notation, $F^{f/\text{POR}}$, denotes the rule that uses F^f for within-decision learning and POR for cross-decision learning. Although we do not select a favorite among the $F^{f/\text{POR}}$ rules here since they all induce the same dynamic for parallel bandits, the selection of f for within-decision learning becomes important for general extensive form bandits (see, in particular, the Centipede Bandit of chapter 8.4.1) where different f do induce different dynamics.

On the other hand, neither PRR nor PIR is intuitive to use under cross-decision learning. Both of these rules consider imitating play at the sampled decision ℓ based entirely (for PRR) or partially (for PIR) on payoffs realized at an unrelated decision $k \neq \ell$. Thus it is somewhat surprising that the playwise imitative rule F^{PRR}, which determines switching probabilities at the sampled decision solely by applying the copy of PRR associated to the experienced decision, satisfies (4.6.2) in theorem 4.6.3 and so is a good behavioral rule when there is a unique best strategy.[35] This is despite the fact that F^{PRR} is an elementary example of a behavioral rule that is not subbandit monotone. For instance, in the two-decision parallel bandit of figure 4.6.2 that has two actions at each decision and a unique optimal strategy, consider the highly correlated population where almost all individuals who use the best action at one decision use the worst at the other. Then cross-decision learning under F^{PRR} has a net effect of decreasing the proportion of the population who use the best action at both decisions.

Remark 4.6.5   The preceding counterintuitive results for F^{PRR} illustrate that it is dangerous to assume good behavioral rules exist simply because we can construct a rule F that is playwise imitative and satisfies (4.6.2). That is, the converse statement of theorem 4.6.3 leaves open the possibility that such an F may not make the set of best strategies asymptotically stable in all parallel bandits that do not have a unique best strategy. As seen already, this is mostly a technical issue in this section since we have explicitly constructed many good behavioral rules (e.g., the $F^{f/\text{POR}}$ rules). However, the issue becomes more important for the general extensive form bandits of chapter 8.4 since there are then rules that satisfy the conditions that correspond to those in theorem 4.6.3 but

---

35. Specifically, F^{PRR} is given by $F^{\text{PRR}}(e, z, x, w, y)_{e\backslash w} = (\omega - x)/(\omega - \alpha)$ if $w \neq z$. Thus $F^{\text{PRR}}(e\backslash w, e\backslash z) - F^{\text{PRR}}(e\backslash z, e\backslash w) = \sum_{z'\in Z}(\gamma(z', e\backslash w) - \gamma(z', e\backslash z))(\omega - \pi_{z'}/\omega - \alpha) = \rho_k(\pi_z - \pi_w)/(\omega - \alpha) = [\pi(e\backslash z) - \pi(e\backslash w)]/(\omega - \alpha)$.

none that always makes the set of best strategies asymptotically stable (see theorem 8.4.2 and remark 8.4.5).

4.7 Asymmetric Games with Two Roles

In this section we consider asymmetric games with $N = 2$ and $\rho(u_k, u_\ell) > 0$ for all $1 \leq k, \ell \leq 2$. Thus we consider games that are neither truly asymmetric nor truly symmetric. Sections 4.7.1 and 4.7.2 respectively emphasize two different aspects of these games: as models of truly asymmetric games with mistakes and as models of two-species intra- and inter-specific frequency-dependent evolution respectively. The emphasis in section 4.7.1 is on the added complexities that arise for the ES structure of asymmetric games that are neither truly asymmetric nor truly symmetric, whereas section 4.7.2 develops the two-species ESS concept and its dynamic consequences for general two-species frequency-dependent interactions.

4.7.1 A Family of Asymmetric Games

Theorems 4.5.3i and 4.6.1 state that ESSets are equivalent to local ESSets when the game is either truly asymmetric or truly symmetric. We will show that this statement is not true for general asymmetric games by considering the family of asymmetric games given in figure 4.7.1 that

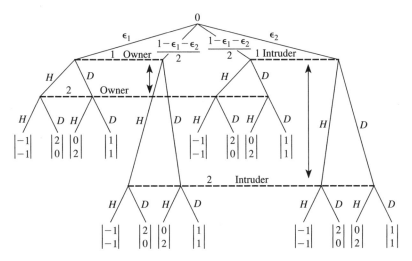

Figure 4.7.1
Owner-Intruder Game with mistakes.

are parameterized by ε_1 and ε_2. The two roles here are called Owner (u_1) and Intruder (u_2). One interpretation of the parameters is that player one in an Owner-Intruder Game makes a mistake in his role identification; namely, with probability ε_1 (ε_2 respectively), he mistakenly considers himself an intruder (an owner respectively).

The payoffs indicated in figure 4.7.1 assume that each $A_{k\ell}$ is the Hawk-Dove Game matrix $A = \begin{bmatrix} -1 & 2 \\ 0 & 1 \end{bmatrix}$ that, as a symmetric normal form game, has an ESS at $(\frac{1}{2}, \frac{1}{2})$. The ES structure of the asymmetric game can be analyzed for general parameters satisfying $0 \le \varepsilon_1 + \varepsilon_2 \le 1$. For instance, if ε_1 and ε_2 are sufficiently small (explicitly, if $\varepsilon_1 + 3\varepsilon_2 < 1$ and $3\varepsilon_1 + \varepsilon_2 < 1$), it can be shown that HD and DH are still strict[36] NE that are the only connected ESSets of this perturbation of the Owner-Intruder Game. On the other hand, the line segment

$$E = \{ p \in \Delta^4 \,|\, p^O = p^I = (\tfrac{1}{2}, \tfrac{1}{2}) \}$$

is always a set of NE. Furthermore, if $\varepsilon_1 + 3\varepsilon_2 > 1$ and $3\varepsilon_1 + \varepsilon_2 > 1$, then the connected NE component E is the only ESSet. This includes the truly symmetric game (i.e., $\varepsilon_1 + \varepsilon_2 = 1$) when the only interactions are either between two owners or between two intruders.

For our purposes it is sufficient to consider the continuum of asymmetric games between truly asymmetric and truly symmetric games parameterized by $\varepsilon_1 = \varepsilon_2 \equiv \varepsilon$ where $0 \le \varepsilon \le \frac{1}{2}$. The ES structure mentioned above becomes clear for this class of games through its 4×4 payoff matrix

$$M = \begin{array}{c} HH \\ HD \\ DH \\ DD \end{array} \begin{bmatrix} -1 & 1/2 & 1/2 & 2 \\ -1/2 & 1 - 2\varepsilon & 2\varepsilon & 3/2 \\ -1/2 & 2\varepsilon & 1 - 2\varepsilon & 3/2 \\ 0 & 1/2 & 1/2 & 1 \end{bmatrix}$$

and the following expression for $p \cdot M\hat{p} - \hat{p} \cdot M\hat{p}$ when $p \in E$:

$$
\begin{aligned}
p \cdot M\hat{p} &- \hat{p} \cdot M\hat{p} \\
&= \varepsilon[(p^O - \hat{p}^O) \cdot A\hat{p}^O + (p^I - \hat{p}^I) \cdot A\hat{p}^I] \\
&\quad + \left(\frac{1}{2} - \varepsilon \right) [(p^O - \hat{p}^O) \cdot A\hat{p}^I + (p^I - \hat{p}^I) \cdot A\hat{p}^O]
\end{aligned}
$$

---

36. We already know that these are strict NE for the truly asymmetric game when $\varepsilon_1 = \varepsilon_2 = 0$ by chapter 3.4.1 where this game is called the Symmetrized Owner-Intruder Game.

$$= \left(\frac{1}{2} - \varepsilon\right) [(p^O + p^I - \hat{p}^O - \hat{p}^I) \cdot A(\hat{p}^O + \hat{p}^I - p^O - p^I)]$$

$$+ \left(2\varepsilon - \frac{1}{2}\right) [(p^O - \hat{p}^O) \cdot A(\hat{p}^O - p^O) + (p^I - \hat{p}^I) \cdot A(\hat{p}^I - p^I)].$$

Specifically, when $0 \leq \varepsilon < \frac{1}{4}$, the strict NE, HD and DH, are the only connected ESSets for the payoff matrix above. Their basins of attraction are separated by the invariant triangle $\{p \in \Delta^4 \mid p_{12} = p_{21}\} = \{p \in \Delta^4 \mid p^O = p^I\}$ with vertices $(0, \frac{1}{2}, \frac{1}{2}, 0)$, $(1, 0, 0, 0)$ and $(0, 0, 0, 1)$. For $\frac{1}{4} < \varepsilon \leq \frac{1}{2}$, E is the (unique) ESSet since all the terms such as $(p^O - \hat{p}^O) \cdot A(\hat{p}^O - p^O)$ in the expansion above of $p \cdot M\hat{p} - \hat{p} \cdot M\hat{p}$ are nonnegative for the Hawk-Dove payoff matrix. Thus E is globally asymptotically stable under the asymmetric replicator dynamic (4.4.1). Finally, for $\varepsilon = \frac{1}{4}$, the triangle $\{p \in \Delta^4 \mid p^O + p^I = (1, 1)\} = \{p \in \Delta^4 \mid p_{11} = p_{22}\}$ with vertices $(\frac{1}{2}, 0, 0, \frac{1}{2})$, $(0, 1, 0, 0)$ and $(0, 0, 1, 0)$ is the unique ESSet. Furthermore this triangle is globally asymptotically stable since the payoffs now satisfy $p \cdot M\hat{p} = \frac{1}{4}(p^O + p^I) \cdot A(\hat{p}^O + \hat{p}^I)$, and so the dynamic trajectories induced on the one-dimensional simplex Δ^2 of vectors of the form $\frac{1}{2}(p^O + p^I)$ are those of the symmetric replicator dynamic (2.1.2) with respect to the payoff matrix $\frac{1}{4}A$.

The ES structure above shows that ESSets are no longer equivalent to local ESSets for asymmetric games that are neither truly asymmetric nor truly symmetric. Specifically, to determine local ESSets in figure 4.7.1, the game induced at role u_1 by any $p \in E$ is

$$
\begin{array}{c}
 \quad Hp^I \qquad Dp^I \\
\text{Owners} \quad
\begin{array}{c} H \\ D \end{array}
\left[
\begin{array}{cc}
\frac{1}{4} - \frac{3}{2}\varepsilon & \frac{1}{4} + \frac{3}{2}\varepsilon \\
\frac{1}{4} - \frac{1}{2}\varepsilon & \frac{1}{4} + \frac{1}{2}\varepsilon
\end{array}
\right].
\end{array}
$$

Thus $p^{O*} = (\frac{1}{2}, \frac{1}{2})$ is an ESS of this induced game for every $\varepsilon > 0$. Similarly $p^{I*} = (\frac{1}{2}, \frac{1}{2})$ is an ESS of the game induced at role u_2 in figure 4.7.1 by any $p \in E$. That is, $E = \text{proj}^{-1}[(p^{O*}, p^{I*})]$ is a local ESS for any $\varepsilon > 0$, but it is an ESSet if and only if $\varepsilon > \frac{1}{4}$ if and only if it is globally asymptotically stable. Thus the converse of theorem 4.2.2 is not true in general.

Remark 4.7.1 The preceding construction generalizes to any $n \times n$ symmetric normal form game A with strategy set S in place of the Hawk-Dove Game. If A has an interior ESS p^*, then the symmetrization of the bimatrix game (A, A) has a saddle point for the asymmetric replicator dynamic at the unique point on the Wright manifold that projects to (p^*, p^*) since the eigenvalues are those for A together with their negatives. Thus small mistake probabilities in role identification of this truly asymmetric game maintain the instability of the NE component $E = \{p \in \Delta(S \times S) \mid p^1 = p^* = p^2\}$, even though E automatically becomes a local ESSet. As the symmetric interactions become more predominant, E eventually emerges as an ESSet that is then globally asymptotically stable.

4.7.2   Two-Species Evolutionarily Stable Strategies

As noted in section 4.4.1, the asymmetric replicator dynamic for an asymmetric game with two roles induces the two-species replicator dynamic (4.4.4) on the Wright manifold. In this section we consider the special case where $\rho(u_k, u_\ell) = \frac{1}{4}$ for all $1 \leq k, \ell \leq 2$. [37] If $|S_1| = n$ and $|S_2| = m$ and we denote p^1 and p^2 by $p \in \Delta^n$ and $q \in \Delta^m$ respectively, the two-species replicator dynamic becomes

$$\dot{p}_i = p_i(e_i - p) \cdot (Ap + Bq),$$
$$\dot{q}_j = q_j(f_j - q) \cdot (Cp + Dq),$$
(4.7.1)

where $A \equiv \frac{1}{4}A_{11}$ and $D \equiv \frac{1}{4}A_{22}$ are payoff matrices of the appropriate size corresponding to intraspecific interactions and $B \equiv \frac{1}{4}A_{12}$ and $C \equiv \frac{1}{4}A_{21}$ refer to interspecific interactions. Thus figure 4.7.2 yields a dynamic on $\Delta^2 \times \Delta^3$.

If we assume that individuals engage in one random interspecific and one random intraspecific interaction per unit time,[38] the dynamic (4.7.1) models two-species frequency-dependent evolution (see Notes). Suppose that (p^*, q^*) is a rest point of (4.7.1). If $E \equiv \{\hat{p} \in \Delta^{nm} \mid \hat{p}^1 = p^*, \hat{p}^2 = q^*\}$ is an ESSet of the asymmetric game, then by section 4.4, (p^*, q^*) is asymptotically stable for (4.7.1). From definition 2.6.3 of chapter 2, E is an ESSet if and only if

$$p^* \cdot (Ap + Bq) + q^* \cdot (Cp + Dq) > p \cdot (Ap + Bq) + q \cdot (Cp + Dq)$$
(4.7.2)

---

37. The asymmetric game in section 4.7.1 when $\varepsilon_1 = \varepsilon_2 = 1/4$ (see figure 4.7.1) is an example of such a game where both species have two pure strategies. Figure 4.7.2 shows the extensive form when $|S_1| = 2$ and $|S_2| = 3$.
38. In particular, population sizes of both species remain in the same ratio over time. Here it is easiest to assume the population sizes are equal.

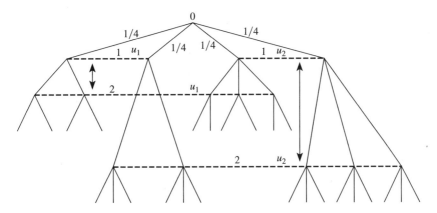

Figure 4.7.2
Extensive form of an asymmetric two-role game with two strategies in role u_1 and three in role u_2.

for all $(p, q) \in \Delta^n \times \Delta^m$ sufficiently close (but not equal) to (p^*, q^*). The following definition introduces the weaker concept of a two-species ESS that is sufficient to guarantee asymptotic stability for (4.7.1) by theorem 4.7.3.

Definition 4.7.2 $(p^*, q^*) \in \Delta^n \times \Delta^m$ *is a* two-species ESS *if, for all* $(p, q) \in \Delta^n \times \Delta^m$ *sufficiently close (but not equal) to* (p^*, q^*),

$$\text{either} \quad p^* \cdot (Ap + Bq) > p \cdot (Ap + Bq)$$
$$\text{(4.7.3)}$$
$$\text{or} \quad q^* \cdot (Cp + Dq) > q \cdot (Cp + Dq).$$

Theorem 4.7.3 *A two-species ESS* (p^*, q^*) *is asymptotically stable for* (4.7.1). *If* (p^*, q^*) *is in the interior of* $\Delta^n \times \Delta^m$, *then it is a two-species ESS if and only if there exists an* $r > 0$ *such that*

$$p^* \cdot (Ap + Bq) + rq^* \cdot (Cp + Dq) > p \cdot (Ap + Bq) + rq \cdot (Cp + Dq)$$
$$\text{(4.7.4)}$$

for all other $(p, q) \in \Delta^n \times \Delta^m$. *If* (p^*, q^*) *satisfies* (4.7.4), *it is globally asymptotically stable for* (4.7.1).

Proof We prove only those statements related to an interior (p^*, q^*) (see Notes). Clearly, (4.7.4) implies that (p^*, q^*) is a two-species ESS according to definition 4.7.2.

Now suppose that (p^*, q^*) is a two-species ESS in the interior of $\Delta^n \times \Delta^m$. Then (4.7.4) is equivalent to the fact that there is some line through the origin of $\mathbf{R}^2$ with negative slope (in fact, with slope $-1/r$) such that the compact set

$$K = \{((p^* - p) \cdot (Ap + Bq), (q^* - q) \cdot (Cp + Dq)) \mid (p, q) \in \Delta^n \times \Delta^m\}$$

lies entirely above the line except for the point $(0, 0)$ that corresponds to (p^*, q^*). On the other hand, definition 4.7.2 is equivalent to the statement that no points in K lie in quadrant III except $(0, 0)$. Suppose that there is no such $r > 0$. By the compactness of K, there must exist (p_1, q_1) and (p_2, q_2) in $\Delta^n \times \Delta^m$ that correspond to points in K that are in quadrants II and IV, respectively, and lie on the same line through the origin. Since (p^*, q^*) is in the interior of $\Delta^n \times \Delta^m$, $(p^* - p) \cdot (Ap^* + Bq^*) = 0$ and $(q^* - q) \cdot (Cp^* + Dq^*) = 0$ for all $(p, q) \in \Delta^n \times \Delta^m$.[39]

Let $p_\alpha = p^* + x_\alpha$ and $q_\alpha = q^* + y_\alpha$ for $\alpha = 1, 2$ be strategies in Δ^n and Δ^m respectively. Then x_α and y_α are in $X^n = \{x \in \mathbf{R}^n \mid \sum x_i = 0\}$ and Y^m respectively. Furthermore

$$x_1 \cdot (Ax_1 + By_1) = (p_1 - p^*) \cdot (A(p_1 - p^*) + B(q_1 - q^*))$$

$$= -(p^* - p_1) \cdot (Ap_1 + Bq_1),$$

$$y_1 \cdot (Cx_1 + Dy_1) = -(q^* - q_1) \cdot (Cp_1 + Dq_1),$$

and there are similar equalities for (x_2, y_2). If (x_1, y_1) and (x_2, y_2) are linearly dependent in $X^n \times Y^m$ (i.e., $(x_1, y_1) = \lambda(x_2, y_2)$ for some $\lambda \in \mathbf{R}$), then

$$x_1 \cdot (Ax_1 + By_1) = \lambda^2 x_2 \cdot (Ax_2 + By_2),$$

$$y_1 \cdot (Cx_1 + Dy_1) = \lambda^2 y_2 \cdot (Cx_2 + Dy_2). \tag{4.7.5}$$

Linear independence follows since (4.7.5) contradicts the choice of (p_1, q_1) and (p_2, q_2) in different quadrants.

The equations in (4.7.5) also show that, by taking suitable positive scalar multiples of (x_1, y_1) and (x_2, y_2), we may assume that

$$(x_1 \cdot (Ax_1 + By_1), y_1 \cdot (Cx_1 + Dy_1)) = -(x_2 \cdot (Ax_2 + By_2), y_2 \cdot (Cx_2 + Dy_2)),$$

and that $(p^*, q^*) + (x, y) \in \Delta^n \times \Delta^m$ for all (x, y) of the form $\cos \theta (x_1, y_1) + \sin \theta (x_2, y_2)$ for all $0 \le \theta \le 2\pi$. By linear independence, $(x, y) \ne (0, 0)$

---

39. Otherwise, p and q can be altered independently in such a way that both these expressions are nonpositive, contradicting the definition of a two-species ESS.

for any θ. By the double angle formulas of trigonometry,

$$
\begin{aligned}
x \cdot (Ax + By) &= (\cos\theta x_1 + \sin\theta x_2) \cdot (A(\cos\theta x_1 + \sin\theta x_2) \\
&\quad + B(\cos\theta y_1 + \sin\theta y_2)) \\
&= x_1 \cdot (Ax_1 + By_1)\cos^2\theta + x_2 \cdot (Ax_2 + By_2)\sin^2\theta \\
&\quad + (x_1 \cdot (Ax_2 + By_2) + x_2 \cdot (Ax_1 + By_1))\cos\theta\sin\theta \\
&= x_1 \cdot (Ax_1 + By_1)\cos 2\theta + \tfrac{1}{2}(x_1 \cdot (Ax_2 + By_2) \\
&\quad + x_2 \cdot (Ax_1 + By_1))\sin 2\theta.
\end{aligned}
$$

By a similar calculation,

$$
\begin{aligned}
y \cdot (Cx + Dy) &= y_1 \cdot (Cx_1 + Dy_1)\cos 2\theta \\
&\quad + \tfrac{1}{2}(y_1 \cdot (Cx_2 + Dy_2) + y_2 \cdot (Cx_1 + Dy_1))\sin 2\theta.
\end{aligned}
$$

Consider the points $(x \cdot (Ax + By), y \cdot (Cx + Dy))$ in K as θ varies. When $\theta = 0$, the point is $-((p^* - p_1) \cdot (Ap_1 + Bq_1), (q^* - q_1) \cdot (Cp_1 + Dq_1))$, and this is in quadrant IV. Similarly, when $\theta = \pi/2$, the point is in quadrant II. Thus, for some θ_0 between 0 and $\pi/2$, the point has zero first component, and since (p^*, q^*) is a two-species ESS, negative second. Then, for $\theta = \theta_0 + \pi/2$, the point has zero first component and positive second, which is a contradiction. Thus (4.7.4) holds.

To complete the proof, suppose that (4.7.4) holds. Consider the non-negative function $V : \Delta^n \times \Delta^m \to \mathbf{R}$ given by

$$
V(p, q) = \prod_{i=1}^{n}(p_i)^{p_i^*} \left(\prod_{j=1}^{m}(q_j)^{q_j^*} \right)^r.
$$

Then V has a global maximum at (p^*, q^*), and by the analogous calculation using (4.7.1) as in chapter 2.7,

$$
\dot{V}(p, q) = V(p, q)\,[(p^* - p) \cdot (Ap + Bq) + r(q^* - q) \cdot (Cp + Dq)].
$$

Thus $\dot{V}(p, q) > 0$ for all (p, q) in the interior of $\Delta^n \times \Delta^m$ except at (p^*, q^*), and so V is a strict Lyapunov function which proves the global asymptotic stability of (p^*, q^*) under (4.7.1). ∎

There are two important special cases of the theory developed above where (4.7.2) and (4.7.3) are equivalent. First, suppose that there is no intraspecific selection pressure (i.e., the entries in A are all equal as are all the entries in D). Since $p^* \cdot Ap = p \cdot Ap$ for all $p \in \Delta^n$, (4.7.3) with $(p, q) = (p, q^*)$ sufficiently close (but not equal) to (p^*, q^*) implies that $p^* \cdot Bq^* > p \cdot Bq^*$. Similarly $q^* \cdot Cp^* > q \cdot Cp^*$. Clearly, (p^*, q^*) is a two-species ESS if and only if it is a strict NE (cf. definition 3.1.1 of chapter 3) of the bimatrix game (B, C) that ignores intraspecific interactions.

Second, if there are no interspecific selection pressures, (4.7.3) implies that $p^* \cdot Ap > p \cdot Ap$ and $q^* \cdot Dq > q \cdot Aq$ for all $p \neq p^*$ and $q \neq q^*$ sufficiently close to (p^*, q^*). That is, (p^*, q^*) is a two-species ESS if and only if p^* is an ESS for the symmetric game with payoff matrix A and q^* is an ESS for the symmetric game with payoff matrix D (cf. theorem 2.7.1 of chapter 2) if and only if (p^*, q^*) satisfies (4.7.2).

In either the case of no interspecific selection or of no intraspecific selection, dynamic stability results follow from the relevant theorems in chapters 2 and 3 respectively. On the other hand, it is clear from the comparison of (4.7.4) to (4.7.2) that two-species ESSs do not always correspond to ESSets of the asymmetric game when there are bona fide intra- and interspecific selection pressures. In fact the following example shows that in an asymmetric game, the NE component corresponding to a two-species ESS is not always asymptotically stable off the Wright manifold.

Example 4.7.4   (A Perturbed Buyer-Seller Game)   Consider the Buyer-Seller Game with bimatrix[40]

$$
\begin{array}{cc}
 & \text{Seller} \\
 & \begin{array}{cc} H & C \end{array} \\
\text{Buyer} \begin{array}{c} T \\ I \end{array} & \begin{bmatrix} 5,4 & 1,6 \\ 4,0 & 2,-2 \end{bmatrix}
\end{array}.
$$

From chapter 3.3.1, $p^* = (\frac{1}{2}, \frac{1}{2}) = q^*$ is a neutrally stable rest point of the bimatrix replicator dynamic that now models interspecific interactions with $B = \begin{bmatrix} 5 & 1 \\ 4 & 2 \end{bmatrix}$ and $C = \begin{bmatrix} 4 & 0 \\ 6 & -2 \end{bmatrix}$.[41] If we perturb the game by adding intraspecific interactions with 2×2 payoff matrices for which p^* is an interior ESS for A and q^* for D, intuitively (p^*, q^*) should be asymptotically stable. In fact we will see that (p^*, q^*) becomes a two-species ESS, although $E = \{\hat{p} \in \Delta^{nm} \mid \hat{p}^1 = p^*, \hat{p}^2 = q^*\}$ is not an ESSet of the

---

40. One payoff entry in the bimatrix was changed from those given in chapter 3.3.1 to simplify the mathematical calculations. This change does not affect the qualitative features of the NE structure or the bimatrix replicator dynamic.

41. Note that so far in this example, C is used to denote two different things; namely this 2×2 payoff matrix or the Seller's strategy "Cheat." Its meaning will be clear from the context in which it is used.

asymmetric game since it is not asymptotically stable for the asymmetric replicator dynamic.

The NE component of the asymmetric game based on A, B, C, D is

$$E = \left\{ \left(\tfrac{1}{4} + \lambda, \tfrac{1}{4} - \lambda, \tfrac{1}{4} - \lambda, \tfrac{1}{4} + \lambda \right) \mid |\lambda| \leq \tfrac{1}{4} \right\},$$

when the pure strategies are ordered as TH, TC, IH, IC. From chapter 3.4.1 we know the points of E for which $\lambda < 0$ are unstable for the Buyer-Seller Game. Thus, if the additional intraspecific interactions are sufficiently small, we expect these points to remain unstable when λ is sufficiently small. The mathematical details for these assertions follow:

Let $A = \varepsilon \begin{bmatrix} -1 & 2 \\ 0 & 1 \end{bmatrix} = D$ where $\varepsilon > 0$. First, with $p^* - p = (x, -x)$ and $q^* - q = (y, -y)$, $(p^* - p) \cdot (Ap + Bq) = -2\varepsilon x^2 + 2xy$ and $(q^* - q) \cdot (Cp + Dq) = -2\varepsilon y^2 - 4xy$. Thus

$$(p^* - p) \cdot (Ap + Bq) + \tfrac{1}{2}(q^* - q) \cdot (Cp + Dq) = -\varepsilon(2x^2 + y^2),$$

and (p^*, q^*) is a two-species ESS for all $\varepsilon > 0$ since it satisfies (4.7.4) with the parameter $r = \tfrac{1}{2}$.

From (2.7.2) the linearization of the asymmetric replicator dynamic about $(\tfrac{1}{4} + \lambda, \tfrac{1}{4} - \lambda, \tfrac{1}{4} - \lambda, \tfrac{1}{4} + \lambda) \in \Delta^4$ is given by the 4×4 matrix

$$L = \begin{bmatrix} -\left(\varepsilon + \tfrac{1}{2}\right)\left(\tfrac{1}{4} + \lambda\right) & -\tfrac{3}{2}\left(\tfrac{1}{4} + \lambda\right) & \tfrac{3}{2}\left(\tfrac{1}{4} + \lambda\right) & \left(\varepsilon + \tfrac{1}{2}\right)\left(\tfrac{1}{4} + \lambda\right) \\ \tfrac{3}{2}\left(\tfrac{1}{4} - \lambda\right) & \left(\tfrac{1}{2} - \varepsilon\right)\left(\tfrac{1}{4} - \lambda\right) & \left(\varepsilon - \tfrac{1}{2}\right)\left(\tfrac{1}{4} - \lambda\right) & -\tfrac{3}{2}\left(\tfrac{1}{4} - \lambda\right) \\ -\tfrac{3}{2}\left(\tfrac{1}{4} - \lambda\right) & \left(\varepsilon - \tfrac{1}{2}\right)\left(\tfrac{1}{4} - \lambda\right) & \left(\tfrac{1}{2} - \varepsilon\right)\left(\tfrac{1}{4} - \lambda\right) & \tfrac{3}{2}\left(\tfrac{1}{4} - \lambda\right) \\ \left(\varepsilon + \tfrac{1}{2}\right)\left(\tfrac{1}{4} + \lambda\right) & \tfrac{3}{2}\left(\tfrac{1}{4} + \lambda\right) & -\tfrac{3}{2}\left(\tfrac{1}{4} + \lambda\right) & -\left(\varepsilon + \tfrac{1}{2}\right)\left(\tfrac{1}{4} + \lambda\right) \end{bmatrix},$$

which has eigenvalues $0, 0, -\tfrac{\varepsilon}{2} - \lambda \pm \tfrac{1}{2}\sqrt{16\lambda^2\varepsilon^2 + 36\lambda^2 + 4\lambda\varepsilon} - 2$. Thus, for positive ε sufficiently small so that there is a λ for which $-\tfrac{1}{4} < \lambda < -\tfrac{\varepsilon}{2}$, L has eigenvalues with positive real part, and so the corresponding point in E is unstable.

Remark 4.7.5 The analysis in this section has concerned interior two-species ESSs for the most part. The characterization (4.7.4) given in theorem 4.7.4 can be extended to those ESSs on the boundary that are regular.[42] Specifically, (p^*, q^*) is a regular two-species ESS if and only if it is a quasi-strict NE that satisfies (4.7.4) for all other $(p, q) \in \text{supp}(p^*) \times \text{supp}(q^*)$. This characterization is especially appealing in the case that one component of (p^*, q^*) is a pure strategy.

---

42. A two-species ESS is *regular* if it is also a quasi-strict NE (cf. theorem 2.7.4 in chapter 2).

For instance, if q^* is a pure strategy and p^* is in the interior of Δ^n, then (p^*, q^*) is a regular two-species ESS if and only if $q \cdot (Cp^* + Dq^*) < q^* \cdot (Cp^* + Dq^*)$ whenever $q \neq q^*$ and p^* is a (single-species) ESS for the game induced in species one by fixing species two at q^*. Furthermore, if p^* and q^* are both pure strategies, (p^*, q^*) is a regular two-species ESS if and only if it is a strict NE.

4.8   A Hierarchical Hawk-Dove Game

General asymmetric games with more than two roles (i.e., $N > 2$) are difficult to analyze either for their ES structure or for their dynamic behavior (see Notes). Sections 4.2.1 and 4.5.1 considered these questions for a three-role truly asymmetric game where each role had two possible pure strategies and payoff matrices were independent of role assignment. In this section we consider a particular N-role asymmetric game that is neither truly asymmetric nor truly symmetric where each role has two possible pure strategies, Hawk or Dove. Figure 4.8.1 gives the three-role extensive form version of this game.

Each role now corresponds to a tier in the structured population. We assume that when two Hawks compete, the individual in the higher tier has a better chance of winning the resource and that this probability

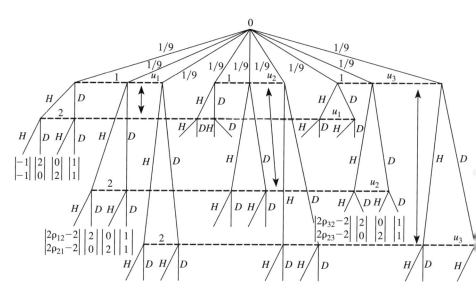

Figure 4.8.1
Three-tier hierarchical Hawk-Dove Game when $V = 2 = C$.

of winning increases as the number of tiers between them increases. Furthermore payoffs in all other pairwise contests are independent of the players' tiers. Specifically, let $\rho_{k\ell}$ be the probability a Hawk in tier k wins the resource in a contest against a Hawk in tier ℓ (in particular, $\rho_{\ell\ell} = \frac{1}{2}$ and $\rho_{k\ell} + \rho_{\ell k} = 1$). Our assumption becomes $\rho_{k\ell} > \rho_{k+1,\ell}$ and $\rho_{k\ell} > \rho_{k,\ell-1}$ whenever all subscripts are between the highest and lowest tiers, 1 and N, respectively. From the Hawk-Dove Game of chapter 2.2, the payoff matrix $A_{k\ell}$ is then given by

$$A_{k\ell} = \begin{bmatrix} V\rho_{k\ell} - C & V \\ 0 & \dfrac{V}{2} \end{bmatrix}, \tag{4.8.1}$$

where $C > V\rho_{k\ell} > 0$. These payoffs when $N = 3$ are indicated in figure 4.8.1.[43]

Hierarchical Hawk-Dove Games are elementary biological models of populations that are structured on such characteristics as individual size. For instance, suppose that there are N possible sizes of individuals in a population and that the expected outcome of Hawk–Hawk contests is based on relative size (e.g., a larger combatant on average does better than a smaller one). The Hierarchical Hawk-Dove Game then models the situation where each individual knows his own size but not that of his opponent.

When $N = 1$, we have the (symmetric) Hawk-Dove Game, and so the population evolves to the mixed-strategy ESS, $(V/2, C - V/2)/C$. When $N > 1$, we will see that there is a threshold tier such that eventually all individuals at higher tiers play Hawk and all individuals at lower tiers play Dove.[44] In fact we will see that this limiting behavior corresponds to a globally asymptotically stable ESS of this asymmetric game. To show these results, we first describe an algorithm to construct a NE of the Hierarchical Hawk-Dove Game. The algorithm repeatedly uses the fact that from (4.8.1),

$$\pi_k(D, p) = \pi_\ell(D, p) \text{ and } \pi_k(H, p) \geq \pi_{k+1}(H, p)$$

for all $p \in \Delta(S)$ whenever all subscripts are between 1 and N.

---

43. The notation $\rho_{k\ell}$ is not to be confused with the probability $\rho(u_k, u_\ell)$ that nature assigns roles u_k and u_ℓ to players one and two respectively. We assume there are the same number of individuals in each role and that there are random pairwise contests. That is, we assume $\rho(u_k, u_\ell) = 1/N^2$ for all $1 \leq k, \ell \leq N$ (and so we can ignore this factor by including it in each payoff matrix $A_{k\ell}$).

44. At this threshold tier, the average local behavior strategy may be mixed.

Step 1 Set p^* to the pure strategy, denoted $HH\ldots H$, that plays Hawk in each tier. If $\pi_N(H, p^*) \geq \pi_N(D, p^*)$,[45] then $\pi_k(H, p^*) \geq \pi_N(H, p^*) \geq \pi_N(D, p^*) = \pi_k(D, p^*)$ for all k, and so p^* is a NE and we stop.

If $\pi_N(H, p^*) < \pi_N(D, p^*)$, then we compare $\pi_N(H, p^*\backslash D^N)$ to $\pi_N(D, p^*\backslash D^N)$ where $p^*\backslash D^N$ plays Hawk in each tier except the last (i.e., tier N) where it plays Dove. If $\pi_N(H, p^*\backslash D^N) \geq \pi_N(D, p^*\backslash D^N)$, then there is a unique (mixed) strategy M in Δ^2 such that $\pi_N(H, p^*\backslash M^N) = \pi_N(D, p^*\backslash M^N)$.[46] $p^*\backslash M^N$ is a NE since $\pi_k(H, p^*\backslash M^N) \geq \pi_N(H, p^*\backslash M^N) = \pi_N(D, p^*\backslash M^N) = \pi_k(D, p^*\backslash M^N)$ and we stop. Otherwise (i.e., if $\pi_N(H, p^*\backslash D^N) < \pi_N(D, p^*\backslash D^N)$), we replace p^* by $p^*\backslash D^N$ and we proceed to the next step.

Step 2 If $\pi_{N-1}(H, p^*) \geq \pi_{N-1}(D, p^*)$, then $\pi_k(H, p^*) \geq \pi_{N-1}(H, p^*) \geq \pi_{N-1}(D, p^*) = \pi_k(D, p^*)$ for all $1 \leq k \leq N-1$ and $\pi_N(D, p^*) > \pi_N(H, p^*)$. Thus p^* is a NE and we stop.

If $\pi_{N-1}(H, p^*) < \pi_{N-1}(D, p^*)$, then we compare $\pi_{N-1}(H, p^*\backslash D^{N-1})$ to $\pi_{N-1}(D, p^*\backslash D^{N-1})$. If $\pi_{N-1}(H, p^*\backslash D^{N-1}) \geq \pi_{N-1}(D, p^*\backslash D^{N-1})$, then $p^*\backslash M^{N-1}$ is a NE where M is a unique (mixed) strategy in Δ^2 that satisfies $\pi_{N-1}(H, p^*\backslash M^{N-1}) = \pi_{N-1}(D, p^*\backslash M^{N-1})$. This follows from the facts that if $1 \leq k \leq N-1$, then

$$\pi_k(H, p^*\backslash M^{N-1}) \geq \pi_{N-1}(H, p^*\backslash M^{N-1}) = \pi_{N-1}(D, p^*\backslash M^{N-1})$$

$$= \pi_k(D, p^*\backslash M^{N-1}),$$

and when $k = N$,

$$\pi_N(D, p^*\backslash M^{N-1}) = \pi_{N-1}(D, p^*\backslash M^{N-1}) = \pi_{N-1}(H, p^*\backslash M^{N-1})$$

$$\geq \pi_N(H, p^*\backslash M^{N-1}).$$

Finally, if $\pi_{N-1}(H, p^*) < \pi_{N-1}(D, p^*)$ and $\pi_{N-1}(H, p^*\backslash D^{N-1}) < \pi_{N-1}(D, p^*\backslash D^{N-1})$, then we replace p^* by $p^*\backslash D^{N-1}$, and we proceed to the next step.

---

45. Note that this can never happen given our assumption that $V\rho_{k\ell} - C < 0$. We include this case only for the sake of completeness when comparing this first step to the other steps in the algorithm.

46. In fact $M = (\alpha, 1 - \alpha)$ where $\alpha = [\pi_N(H, p^*\backslash D) - \pi_N(D, p^*\backslash D)]/[\pi_N(H, p^*\backslash D) - \pi_N(D, p^*\backslash D) + \pi_N(D, p^*) - \pi_N(H, p^*)]$.

We continue these steps until we compare, if necessary, $\pi_1(H, p^*)$ to $\pi_1(D, p^*)$ where $p^* = HD\ldots D$. Since $\pi_1(H, p^*\backslash D^1) > \pi_1(D, p^*\backslash D^1)$, the final replacement that then yields a NE p^* will never have all individuals at every tier playing Dove (or, as noted above, Hawk). Furthermore, at whatever tier we stop, all individuals above this tier play Hawk and below play Dove (i.e., we stop at the threshold tier).

The algorithm described above constructs a single NE p^*. Furthermore, since $p^* \in \Delta(S)$ induces a mixed local behavior strategy in at most one tier, no other $p \in \Delta(S)$ can induce the same local behavior strategy. Thus, if $p \neq p^*$, then $p^{*k} \neq p^k$ for some k. We use this fact to show that $\pi(p^* - p, p) > 0$ for all $p \neq p^*$.[47] Notice that if $\pi(p^* - p, p^* - p) = \pi(p^* - p, p^*) - \pi(p^* - p, p)$ is negative, then $\pi(p^* - p, p) > 0$ since p^* a NE implies $\pi(p^* - p, p^*) \geq 0$. Now, with $p^{*k} - p^k \in X^2$ written as $(x^k, -x^k)$,

$$\pi(p^* - p, p^* - p) = \sum_{k,\ell} (x^k, -x^k) \cdot A_{k\ell}(x^\ell, -x^\ell)$$

$$= \sum_{k,\ell} (V\rho_{k\ell} - C - V + V/2)x^k x^\ell$$

$$= -C \sum_k (x^k)^2 + \sum_{k=1}^{N}\sum_{\ell=1}^{k-1} (V\rho_{k\ell} + V\rho_{\ell k} - 2C - V)x^k x^\ell$$

$$= -C \sum_{k,\ell} x^k x^\ell = -C \left(\sum_k x^k\right)^2. \tag{4.8.2}$$

Thus $\pi(p^* - p, p^* - p) < 0$ whenever $p \neq p^*$, and this completes the proof that p^* is an ESS and so asymptotically stable for the replicator dynamic (2.1.2). In fact, by theorem 2.7.4 in chapter 2, p^* is globally asymptotically stable for the replicator, best response and fictitious play dynamics.[48]

---

47. Here $\pi(p^* - p, p)$ is a shortened notation for $\pi(p^*, p) - \pi(p, p)$. Recall that $\pi(p^*, p)$ is the expected payoff to strategy p^* in a contest against p and that we have ignored the factor $\rho(u_k, u_\ell) = 1/N^2$.

48. Notice that $\pi(p^* - p, p^* - p) < 0$ whenever $p \neq p^*$ as long as $C > 0$. A careful examination of the above discussion shows the algorithm to find the globally asymptotically stable ESS is still correct even if $V\rho_{k\ell} > C > 0$ for some k and ℓ. That is, hierarchical games do not have to be based on the Hawk-Dove Game. For instance, if $V\rho_{N1} > C > 0$, then $HH\ldots H$ is the ESS and, in this case, also a strict NE.

4.9   Appendix A

Proof of Theorem 4.4.2

Let us first show (4.4.6). From (4.4.5),

$$
\dot{p}^1_{i_1} = \sum_{j_2,\dots,j_N} \dot{p}_{i_1 j_2 \dots j_N}
$$

$$
= \sum_{j_2,\dots,j_N} \sum_{\ell=1}^{N} \rho(u_1, u_\ell) \left[\sum_{j_1} p_{j_1 j_2 \dots j_N} BR^1_{i_1}(p) - p_{i_1 j_2 \dots j_N} \right]
$$

$$
+ \sum_{j_2,\dots,j_N} \sum_{\ell=1}^{N} \rho(u_2, u_\ell) \left[\sum_{j'_2} p_{i_1 j'_2 j_3 \dots j_N} BR^2_{j_2}(p) - p_{i_1 j_2 \dots j_N} \right]
$$

$$
+ \cdots + \sum_{j_2,\dots,j_N} \sum_{\ell=1}^{N} \rho(u_N, u_\ell) \left[\sum_{j'_N} p_{i_1 j_2 j_3 \dots j'_N} BR^2_{j_N}(p) - p_{i_1 j_2 \dots j_N} \right]
$$

$$
= \sum_{\ell=1}^{N} \rho(u_1, u_\ell) \left[BR^1_{i_1}(p) - p^1_{i_1} \right].
$$

This is because $\sum_{j_2,\dots,j_N} \sum_{\ell=1}^{N} \rho(u_2, u_\ell)[\sum_{j'_2} p_{i_1 j'_2 j_3 \dots j_N} BR^2_{j_2}(p) - p_{i_1 j_2 \dots j_N}] = \sum_{\ell=1}^{N} \rho(u_2, u_\ell) \cdot \sum_{j_2,\dots,j_N} [p_{i_1 j_2 \dots j_N} - p_{i_1 j_2 \dots j_N}] = 0$, and so on.

The remainder of the proof is restricted to the case $N = 3$. To complete the proof in general requires induction on N. Consider the expression $d[p_{i_1 i_2 i_3} - p^1_{i_1} p^2_{i_2} p^3_{i_3}]/dt$. By (4.4.5) and (4.4.6), this equals

$$
\sum_{\ell=1}^{N} \rho(u_1, u_\ell) \left[\sum_{j_1} p_{j_1 i_2 i_3} BR^1_{i_1}(p) - p_{i_1 i_2 i_3} \right]
$$

$$
- \sum_{\ell=1}^{N} \rho(u_1, u_\ell) \left[BR^1_{i_1}(p) - p^1_{i_1} \right] p^2_{i_2} p^3_{i_3}
$$

$$
+ \sum_{\ell=1}^{N} \rho(u_2, u_\ell) \left[\sum_{j_2} p_{i_1 j_2 i_3} BR^2_{i_2}(p) - p_{i_1 i_2 i_3} \right]
$$

$$
- \sum_{\ell=1}^{N} \rho(u_2, u_\ell) \left[BR^2_{i_2}(p) - p^2_{i_2} \right] p^1_{i_1} p^3_{i_3}
$$

$$
+ \sum_{\ell=1}^{N} \rho(u_3, u_\ell) \left[\sum_{j_3} p_{i_1 i_2 j_3} BR^3_{j_2}(p) - p_{i_1 i_2 i_3} \right]
$$

$$- \sum_{\ell=1}^{N} \rho(u_3, u_\ell) \left[BR^3_{i_3}(p) - p^3_{i_3} \right] p^1_{i_1} p^2_{i_2}$$

$$= \sum_{\ell=1}^{N} \rho(u_1, u_\ell) \left[\left(\sum_{j_1} p_{j_1 i_2 i_3} - p^2_{i_2} p^3_{i_3} \right) BR^1_{i_1}(p) - \left(p_{i_1 i_2 i_3} - p^1_{i_1} p^2_{i_2} p^3_{i_3} \right) \right]$$

$$+ \sum_{\ell=1}^{N} \rho(u_2, u_\ell) \left[\left(\sum_{j_2} p_{i_1 j_2 i_3} - p^1_{i_1} p^3_{i_3} \right) BR^2_{i_2}(p) - \left(p_{i_1 i_2 i_3} - p^1_{i_1} p^2_{i_2} p^3_{i_3} \right) \right]$$

$$+ \sum_{\ell=1}^{N} \rho(u_3, u_\ell) \left[\left(\sum_{j_3} p_{i_1 i_2 j_3} - p^1_{i_1} p^2_{i_2} \right) BR^3_{i_3}(p) - \left(p_{i_1 i_2 i_3} - p^1_{i_1} p^2_{i_2} p^3_{i_3} \right) \right].$$

By the same argument used in (3.4.4) of chapter 3, $d[\sum_{j_1}(p_{j_1 i_2 i_3} - p^2_{i_2} p^3_{i_3})]/dt = -\sum_{\ell=1}^{N}(\rho(u_2, u_\ell) + \rho(u_3, u_\ell)) \sum_{j_1}(p_{j_1 i_2 i_3} - p^2_{i_2} p^3_{i_3})$. Thus $\sum_{j_1}(p_{j_1 i_2 i_3} - p^2_{i_2} p^3_{i_3}) = B_{23} e^{-c_{23} t}$, where $c_{23} \equiv \sum_{\ell=1}^{N}(\rho(u_2, u_\ell) + \rho(u_3, u_\ell))$ and B_{23} is some constant.

That is,

$$\frac{d}{dt} \left[p_{i_1 i_2 i_3} - p^1_{i_1} p^2_{i_2} p^3_{i_3} \right]$$

$$= - \sum_{\ell=1}^{N} (\rho(u_1, u_\ell) + \rho(u_2, u_\ell) + \rho(u_3, u_\ell)) \left[p_{i_1 i_2 i_3} - p^1_{i_1} p^2_{i_2} p^3_{i_3} \right]$$

$$+ \sum_{\ell=1}^{N} \rho(u_1, u_\ell) B_{23} e^{-c_{23} t} BR^1_{i_1}(p) + \sum_{\ell=1}^{N} \rho(u_2, u_\ell) B_{13} e^{-c_{13} t} BR^2_{i_2}(p)$$

$$+ \sum_{\ell=1}^{N} \rho(u_3, u_\ell) B_{12} e^{-c_{12} t} BR^3_{i_3}(p).$$

Let $c_{123} \equiv \sum_{\ell=1}^{N} (\rho(u_1, u_\ell) + \rho(u_2, u_\ell) + \rho(u_3, u_\ell))$. Then

$$\left| p_{i_1 i_2 i_3}(t) - p^1_{i_1}(t) p^2_{i_2}(t) p^3_{i_3}(t) \right|$$

$$\leq e^{-c_{123} t} \int_0^t e^{c_{123} s} \left| B_{23} e^{-c_{23} s} BR^1_{i_1}(p) + B_{13} e^{-c_{13} s} BR^2_{i_2}(p) \right.$$

$$\left. + B_{12} e^{-c_{12} s} BR^3_{i_3}(p) \right| ds$$

$$\leq 3 \max \left\{ \frac{|B_{23}|}{\sum_{\ell=1}^{3} \rho(u_1, u_\ell)}, \frac{|B_{13}|}{\sum_{\ell=1}^{3} \rho(u_2, u_\ell)}, \frac{|B_{12}|}{\sum_{\ell=1}^{3} \rho(u_3, u_\ell)} \right\}$$

$$\times e^{-\left(\min_k \left(\sum_{\ell=1}^{3} \rho(u_k, u_\ell) \right) \right) t}.$$

That is, $|p_{i_1 i_2 i_3}(t) - p_{i_1}^1(t) p_{i_2}^2(t) p_{i_3}^3(t)| \le B \exp(-ct)$ for some constants B and c that can be chosen independent of the initial conditions. Thus all trajectories converge to the Wright manifold.

Furthermore, by a similar induction argument, if $p_{i_1 i_2 i_3}(t) - p_{i_1}^1(t) p_{i_2}^2(t)$ $p_{i_3}^3(t)$ is close to 0 initially, the constants B_{ij} above are also close to 0. Thus $p_{i_1 i_2 i_3}(t) - p_{i_1}^1(t) p_{i_2}^2(t) p_{i_3}^3(t)$ will remain close to 0, and so the Wright manifold is globally asymptotically stable. ∎

4.10   Appendix B

Proof of Lemma 4.5.2

The proof is based on Liouville's formula for the divergence of a vector field (for a dynamical system). In particular, for any subset H of initial conditions, this formula shows the volume of $\{p(t) \mid p(0) \text{ is in } H\}$ is independent of t if the vector field has zero divergence (see Notes). To apply this method to the N-player replicator dynamic (4.4.4), we first divide the vector field by $\prod(p) \equiv \prod_{k=1}^{N} \prod_{i_k=1}^{|S_k|} p_{i_k}^k$. Since $\prod(p) > 0$ for all p in the interior of the strategy space $\Delta(S_1) \times \cdots \times \Delta(S_N)$, a closed set H in this interior will be asymptotically stable under (4.4.4) if and only if it is asymptotically stable under the transformed vector field.

The divergence of the transformed dynamic restricted to $\Delta(S_1) \times \cdots \times \Delta(S_N)$ is given by

$$\sum_{k=1}^{N} \sum_{i_k=1}^{|S_k|-1} \frac{\partial \dot{p}_{i_k}^k}{p_{i_k}^k},$$

where $\dot{p}_{i_k}^k$ equals the final expression of (4.4.4) divided by $\prod(p)$ and $p_{i|S_k|}^k$ is replaced by $1 - \sum_{i_k=1}^{|S_k|-1} p_{i_k}^k$ due to the invariance of the strategy space. Consider the contribution to the divergence from species one (i.e., $k = 1$). Since the game is truly asymmetric, the quotient rule implies that $(\prod(p))^2 \sum_{i_1=1}^{|S_1|-1} \partial \dot{p}_{i_1}^1 / p_{i_1}^1$ equals

$$\sum_{i_1=1}^{|S_1|-1} \left\{ \begin{array}{l} \left[\sum_{\ell=2}^{N} \rho(u_1, u_\ell) \left[(e_{i_1} - p^1) \cdot A_{1\ell} p^\ell + p_{i_1}^1 \left(-e_{i_1} \cdot A_{1\ell} p^\ell + e_{|S_1|_1} \cdot A_{1\ell} p^\ell \right) \right] \prod(p) \\ - p_{i_1}^1 \sum_{\ell=2}^{N} \rho(u_1, u_\ell)(e_{i_1} - p^1) \cdot A_{1\ell} p^\ell \left[\dfrac{\prod(p)}{p_{i_1}^1} - \dfrac{\prod(p)}{p_{|S_1|_1}^1} \right] \end{array} \right\}$$

$$= \sum_{\ell=2}^{N} \rho(u_1, u_\ell) \left\{ \begin{array}{l} \left[-p^1 \cdot A_{1\ell} p^\ell + p_{|S_1|_1}^1 e_{|S_1|_1} \cdot A_{1\ell} p^\ell + \left(1 - p_{|S_1|_1}^1 \right) e_{|S_1|_1} \cdot A_{1\ell} p^\ell \right] \prod(p) \\ + \dfrac{\prod(p)}{p_{|S_1|_1}^1} \left[p^1 \cdot A_{1\ell} p^\ell - p_{|S_1|_1}^1 e_{|S_1|_1} \cdot A_{1\ell} p^\ell - \left(1 - p_{|S_1|_1}^1 \right) p^1 \cdot A_{1\ell} p^\ell \right] \end{array} \right\}$$

$$= \sum_{\ell=2}^{N} \rho(u_1, u_\ell) \left\{ -p^1 \cdot A_{1\ell} p^\ell + e_{|s_1|_1} \cdot A_{1\ell} p^\ell - e_{|s_1|_1} \cdot A_{1\ell} p^\ell + p^1 \cdot A_{1\ell} p^\ell \right\} \prod(p)$$

$$= 0.$$

The analogous expressions for the other $N-1$ players are also zero, and so the divergence vanishes at all interior p.

If H is a closed asymptotically stable set contained in the interior of $\Delta(S_1) \times \cdots \times \Delta(S_N)$, then its volume is finite (by compactness) and its basin of attraction would have larger volume, a contradiction to Liouville's formula. Thus any closed asymptotically stable set H contains points on a boundary face of $\Delta(S_1) \times \cdots \times \Delta(S_N)$. Since this face is invariant under (4.4.4), its intersection with H is a closed asymptotically stable set under the dynamic restricted to a lower dimensional face. By continuing this argument, we finally conclude that H contains a pure strategy. ∎

4.11 Notes

Asymmetric two-player games were introduced by Selten (1980) and in extensive form by Selten (1983). This terminology may cause confusion for some readers since bimatrix games (not their symmetrizations) are often called asymmetric in the literature. The terminology is from van Damme (1991), and the basic notation is similar to his although the approach taken is closer to that in Balkenborg (1994) who extended many of the concepts to n-player asymmetric games. Local ESSs (but not local ESSets) were defined as local stable strategies (or LSS) by Selten (1983) and van Damme (1991). The definition of SESets (definition 4.3.1) and their characterization (theorem 4.3.2) are from Balkenborg (1994). Ritzberger and Weibull (1995) analyze the stability consequences of sets that are closed under (weakly) better replies. The Wright manifold of an asymmetric game is a special case of that for general extensive form games given in Cressman (2000).

Truly asymmetric games were defined by van Damme (1991) where the parts of theorem 4.5.3 relevant for strict NE were stated. Balkenborg (1994) proved the remainder of theorem 4.5.3 using a different approach than that taken in this text. Linear incentive games were introduced by Selten (1995). The proof of lemma 4.5.2 (appendix B) is from Ritzberger and Weibull (1995; see also Weibull 1995 and Hofbauer and Sigmund 1988, 1998). Truly symmetric games and theorems 4.6.1 and 4.6.2 are straightforward generalizations of concepts introduced in Cressman et al. (2000), and the counterexample of section 4.6.1 is from Chamberland and Cressman (2000). Section 4.6.2 on parallel bandits is based on Cressman and Schlag (1998b).

The interpretation in section 4.7.1 of two-role asymmetric games as truly asymmetric games with mistakes was considered by van Damme (1991; see also Binmore and Samuelson 2001). Taylor (1979) and Schuster et al. (1981) introduced the dynamic (4.7.1) for two-species frequency dependent evolution. Cressman (1992) developed the two-species ESS concept of section 4.7.2 (see Cressman et al. 2001 for the N-species ESS concept). The asymptotic stability of a two-species ESS as well as the characterization of interior ones through (4.7.4) was proved by Cressman (1996). Hierarchical Games have received some attention in the biological literature (e.g., Crowley 2000) but not from the perspective of an extensive form game.

5

Natural Selection with Multiple Loci

This chapter applies the theory of asymmetric games developed in the previous chapter to the multi-locus theory of natural selection. We generalize the single-locus continuous-time natural selection model of chapter 2.8.2 to multiple loci by incorporating the effects of recombination that model the reassociation of genes at different loci during the reproductive process. After developing the general continuous-time selection-recombination equation in the first section, the remainder of this chapter considers the special case of additive fitness among the loci. Natural selection then corresponds to a truly symmetric game for which the Wright manifold has new significance when there are positive recombination effects (see theorems 5.3.1 and 5.4.1).

5.1 Continuous-Time Selection-Recombination

Suppose that there are N loci ($N \geq 2$) and that locus k has n_k possible alleles $A_1^k, \ldots, A_{n_k}^k$. A *gamete* specifies one allele (or *gene*) at each locus (e.g., $A_{i_1}^1 A_{i_2}^2 \cdots A_{i_N}^N$ is the gamete with allele $A_{i_k}^k$ at locus k). Let p_i, where $i = (i_1, \ldots, i_N)$, be the frequency of gamete $A_{i_1}^1 A_{i_2}^2 \cdots A_{i_N}^N$. An individual in the population is then a *zygote* (i.e., a pair of gametes) that is represented by its genotype $A_{i_1}^1 A_{i_2}^2 \cdots A_{i_N}^N \backslash A_{j_1}^1 A_{j_2}^2 \cdots A_{j_N}^N$. As in chapter 2.8.2 we assume that genotypic frequencies are in Hardy-Weinberg proportions (i.e., the frequency of genotype $A_{i_1}^1 A_{i_2}^2 \cdots A_{i_N}^N \backslash A_{j_1}^1 A_{j_2}^2 \cdots A_{j_N}^N$ is $p_i p_j$). Without recombination, this leads to the continuous-time selection component $\dot{p}_i = p_i (e_i - p) \cdot Mp$ where M is a square matrix of order $\prod_{k=1}^N n_k$ with entries the Malthusian fitness parameters m_{ij}.

Recombination involves a reassociation of the genes of the two parental gametes during the birth process. Recall, from chapter 2.8.2, that m_{ij} is composed of a birth (fertility) and death (mortality) rate for individuals of genotype $A_{i_1}^1 A_{i_2}^2 \cdots A_{i_N}^N \backslash A_{j_1}^1 A_{j_2}^2 \cdots A_{j_N}^N$. Let $b_{i \backslash j, j \backslash i}^l$ be the component of fertility (i.e., the birth rate) for the genotype corresponding to gametes with frequencies $p_{i\backslash j}^I$ and $p_{j\backslash i}^I$.[1] Let $L = \{1, \ldots, N\}$ index the N loci, I be a proper subset of L that has $\{1\}$ as a subset and $L\backslash I \equiv \{k \in L \mid k \notin I\}$. Let r_I denote the probability of reassociation of the genes at the loci in I, inherited from one gamete, with the genes at the loci in $L\backslash I$ inherited from the parent's other gamete. For example, a zygote formed from gametes $A_{i_1}^1 A_{i_2}^2 \cdots A_{i_N}^N$ and $A_{j_1}^1 A_{j_2}^2 \cdots A_{j_N}^N$ will have unordered genotype $A_{i_1}^1 A_{i_2}^2 \cdots A_{i_N}^N \backslash A_{j_1}^1 A_{j_2}^2 \cdots A_{j_N}^N$ with probability $1 - \sum_I r_I$ and genotype $A_{i_1}^1 A_{j_2}^2 \cdots A_{j_N}^N \backslash A_{j_1}^1 A_{i_1}^2 \cdots A_{i_N}^N$ with probability $r_{\{1\}}$, and so on.

We will assume that birth rates of all genotypes with the same gene pairs at each locus are equal. This assumption of no *position effects* means that $b_{ij} \equiv b_{i\backslash i, j\backslash j}^I = b_{i\backslash j, j\backslash i}^I$ for all i, j, and I. Consider the rate of change in the frequency p_i of $A_{i_1}^1 A_{i_2}^2 \cdots A_{i_N}^N$ gametes. These gametes are lost at a rate of $\sum_I r_I \sum_j b_{ij} p_i p_j$ due to their recombination with other gametes. However, $A_{i_1}^1 A_{i_2}^2 \cdots A_{i_N}^N$ gametes are also formed through recombination. For instance, the ordered genotype $A_{i_1}^1 A_{j_2}^2 \cdots A_{j_N}^N \backslash A_{j_1}^1 A_{i_1}^2 \cdots A_{i_N}^N$ occurs with probability $p_{i\backslash j}^{\{1\}} p_{j\backslash i}^{\{1\}}$ and recombines to form the gamete $A_{i_1}^1 A_{i_2}^2 \cdots A_{i_N}^N$ with probability $r_{\{1\}}$. That is, $A_{i_1}^1 A_{i_2}^2 \cdots A_{i_N}^N$ gametes are gained through these reassociations at a rate of $r_{\{1\}} b_{ij} p_{i\backslash j}^{\{1\}} p_{j\backslash i}^{\{1\}}$. Overall, there is a gain of $\sum_I r_I \sum_j b_{ij} p_{i\backslash j}^I p_{j\backslash i}^I$, where I ranges over all proper subsets of L that include $\{1\}$ as a subset. Thus the *continuous-time selection-recombination equation* becomes

$$\dot{p}_i = p_i(e_i - p) \cdot Mp - \sum_I r_I \sum_j b_{ij} \left(p_{i\backslash j}^I p_{j\backslash i}^I - p_{i\backslash j}^I p_{j\backslash i}^I \right). \qquad (5.1.1)$$

This is an autonomous dynamical system that leaves the state space of gametic frequencies forward invariant.

The dynamical analysis in the following section assumes there is no recombination (i.e., $r_I = 0$ for all I). That is, we consider the *continuous-time selection equation*

$$\dot{p}_i = p_i(e_i - p) \cdot Mp. \qquad (5.1.2)$$

There is then *tight linkage* among the loci, which implies that the entire gamete can be considered as a single allele (or gene complex). Our treatment of recombination begins in section 5.3.

---

1. The notation here is consistent with chapter 4.4 where $p_{i\backslash j}^I$ is the frequency of the strategy that takes action $A_{i_k}^k$ for all $k \in I$ and action $A_{j_k}^k$ for all $k \in L\backslash I$.

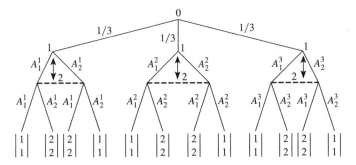

Figure 5.2.1
Symmetric extensive form of a three-locus two-allele system.

5.2 Symmetric Extensive Form with Additive Fitness

There is *additive fitness* among loci if, for all $i = (i_1, \ldots, i_N)$ and $j = (j_1, \ldots, j_N)$,

$$m_{ij} = m_{i_1 j_1}^1 + \cdots + m_{i_N j_N}^N, \tag{5.2.1}$$

where $m_{i_k j_k}^k$ is then the Malthusian fitness parameter for genotype $A_{i_k}^k A_{j_k}^k$ in the square matrix M_{kk} of order n_k at locus k. The remainder of the chapter assumes that fitness is additive.

Every N-locus system with additive fitness can be represented in extensive form as in figure 5.2.1 above. This consists of an initial move by nature (player 0) that takes each of N possible actions with probability $1/N$. The kth action by nature leads to a two-player subgame with the symmetric payoff matrix[2] M_{kk} which models natural selection at a single locus as considered in chapter 2.8. Overall, we then have the extensive form of a truly symmetric two-player game considered in chapter 4.6 with $|S_k| = n_k$ for all $1 \leq k \leq N$. We will adopt the notation used there to write the state space of gametic frequencies as $\Delta(S_1 \times \cdots \times S_N)$.

Remark 5.2.1 The preceding discussion shows that the asymmetric replicator dynamic for a truly symmetric game with N information situations where each subgame has a symmetric payoff matrix is the model of N-locus natural selection where fitness is additive among loci and there is no recombination.

---

2. Strictly speaking, the entries in each M_{kk} should be scaled by a factor N in order that the notation of chapter 4.6 match (5.2.1) above. We have ignored this nuisance factor since it plays no role in our analysis.

The case of no recombination is usually dismissed as uninteresting in the population genetics literature, through the simple observation that the theory developed in chapter 2.8 applies, since this case is equivalent to single-locus natural selection with $\prod_{k=1}^{N} n_k$ alleles. However, considered in this traditional way as a single-locus model, the system is highly nongeneric (in the set of symmetric normal form games with symmetric payoff matrix M) compared to the typical system in chapter 2.8.2 where most initial population polymorphisms evolve to an ESS of M.

Example 5.2.2 Consider a three-locus, two-allele system with additive fitness and no recombination. Suppose that each of the three loci separately have an interior ESS. Then, by theorem 4.6.2, the 8×8 payoff matrix has a single four-dimensional ESSet and no ESS. Specifically, if $M_{kk} = \begin{bmatrix} 1 & 2 \\ 2 & 1 \end{bmatrix}$ as in figure 5.2.1 for $k \in \{1, 2, 3\}$, each M_{kk} has ESS $(\frac{1}{2}, \frac{1}{2})$, whereas the only ESSet of M is

$$E = \left\{ p \in \Delta^8 \,\middle|\, \frac{1}{2} = \sum_{\beta\gamma} p_{1\beta\gamma} = \sum_{\alpha\gamma} p_{\alpha 1 \gamma} = \sum_{\alpha\beta} p_{\alpha\beta 1} \right\},$$

where $p_{\alpha\beta\gamma}$ is the frequency of the strategy with multi-index (α, β, γ). The only immediate consequence from chapter 2.8 is that all initial polymorphisms evolve to some point in E.

From the theory developed in chapter 4.6, we know the ES structure for general truly symmetric games can best be described by treating the loci separately. To this end, for each $p \in \Delta(S_1 \times \cdots \times S_N)$ of our N-locus system, the frequency of allele $A_{i_k}^k$ at locus k is given by the projection map

$$p \mapsto (p^1, \ldots, p^N)$$

onto $\Delta(S_1) \times \cdots \times \Delta(S_N)$. In particular, almost all initial points evolve to some p^* where p^{k*} is in an ESSet of M_{kk} for all k.

The general theory also gives a more exact description of the limit point p^*. In analogy to the generalized Wright manifold of chapter 3.4.1, define W_K as follows:

$$\{p \mid p_{i\backslash i}^I p_{j\backslash j}^I = K_{ij}^I p_{i\backslash j}^I p_{j\backslash i}^I \text{ for all subsets } I \subset L \text{ and multi-indexes } i, j\}$$

$$(5.2.2)$$

Then W_K is invariant, under the continuous-time selection equation (5.1.2), for each set of positive constants K^I_{ij} for which W_K intersects the interior of $\Delta(S_1 \times \cdots \times S_N)$. Furthermore there is a unique point p^*_K in each generalized Wright manifold W_K that projects to $(p^{1*}, \ldots, p^{N*})$. Thus $p(0)$ converges to the unique point p^*_K that lies on the same generalized Wright manifold as $p(0)$.

The following theorem summarizes the results above:

Theorem 5.2.3 *Every initial polymorphism of a multi-locus system with additive fitness and no recombination evolves under the continuous-time selection equation (5.1.2) to a point on the same generalized Wright manifold as the initial polymorphism where the allelic frequencies at each locus are at a NE. Almost all these limit points project to an element of an ESSet of M_{kk} for each locus k which, generically, will be an ESS of M_{kk}.*

In general, the ES set structure of a multi-locus system can be quite complicated (especially when some subgames of the extensive form have multiple ESSets). However, an interesting special case occurs when each of the N subgames has an ESS p^{k*} in the interior of $\Delta(S_k)$.[3] Then p^{k*} is also the unique NE of M_{kk}. The only ESSet is the hyperplane $E = \{p \mid p^k = p^{k*} \text{ for all } k\}$ through the interior of $\Delta(S_1 \times \cdots \times S_N)$. By chapter 2.8.2 and theorem 5.2.3, every initial polymorphism $p(0)$ evolves along its generalized Wright manifold to the unique point in E where each locus attains its maximum mean fitness.

The Wright manifold, where all $K^I_{ij} = 1$, has further special properties. If $p(0)$ is on the Wright manifold W, the continuous-time selection equation induces the replicator dynamic (with respect to M_{kk}) for p^k at each locus k. That is, on W, continuous-time natural selection reduces to analyzing natural selection acting on the gene frequency at each locus separately. In particular, for example 5.2.2 based on figure 5.2.1, every initial polymorphism lying in W evolves to $p_{\alpha\beta\gamma} = \frac{1}{8}$ for all multi-indexes (α, β, γ).

The Wright manifold plays an even more central role in the following two sections where recombination effects are considered. It is then often called the *linkage-equilibrium manifold* for reasons that will become apparent in the following section.

---

3. For multi-alleles at a single locus k, polymorphic ESS's are unexpected if $n_k \geq 3$ and payoff entries are random (see Notes). For $n_k = 2$, an interior ESS exists if and only if the heterozygote at locus k is *overdominant* (i.e., the viability of the heterozygote, $A^k_1 A^k_2$, is higher than that of either homozygote, $A^k_1 A^k_1$ or $A^k_2 A^k_2$).

5.3   Recombination

In this section we consider recombination in the absence of selection for the continuous-time model. That is, we assume that all birth rates are equal (normalized to 1) as well as all death rates. For simplicity, we will assume that all $r_I > 0$ in this section. From (5.1.1), the *continuous-time recombination equation* for N loci is

$$\dot{p}_i = -\sum_I r_I \sum_j \left(p^I_{i\backslash i} p^I_{j\backslash j} - p^I_{i\backslash j} p^I_{j\backslash i} \right)$$

$$= -\left(\sum_I r_I \right) p_i + \sum_I r_I \sum_j \left(p^I_{i\backslash j} p^I_{j\backslash i} \right). \tag{5.3.1}$$

From (5.3.1), it is clear that every point p^* on the Wright manifold is a rest point of the recombination equation since it satisfies $p^I_{i\backslash i} p^I_{j\backslash j} = p^I_{i\backslash j} p^I_{j\backslash i}$ for every i, j and I. The converse is also true since, by theorem 5.3.1 below, every trajectory converges to a unique point on the Wright manifold. Furthermore, for every $p \in \Delta(S_1 \times \cdots \times S_N)$, $\dot{p}^k_{i_k} = 0$ for all k since, for instance,

$$\dot{p}^1_{i_1} = \sum_{i_2,\ldots,i_N} \dot{p}_i = -\sum_I r_I \sum_{i_2,\ldots,i_N} \sum_{j_1,\ldots,j_N} \left(p_{i_1 i_2 \ldots i_N} p_{j_1 j_2 \ldots j_N} - p^I_{i\backslash i} p^I_{j\backslash j} \right)$$

$$= -\sum_I r_I \left(\sum_{i_2,\ldots,i_N} \sum_{j_1,\ldots,j_N} p_{i_1 i_2 \ldots i_N} p_{j_1 j_2 \ldots j_N} - \sum_{i'_2,\ldots,i'_N} \sum_{j_1, j'_2,\ldots, j'_N} p_{i_1 i'_2 \ldots i'_N} p_{j_1 j'_2 \ldots j'_N} \right).$$

That is, recombination does not alter the allele frequencies at any of the N loci, a result that is biologically intuitive. Thus the limit point for a trajectory with initial state p must be $p^* \in W$ where $p^*_i = p^1_{i_1} p^2_{i_2} \cdots \cdot p^N_{i_N}$.

Theorem 5.3.1   *If all reassociation rates are positive, every trajectory of the N-locus continuous-time recombination equation (5.3.1) converges to the unique point p^* of the Wright manifold W whose gene frequency at each locus equals the initial gene frequency at that locus. Moreover convergence to this point is exponential in the sense that $|p_i - p^*_i| \leq Be^{-ct}$ for some positive constants B and c that are independent of the multi-index i and the initial point $p(0)$. In particular, W is globally asymptotically stable.*

Proof   The proof is quite similar to the proof that the Wright manifold is globally attracting for the asymmetric best response dynamic of chapter 4.4.2. The partial proof presented here is only complete for the two-locus case. In general, the proof relies on rewriting the recombination equation as

$$\frac{d}{dt}(p_i - p_i^*) = -\left(\sum_I r_I\right)(p_i - p_i^*) + \sum_I r_I\left(p_i^I\, p_i^{L\setminus I} - p_i^*\right),$$

where $p_i^I \equiv \sum_j \{p_j | j_k = i_k \text{ for all } k \in I\}$ and then showing each non-homogeneous term, $p_i^I\, p_i^{L\setminus I} - p_i^* = (p_i^I - p_i^{I*})p_i^{L\setminus I} + p_i^{I*}(p_i^{L\setminus I} - p_i^{L\setminus I*})$, is bounded by an exponentially decreasing function.

To illustrate, consider the case $I = \{1, 2\}$. Then

$$\frac{d}{dt}(p_i^I - p_i^{I*}) = \frac{d}{dt}\left(p_i^{\{1,2\}} - p_{i_1}^{1*}\, p_{i_2}^{2*}\right)$$

$$= -\sum_J r_J \sum_{i_3,\dots,i_N} \sum_{j_1,\dots,j_N} \left(p_{i_3\dots i_N}\, p_{j_1\dots j_N} - p_{i\setminus j}^J\, p_{j\setminus i}^J\right).$$

If $J = \{1\}$, then

$$\sum_{i_3,\dots,i_N} \sum_{j_1,\dots,j_N} \left(p_{i_3\dots i_N}\, p_{j_1\dots j_N} - p_{i\setminus j}^J\, p_{j\setminus i}^J\right)$$

$$= \sum_{i_3,\dots,i_N} \sum_{j_1,\dots,j_N} \left(p_{i_3\dots i_N}\, p_{j_1\dots j_N} - p_{i_3 j_2 i_3\dots i_N}\, p_{j_1 i_2 j_3\dots j_N}\right)$$

$$= p_i^{\{1,2\}} - p_{i_1}^{1*}\, p_{i_2}^{2*}.$$

In fact $\sum_{i_3,\dots,i_N} \sum_{j_1,\dots,j_N} (p_{i_3\dots i_N}\, p_{j_1\dots j_N} - p_{i\setminus j}^J\, p_{j\setminus i}^J)$ equals $p_i^{\{1,2\}} - p_{i_1}^{1*}\, p_{i_2}^{2*}$ if $2 \notin J$ and equals 0 if $2 \in J$. Thus

$$\frac{d}{dt}\left(p_i^{\{1,2\}} - p_{i_1}^{1*}\, p_{i_2}^{2*}\right) = -\sum_{2\notin J} r_J\left(p_i^{\{1,2\}} - p_{i_1}^{1*}\, p_{i_2}^{2*}\right),$$

and so decreases to zero exponentially. Similarly

$$\frac{d}{dt}\left(p_i^{L\setminus I} - p_i^{L\setminus I*}\right) = -\sum_{2\notin J} r_J\left(p_i^{L\setminus I} - p_i^{L\setminus I*}\right)$$

also decreases to zero exponentially, and so $p_i^I\, p_i^{L\setminus I} - p_i^*$ is exponentially decreasing as well. The proof for general I is left to the reader. ∎

The details above complete the proof in the two-locus case since $J = \{1\}$ is the only proper subset of $\{1, 2\}$ containing $\{1\}$. For the two-locus case, $r \equiv r_{\{1\}}$ is called the *crossover rate* between the two loci and

$D_i = -r(p_i - p_{i_1}^1 p_{i_2}^2)$ measures the *linkage disequilibrium* in gamete i. $W = \{p \mid D_i = 0 \text{ for all } i\}$ is then the linkage-equilibrium manifold.

5.4   Selection and Recombination

From section 5.2 the continuous-time selection equation (5.1.2) with additive fitness reduces on the Wright manifold W to analyzing natural selection acting on the gene frequencies at each locus separately. Heuristically, since W also consists of equilibrium points of the recombination equation, this statement should also be true for the selection-recombination process (5.1.1) under additive fitness. The main result, theorem 5.4.1 below, shows this intuition goes a long way to understanding trajectories that are not on W as well.

From the method used in section 5.3, the recombination term $-\sum_I r_I \sum_j b_{ij}(p_{i\setminus i}^I p_{j\setminus j}^I - p_{i\setminus j}^I p_{j\setminus i}^I)$ in (5.1.1) still satisfies $\dot{p}_{i_k}^k = 0$ for all k. Thus, since fitness is additive, the mean fitness, $p \cdot Mp$, evolves according to the selection term $p_i(e_i - p) \cdot Mp$ in (5.1.1). In particular, $p \cdot Mp$ is strictly increasing at each point where the selection equation (5.1.2) is not at rest. Moreover the ω-limit points of any trajectory of (5.1.1) must form a closed set Ω of rest points of (5.1.2) that all have the same mean fitness. In fact Ω consists of a single point p^* as stated in the following theorem. Then p^* must also be a rest point of the recombination component and so is on the Wright manifold W by theorem 5.3.1.

Theorem 5.4.1 *Suppose that we have an N-locus system with additive fitness, no position effects and all reassociation rates and birth rates positive. Then every trajectory of the continuous-time selection-recombination equation (5.1.1) converges to a unique point p^* on the Wright manifold W. Moreover p^* is a rest point of the corresponding selection equation with no recombination that generically yields ESS allelic frequencies at each locus.*

Proof We only provide a proof when the ω-limit points Ω of the trajectory contains an element p^* in the interior of $\Delta(S_1 \times \cdots \times S_N)$ and each M_{kk} has a unique interior NE. Since Ω consists of rest points of (5.1.2), p^* is a NE. Thus p^{k*} is a NE of M_{kk} for all k which implies that $\dot{p}_{i_k}^{k*} = 0$ (e.g., $\dot{p}_{i_1}^{1*} = \sum_{i_2,\dots,i_N} \dot{p}_{i_1 i_2 \dots i_N}^* = \sum_{i_2,\dots,i_N} p_i^*(e_i - p^*) \cdot Mp^* = \sum_{i_2,\dots,i_N} p_i^*(e_{i_k} - p^{k*}) \cdot M_{kk} p^{k*} = 0$). Thus, since the trajectory of (5.1.1) with initial point p^* is completely contained in Ω, this trajectory is a subset of $\{p \mid p^k = p^{k*} \text{ for all } k\}$. Therefore the trajectory with initial point p^* converges to a point in W by theorem 5.3.1. Relabel this point in W as p^*. In fact p^* is globally asymptotically stable with respect to

$\{p \mid p^k = p^{k*}$ for all $k\}$ for the recombination equation since the Wright manifold is globally asymptotically stable by theorem 5.3.1. Thus Ω has no points outside this set and this completes the proof. ∎

5.5 Notes

The continuous-time multi-locus selection-recombination equation is given in Akin (1979; see also Shahshahani 1979) where the complete proofs of the theorems in this chapter are also provided from a more traditional population genetics perspective. The approach taken here is closer to Cressman (1999). The statements of the theorems are all valid (with the exception of the invariance of the (generalized) Wright manifold in theorem 5.2.3) for the discrete-time selection-recombination equation with additive fitness (Lyubich 1992). The distribution of ESSs for random symmetric payoff matrices was investigated by Haigh (1989).

It is well known (Nagylaki 1992) that multi-locus natural selection with *epistasis* (i.e., relationships between loci that affect fitness such as the presence of a modifier locus) can exhibit dynamics that are more complicated than ours (nonconvergence of trajectories, decrease in population mean fitness, limit cycles etc.). Cressman (1999) points out that when there is additive epistasis (i.e., fitness is not additive among loci), there is no truly symmetric game representation of natural selection that has each information set corresponding to a locus. Nagylaki et al. (1999) prove that under sufficiently weak epistasis and positive recombination, a *quasi–linkage-equilibrium manifold* exists close to the Wright manifold that is invariant and contains all limit points of the trajectories.

6

Extensive Form Games

In the extensive form games considered in the previous chapters, a player's choice at a decision point cannot depend on his actions at previous decision points in the same game. For these "one-shot" games it was not essential to have a formal definition of extensive form games in order to appreciate the special properties that the extensive form tree structure imparts on the analysis of the game.

As we will see in the following chapters, the extensive form becomes even more central to the analysis when there is a sequential aspect to a player's actions in the game. For instance, in the Two-Message Symmetric Signaling Game of figure 6.0.1 analyzed in chapter 7.2.2, player one may condition his choice of H or D at stage two on the messages (m_1 or m_2) both he and his opponent sent at stage

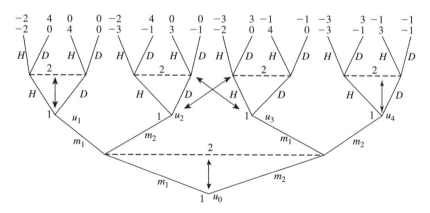

Figure 6.0.1
Two-Message Symmetric Signaling Game.

one.[1] Since, for the most part, these are the types of games analyzed in the remainder of the book, it is now appropriate to give the formal definition of extensive form games. The extensive form game of figure 6.0.1 has the additional property, indicated there by the double arrows $\longleftrightarrow$, of being symmetric (see section 6.4)—an issue that is ignored for the first three sections when referring to this game.

6.1   N-Player Extensive Form Games

A *(finite) N-player extensive form game* is a sextuple $\Gamma = (K, P, U, C, \rho, \pi)$ where the six constituents are defined as follows.[2]

Game Tree K   The game tree K is a finite tree with a distinguished vertex called the *origin* or *root* of K. The sequence of edges and vertices connecting the root to a vertex x is called the *path to x*. We say vertex y *comes before* x (or that x *comes after* y or that x *follows* y) if y is different from x and on the path to x. An *endpoint* is a vertex z such that no vertex comes after z. The set of all endpoints is denoted by Z. A *decision point* is a vertex that is not an endpoint. The set of all decision points is denoted by X. A path to an endpoint is called a *play*. An *alternative* (or *action*) at a decision point x is an edge that connects x to a vertex after x.

Player Partition P   The player partition P is a partition of X into $N+1$ sets $P_0, P_1, \ldots, P_N$ where P_0 is the *random decision set* (or *set of decisions by nature*) and P_n $(1 \leq n \leq N)$ is the *set of decisions of player n*. In the two-player extensive form game of figure 6.0.1 (with symmetry ignored), there are no random decision points (i.e., $P_0 = \{\}$). This game has root labeled u_0 that is a decision point of player one with two alternatives (labeled m_1 and m_2). The decision points along any path from the root alternate between the two players and are labeled accordingly.

---

1. In the dynamic analysis of our Symmetric Signaling Games, the only relevant aspects of these messages are their cost to the sender and that both players recognize which message is sent. In particular, the content of the message is irrelevant. The payoffs given in figure 6.0.1 model a two-strategy game with payoff matrix $\begin{bmatrix} -2 & 4 \\ 0 & 0 \end{bmatrix}$ that follows possible messages m_1 and m_2 with associated costs 0 and 1 respectively.

2. These are the traditional formal definitions of the six constituents (see Notes). Readers less familiar with this formal approach should repeatedly refer to an extensive form diagram (e.g., figure 6.0.1) to see how these concepts are reflected in specific examples.

Information Partition U The information partition U is an N-tuple $(U_1, \ldots, U_N)$ where U_n is a partition of P_n into *information sets* of player n such that each information set u satisfies the following two conditions:

i. Every path intersects u at most once.

ii. All decision points in u have the same number of alternatives.

Each decision point $x \in P_0$ forms a (singleton) information set $u = \{x\}$, called an *information set of nature*. Player information sets that contain more than one point are joined by dashed lines (see figure 6.0.1) and labeled by the appropriate player number. Thus in figure 6.0.1 player two has five information sets with two decision points each and two alternatives at each decision point.

Choice Partition C A *choice c* at information set u assigns exactly one alternative to each $x \in u$. The choice partition at u, C_u, is a set of choices at u so that every alternative at each $x \in u$ is assigned to exactly one choice. The choice partition C is the collection of choice partitions at u, $\bigcup C_u$, where the union is taken over all information sets u. For instance, the choice partition in figure 6.0.1 assigns exactly two choices (H or D) at each (player) information set at stage two and these are labeled along the possible alternatives. Thus, if player two chooses H at one decision point in the top left-hand information set of figure 6.0.1, he must choose H at the other decision point in there as well.

Probability Assignment ρ At each information set of nature (i.e., at each $u = \{x\}$ where $x \in P_0$), the probability assignment specifies a positive probability to all choices at u.[3] In the game tree these are indicated as positive numbers along the alternatives at x.

Payoff Function π The payoff function assigns, for all endpoints $z \in Z$, real numbers $\pi_n(z)$ to each player n. $\pi_n(z)$ is called the *payoff to player n at z*. These numbers are shown above the endpoints of figure 6.0.1 with the payoff of player one above that of player two.

Throughout the book we will restrict attention to extensive form games that satisfy two conditions. The first is that there are at least

---

3. At any information set u that is a singleton $\{x\}$, a choice at u is the same as an alternative at x. Sometimes "the choice c at x" is used even when $\{x\}$ is not a singleton player information set instead of the more rigorous expression "the choice at the information set containing the decision point x that assigns the alternative specified by c at x."

two alternatives at each decision point of Γ. The second is that at every player decision point, this player knows which of his information sets he has previously encountered and what choice he made at each of these information sets. To formalize this, we say that a choice c at information set u *comes before decision point* x if one of the alternatives assigned by c is on the path to x. Furthermore we say that Γ has *perfect recall* if, for all information sets u, v of player n, all decision points x, $y \in v$, and all choices $c \in C_u$, c comes before x if and only if c comes before y. That is, we will restrict attention to finite N-player extensive form games Γ of perfect recall where each decision point has at least two alternatives.

Perfect recall defines a partial order on the information sets, U_n, of player n. Specifically, if u and v are information sets of player n, $u \prec v$ if some choice at information set u comes before a decision point in v. We say that u and v are *disjoint information sets* of player n if they are unrelated under this partial order (i.e., if it is not true that $u = v, u \prec v$ or $v \prec u$).

6.1.1   Strategies and Payoffs

Suppose that Γ is a finite N-player extensive form game of perfect recall. The *pure strategies of player* $n \in \{1, \ldots, N\}$, denoted $e_{n,i}$, specify a choice at each of the information sets of this player. The set of all pure strategies of player n is denoted by S_n. *Mixed strategies of player* n are probability vectors $p_n \in \Delta_n \equiv \Delta(S_n)$ whose ith coordinate $p_{n,i}$ specifies the probability that strategy $e_{n,i}$ is used. The vertices of this $(|S_n| - 1)$-dimensional simplex represent the pure strategies of player n. The *strategy space* for Γ is then the set of *mixed strategy combinations* p in $\Delta \equiv \times_{n=1}^{N} \Delta_n = \{p = (p_1, \ldots, p_N) \mid p_n \in \Delta_n\}$.[4] A *pure strategy combination* e is an N-tuple $(e_1, \ldots, e_N)$ in Δ such that all of its components are pure strategies.

Let $\gamma(x, e)$ be the *probability vertex x is reached* if the players are using pure strategy combination e. That is, $\gamma(x, e) = 0$ if, at some player decision point on the path to x, pure strategy combination e assigns an alternative that is not on this path. Otherwise, $\gamma(x, e)$ is the product

---

4. For two-player extensive form games (i.e., $N = 2$), we often revert to the notation used in chapters 2 and 3. For instance, a mixed-strategy combination $(p_1, p_2) \in \Delta_1 \times \Delta_2$ can be denoted as (p, q). This has the advantage of avoiding the possible ambiguity between the notation $p_2 \in \Delta_2$ in this chapter conflicting with that in chapter 2 where p_2 is the second component of the probability vector p for either player in a symmetric normal form game.

of all probabilities assigned to the alternatives at the random decision points along the path to x. Furthermore $\gamma(x, p) \equiv \sum_e p(e)\gamma(x, e)$ where $p(e) \equiv \prod_{n=1}^{N}\{p_{n,i} \mid e_n = e_{n,i}\}$ is then the standard extension to mixed strategies in Δ and is called the *realization probability of x under p*. A vertex x is called *reachable under p* if $\gamma(x, p) > 0$ (if $x \in X$, we also say p *reaches the information set u* that contains x). The strategy combination $p \in \Delta$ is *pervasive* if all player information sets are reachable under p. Every completely mixed strategy combination is pervasive. An information set u for player n is *relevant for p_n* if some decision point $x \in u$ is reachable under some strategy combination of the form $p \backslash p_n$, where $p \backslash p_n$ is the same strategy combination as p except that player n uses strategy p_n. Clearly, if p is pervasive, then every information set of player n is relevant for p_n. The converse is not true.

For a fixed $p \in \Delta$, $\gamma(z, p)$ defines a probability distribution on Z, called the *outcome of p*. If the outcome of p assigns probability 1 to a particular endpoint (e.g., if p is a pure strategy and there are no random decision points), then we speak of the *outcome path of p*. The outcome of p uniquely determines $\gamma(x, p)$ at each decision point x; namely $\gamma(x, p) = \sum_{z \text{ follows } x} \gamma(z, p)$. Through the outcome of p, the payoff function $\pi_n(z)$ of player n defined above at all endpoints z extends to a payoff function, $\pi_n(p)$, for strategy combinations p as well by

$$\pi_n : \Delta \to R,$$

$$p \mapsto \sum_{z \in Z} \gamma(z, p)\pi_n(z).$$

The *normal form of Γ* is the strategy set Δ together with this payoff function.[5]

For most interesting extensive form games where some player has at least two information sets, there are many p that have the same outcome.[6]

---

5. Strictly speaking, the normal form of Γ consists of the set of pure strategy combinations in Δ together with the payoff functions π_n restricted to these strategies (see section 6.2 below). What is called the normal form here is then the usual extension of these payoff functions to the strategy space.

6. Suppose that u and v are information sets of player n. If $u \prec v$, the set of pure strategies combinations that have a given outcome that reaches u but not v is never a singleton set since pure strategies of player n specify a choice at all his information sets regardless of whether this information set can be reached by this strategy. The fact not all information sets can be reached by every pure strategy combination follows from our assumptions of perfect recall and at least two alternatives at each decision point. In addition, if u and v are disjoint, there are always strategy combinations with different (completely) mixed strategies of player n that have the same outcome.

This causes difficulties in the usual interpretation of several standard game theory concepts. Two important approaches to alleviate these difficulties are through the reduced-strategy normal form introduced in section 6.2 below or through the introduction of behavior strategies as follows. For instance, in figure 6.0.1, there are $2^5 = 32$ pure strategies of player one (and of player two) corresponding to a binary choice at each of his five information sets. Thus Δ_1 is 31-dimensional. On the other hand, the set of behavior strategies of player one is only 5-dimensional.

A *behavior strategy* b_n of player n for Γ assigns a probability distribution b_n^u on C_u for every information set $u \in U_n$ of this player. b_n^u is called the *local behavior strategy* of player n at his information set u. A *behavior strategy combination* b is then an N-tuple of behavior strategies, one for each player. Pure strategy combinations are in 1–1 correspondence with behavior strategy combinations that assign a unique choice at all player information sets and so can also be called *pure behavior strategy combinations*. The *mixed representative* $p \in \Delta$ of a behavior strategy combination b has components $p_n \in \Delta_n$ with $p_{n,i}$ equal to the product of all probabilities over the information sets u of player n that b_n makes the same choice as $e_{n,i}$ at u. A behavior strategy combination and its mixed representative are *realization equivalent* in the sense that the probability any vertex is reached is the same for both strategies (equivalently, they both yield the same outcome). Similarly every mixed strategy combination p has a realization equivalent behavior strategy combination b. Specifically, if c is a choice at an information set u of player n, take

$$b_n^u(c) \equiv \frac{\sum_i \{p_{n,i} \mid u \text{ is relevant for } e_{n,i} \text{ and } e_{n,i} \text{ makes choice } c \text{ at } u\}}{\sum_i \{p_{n,i} \mid u \text{ is relevant for } e_{n,i}\}}$$

(6.1.1)

if u is relevant for p_n and $b_n^u(c) \equiv \sum_i \{p_{n,i} \mid e_{n,i} \text{ makes choice } c \text{ at } u\}$ otherwise.

If p is pervasive, it has only one realization equivalent behavior strategy combination. On the other hand, there are typically many mixed strategy combinations that have the same realization equivalent behavior strategy combination. In any event, the payoff $\pi_n(b)$ for player n given behavior strategy b is the payoff $\pi_n(p)$ for any mixed strategy combination that yields the same outcome.

6.1.2 *Nash Equilibria, Subgames, and Backward Induction*

Nash equilibria for extensive form games can either be defined through normal form strategy combinations or through behavior strategy combinations. For the former approach, $p \in \Delta$ is a NE of Γ if, for all $1 \leq n \leq N$, $\pi_n(p \backslash p'_n) \leq \pi_n(p)$ for all $p'_n \in \Delta_n$. Since these payoff comparisons do not depend on behavior at information sets of the other players that are not relevant for p, every other strategy combination that differs from p only at irrelevant information sets is also a NE. In particular, p is a NE of Γ if and only if its realization equivalent behavior strategy combination given by (6.1.1) is also a NE. In the literature the NE analysis is often done through this latter behavior strategy approach. However, since there is no definitive behavior strategy dynamic (e.g., see the discussions in chapter 4.6.1 and immediately following theorem 6.3.3 below with specific reference to the replicator dynamic), the normal form approach is essential for us as well.

We will be particularly interested in the subgame structure of Γ. Suppose that u is an information set for Γ that consists of a single decision point $\{x\}$. If every information set of Γ is either a subset of the decision points in the subtree Γ_u of Γ that has its root at u or is completely disjoint from this subtree, then the restriction of Γ to Γ_u constitutes an N-player extensive form game, called the *subgame Γ_u of Γ with root u*. A strategy combination p *reaches the subgame* Γ_u if p reaches the information set u.

All of the concepts introduced in section 6.1 above apply to Γ_u. Let us denote mixed-strategy combinations in Γ_u by p^u and payoff functions to player n by $\pi_n^u(p^u)$, and so on. Then a *truncated game* $\Gamma_{-u}(p^u)$ can be defined for any mixed-strategy combination p^u in Γ_u by replacing in Γ the subtree Γ_u with an endpoint that has payoff $\pi_n^u(p^u)$ for each player n. Behavior strategy combinations b of Γ obviously induce behavior strategy combinations b^u in Γ_u and b^{-u} in $\Gamma_{-u}(p^u)$ since any given information set is completely contained in exactly one of these extensive form games.[7]

A behavior strategy combination b of Γ is a *subgame perfect NE* if, for every subgame Γ_u of Γ (including Γ itself), the restriction of b to Γ_u is a NE of Γ_u. *Backward induction*, a fundamental technique that we will use to analyze different aspects of extensive form games, can be applied

---

7. The notation b^u refers to a behavior strategy combination in Γ_u (i.e., a local behavior strategy at all player information sets of Γ_u), whereas b_n^u is a single local behavior strategy of player n at his information set u.

as follows to the subgame NE structure to show at least one subgame perfect NE exists: Start at the *minimal subgames* of Γ (i.e., subgames that contain no proper subgames). Find a behavior strategy NE for these minimal subgames (since every normal form game has at least one NE), truncate Γ with respect to these NE at the minimal subgames, and then proceed inductively on the minimal subgames of the truncation. This yields a behavior strategy combination of Γ that is a subgame perfect NE.[8] The following theorem summarizes well-known results (see Notes) based on the discussion above:

Theorem 6.1.1   *If b^u is a NE in Γ_u and b^{-u} is a NE in $\Gamma_{-u}(b^u)$, then b is a NE for Γ.[9] If p is a NE and Γ_u is reachable by p, then p induces through (6.1.1) a NE p^u in Γ_u and a NE in the truncated game $\Gamma_{-u}(p^u)$. In particular, a pervasive NE is subgame perfect. Every N-player extensive form game Γ has at least one subgame perfect NE.*

For instance, ignoring symmetry in figure 6.0.1, one (of many) subgame perfect NE has player one choosing H at all four of his second-stage information sets (which are roots of subgames) and player two choosing D at all four of his. Truncation produces a one-stage asymmetric Prisoner's Dilemma Class Game with bimatrix

$$\begin{bmatrix} 4,0 & 4,-1 \\ 3,0 & 3,-1 \end{bmatrix},$$

and so both players must choose message m_1 at their initial decision point as it is the unique NE.

Remark 6.1.2   The above backward induction procedure is often used as a static equilibrium selection technique to discard NE that are not subgame perfect. The method becomes more controversial as the number of decision points that are not reachable by the subgame perfect NE increases. Backward induction is also called *dynamic programming*. This latter terminology is somewhat misleading (and is not used hereafter) since its application above is to the static NE structure. It would be more appropriately used when the same technique is applied later

---

8. This follows from the first statement of theorem 6.1.1. The proofs of the first two statements of theorem 6.1.1 are straightforward and so are left to the reader.

9. The converse is not true. Although a NE b must induce a NE in every subgame reached by b, it need not induce a NE in the other subgames Γ_u (even if u is an information set of player n that is relevant for b_n).

(e.g., chapter 7.3) to the ESS and/or dynamic stability structure of the subgames.

6.2 Normal Forms and the Replicator Dynamic

The normal form of Γ given above through the payoff functions $\pi_n(p)$ can also be defined as follows to more easily introduce the concept of the reduced-strategy normal form: The *(standard) normal form of the N-player extensive form game* Γ is the N-player normal form game with pure strategy set $S \equiv S_1 \times \cdots \times S_N$ and payoff functions $\pi_n(e)$ for every $e \in S$. The preceding section suggests that choices at information sets that are not relevant for a pure behavior strategy combination have no effect on the NE structure of Γ. To make this explicit (see theorem 6.2.1 below), perfect recall allows us to define inductively reduced sets of pure strategies and through this a reduced-strategy normal form as follows:

A pure strategy[10] e_n in the *reduced-strategy set* T_n *of pure strategies of player n* specifies a choice at each of the information sets u of player n which are relevant given the choices already made by e_n at information sets $v \prec u$ of player n. The *reduced-strategy normal form of the N-player extensive form game* Γ is the N-player normal form game with pure strategy set $T = T_1 \times \cdots \times T_N$ and payoff functions $\pi_n(e) \equiv \pi_n(\hat{e})$ for some $\hat{e} \in S$ that restricts to $e \in T$ at those information sets of player n that are relevant for e_n (this function is independent of the choice of $\hat{e}$ by perfect recall). Each pure strategy combination $e \in T$ in the reduced-strategy normal form corresponds to the set of all such $\hat{e} \in S$. The correspondence extends to mixed-strategy combinations as well. Specifically, the normal form strategy combination $\hat{p}$ is identified with the reduced-strategy normal form strategy combination p given by

$$p_{n,i} \equiv \sum \{\hat{p}_{n,i} \mid e_{n,i} \text{ corresponds to } \hat{e}_{n,i}\}. \tag{6.2.1}$$

Then p corresponds to the set of all such $\hat{p}$.

A straightforward application of this correspondence (and of the equality $\pi_n(p) \equiv \pi_n(\hat{p})$ whenever $\hat{p}$ is identified with p) to definition 4.3.1 in chapter 4 yields the following result.

---

10. We typically use the same notation for (pure) strategies in the reduced-strategy normal form as in the (standard) normal form. Only in this paragraph do we distinguish notationally these two normal forms by using $\hat{e}$, etc., for the standard normal form.

Theorem 6.2.1 *Each NE of the reduced-strategy normal form corresponds to a set of NE in the standard normal form. F is an SESet of the standard normal form of an N-player extensive form game* Γ *if and only if F corresponds to an SESet of the reduced-strategy normal form of* Γ.

The standard evolutionary dynamics for the two normal forms are also closely related. The *replicator dynamic of the N-player extensive form game* Γ is the dynamic on $\times_{n=1}^{N} \Delta(S_n)$ given by

$$\dot{p}_{n,i} = p_{n,i}[\pi_n(p\backslash e_{n,i}) - \pi_n(p)], \tag{6.2.2}$$

where $p\backslash e_{n,i}$ is the mixed-strategy combination p except for player n who uses pure strategy $e_{n,i}$. If $e_{n,i}$ and $e_{n,j}$ correspond to the same pure strategies in the reduced-strategy set of player n, then

$$\frac{d}{dt}\left(\frac{p_{n,i}}{p_{n,j}}\right) = \left(\frac{p_{n,i}}{p_{n,j}}\right)[\pi_n(p\backslash e_{n,i}) - \pi_n(p\backslash e_{n,j})] = 0,$$

and so the ratios $p_{n,i}/p_{n,j}$ are constant for all time. Thus any trajectory of (6.2.2) becomes a trajectory of the *reduced-strategy normal form N-player replicator dynamic* where $p_{n,i}$ for a pure strategy $e_{n,i}$ in the reduced pure strategy set is the sum of the frequencies given in (6.2.1). Conversely, given a trajectory C of the reduced form N-player replicator dynamic and an initial collection of ratios $p_{n,i}/p_{n,j}$ for all $e_{n,i}$ and $e_{n,j}$ that correspond to the same pure strategies in the reduced-strategy set, there is a unique trajectory of (6.2.2) corresponding to C.[11]

A similar correspondence exists for the best response dynamics of the standard and reduced-strategy normal forms when appropriate tie-breaking rules for the standard normal form are used that maintain these ratios. For arbitrary tie-breaking rules that do not maintain these ratios, best response trajectories of the standard normal form still project to best response trajectories of the reduced-strategy normal form.[12] Furthermore trajectories of a monotone selection dynamic for the standard normal form project to trajectories of a monotone selection dynamic for the reduced-strategy normal form when vector fields at strategies that have the same projection are consistent.

---

11. It is not always explicitly stated when the reduced form replicator dynamic is being considered in the following chapters. The reader will be able to determine this from the surrounding context.

12. Care must be taken here to ensure that the tie-breaking rules for the standard normal form assign the same (reduced form) best response at two points that project to the same point. Otherwise, a single best response trajectory may intersect itself. Similar considerations also apply to monotone selection dynamics.

There are relative advantages and disadvantages to each of these normal forms. The reduced-strategy normal form is often used to eliminate "spurious" duplication of strategies that needlessly complicates the analysis. For instance, if player one has disjoint information sets in Γ that follow another of his information sets, then Γ can have no strict NE in its standard normal form (and so no singleton asymptotically stable rest point for the replicator dynamic) but can have strict NE in the reduced-strategy normal form. On the other hand, an obvious disadvantage of the reduced-strategy normal form is that pure strategies are no longer in 1–1 correspondence with behavior strategy combinations which leads to problems with the concept of subgame perfect NE (except in the special case that a subgame perfect NE exists for which the root of every subgame is relevant). A further advantage of the standard normal form becomes clear when the population adjustment process is based on observed play (see chapter 8.4).

Remark 6.2.2 There are other "reduced" normal forms considered in the literature (see Notes). In an N-player normal form game, two pure strategies of player n ($e_{n,i}$ and $e_{n,j}$) are equivalent if they have the same payoff function (i.e., $\pi_n(p \backslash e_{n,i}) = \pi_n(p \backslash e_{n,j})$ for all $p \in \Delta$). Only one copy of equivalent pure strategies are taken for the *semireduced normal form* of an N-player normal form game. The *reduced normal form* of an N-player normal form game goes further by also deleting, for each player n, every pure strategy whose payoff function is a strict convex combination of those given by other pure strategies. Since $\hat{e}_{n,i}$ and $\hat{e}_{n,j}$ in S_n are equivalent pure strategies of player n if they both restrict to $e_n \in T_n$, the (semi-)reduced normal form of the normal form of an extensive form game Γ is a reduction of the reduced-strategy normal form Γ. On the other hand, for almost all payoff assignments to the endpoints of a fixed extensive form structure, all of these reduced normal forms agree.

6.3 The Wright Manifold and Replicator Dynamic

The Wright manifold in its various guises has played an increasingly central role for the dynamic analyses of the previous chapters starting with the symmetrized bimatrix games of chapter 3.4. As discussed below (see theorem 6.3.2), these Wright manifolds in chapter 3 can be obtained by looking at the subgame structure of the extensive form of the symmetrized bimatrix game (with the symmetry ignored). We start by defining the Wright manifold for any subgame of an extensive form game Γ.

Suppose that Γ_u is a subgame of Γ and that $e_{n,i}$ and $e_{n,j}$ are (normal form) pure strategies of player n for which u is a relevant information set. Let $e^u_{n,i\backslash j}$ be the pure strategy in Γ of player n that makes the same choice as $e_{n,j}$ at all player n information sets in the subgame Γ_u and the same choice as $e_{n,i}$ at all other player n information sets. Notice that both $e_{n,i}$ and $e_{n,j}$ (and so $e^u_{n,i\backslash j}$) make the same choice at each decision point of player n on the path to u. Let $p^u_{n,i\backslash j}$ be the frequency of pure strategy $e^u_{n,i\backslash j}$ (at time t). In particular, $e^u_{n,i\backslash i} = e_{n,i}$ and $p^u_{n,i\backslash i} = p_{n,i}$.[13]

Definition 6.3.1 *Suppose that Γ_u is a subgame of a finite N-player extensive form game Γ with perfect recall. The Wright manifold with respect to Γ_u, W^u, is the set of strategies p in the interior of Δ satisfying*

$$p^u_{n,i\backslash i} p^u_{n,j\backslash j} = p^u_{n,i\backslash j} p^u_{n,j\backslash i} \tag{6.3.1}$$

whenever u is relevant for both $e_{n,i}$ and $e_{n,j}$. The Wright manifold, W, of Γ consists of all interior strategies that are in W^u for all subgames Γ_u of Γ.

Let us apply definition 6.3.1 to the symmetrized bimatrix games Γ of chapter 3.4. As a two-player game, Γ has two subgames following an initial move by nature; namely the left-hand subgame (where player one is the row player and player two is the column player) and the right-hand subgame (where the player roles are reversed). For either subgame, Γ_u, a completely mixed strategy combination $(p, q) \in \Delta_1 \times \Delta_2$, is in W^u if and only if $p_{ij} p_{k\ell} = p_{i\ell} p_{kj}$ (and the analogous equation for q), where p_{ij} is the frequency of the pure strategy of player one that chooses action i in the left-hand subgame and action j in the right-hand subgame. Thus the Wright manifold, W, of Γ is the set of all mixed representatives of completely mixed behavior strategies (i.e., $p_{ij} = p^1_i p^2_j$ and a similar equation for q).[14] That is, we have the following result:

Theorem 6.3.2 *The Wright manifold for a symmetrized bimatrix game is the set of all mixed representatives of completely mixed behavior strategies.*

---

13. The construction of the strategy $e^u_{n,i\backslash j}$ (and its frequency $p^u_{n,i\backslash j}$) from $e_{n,i}$ and $e_{n,j}$ is closely related to the fact that for each player, $\{e \in S \mid e \text{ reaches } u\}$ is a strategically independent set (see Notes) of the normal form of Γ whenever Γ_u is a subgame of Γ. Strategic independence is also important for other information sets u (see remark 6.3.4 below).

14. This was only shown in chapter 3.4 for the strategies of player one since the symmetry of the game was emphasized there. Elements (p, q) of the Wright manifold defined above are precisely those whose separate components, p and q, are elements of the Wright manifold considered in chapter 3.4. We will see this connection again in section 6.4 when we define the Wright manifold of general symmetric extensive form games.

In chapter 3.4 we also showed that the symmetrized replicator dynamic was invariant on the Wright manifold of Γ, becoming the bimatrix replicator dynamic up to the factor $\frac{1}{2}$. For a general extensive form game with subgame Γ_u, let $K^u(p \backslash e_{n,i})$ be the probability that u is reached when strategy $p \backslash e_{n,i}$ is used (for symmetrized bimatrix games, $K^u(p \backslash e_{n,i}) = \frac{1}{2}$ for each subgame Γ_u since this is the probability assigned by nature to reach subgame Γ_u). The general result becomes:

Theorem 6.3.3 *(i) If Γ_u is a subgame of Γ, then W^u is invariant for the replicator dynamic (6.2.2). Thus, the Wright manifold W is also invariant for the replicator dynamic (6.2.2).*

(ii) The replicator dynamic (6.2.2) restricted to W^u induces an adjusted *replicator dynamic for the N-player extensive form game Γ_u; namely*

$$\dot{p}^u_{n,i} = K^u(p \backslash e_{n,i}) p^u_{n,i} \left(\pi^u_n(p^u \backslash e^u_{n,i}) - \pi^u_n(p^u) \right), \tag{6.3.2}$$

where $e_{n,i}$ is any pure strategy for which u is relevant and $p^u_{n,i}$ is the frequency of pure strategy $e^u_{n,i}$ of player n in Γ_u.[15]

Proof Let Γ_u be a subgame of Γ with corresponding Wright manifold W^u.

(i) If u is relevant for pure strategies $e_{n,1}$ and $e_{n,2}$ of player n, from (6.2.2),

$$\frac{d}{dt} \left(p^u_{n,1 \backslash 1} p^u_{n,2 \backslash 2} - p^u_{n,1 \backslash 2} p^u_{n,2 \backslash 1} \right)$$

$$= p^u_{n,1 \backslash 1} p^u_{n,2 \backslash 2} \left[\pi_n(p \backslash e^u_{n,1 \backslash 1}) - \pi_n(p) + \pi_n(p \backslash e^u_{n,2 \backslash 2}) - \pi_n(p) \right]$$

$$- p^u_{n,1 \backslash 2} p^u_{n,2 \backslash 1} \left[\pi_1(p \backslash e^u_{n,1 \backslash 2}) - \pi_n(p) + \pi_2(p \backslash e^u_{n,2 \backslash 1}) - \pi_n(p) \right].$$

W^u is invariant if the derivative above is zero when $p \in W^u$. On W^u, the right-hand side simplifies to

$$p^u_{n,1 \backslash 1} p^u_{n,2 \backslash 2} \left[\pi_n(p \backslash e^u_{n,1 \backslash 1}) + \pi_n(p \backslash e^u_{n,2 \backslash 2}) - \pi_n(p \backslash e^u_{n,1 \backslash 2}) - \pi_n(p \backslash e^u_{n,2 \backslash 1}) \right].$$

On the other hand, if u is relevant for both e_i and e_j, then

$$\pi_n(p \backslash e^u_{n,i \backslash j}) = \sum_{\substack{z \text{ follows } u}} \gamma(z, p \backslash e_{n,j}) \pi_n(z) + \sum_{\substack{z \text{ does not} \\ \text{follow } u}} \gamma(z, p \backslash e_{n,i}) \pi_n(z),$$

---

15. The notation $p^u_{n,i}$ is not to be confused with $p^u_{n,i \backslash i}$ in (6.3.1). They refer to frequencies of pure strategies in the extensive form games Γ_u and Γ respectively. Each p in the interior of Δ induces a mixed strategy combination in Γ_u according to formula (6.3.3) given in the proof of theorem 6.3.3.

where $z \in Z$, the set of endpoints of Γ. Note that this last equation relies on the fact $e_{n,i}$ and $e_{n,j}$ make the same choices at all decision points of player n on the path to u. Clearly, the required derivative is zero.

The final statement of part (i) of the theorem follows immediately from definition 6.3.1.

(ii) To prove that induced dynamics are an adjusted replicator, any point p in the interior of Δ induces a point p^u in the interior of the normal form strategy simplex for Γ_u. Specifically, in analogy to (6.1.1), if $e_{n,i}^u$ is a pure strategy of player n for Γ_u, let the corresponding components of p_n^u be defined by

$$p_{n,i}^u = \frac{\sum_j \left\{ p_{n,j} \mid u \text{ is relevant for } e_{n,j} \text{ and } e_{n,j} \text{ restricts to } e_{n,i}^u \text{ on } \Gamma_u \right\}}{\sum_j \{ p_{n,j} \mid u \text{ is relevant for } e_{n,j} \}}.$$

$$(6.3.3)$$

Recall that the information set u is *relevant* for $e_{n,j}$ (or for a mixed strategy p_n with $p_{n,j} > 0$) if there is some pure strategy $e \in \Delta$ with nth component $e_{n,j}$ such that the outcome path e goes through u. The remainder of the proof, given in the appendix, develops (6.3.2) by taking the derivative of (6.3.3). A crucial step is to show that only those $z \in Z$ that follow u affect this derivative.   ∎

The Wright manifold is nontrivial since it includes all mixed representatives of completely mixed behavior strategies. That is, a $p \in \Delta$ is automatically in W if $p_{n,i}$ is the product of probabilities, over the information sets of player n, that p_n chooses the action specified by $e_{n,i}$ at each such information set since these p clearly satisfy definition 6.3.1. If W equals the set of mixed representatives as in theorem 6.3.2, the replicator dynamic on W induces a behavior strategy dynamic through (6.3.2) at each player information set. Unfortunately, we cannot expect the replicator dynamic to restrict so naturally to a behavior strategy dynamic for all extensive form games. For instance, Γ may have few, if any, subgames (e.g., all the explicit asymmetric games considered in chapter 4 that were not truly symmetric) in which case the Wright manifold will typically be much larger than the set of mixed representatives.

On the other hand, the proof above shows that the invariance of W^u for player n only relies on the fact both $e_{n,i}$ and $e_{n,j}$ make the same choice at each decision point of player n on the path to u. This observation, together with perfect recall, means that a *Wright manifold with respect to information set u for player n, W_n^u*, can be defined for any information set u of player n even when it is not the root of a sub-game of Γ. If W_n^u is taken to be the set of all p in the interior of Δ for which $p_{n,i\setminus i}^u p_{n,j\setminus j}^u = p_{n,i\setminus j}^u p_{n,j\setminus i}^u$ whenever u is relevant for both $e_{n,i}$ and $e_{n,j}$, then W_n^u is indeed invariant for the replicator dynamic (6.2.2). The *Wright manifold for player n*, W_n, is the set of all interior strategies that are in W_n^u for all information sets u of player n. This construction is especially important for the asymmetric games of chapter 4. For example, in the Age-Structured Owner-Intruder Game, there are no subgames but the Wright manifold considered there is closely connected to the Wright manifold of each player (see theorem 6.4.4 below) and is still the set of completely mixed strategy representatives.

Remark 6.3.4   The Wright manifold W_n^u of player n can be described intuitively as those strategy combinations whose conditional strategies for player n at those information sets of player n that follow u (or equal u) are independent of choices at player n information sets v that are disjoint from u. To formalize this, any pure strategy $e_{n,i}$ for player n can be split at u by writing it as $e_{n,i_1\setminus i_2}^u$ where i_1 refers to choices at information sets of player n that are disjoint from u and i_2 refers to the others.

   If u is relevant for $e_{n,i} = e_{n,i_1\setminus i_2}^u$, then it will be relevant for all e_j of the form $e_{n,j_1\setminus i_2}^u$. The frequency of a strategy in Γ_u indexed by i_2 conditional on using choices indexed by j_1 disjoint from u is $p_{n,j_1\setminus i_2}^u / \sum_{j_2} p_{n,j_1\setminus j_2}^u$, where j_2 are those indexes for which u is relevant for $e_{n,j_1\setminus j_2}^u$. These conditional strategy frequencies do not depend on j_1 if

$$\frac{p_{n,i_1\setminus i_2}^u}{\sum_{j_2} p_{n,i_1\setminus j_2}^u} = \frac{p_{n,j_1\setminus i_2}^u}{\sum_{j_2} p_{n,j_1\setminus j_2}^u}$$

for all j_1. From (6.3.1) this equation holds for all $p \in W_n^u$. In fact this independence of conditional strategies on W_n^u holds when both sides of this equation are summed over a subset of $i_2's$. In particular, on W_n^u, the conditional frequency distribution of a behavior strategy of player n at a fixed information set of player n following or equal to u is independent of choices that are disjoint from u.

   By remark 6.3.4 applied to the Wright manifold for Γ, W can be understood heuristically as the set of completely mixed strategies for which the expected strategy used by any player in any subgame Γ_u of Γ does not depend on what choice was used at information sets that are disjoint from u. For instance, p is in the Wright manifold of the

symmetrized Buyer-Seller Game of chapter 3.4 if the relative frequency
of player one individuals who are Honest as a seller conditioned on
using Trust as a buyer is the same as that conditioned on using Inspect
as a buyer. That is, for player one, $p \in W$ if and only if it is a completely
mixed strategy that satisfies $p_{HT}/(p_{HT} + p_{CT}) = p_{HI}/(p_{HI} + p_{CI})$. It is
easy to verify that such p are given precisely by the set W defined in
definition 6.3.1.

6.4   Symmetric Extensive Form Games

A *symmetric extensive form game* Γ is a two-player extensive form game
together with a *symmetry* f that maps the choice partition onto itself and
satisfies the following six properties (here C_i denotes the set of choices
of player i):

   i. If $c \in C_0$, then $f(c) \in C_0$ and $\rho(f(c)) = \rho(c)$.

  ii. If $c \in C_1$, then $f(c) \in C_2$.

 iii. $f(f(c)) = c$ for every $c \in C$.

 iv. For every information set $u \in U$, there is an $f(u) \in U$ such that every
choice at u is mapped onto a choice at $f(u)$.

  v. For every endpoint $z \in Z$, there is an $f(z) \in Z$ such that the choices
on the path to $f(z)$ are the image under f of the choices on the path to z.

 vi. $\pi_1(f(z)) = \pi_2(z)$ and $\pi_2(f(z)) = \pi_1(z)$ for every $z \in Z$.

Every symmetry f of a symmetric extensive form game is *subgame
preserving*.[16] That is, for every subgame Γ_u of Γ, there is another subgame Γ_v of Γ such that every information set in Γ_u is mapped under
f onto an information set in Γ_v. A subgame that is mapped onto itself
under f is called a *symmetric subgame*; otherwise, it is *an asymmetric subgame*. The Two-Message Signaling Game of figure 6.0.1 is a symmetric
extensive form game, the symmetry is indicated by double arrows join-
ing information sets of players one and two. The subgames Γ_{u_1} and Γ_{u_4}
are symmetric,[17] whereas Γ_{u_2} and Γ_{u_3} are asymmetric.

The symmetry f also maps the pure strategies of player one onto
the pure strategies of player two (and vice versa) in the obvious way.
That is, if e_1 is the pure strategy of player one that takes choice c_u
at information set u of player one, then $f(e_1)$ is the pure strategy of

---

16. This result relies on the assumption that every decision point of Γ has at least two
alternatives.

17. Γ_{u_0} is trivially symmetric since it is the entire game.

player two that takes choice $f(c_u)$ at information set $f(u)$ of player two. When the normal form strategy sets of both players are so identified (and labeled S), payoffs are independent of player designation (i.e., $\pi_1(e_i, e_j) = \pi_2(e_j, e_i) \equiv \pi(e_i, e_j)$) by condition vi above, and so we have a symmetric normal form game.

The terminology and techniques developed in the previous sections can be applied, with minor adjustments, to these symmetric normal form games. For instance, a strategy $p \in \Delta(S)$ in a symmetric extensive form game is *pervasive* if (p, p) is pervasive for the two-player extensive form game. In fact p is pervasive if and only if every information set of player one is relevant for p. A behavior strategy (of player one) is pervasive if its mixed strategy representative is pervasive. The statements in theorem 6.1.1 also require minor adjustments. For instance, to conclude that every symmetric extensive form game has at least one symmetric subgame perfect NE, backward induction applied to minimal symmetric subgames must take a symmetric NE, whereas any two-player NE of an asymmetric subgame is permissible by assigning one of these strategies to player one in this subgame and the other to player one in its symmetric image.

Again, we do not expect singleton ESSs in the standard symmetric normal form due to spurious duplication of strategies. One attempt to eliminate this problem is through the following definition and theorem based on behavior strategies. Here the expected payoff to behavior strategy b interacting with behavior strategy b', denoted $\pi(b, b')$, is $\pi_1(p, q)$ where p and q are the mixed strategy representatives of b and b' respectively.

Definition 6.4.1 *The behavior strategy b is a* direct ESS *of a symmetric extensive form game Γ if*

i. $\pi(b', b) \leq \pi(b, b)$ *for all behavior strategies b' (i.e., b is a symmetric NE) and*

ii. *if $\pi(b', b) = \pi(b, b)$, then $\pi(b', b') < \pi(b, b')$ whenever $b' \neq b$.*

Some symmetric extensive form games have a direct ESS but no (normal form) ESS, while others have an ESS that is not direct. As an example of the former, consider a truly symmetric game Γ of chapter 4.6 that has two strategies in each of two information situations (i.e., there are $N = 2$ roles). Theorem 4.6.1 of chapter 4, expressed in the terminology of this section for symmetric extensive form games, states that if both proper subgames have an interior ESS, these combine to form a direct ESS b^* for Γ. However, there is no ESS for Γ since b^* corresponds to a one dimensional ESSet E (i.e., a line segment), all of whose points induce b^* in these subgames. Elementary examples of the latter phenomenon occur when strict NE exist in the reduced-strategy normal form that do not reach all information sets.[18] The following theorem shows such strict NE do not induce direct ESSs since they are not pervasive:

Theorem 6.4.2   *A behavior strategy is a direct ESS if and only if it is pervasive and corresponds to an ESSet of the game's normal form. In particular, a direct ESS is a subgame perfect NE.*

Proof   Suppose that b^* is a direct ESS. If an information set u of player one is not relevant for the mixed representative of b^*, then there are other behavior strategies $b' \neq b^*$ that are realization equivalent[19] to b^* by (6.1.1). This contradicts condition ii of definition 6.4.1, and so b^* must be pervasive. Let $E \equiv \{p^* \mid p^*$ is realization equivalent to $b^*\}$. Since every information set of player one is relevant for b^*, E is a set of NE by condition i. Furthermore, if $p' \notin E$ and $\pi(p', p^*) = \pi(p^*, p^*)$, then p' is realization equivalent to $b' \neq b^*$ which satisfies $\pi(b', b^*) = \pi(b^*, b^*)$. Thus, by condition ii, $\pi(b', b') < \pi(b, b')$, which implies $\pi(p', p') < \pi(p^*, p')$. That is, E is an ESSet.

The converse is straightforward, and the final statement of the theorem is a corollary of theorem 6.1.1.   ∎

The statement of theorem 6.4.2 does not specify which normal form is taken for Γ. The reason for this ambiguity is that we have the following analogues of theorems 6.1.1 and 6.2.1 (whose straightforward proof is again left to the reader):

Theorem 6.4.3   *A subset E of $\Delta(S)$ is an ESSet of the normal form of a symmetric extensive form game Γ if and only if E corresponds to an ESSet of the reduced-strategy normal form of Γ. If p is an ESS of the (reduced) normal form of Γ and Γ_u is reachable by p, then p induces an ESS p^u in Γ_u as well as an ESS in the truncated game $\Gamma_{-u}(p^u)$.*[20]

The results of sections 6.2 and 6.3 concerning the replicator dynamic and the Wright manifold also apply to symmetric extensive form games

---

18. Payoffs for the elementary symmetric extensive form game of figure 7.1.1 in chapter 7 are easily modified to satisfy this.

19. That is, (b', b') is realization equivalent to (b^*, b^*) for the two-player extensive form game obtained when symmetry is ignored.

20. The converse of this statement is not true (see chapter 7.1). In fact examples given there show backward induction applied to the ESS structure of the subgames does not necessarily yield an ESS of Γ even when this NE is pervasive.

Γ. Dynamic trajectories $(p(t), q(t))$ in these two-player games are *symmetric* if $p(t) = q(t)$ for all t. In particular, all trajectories of the replicator dynamic (6.2.2) are symmetric if they are so at time $t = 0$, thus defining the *symmetric replicator dynamic* for Γ. Similarly the Wright manifold of definition 6.3.1 can be restricted to the symmetric interior strategies in the strategy simplex which is identified with $\Delta(S)$. Theorem 6.3.3 remains valid for these revised definitions.

The discussion surrounding remark 6.3.4 applied to symmetric extensive form games is especially relevant for the asymmetric games of chapter 4 as summarized in theorem 6.4.4 below. In general, for any information set u of player one in a symmetric extensive form game Γ, the Wright manifold with respect to information set u of player one, W_1^u, consists of those strategies p in $\Delta(S)$ that satisfy $p_{i \setminus i}^u p_{j \setminus j}^u = p_{i \setminus j}^u p_{j \setminus i}^u$ whenever u is relevant for both e_i and e_j. The Wright manifold of player one, W_1, of Γ is then the set of all interior strategies that are in W_1^u for all information sets of Γ for player one. It is invariant under the symmetric replicator dynamic.[21] From this perspective, the results in chapter 4.4 become as follows:

Theorem 6.4.4   *The Wright manifold of player one for the extensive form of an asymmetric game with N roles is the set of all mixed representatives of completely mixed behavior strategies. The symmetric replicator dynamic is invariant on this set where it induces the N-species behavior strategy dynamic (4.4.4).*

If information set u of player one is the root of a subgame Γ_u of the symmetric extensive form game Γ, there is additional structure on the dynamics (whether Γ_u is a symmetric or asymmetric subgame) that is used repeatedly in chapter 7. Recall that the Wright manifold, W, of Γ is the set of all interior strategies that are in W_1^u for all subgames Γ_u of Γ. It is invariant under the symmetric replicator dynamic.

If Γ_u is a symmetric subgame of Γ, the symmetric replicator dynamic on W^u induces the rescaled symmetric replicator dynamic (6.4.1) on Γ_u that is adjusted by the factor $K^u(p)$:[22]

$$\dot{p}_i^u = K^u(p) p_i^u \left(\pi^u \left(e_i^u, p^u \right) - \pi^u(p^u, p^u) \right). \tag{6.4.1}$$

---

21. We can ignore the strategy of player two in these calculations since, by symmetry, the strategies of player one and player two can be identified.
22. From theorem 6.3.3ii, $K^u(p)$ is the probability u is reached when strategy p is used by player two (and player one takes all the correct alternatives that lead to u).

As an elementary example, consider the truly symmetric game Γ of figure 4.6.1 in chapter 4. The Wright manifold is $W = \{p \in \Delta^9 \mid p_{ik} = p_i^u p_k^v\}$, the set of mixed representatives of the completely mixed behavior strategies of Γ. On both proper (symmetric) subgames, $K^u(p) = \frac{1}{2}$, and so the replicator dynamic restricted to W actually induces the replicator dynamic on each. Since $p_0^* = (10, 8, 11)/29$ is globally asymptotically stable in each subgame, the unique point $p^* \in W$ that induces p_0^* in these two subgames is globally asymptotically stable on W for the symmetric replicator dynamic. Thus the unstable NE reported in chapter 4.6.1 is forced to be a point in the four-dimensional NE set that is not on the Wright manifold.

For asymmetric subgames the analysis is complicated by the fact pay-offs $\pi_1^u(p^u \backslash e_{1,i}^u)$ in (6.3.2) depend on the strategy of player two in sub-game Γ_u which, by symmetry, is the same as the strategy of player one in subgame $\Gamma_{f(u)}$. Thus we obtain an adjusted bimatrix replicator dynamic that combines Γ_u and its symmetric image:

$$
\begin{aligned}
\dot{p}_i^u &= K^{f(u)}(p) p_i^u \left(\pi^u \left(e_i^u, p^{f(u)} \right) - \pi^u \left(p^u, p^{f(u)} \right) \right), \\
\dot{p}_i^{f(u)} &= K^u(p) p_i^{f(u)} \left(\pi^{f(u)} \left(e_i^{f(u)}, p^u \right) - \pi^{f(u)} \left(p^{f(u)}, p^u \right) \right).
\end{aligned}
\tag{6.4.2}
$$

Since the factor $K^{f(u)}(p)$ adjusting the replicator dynamic is typically dif-ferent in Γ_u than $K^u(p)$ in $\Gamma_{f(u)}$, this is not simply the rescaled bimatrix replicator dynamic (see chapter 7.2 where explicit expressions for these factors are given for symmetric extensive form games with the tree structure of figure 6.0.1).

6.5   Appendix

Proof of Theorem 6.3.3ii

To prove (6.3.2), fix a pure strategy $e_{n,1}^u$ of player n in Γ_u. From (6.2.2) and (6.3.3),

$$
\begin{aligned}
\dot{p}_{n,1}^u &= \frac{\sum_{i,j}(\dot{p}_{n,i} p_{n,j} - p_{n,i} \dot{p}_{n,j})}{\left(\sum p_{n,j} \right)^2} \\
&= \frac{\sum_{i,j} p_{n,i} p_{n,j} (\pi_n(p \backslash e_{n,i}) - \pi_n(p \backslash e_{n,j}))}{\left(\sum_j p_{n,j} \right)^2},
\end{aligned}
\tag{6.5.1}
$$

where the summations for the remainder of this proof are over i and j for which u is relevant for both $e_{n,i}$ and $e_{n,j}$ with $e_{n,i}$ restricting to $e_{n,1}^u$ on Γ_u. The two terms in the numerator are weighted sums of payoffs over the paths of Γ (e.g., $\sum_{i,j} p_{n,i} p_{n,j} \pi_n(p \backslash e_{n,i}) = \sum_{z \in Z} \sum_{i,j} p_{n,i} p_{n,j} \gamma(z, p \backslash e_{n,j}) \pi_n(z)$).

First, consider those endpoints z that do not follow u and write $e_{n,j}$ as $e_{n,j_1 \backslash j_2}^u$ where j_1 refers to choices at those information sets of player one that are disjoint from u (i.e., no path goes through u and this information set) and j_2 refers to the others. Then, on W^u,

$$\sum_{i,j} p_{n,i} p_{n,j} \gamma(z, p \backslash e_{n,j}) \pi_n(z) = \sum_{i,j_1,j_2} p_{n,i \backslash j_2}^u p_{n,j_1 \backslash 1} \gamma(z, p \backslash e_{n,i \backslash j_2}^u) \pi_n(z)$$

$$= \sum_{i,j} p_{n,i \backslash i}^u p_{n,j \backslash j}^u \gamma(z, p \backslash e_{n,i \backslash i}^u) \pi_n(z).$$

Therefore the numerator in (6.5.1) for $p_{n,1}^u$ is zero for these paths.

Thus, on W^u, $\dot{p}_{n,1}^u$ is given by

$$\frac{\sum_{i,j} \sum_{z \text{ follows } u} p_{n,i} p_{n,j} \left(\gamma(z, p \backslash e_{n,i \backslash i}^u) - \gamma(z, p \backslash e_{n,j \backslash j}^u) \right) \pi_n(z)}{\left(\sum_j p_{n,j} \right)^2}$$

$$= \frac{\sum_{z \text{ follows } u} \left(\sum_j p_{n,j} \sum_i p_{n,i} \gamma(z, p \backslash e_{n,i \backslash i}^u) - \sum_i p_{n,i} \sum_j p_{n,j} \gamma(z, p \backslash e_{n,j \backslash j}^u) \right) \pi_n(z)}{\left(\sum p_{n,j} \right)^2}$$

$$= \frac{\sum_{z \text{ follows } u} \pi_n(z) \left(p_{n,1}^u \gamma(z, p \backslash e_{n,1}) - p_{n,1}^u \sum_j p_{n,j} \gamma(z, p \backslash e_{n,j}) \right)}{\sum p_{n,j}}.$$

If z follows u, then $\gamma(z, p \backslash e_{n,j})$ is equal to the positive probability endpoint z is reached in the subgame times the probability $K^u(p \backslash e_{n,j})$ that u is reached under the strategy $p \backslash e_{n,j}$. Since p is in the interior of Δ, $K^u(p \backslash e_{n,j}) = K^u(p \backslash e_{n,i})$ for all i and j under consideration. Thus

$$\dot{p}_{n,1}^u = K^u(p \backslash e_{n,i}) p_{n,1}^u \left(\pi_n^u(p^u \backslash e_{n,1}^u) - \pi_n^u(p^u) \right),$$

where π_n^u is the payoff function for player n in the subgame Γ_u. This is the replicator dynamic (up to the factor $K^u(p \backslash e_{n,i})$) on the subgame Γ_u. ■

6.6 Notes

The terminology introduced in this chapter for extensive form games follows for the most part the traditional approach of Kuhn (1953) and, when the game is symmetric, of Selten (1983; see also van Damme 1991). This terminology is based primarily on the information partition.

Recently Ritzberger (1999) defined extensive form games through the choice partition, showing that the original definition overspecifies the six constituents. Ritzberger also characterized the perfect recall concept in several different ways that clarify its connection with rationality assumptions. The backward induction procedure applied to the NE structure of games is often attributed to Zermelo (1913), although this seems to be undeserved (Schwalbe and Walker 2001). It certainly appears in Kuhn (1953) and, more explicitly, in Selten (1975) where the concept of subgame perfection is also discussed. Kuhn also proved most of the statements in theorem 6.1.1.

The Two-Message Symmetric Signaling Game (figure 6.0.1) is from Kim (1995). Although the phrase "reduced-strategy normal form" appears to be new, the concept of a reduced-strategy set is not (Osborne and Rubinstein 1994). The (semi-)reduced normal form is quite common (e.g., van Damme 1991; Mailath et al. 1993). Strategically independent sets were introduced by Mailath et al. (1993) as a means to develop the concepts of information sets and subgame perfection in normal form games (see also chapter 1.5). The Wright manifold concept for general extensive form games and the analysis of the replicator dynamic in sections 6.2 to 6.4 is from Cressman (2000; see also Cressman et al. 2000). Direct ESSs for symmetric extensive form games were introduced by Selten (1983) with further static properties developed in van Damme (1991). The related concept of *limit ESS* in these references (see also Samuelson 1991), which was introduced to widen the ESS concept to select certain nonpervasive NE, is ignored in this book.

7   Simultaneity Games

In this chapter and the next we analyze the dynamics of extensive form games that exhibit a high degree of subgame decomposability by applying the theory developed in chapter 6.

A *(symmetric) simultaneity game* is a symmetric extensive form game that involves several rounds (or *stages*) between the same two players such that at the beginning of each stage, both players know all actions that have already occurred in the previous stages but not the opponent's action in the current stage. Thus the extensive form of a simultaneity game has many subgames; namely the initial decision point at each stage is a singleton information set that is the root of a subgame. Although moves by nature are allowed at any stage of the game (in which case we assume these occur at the beginning of each stage and that both players know these moves), for the most part we restrict our analysis to simultaneity games that have only player decision points. We arbitrarily assume that player one makes his decision before player two at each stage. Thus, to model simultaneous moves, each information set of player two consists of exactly those decision points that immediately follow a player one decision point. Along any path of the game tree, actions alternate between the two players with exactly one action per player at each stage.

Most of this chapter analyzes specific examples of simultaneity games, emphasizing those aspects of the extensive form game tree that simplify the dynamic and static evolutionary analysis. Specifically, sections 7.1 and 7.2 deal exclusively with two-stage games, while sections 7.4 and 7.5 consider multi-stage examples. The exception is section 7.3 that develops the general theory of asymptotic stability under the symmetric replicator dynamic for simultaneity games.

Equilibrium selection through asymptotic stability is a central theme throughout the chapter. Thus much of our dynamic analysis focuses on subgame perfect NE due to the following result:

Theorem 7.0.1 *If p^* is an asymptotically stable symmetric NE of the standard normal form of a symmetric extensive form game Γ under the symmetric replicator dynamic, then p^* is pervasive. Moreover p^* has one realization equivalent behavior strategy, and this is subgame perfect. If p^* is an asymptotically stable symmetric NE of the reduced-strategy normal form of a symmetric extensive form game under the symmetric replicator dynamic, then p^* is subgame perfect.*[1]

Proof If p^* is asymptotically stable for the standard normal form, then (p^*, p^*) must reach all player one information sets (i.e., p^* is pervasive). Otherwise, consider a $p \neq p^*$ that induces the same behavior strategy at all player one information sets reachable by (p^*, p^*). Then any convex combination of p and p^* is a rest point of the replicator dynamic and so none are asymptotically stable.

Since p^* is pervasive, it has a unique realization equivalent behavior strategy. By theorem 6.1.1 of chapter 6 adjusted to symmetric extensive form games, p^* is subgame perfect. The same argument applies for the reduced-strategy normal form except that (p^*, p^*) must only reach all player one information sets relevant for p^*.   ∎

7.1   Elementary Two-Stage Simultaneity Games

Consider a two-stage simultaneity game, Γ, where both players simultaneously choose between L and R at the first stage. If both choose R, a second stage is reached (otherwise, the game ends) where a simultaneous choice is made between ℓ and r. The extensive form game tree for Γ is given in figure 7.1.1 where two different explicit payoff specifications are also provided. The reduced-strategy normal form of Γ has three pure strategies $S = \{L, [R, \ell], [R, r]\}$ for both players where

---

1. The phrase "p^* is subgame perfect" is a slight abuse of notation that is used throughout the chapter. Any reduced-strategy p defines a unique local behavior strategy at each player one information set that is relevant for p. By extending this for p^* to a behavior strategy that is subgame perfect in all subgames not relevant for p^*, we construct a realization equivalent strategy that is subgame perfect.

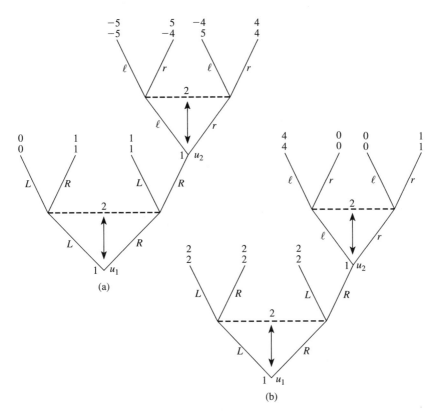

Figure 7.1.1
Elementary two-stage simultaneity games.

these are

L—play L at stage 1.

$[R, \ell]$—play R at stage 1 and ℓ at stage 2 if it is reached.

$[R, r]$—play R at stage 1 and r at stage 2 if it is reached.

The 3×3 payoff matrices for the games in figure 7.1.1a and b respectively are

$$\begin{bmatrix} 0 & 1 & 1 \\ 1 & -5 & 5 \\ 1 & -4 & 4 \end{bmatrix} \quad \text{and} \quad \begin{bmatrix} 2 & 2 & 2 \\ 2 & 4 & 0 \\ 2 & 0 & 1 \end{bmatrix}.$$

The static and dynamic stability properties of the equilibria in Δ^3 for both these games can be obtained readily from their normal forms.

However, to emphasize the extra structure imposed through the games' extensive form, we will begin by discussing these properties through the subgame structure of figure 7.1.1. Specifically, we apply backward induction to the NE and ESS of the subgames and their truncations for these two games in turn.

For figure 7.1.1a the symmetric subgame Γ_{u_2} has payoff matrix A^{u_2} given by

$$
\begin{array}{cc}
 & \ell \quad r \\
\begin{array}{c} \ell \\ r \end{array} & \begin{bmatrix} -5 & 5 \\ -4 & 4 \end{bmatrix},
\end{array}
$$

with a unique symmetric NE $p^{u_2*} = (\frac{1}{2}, \frac{1}{2})$ that also happens to be a mixed ESS. In the truncated game, $\Gamma_{-u_2}(p^{u_2*})$, with information set u_2 replaced by the payoff 0 received by both players who use p^{u_2*} whenever stage 2 is reached, the single-stage payoff matrix is

$$
\begin{array}{cc}
 & L \quad R \\
\begin{array}{c} L \\ R \end{array} & \begin{bmatrix} 0 & 1 \\ 1 & 0 \end{bmatrix}.
\end{array}
$$

Thus $\Gamma_{-u_2}(p^{u_2*})$ also has a unique symmetric NE $(\frac{1}{2}, \frac{1}{2})$ that also happens to be a mixed ESS. Combining these results shows that Γ has a unique symmetric subgame perfect NE; namely the pervasive NE $p^* = (\frac{1}{2}, \frac{1}{4}, \frac{1}{4})$ that plays L at stage 1 half the time and, if the game reaches stage 2, plays ℓ with probability $\frac{1}{2}$. One might intuitively expect that p^* is also an ESS of Γ. Clearly, $\pi(p, p^*) = \pi(p^*, p^*)$ for all $p \in \Delta^3$. However, $\pi(p^*, e_3) < \pi(e_3, e_3)$, which violates the ESS requirement for a mixed NE. Thus p^* is not an ESS, and in fact Γ has no ESS for figure 7.1.1a. This example shows the converse to the final statement in theorem 6.4.3 of chapter 6 is not true (i.e., backward induction applied to the ESS structure of the subgames and their truncations for symmetric extensive form games does not necessarily yield an ESS of the entire game).

For figure 7.1.1b the symmetric subgame Γ_{u_2} is a Coordination Game with three symmetric NE $(1, 0)$, $(0, 1)$, and $(\frac{1}{5}, \frac{4}{5})$. Only the two pure strategies are ESSs. The truncated 2×2 games are now

$$
\begin{bmatrix} 2 & 2 \\ 2 & 4 \end{bmatrix}, \quad \begin{bmatrix} 2 & 2 \\ 2 & 1 \end{bmatrix}, \quad \text{and} \quad \begin{bmatrix} 2 & 2 \\ 2 & \frac{4}{5} \end{bmatrix}
$$

respectively. Each has a unique symmetric NE $((0, 1)$, $(1, 0)$, and $(1, 0)$ respectively) and all are ESSs. Thus $(0, 1, 0)$ and $(1, 0, 0)$ are symmetric

NE of Γ that are readily shown to be the only ones. The former is a pervasive ESS, while the latter is neither pervasive nor an ESS.

The dynamic stability of symmetric NE for the symmetric replicator dynamic is easy to describe for these two games by considering the dynamic induced on the subgame Γ_{u_2}. From first principles

$$
\begin{aligned}
\dot{p}_\ell^{u_2} &= \frac{d}{dt}\left(\frac{p_{[R,\ell]}}{p_{[R,\ell]} + p_{[R,r]}}\right) \\
&= (\dot{p}_{[R,\ell]}p_{[R,r]} - \dot{p}_{[R,r]}p_{[R,\ell]})/(p_{[R,\ell]} + p_{[R,r]})^2 \\
&= p_{[R,\ell]}p_{[R,r]}\pi([R,\ell] - [R,r], p)/(p_{[R,\ell]} + p_{[R,r]})^2 \qquad (7.1.1) \\
&= p_{[R,\ell]}p_{[R,r]}\left(e_\ell^{u_2} - e_r^{u_2}\right) \cdot A^{u_2}p^{u_2}/(p_{[R,\ell]} + p_{[R,r]}) \\
&= p_R^{u_1}p_\ell^{u_2}p_r^{u_2}\left(e_\ell^{u_2} - e_r^{u_2}\right) \cdot A^{u_2}p^{u_2} \\
&= p_R^{u_1}p_\ell^{u_2}\left(e_\ell^{u_2} - p^{u_2}\right) \cdot A^{u_2}p^{u_2},
\end{aligned}
$$

where $p_R^{u_1} \equiv p_{[R,\ell]} + p_{[R,r]}$ is the frequency action R is used at the first-stage information sets if the population is in state p.[2] This is the rescaled symmetric replicator dynamic for Γ_{u_2} up to the nonnegative factor $p_R^{u_1}$.

If $p_R^{u_1} \nrightarrow 0$, the induced one-dimensional dynamic in the second-stage subgame has asymptotically stable rest points that correspond to ESSs of Γ_{u_2}. Thus, if we start sufficiently close to a pervasive p^* so that p^{u_2} is close to an asymptotically stable p^{u_2*} and the truncated two-strategy game $\Gamma_{-u_2}(p^{u_2*})$ has an asymptotically stable rest point (i.e., an ESS) at p^{u_1*}, then p^* is asymptotically stable. This is what happens for the pervasive NE $p^* = (\frac{1}{2}, \frac{1}{4}, \frac{1}{4})$ of figure 7.1.1a and for the pervasive NE $p^* = (0, 1, 0)$ of figure 7.1.1b.

On the other hand, if $p_R^{u_1} \to 0$ as for the symmetric NE $(1, 0, 0)$ of figure 7.1.1b, we cannot conclude immediately from (7.1.1) that p^{u_2} converges to the corresponding ESS $(0, 1)$ of Γ_{u_2} (i.e., that $p_\ell^{u_2}$ converges to 0). However, further analysis shows that for any initial value $0 < p_\ell^{u_2} < \frac{1}{5}$, $p_\ell^{u_2}$ monotonically decreases to 0 for any such interior trajectory of the replicator dynamic. These properties are suggested in the following phase portraits (figure 7.1.2) which also show that $(1, 0, 0)$ is not asymptotically stable for figure 7.1.1b.

---

2. This is actually equation (6.4.1) in chapter 6 for the subgame Γ_{u_2}. The reason is that the Wright manifold W^{u_2} for this example is all of $\Delta(S)$. From this perspective, $p_R^{u_1}$ is the factor $K^{u_2}(p)$ that gives the probability u_2 is reached when player one plays R at u_1 and p is used by player two.

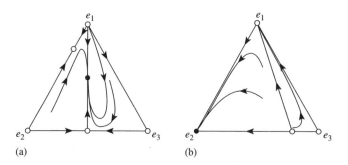

Figure 7.1.2
Phase portraits for the extensive games in figure 7.1.1.

7.2   Two-Stage Two-Strategy Games

In this section we consider two-stage simultaneity games Γ such as that given by the Two-Message Symmetric Signaling Game at the beginning of chapter 6. Specifically, a *two-stage two-strategy game* has the tree structure of this example with no moves by nature, payoffs are cumulative between stages, and all payoffs from the second-stage subgames are based on the same 2×2 game having payoff matrix $\begin{bmatrix} a & b \\ c & d \end{bmatrix}$. For instance, in figure 6.0.1 of chapter 6, the second stage subgames all have strategies H and D with payoff matrix $\begin{bmatrix} -2 & 4 \\ 0 & 0 \end{bmatrix}$, and the first stage game has strategies m_1 and m_2 with payoff matrix $\begin{bmatrix} 0 & 0 \\ -1 & -1 \end{bmatrix}$. The complete dynamic analysis is substantially more difficult than that for the elementary games of section 7.1 (see remark 7.2.2 at the end of section 7.2.1 below). We therefore restrict our attention to the symmetric replicator dynamic on the reduced-strategy normal form Wright manifold W of Γ. For these games, W is the set of completely mixed representatives of Γ (see theorem 7.3.1 below) and is the same as the Wright manifold of player one since each of his information sets corresponds to the root of a subgame.

From chapter 6.4, a calculation similar to (7.1.1) produces the following induced dynamics on the Wright manifold for the second-stage subgames:

$$\dot{p}_\ell^{u_1} = p_L^{u_0} p_\ell^{u_1} \left(e_\ell^{u_1} - p^{u_1} \right) \cdot A^{u_1} p^{u_1}$$

$$\dot{p}_\ell^{u_2} = p_R^{u_0} p_\ell^{u_2} \left(e_\ell^{u_2} - p^{u_2} \right) \cdot A^{u_2} p^{u_3}$$

$$\dot{p}_\ell^{u_3} = p_L^{u_0} p_\ell^{u_3} \left(e_\ell^{u_3} - p^{u_3} \right) \cdot A^{u_3} p^{u_2}$$

$$\dot{p}_\ell^{u_4} = p_R^{u_0} p_\ell^{u_4} \left(e_\ell^{u_4} - p^{u_4} \right) \cdot A^{u_4} p^{u_4}$$

The dynamic on the truncated first-stage game is

$$\dot{p}_L^{u_0} = p_L^{u_0}\left(e_L^{u_0} - p^{u_0}\right) \cdot A^{u_0}(p)p^{u_0},$$

where $A^{u_0}(p)$ is the 2×2 first-stage payoff matrix formed by truncating the four subgames at the second stage with respect to $p^{u_1}, \ldots, p^{u_4}$.

The induced dynamics on symmetric subgames Γ_{u_1} and Γ_{u_4} are again rescaled symmetric replicator dynamics for these symmetric games. The dynamic analysis on the Wright manifold of Γ is considerably simplified for those games whose payoffs are assumed to be generic.[3] Then, for interior trajectories, p^{u_1} and p^{u_4} monotonically evolve in the direction of a NE and so converge to a unique limit point. On the other hand, the dynamics on the asymmetric subgames Γ_{u_2} and Γ_{u_3} are coupled and would be equal to the bimatrix replicator dynamic for the matrix pair (A^{u_2}, A^{u_3}) except for the factors $p_L^{u_0}$ and $p_R^{u_0}$. Although these trajectories can be quite different than those in chapter 3, it is still true that every trajectory of (p^{u_2}, p^{u_3}) converges to a unique limit point (see the proof of theorem 7.2.1 below).

If neither $p_L^{u_0}$ nor $p_R^{u_0}$ converges to zero, the following theorem shows that p^{u_1} and p^{u_4} converge to a NE of A^{u_1} and A^{u_4} respectively while (p^{u_2}, p^{u_3}) converges to a NE of the bimatrix game (A^{u_2}, A^{u_3}). By our assumption of generic payoffs, the truncated first-stage game with respect to these NE has no relevant payoff ties, and so $p_L^{u_0}$ converges to a completely mixed NE of it. That is, p converges to a pervasive subgame perfect NE.

Now suppose that $p_L^{u_0} \to 0$. Although it is still true that p^{u_i} converges to a unique limit point for each second-stage subgame, this limit point need not be a NE of $\Gamma_{u_1}, \Gamma_{u_2}$, or Γ_{u_3}. In the reduced-strategy normal form, let $[R, \ell r]$ denote the pure strategy that chooses R at u_0, ℓ at u_3 and r at u_4, and so on. On the Wright manifold $p_{[R,\ell r]} = p_R^{u_0} p_\ell^{u_3} p_r^{u_4}$, and so the convergence of $p^{u_1}, \ldots, p^{u_4}$ completely determines $p_{[R,\ell r]}$, and so on. That is, p converges to a unique limit point which, by the Folk Theorem of Evolutionary Game Theory, is a NE of Γ that induces a NE in the subgame Γ_{u_4}.

Theorem 7.2.1 *Suppose that Γ is a generic two-stage two-strategy game. Every interior trajectory of the symmetric replicator dynamic on the Wright manifold of Γ converges to a NE. A pervasive NE is asymptotically stable*

---

3. Generic means there are no relevant payoff ties. For second-stage subgames, this requires $(a - c)(b - d) \neq 0$. Furthermore, when Γ is truncated with respect to NE at the second stage, the resultant 2×2 matrix also has no relevant payoff ties.

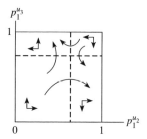

Figure 7.2.1
Flow of the replicator dynamic on the asymmetric subgames Γ_{u_2} and Γ_{u_3} (when there is an interior NE) for two-stage, two-strategy games.

for the reduced-strategy normal form symmetric replicator dynamic of Γ if and only if it is given by backward induction on the ESS structure of the second-stage subgames[4] and of the resultant truncated first-stage symmetric game.

Proof   The final statement is a special case of theorem 7.3.3 below applied to the Wright manifold since subgame asymptotically stable NE are ESSs when there are only two strategies. By the discussion above, the remainder of the theorem will be proved by showing every interior trajectory induces a pair (p^{u_2}, p^{u_3}) that converges to a unique limit point. This result follows from the phase portraits for the nondegenerate bimatrix games considered in chapter 3.3.1 under monotone selection dynamics. The qualitative direction of the evolution for the bimatrix replicator dynamic is all that we need. For instance, if there is no interior NE of the bimatrix game (A^{u_2}, A^{u_3}), then we are in case 3.[5] Thus $p_1^{u_2}$ and $p_1^{u_3}$ are both monotonically decreasing and so have a unique limit point.

If there is an interior NE of the bimatrix game (A^{u_2}, A^{u_3}), then we must be in case 1 of chapter 3.3.1 (i.e., Buyer-Seller Games are not possible for the asymmetric second-stage subgames). With suitable ordering of the two strategies of player one in this bimatrix game, (p^{u_2}, p^{u_3}) evolves in the directions indicated in the four quadrants formed by the interior NE in figure 7.2.1 (i.e., the direction of evolution is that of the

---

4. That is, the NE induce ESSs in the symmetric subgames Γ_{u_1} and Γ_{u_4} and an ESS of the symmetrized bimatrix game (A^{u_2}, A^{u_3}). By chapter 3, this latter ESS is a strict NE of the asymmetric subgames Γ_{u_2} and Γ_{u_3}.
5. Since this is a symmetric bimatrix game (i.e., $A^{u_2} = A^{u_3}$), only figure 3.3.3 with $\alpha < 0$ is relevant. That is, with suitable ordering of the two strategies in this bimatrix game, all trajectories are evolving downward and to the left.

Owner-Intruder Game). Since each trajectory evolves in the interior of this square, it is clear there can be no interior periodic trajectories. In particular, each trajectory converges to a unique limit point.   ∎

7.2.1 Two-Stage Two-Strategy Repeated Games

A two-stage repeated game has the same normal form game at the first stage game as at each of the second stage subgames (and cumulative payoffs). We will speak of the Two-Stage Prisoner's Dilemma Class, Two-Stage Coordination Class, and Two-Stage Hawk-Dove Class when the payoffs of the single-stage games satisfy the obvious conditions. The analysis of Two-Stage Prisoner's Dilemma Class Games is contained in section 7.5 without the aid of theorem 7.2.1, and an example of a two-stage game with Coordination Games in the second stage is considered in section 7.2.3. Here we will illustrate the above theory by applying it to the Two-Stage Hawk-Dove Game. The extensive form of Γ, based on each single-stage game having payoff matrix $\begin{bmatrix} (V/2)-C & V \\ 0 & V/2 \end{bmatrix}$ with $C > \frac{V}{2}$, is given in figure 7.2.2.

There are two pervasive NE of Γ given by backward induction on the ESS structure of the second-stage subgames and the resultant truncated first-stage game. At the second-stage asymmetric subgames these play "H at u_2 and D at u_3" and "D at u_2 and H at u_3" respectively. Of course, at the second-stage symmetric subgames Γ_{u_1} and Γ_{u_4}, both NE

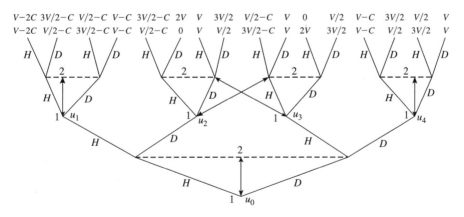

Figure 7.2.2
Two-Stage Hawk-Dove Game.

play the mixed strategy ESS $(V/2, C - V/2)/C$. The resultant truncated
first-stage games have payoff matrices

$$
\begin{bmatrix}
-\dfrac{1}{C}\left(C - \dfrac{V}{2}\right)^{2} & 2V \\[2ex]
0 & \dfrac{V}{2C}\left(2C - \dfrac{V}{2}\right)
\end{bmatrix}
\quad \text{and} \quad
\begin{bmatrix}
-\dfrac{1}{C}\left(C - \dfrac{V}{2}\right)^{2} & V \\[2ex]
V & \dfrac{V}{2C}\left(2C - \dfrac{V}{2}\right)
\end{bmatrix}
$$

respectively whose only ESSs are the mixed strategies $(V^2 + 4VC, 4[C - V/2]^2)/(2V^2 + 4C^2)$ and $(V^2, 4[C - V/2]^2 + 4VC)/(2V^2 + 4C^2)$ respectively.

Thus backward induction on the ESS structure yields two pervasive NE. A tedious calculation verifies that unlike the counterexample in figure 7.1.1a, these two NE are in fact ESSs of the reduced-strategy normal form. Another calculation shows there is only one other symmetric NE outcome; namely the pervasive NE that plays the mixed behavior strategy ESS $(V/2, C - V/2)/C$ at all five information sets of player one. By theorem 7.2.1, every interior trajectory of the symmetric replicator dynamic on the Wright manifold converges to one of these three NE, only the first two of which are asymptotically stable.

Remark 7.2.2   Convergence of general interior trajectories of the symmetric replicator dynamic off the Wright manifold is an open problem for generic two-stage two-strategy repeated games. Computer simulations support this conjecture (see Notes). For instance, the basins of attraction of the two reduced-strategy normal form ESSs for the Two-Stage Hawk-Dove Game appear to be two regions of Δ^8 that are separated by a six-dimensional surface (of measure zero) and that initial points on this surface evolve to the NE component corresponding to the unstable NE outcome. Of course, this optimism must be tempered by the possibility of the type of counterexample reported in chapter 4.6.1 where global asymptotic stability of a single NE on the Wright manifold does not imply convergence of other interior trajectories off the Wright manifold.

The final statement of theorem 7.2.1 is not true if the backward induction process leads to a nonpervasive NE (even if we consider stability of its NE component). For example, for the Two-Stage Prisoner's Dilemma Game, the limit points of the replicator dynamic are a whole line segment of NE on an edge, but this is not asymptotically stable (see remark 7.5.4 at the end of section 7.5.1 below).

7.2.2 Symmetric Signaling Games

In this section we consider a model of preplay communication in symmetric games where players attempt to "signal" their intentions of what strategy they will play in the "base game" by first sending one of N messages $\{m_1, \ldots, m_N\}$. We call these symmetric signaling games (see Notes). Specifically, we consider one class of such games whose extensive form is a two-stage simultaneity game where each player has a choice of N messages at the first stage and, following each pair of choices, there is the same normal form base game with two possible strategies (see figure 7.2.3 below). If there is no cost to sending a signal, we have a *cheap talk game* as in section 7.2.3. In this section we consider symmetric signaling games where each message m_i has an associated nonnegative cost. We assume that no two of these costs are the same and then order the messages by $m_1 < m_2 < \cdots < m_N$, where, by a slight abuse of notation, m_i also denotes the cost of the ith message. Without loss of generality, we can assume $m_1 = 0$.

The Two-Message Symmetric Signaling Game Γ of figure 6.0.1 in chapter 6 models a two-strategy base game with strategies H and D

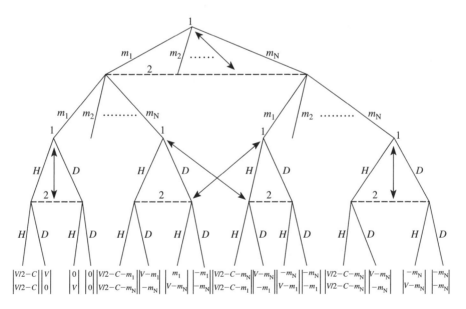

Figure 7.2.3
N-Message Symmetric Signaling Game.

and payoff matrix $\begin{bmatrix} -2 & 4 \\ 0 & 0 \end{bmatrix}$ following messages m_1 and m_2 with associated costs 0 and 1 respectively. The base game has the unique symmetric NE, $p^* = (\frac{2}{3}, \frac{1}{3})$, that is an ESS. It is straightforward to show there are exactly three symmetric NE outcomes;[6] namely

1. Choose m_1 at the first stage and p^* in Γ_{u_1}.

2. Choose m_2 at the first stage and p^* in Γ_{u_4}.

3. Choose m_1 and m_2 at the first stage with frequencies $\frac{1}{4}$ and $\frac{3}{4}$ respectively, p^* at u_1 and u_4, D at u_2 and H at u_3.

By theorem 7.2.1, every interior trajectory of the symmetric replicator dynamic on the Wright manifold of Γ converges to one of these NE.[7] Moreover, since the third outcome is the only pervasive NE that is given by backward induction on the game's ESS structure (in fact it corresponds to an ESS in the reduced-strategy normal form), this is the only NE outcome selected via asymptotic stability. That is, the solution of the Two-Message Symmetric Signaling Game from the dynamic perspective illustrates the "handicap principle"; namely the player who wins the contest (i.e., plays H) in the two second-stage asymmetric subgames must handicap himself by sending the more costly message m_2 (see Notes).

The remainder of this section applies the approach above to a more general class of symmetric signaling games that has base game strategies H and D and payoff matrix $\begin{bmatrix} (V/2)-C & V \\ 0 & 0 \end{bmatrix}$ with $C > V/2$ and message set $\{m_1, \ldots, m_N\}$. Notice that the base game is the Hawk-Dove Game except that the payoffs when two Doves compete is 0 and that, in the Two-Message Symmetric Signaling Game, $V = C = 4$.[8]

Consider the behavioral strategy b^* that plays the ESS strategy $p^* = (V, C - V/2)/(C + V/2)$ with expected payoff 0 at the N symmetric

---

6. For instance, the first NE outcome listed is the outcome that results when the only subgame perfect NE that specifies p^* at all four second-stage subgames is taken.

7. The proof actually shows each of the three NE components attract some initial interior points and so none are globally asymptotically stable.

8. The standard Hawk-Dove Game is not taken here as the base game for technical reasons. This anomalous payoff of 0 can be justified if one assumes two Doves compete in a Continuous War of Attrition whose expected payoff is in fact 0 (see section 7.4.2 below). Alternatively, a similar analysis is possible for the standard Hawk-Dove Game if $N > 2$, though the calculations become somewhat more complicated.

Since the base game of figure 7.2.3 has two strategies, the proof of theorem 7.2.1 implies that all trajectories induced in the second-stage subgames by the replicator dynamic on the Wright manifold have a unique limit point. However, we can no longer assert the trajectories on the Wright manifold of Γ converge when there are $N > 2$ messages since the truncated game is then a symmetric normal form game with three or more strategies.

second-stage subgames and the strict NE H (respectively D) at the information set in the asymmetric second-stage subgames corresponding to the message with the higher (respectively lower) cost. Truncation with respect to b^* yields the first-stage game with $N \times N$ payoff matrix $A^{u_0}(b^*)$ given by

$$
\begin{array}{c}
 \\
m_1 \\
m_2 \\
\vdots \\
m_N
\end{array}
\begin{array}{cccc}
m_1 & m_2 & \cdots & m_N \\
\left[\begin{array}{cccc}
0 & 0 & \cdots & 0 \\
V - m_2 & -m_2 & \cdots & -m_2 \\
\vdots & \vdots & & \vdots \\
V - m_N & V - m_N & \cdots & -m_N
\end{array}\right].
\end{array}
$$

These entries are the net payoffs resulting from the cost m_i to player i offset by a gain V only when m_i plays against m_j with $i > j$.

If $V > m_N$, then this game has the symmetric NE $b^{*u_0} \equiv (m_2, m_3 - m_2, \ldots, m_N - m_{N-1}, V - m_N)/V$ which is an ESS in the interior of Δ^N since $A^{u_0}(b^*)$ is negative definite on X^N (specifically, $x \cdot A^{u_0}(b^*)x = (V/2)\sum_{i \neq j} x_i x_j = -(V/2)\sum_{i=1}^{N} x_i^2$ for all $x \in X^N$). Thus b^* corresponds to a single pervasive NE p^* in the reduced-strategy normal form of Γ that is formed through the backward induction process on its ESS structure. By theorem 7.3.3 in section 7.3.2 below, p^* is asymptotically stable. Asymptotic stability also follows from the fact p^* is an ESS when $V > m_N$.[9] In any case, a solution selected from the dynamic perspective again satisfies the handicap principle.

If $m_{K+1} > V > m_K$ for some $1 \leq K < N$, then pure strategies $m_{K+1}, \ldots, m_N$ are strictly dominated by m_1 in $A^{u_0}(b^*)$ and so cannot be in the support of any of its symmetric NE. In fact $A^{u_0}(b^*)$ has a unique symmetric NE, which must be an ESS by negative definiteness, given by $b^{*u_0} \equiv (m_2, m_3 - m_2, \ldots, m_K - m_{K-1}, V - m_K, 0, \ldots, 0)/V$. Thus the theory developed in this section is not directly applicable to the nonpervasive behavior strategy NE b^*. However, since $V - m_i$ is the highest payoff possible to a player who uses message m_i when competing against someone using message m_j with $i > j$, b^{*u_0} remains an ESS of $A^{u_0}(b)$ formed by a truncation with respect to any behavior strategy combination at the second-stage subgames that agrees with b^* whenever both players choose messages in $\{m_1, \ldots, m_K\}$ at the first stage. In fact this set of behavior strategies, all of which yield the same outcome that satisfies

---

9. This result and several others in sections 7.2.2 and 7.2.3 are stated without proof (references for their proofs are given in the Notes).

the handicap principle, is an ESSet.[10] For instance, in the Two-Message Symmetric Signaling Game altered to $m_2 > V = 4$, the set of behavior strategies that plays m_1 at u_0 and $p^* = (\frac{2}{3}, \frac{1}{3})$ at u_1 corresponds to an ESSet of the (reduced-strategy) normal form.

7.2.3   Cheap Talk Games

When preplay communication is costless, the first-stage game obtained by truncating all second-stage subgames with respect to the same symmetric NE yields an $N \times N$ payoff matrix, all of whose entries are equal. Thus all NE outcomes of the base game yield equilibrium outcomes of the corresponding cheap talk game that can be selected from the perspective of evolutionary game theory. On the other hand, cheap talk games are highly nongeneric, and so the theory of section 7.2 is not directly applicable. Let us first examine one of the initial reasons these games were introduced; namely to select the efficient NE outcome when the base game is a symmetric Coordination Game such as $\begin{smallmatrix}\ell\\r\end{smallmatrix}\begin{bmatrix}2 & 0\\0 & 1\end{bmatrix}$. To simplify the discussion, suppose there are two possible messages as in figure 6.0.1 of chapter 6.

The reduced-strategy normal form of this extensive form game, Γ, is an 8×8 symmetric payoff matrix with maximum entry 2. By chapter 2.8, $E \equiv \{p \in \Delta^8 \mid \pi(p, p) = 2\}$ is an ESSet of Γ. E consists of the three edges of Δ^8 joining the vertices $\{e_{[m_2, \ell\ell]}, e_{[m_1, \ell\ell]}\}$, $\{e_{[m_1, \ell\ell]}, e_{[m_1, \ell r]}\}$, and $\{e_{[m_2, \ell\ell]}, e_{[m_2, r\ell]}\}$, which comprise exactly those strategies p that choose the efficient NE outcome ℓ at all second-stage subgames reached by p. Moreover the payoff 1 of the inefficient NE outcome of the base game is never attained by any element of an ESSet (or an asymptotically stable set of rest points). Thus the replicator dynamic appears to select the efficient NE outcome in this game. Unfortunately, there are other ESSets that appear in this cheap talk game. For instance, the pervasive NE in normal form that truncates with respect to the inefficient NE in the symmetric second-stage subgames and the efficient NE in the asymmetric second-stage subgames yields the first stage payoff matrix $\begin{bmatrix}1 & 2\\2 & 1\end{bmatrix}$ with ESS $(\frac{1}{2}, \frac{1}{2})$. Theorem 7.3.3 below shows this is asymptotically stable and therefore, by chapter 2.8, an ESS of Γ.

As a final example of the counterintuitive results that arise in cheap talk games, consider the two-message cheap talk game whose base game payoff matrix $\begin{smallmatrix}\ell\\r\end{smallmatrix}\begin{bmatrix}2 & 1\\2 & 0\end{bmatrix}$ has a single ESS $(1, 0)$. Suppose that E is

---

10. This is also true if $m_{K+1} \geq V > m_K$.

an asymptotically stable set of rest points of this cheap talk game. If no element of E is pervasive, then without loss of generality, $e_{[m_1, \ell\ell]} \in E$. Now $e_{[m_2, r\ell]}$ can invade E since

$$\pi\left(e_{[m_2, r\ell]}, e_{[m_1, \ell\ell]}\right) = 2 = \pi\left(e_{[m_1, \ell\ell]}, e_{[m_1, \ell\ell]}\right),$$

$$\pi\left(e_{[m_1, \ell\ell]}, e_{[m_2, r\ell]}\right) = 1 < \pi\left(e_{[m_2, r\ell]}, e_{[m_2, r\ell]}\right).$$

Thus the edge joining $\{e_{[m_1, \ell\ell]}, e_{[m_2, r\ell]}\}$ is contained in E, and so E has an element that is pervasive. In this case every element in E must choose strategy ℓ at all second-stage subgames, which contradicts the invasion argument above. Thus there is no asymptotically stable set of rest points. In particular, the efficient NE outcome of the base game is not selected on dynamic grounds.

7.3   Asymptotic Stability of Pervasive NE

In the elementary examples of section 7.1, the only pervasive NE[11] that are asymptotically stable under the symmetric replicator dynamic are given by backward induction on the pervasive NE that are asymptotically stable at each step of this process. Similarly the only pervasive NE that are asymptotically stable under the symmetric replicator dynamic restricted to the reduced Wright manifold for the generic two-stage two-strategy games of section 7.2 are also given by backward induction. In this section we prove that this backward induction principle holds for all simultaneity games without moves of nature whether the dynamic is restricted to the Wright manifold or not (theorem 7.3.3). With moves by nature we must restrict to the Wright manifold (theorem 7.3.5).

7.3.1   Simultaneity Games with No Asymmetric Subgames

The stability analysis for these games is simplified considerably by the second statement of the following result. This extends the comment in section 7.1 that the Wright manifold of the elementary simultaneity games considered there is the entire strategy space.

---

11. Our concentration here on pervasive NE is justified by theorem 7.0.1 if the standard normal form is used. Alternatively, if the reduced-strategy normal form is used instead, the results of this section are still important for arbitrary p^* by considering a "pruned" game tree whereby one removes those paths that do not contain an information set of player one relevant for p^*.

Theorem 7.3.1   *The Wright manifold of the reduced-strategy normal form of a simultaneity game Γ is the set of mixed representatives of the completely mixed behavior strategies. If Γ has no asymmetric subgames and no moves by nature, the Wright manifold of the reduced-strategy normal form of Γ is the interior of the entire strategy space $\Delta(T)$.*[12]

Proof   Suppose that u is a final decision point of player one and that L is one of the alternatives at u. For any pure strategy e_i in the reduced-strategy normal form for which u is relevant and any $p \in \Delta(S)$, define p_i^{-u} by

$$p_i^{-u} = \sum \{p_k \mid e_k \text{ restricts to } e_i \text{ on } \Gamma_{-u}\}.$$

If e_i takes action L at u and $p \in W^u$, then $b_1^u(L)p_i^{-u}$ (where $b_1^u(L)$ is given by (6.1.1) in chapter 6) is equal to

$$\frac{\sum_j \{p_j \mid u \text{ is relevant for } e_j \text{ and } e_j \text{ plays } L \text{ at } u\} \sum_k \{p_k \mid e_k \text{ restricts to } e_i \text{ on } \Gamma_{-u}\}}{\sum \{p_j \mid u \text{ is relevant for } e_j\}}$$

$$= \frac{\sum_{j,k} \{p_j p_k \mid u \text{ is relevant for } e_j, e_j \text{ plays } L \text{ at } u \text{ and } e_k \text{ restricts to } e_i \text{ on } \Gamma_{-u}\}}{\sum \{p_j \mid u \text{ is relevant for } e_j\}}$$

$$= \frac{\sum_{j,k} \left\{ p_{j \setminus k}^u p_{k \setminus j}^u \mid u \text{ is relevant for } e_j, e_j \text{ plays } L \text{ at } u \text{ and } e_k \text{ restricts to } e_i \text{ on } \Gamma_{-u} \right\}}{\sum \{p_j \mid u \text{ is relevant for } e_j\}}$$

$$= p_i \frac{\sum_{j,k} \left\{ p_{j \setminus k}^u \mid u \text{ is relevant for } e_j, e_j \text{ plays } L \text{ at } u \text{ and } e_k \text{ restricts to } e_i \text{ on } \Gamma_{-u} \right\}}{\sum \{p_j \mid u \text{ is relevant for } e_j\}}$$

$$= p_i \frac{\sum_j \{p_j \mid u \text{ is relevant for } e_j\}}{\sum_j \{p_j \mid u \text{ is relevant for } e_j\}}. \tag{7.3.1}$$

That is, $b_1^u(L)p_i^{-u} = p_i$. Furthermore, since Γ_u is a subgame of Γ, it is straightforward to verify that p^{-u} is a point in the Wright manifold of Γ_{-u} if p is a point in the Wright manifold of Γ. Thus an induction argument using (7.3.1) applied to the truncated game $\Gamma_{-u}(p^u)$ shows that p_i is the product of probabilities over the information sets u of player one that b_1 makes the same choice as e_i at u. That is, p is the mixed representative of a completely mixed behavior strategy.

12. To emphasize the fact that the results of section 7.3 on asymptotic stability of pervasive NE require the reduced-strategy normal form (to avoid spurious duplication of pure strategies), we will denote the set of pure strategies by T in analogy to the notation used for the reduced normal form of N-player extensive form games in chapter 6.2.

Now suppose that Γ has no asymmetric subgames, no moves by nature, and that u is an information set of player one. Then Γ_u is a symmetric subgame of Γ. The symmetry f must map choices of player one on the path to u onto choices of player two on the path to u (i.e., player two must make the "same" choices as player one at all decision points that come before u). Thus, if u is relevant for e_i and v is an information set of player one disjoint from u, then v is not relevant for e_i, and so e_i does not specify a choice at v in the reduced-strategy normal form of Γ. In particular, $p^u_{i\backslash i} = p^u_{j\backslash i}$ for any pair of pure strategies e_i and e_j for which u is relevant. Thus, by definition 6.3.1 of chapter 6, W^u is $\Delta(T)$. Since this is true for all information sets, u, of player one, the result follows. ∎

For the remainder of this section, assume that $p^* \in \Delta(T)$ is a pervasive NE of the reduced-strategy normal form of a simultaneity game Γ with no asymmetric subgames and no moves by nature. By theorem 7.3.1, the symmetric replicator dynamic for the reduced-strategy normal form of Γ induces the rescaled symmetric replicator dynamic (6.4.1) for any subgame Γ_u of Γ. Furthermore the scaling factor $K^u(p)$ will be arbitrarily close to $K^u(p^*)$ for all p sufficiently close to p^*, and $K^u(p^*) > 0$ since p^* is pervasive. In particular, if p^* is asymptotically stable and Γ_u is a subgame, then p^{*u} will be asymptotically stable under the symmetric replicator dynamic for Γ_u. Also $\{p \in \Delta(T) \mid p^u = p^{*u}\}$ is invariant under the symmetric replicator dynamic for the reduced-strategy normal form of Γ. In fact the restricted dynamic on this invariant set is the symmetric replicator dynamic for the reduced-strategy normal form of the truncated game $\Gamma_{-u}(p^{*u})$. Specifically, each completely mixed strategy p of Γ restricts to a strategy p^{-u} of Γ_u whose components p_i^{-u}, for any pure strategy of Γ_u, is given by

$$p_i^{-u} \equiv \sum_j \{p_j \mid e_j \text{ is a pure strategy of } \Gamma \text{ that restricts to } e_i \text{ on } \Gamma_u\}.$$

Then $\{p^{-u} \mid p \in \Delta(T), p^u = p^{*u}\}$ is the set of strategies for the reduced-strategy normal form of $\Gamma_{-u}(p^{*u})$ on which we have the symmetric replicator dynamic. Moreover p^{*-u} is a pervasive NE of $\Gamma_{-u}(p^{*u})$ that is asymptotically stable. When these results are applied inductively to a subgame, Γ_u, at the last stage, we have one direction of the following result.

Theorem 7.3.2   *Suppose that Γ is a simultaneity game with no asymmetric subgames and with no moves by nature. A pervasive NE, $p^* \in \Delta(T)$ of the reduced-strategy normal form of Γ is asymptotically stable under the symmetric replicator dynamic if and only if p^* is given by backward induction applied to the asymptotically stable pervasive NE of the subgames of Γ and their truncations.*[13]

Proof   The "only if" direction is shown above. For the other direction, suppose that p^* is a pervasive NE given by backward induction applied to the asymptotically stable pervasive NE of the subgames of Γ and their truncations. Let Γ_u be a symmetric subgame of Γ at the last stage. If $\Gamma_u = \Gamma$, there is nothing to prove. Otherwise, $\Gamma_{-u}(p^{*u})$ is a simultaneity game with no asymmetric subgames that has fewer subgames than Γ. Thus, by induction on the number of subgames in Γ, p^{*-u} is asymptotically stable for $\Gamma_{-u}(p^{*u})$. That is, p^* is asymptotically stable on the invariant set $\{p \in \Delta(T) \mid p^u = p^{*u}\}$.

Furthermore, since p^* is pervasive, any $p \in \Delta(T)$ sufficiently close to p^* will have p^u arbitrarily close to p^{*u}. The asymptotic stability of p^{*u} in Γ_u implies p^u remains close to p^{*u} and eventually converges to it. That is, p converges to the compact set $\{p \in \Delta(T) \mid p^u = p^{*u}\}$ on which p^* is asymptotically stable. By the continuous dependence on their initial conditions of trajectories for the replicator dynamic over finite time intervals,[14] the trajectory with initial point p sufficiently close to p^* will stay close and eventually converge to p^*.   ∎

7.3.2   Simultaneity Games with Asymmetric Subgames

The stability analysis for these games is considerably more complicated than that in the previous section since the dynamic induced on an asymmetric subgame is not the rescaled symmetric replicator dynamic (6.4.1). Although it is the adjusted bimatrix replicator dynamic (6.4.2) on the Wright manifold, W is no longer the entire strategy space as can be seen from the two-stage two-strategy simultaneity games considered in section 7.2. However, we still have the following result where asymptotic stability of NE of asymmetric subgames refers to asymptotic stability with respect to their bimatrix replicator dynamic.

---

13. Asymptotic stability in the subgames and their truncations is with respect to the symmetric replicator dynamic. Compare this with theorem 7.3.3 below where the bimatrix replicator dynamic is used in the asymmetric games.
14. That is, for a given finite time interval $[0, t_0]$ and $\varepsilon > 0$, there is a $\delta > 0$ such that $|p(t) - \hat{p}(t)| < \varepsilon$ for all $t \in [0, t_0]$ whenever $|p(0) - \hat{p}(0)| < \delta$.

Theorem 7.3.3   *Suppose that* Γ *is a simultaneity game with no moves by nature. A pervasive NE,* $p^* \in \Delta(T)$ *of the reduced-strategy normal form of* Γ *is asymptotically stable under the symmetric replicator dynamic if and only if* p^* *is given by backward induction applied to the asymptotically stable pervasive NE of the subgames of* Γ *and their truncations.*

Proof   If Γ has no asymmetric subgames, we are done by theorem 7.3.2. Suppose that Γ_u is an asymmetric subgame of Γ and that $p^* \in \Delta(T)$ is given by backward induction applied to the asymptotically stable pervasive NE of the subgames of Γ and their truncations. Let Γ_v be the asymmetric subgame of Γ that is the image of Γ_u under the symmetry f. Then the induced strategy pair (p^{*u}, p^{*v}) is a NE of the bimatrix game Γ_u.

By theorem 3.2.1 of chapter 3, asymptotic stability of (p^{*u}, p^{*v}) under the bimatrix replicator dynamic implies that this is a strict NE pair of Γ_u. Furthermore Γ_u must be a subgame at the last stage (otherwise, p^* is not pervasive due to our assumption that every decision point of Γ has at least two alternatives). Since p^* is a NE and (p^{*u}, p^{*v}) is strict,

$$\pi(e, p^*) < \pi(p^*, p^*)$$

for any pure strategy $e \in T$ for which u is relevant but either chooses a different alternative than p^{*u} at u or than p^{*v} at v. By the linearization technique of chapter 2.7 applied to the reduced-strategy normal form of Γ, asymptotic stability of p^* is determined by restricting the analysis to the pure strategies $e \in T$ that are best replies to p^*. But the symmetric replicator dynamic restricted to those $e \in T$ that agree with (p^{*u}, p^{*v}) whenever u is relevant for e is precisely the symmetric replicator dynamic for the simultaneity game formed by truncating Γ at u and v by p^{*u} and p^{*v} respectively. Repeated application of this technique results in a simultaneity game with no asymmetric subgames. Theorem 7.3.2 then shows that p^* is asymptotically stable.

Conversely, assume p^* is a pervasive asymptotically stable NE of the reduced-strategy normal form of Γ that is not given by backward induction applied to the asymptotically stable pervasive NE of the subgames of Γ and their truncations. Every strategy that is realization equivalent to the unique behavior strategy induced by p^* is also a rest point of the dynamic. Thus asymptotic stability of p^* implies that it must be a mixed representative in the closure of the Wright manifold. Then p^* is also asymptotically stable when the symmetric replicator dynamic is restricted to the Wright manifold of Γ with respect to any subgame

Γ_u of Γ.[15] By the discussion immediately preceding theorem 7.3.2, if Γ_u is symmetric and an analogous argument using the adjusted bimatrix replicator dynamic if Γ_u is asymmetric, p^* induces a pervasive asymptotically stable NE in Γ_u and its truncation.   ■

Remark 7.3.4   Contained in the preceding proof is the fact that all asymmetric subgames of a simultaneity game that has an asymptotically stable pervasive NE must occur at the last stage (cf. theorem 7.0.1). In particular, no repeated game with at least three stages can have an asymptotically stable NE that is pervasive. In fact such games with at least three stages have no asymptotically stable NE whatsoever since the NE component of a nonpervasive NE is never a singleton set even for the two-stage games of section 7.2. Theorems 7.3.2 and 7.3.3 are not true if the replicator dynamic is replaced by a general monotone selection dynamic. For instance, if Γ contains a second-stage asymmetric subgame of the Buyer-Seller Class (or a symmetric subgame such as Rock–Scissors–Paper), a completely mixed NE in this subgame is asymptotically stable for some monotone selection dynamics but not for others.

7.3.3   Simultaneity Games with Moves by Nature

Theorems 7.3.2 and 7.3.3 do not extend directly to simultaneity games that include moves by nature.[16] One reason for this is the technicality that asymptotically stable NE of the subgames may not correspond to a singleton NE point in the reduced-strategy normal form but to a larger NE component (cf. theorem 4.6.1 in chapter 4). The example in chapter 4.6.1 illustrates a more fundamental difficulty introduced through moves by nature; namely the NE component of a p^* given by backward induction applied to pervasive asymptotically stable NE of the subgames is not necessarily asymptotically stable for the entire game. However, if we restrict the dynamic to the Wright manifold, the first statement of theorem 7.3.1 combines with the final paragraph of the proof of theorem 7.3.3 to yield the following result:

---

15. Although the Wright manifold is only formally defined as a subset of completely mixed-strategy combinations, the dynamic extends to pervasive strategies p on the boundary of W since the relevant factors, $K^u(p)$ and/or $K^{f(u)}(p)$ are positive there.

16. Recall that we assume such moves to occur at the beginning of each stage and that both players are aware of all moves by nature that occur before any of their own decision points.

Theorem 7.3.5   *Suppose that Γ is a simultaneity game with moves by nature. A pervasive NE, $p^* \in \Delta(T)$, in the closure of the Wright manifold is asymptotically stable under the symmetric replicator dynamic restricted to the Wright manifold of the reduced-strategy normal form of Γ if and only if p^* is given by backward induction applied to the asymptotically stable pervasive NE of the subgames of Γ and their truncations.*

Theorems 7.3.2, 7.3.3, and 7.3.5 develop the fundamental connection between backward induction and equilibrium selection of pervasive NE via asymptotic stability (i.e., asymptotically stable pervasive NE of the subgames of Γ and their truncations are selected in this manner). The results in chapter 6 easily combine to show the analogous static result that pervasive NE are given by the backward induction technique applied to pervasive NE of the subgames of Γ and their truncations. On the other hand, we have also seen in section 7.1 that the same backward induction principle is not true for the ESS structure of symmetric extensive form games even if the resultant NE is pervasive.

This dynamic theory of equilibrium selection works well in the games considered in section 7.4 since they only have pervasive NE. However, general extensive form games typically have no pervasive NE. This is certainly true of the repeated Prisoner's Dilemma Game of section 7.5 and for most of the perfect information games of chapter 8. As we will see, other methods are then needed to analyze the dynamics. These are introduced in section 7.5 and are central to the two-player extensive form games of chapter 8 as well.

7.4   The War of Attrition

The classic War of Attrition is a two-player symmetric game over a resource of positive value V where the player who waits the longest receives the resource. There is also a cost associated with the length of time a contest lasts. Specifically, the payoff to a pure strategist t (i.e., to a player who is prepared to wait a time $t \geq 0$) is given by

$$\pi(t, t') = \begin{cases} V - t' & \text{if } t > t', \\ -t & \text{if } t < t', \\ \frac{V}{2} - t & \text{if } t = t'. \end{cases} \tag{7.4.1}$$

In section 7.4.2 we briefly consider this game when any t in an interval is a possible waiting time and so the pure strategy set is a continuum. Our main interest there is to compare the results to those in section 7.4.1 where only a finite set of N possible waiting times are available. This

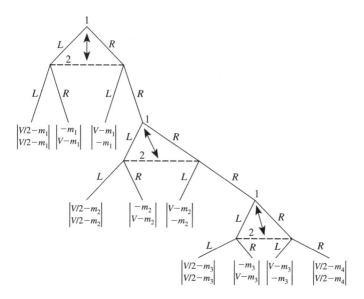

Figure 7.4.1
Three-Stage War of Attrition.

latter game, a Discrete War of Attrition, provides an excellent example on which to apply the theory of simultaneity games with only symmetric subgames developed in section 7.3.1. So too does the Discrete War of Aggression (an altered Discrete War of Attrition where the player who is first to be aggressive wins the resource) that is analyzed in section 7.4.3.

7.4.1   The Discrete War of Attrition

The *N-Stage Discrete War of Attrition* is a symmetric two-player War of Attrition where the players compete over a resource of positive value V and have a discrete set $\{m_1, \ldots, m_{N+1}\}$ of $N + 1$ possible stopping times.[17] At each stage a player may either Leave (L) or Remain (R). The game ends either at the first stage where at least one player leaves or else at stage N if both players never leave. The game's extensive form tree is that of an N-stage simultaneity game with only symmetric subgames. The game tree in figure 7.1.1 of section 7.1 and figure 7.4.1 here are those of the Two-Stage and Three-Stage War of Attrition respectively.

Payoffs (indicated in figure 7.4.1 for $N = 3$) are described as follows: For each stage that both players remain, they incur a nonnegative cost. Let m_i be the total cumulative cost to each player when neither player

---

17. Stopping time $N + 1$ means the players never leave.

leaves before stage i (if both remain for all N stages, the total cost is m_{N+1}). Then $m_{N+1} \geq m_N \geq \cdots \geq m_1 \geq 0$. We also assume that $m_1 = 0$ is the cost if at least one player leaves immediately (i.e., at stage one). If both players leave at the same stage (or if both remain for all N stages), they split the value, $V > 0$, of the resource. Otherwise, the player who remains the longest receives the resource.

As seen in section 7.3.1, the dynamic analysis is simplified considerably by taking into account the subgame structure. Suppose that there is a unique pervasive NE that satisfies the backward induction process[18] of theorem 7.3.2. Let W_i denote the expected payoff at the ith stage of the backward induction process and $W_{N+1} \equiv (V/2) - m_{N+1}$.

For the Three-Stage War of Attrition in figure 7.4.1, $W_4 \equiv (V/2) - m_4$, W_3 is the expected payoff at the asymptotically stable equilibrium of the 2×2 normal form game

$$
\begin{bmatrix}
\dfrac{V}{2} - m_3 & -m_3 \\
V - m_3 & W_4
\end{bmatrix}.
$$

This asymptotically stable equilibrium (which is actually the only ESS as well) is

$$
\begin{cases}
(0, 1) & \text{if } W_4 + m_3 \geq 0, \\
\dfrac{(W_4 + m_3, -V/2)}{W_4 + m_3 - V/2} & \text{if } W_4 + m_3 < 0,
\end{cases}
$$

with expected payoff

$$
W_3 = \begin{cases}
W_4 & \text{if } W_4 + m_3 \geq 0, \\
\dfrac{-m_3(W_4 + m_3) - W_4 V/2)}{W_4 + m_3 - V/2} & \text{if } W_4 + m_3 < 0.
\end{cases}
$$

Similarly W_2 is the expected payoff at the asymptotically stable equilibrium of the 2×2 normal form game

$$
\begin{bmatrix}
\dfrac{V}{2} - m_2 & -m_2 \\
V - m_2 & W_3
\end{bmatrix}.
$$

W_1 can then be calculated by the same method.

---

18. This assumption is true if there is a unique asymptotically stable NE at each stage of the process that with positive probability, plays Remain to the end of any stage that is reached—a result that will be clear shortly.

Since, at each stage i of the backward induction process, the first column of the 2×2 normal form game has its smallest entry $(V/2) - m_i$ on the diagonal, there is always a unique asymptotically stable equilibrium (which is actually the only ESS as well) that plays Remain with positive probability. This probability in fact is 1 if and only if $W_{i+1} + m_i \geq 0$. Thus backward induction leads to a unique symmetric NE p^* that is pervasive since there is positive weight on the strategy Always Remain.

These results are included in the following theorem which also shows p^* is the unique ESS of the N-Stage War of Attrition:[19]

Theorem 7.4.1   *The reduced-strategy normal form of the N-Stage War of Attrition has a unique ESS $p^* \in \Delta^{N+1}$, and this is given by backward induction applied to the game's extensive form. The ESS is pervasive (in fact, $p^*_{N+1} > 0$) and globally asymptotically stable for both the symmetric replicator and best response dynamics. The expected payoff at the ith stage of the backward induction process, W_i, satisfies*

$$W_{N+1} \leq W_N \leq \cdots \leq W_1,$$

where $W_{N+1} \equiv (V/2) - m_N$. Furthermore $-m_i \leq W_i \leq \frac{V}{2} - m_i$ with the latter inequality strict unless $m_i = m_{i+1} = \cdots = m_{N+1}$. In particular, the expected payoff W_1 at the ESS satisfies $0 \leq W_1 \leq (V/2)$, and so neither player is better off at equilibrium than both leaving immediately.[20] The pure strategy that plans to leave at exactly stage i is in the support of p^* if and only if $W_{i+1} + m_i < 0$.

Proof   By the discussion above and theorem 7.3.2, we have already shown that p^* is a pervasive NE that is asymptotically stable for the symmetric replicator dynamic. To complete the proof, let us denote the $N + 1$ pure strategies by $\{L, RL, RRL, \ldots, R \cdots RL, R \cdots RR\}$ where the number of R's in the strategy (up to N) indicate how many stages this player is prepared to wait. If $m_1 = \cdots = m_N = 0$, then p^* is the pure strategy $RR \cdots R$ (i.e., Always Remain), which is clearly an ESS in this case and so asymptotically stable for both the symmetric replicator and best response dynamics by theorem 2.7.4 of chapter 2. Global stability is then a straightforward exercise using weak domination in the reduced-strategy normal form payoff matrix A given in (7.4.2) below when $m_1 = \cdots = m_N = 0$. Furthermore $W_i = (V/2)$ for all i, which

---

19. The theory of section 7.3 does not prove p^* is an ESS since a counterexample such as figure 7.1.1a in section 7.1 has not been ruled out.
20. In fact they are worse off since $W_1 < V/2$ (unless $m_i = 0$ for all i).

clearly satisfies the required inequalities stated in the theorem.

$$
\begin{array}{c}
\begin{array}{ccccc} L & RL & RRL & \cdots & R\cdots R \end{array}\\
\begin{array}{c} L\\ RL\\ RRL\\ \vdots\\ R\cdots R \end{array}
\left[\begin{array}{ccccc}
\dfrac{V}{2} & 0 & 0 & \cdots & 0\\[2mm]
V & \dfrac{V}{2}-m_2 & -m_2 & \cdots & -m_2\\[2mm]
V & V-m_2 & \dfrac{V}{2}-m_3 & \cdots & -m_3\\[2mm]
\vdots & \vdots & \vdots & & \vdots\\[2mm]
V & V-m_2 & V-m_3 & \cdots & \dfrac{V}{2}-m_{N+1}
\end{array}\right].
\end{array}
\tag{7.4.2}
$$

Now assume that $m_i \neq m_j$ for some i, j. We will show that $(p^* - p) \cdot Ap > 0$ for all $p \neq p^*$ in Δ^{N+1}, from which it follows that p^* is an ESS. From (7.4.2),

$$
\begin{aligned}
x \cdot Ax &= \left(\frac{V}{2}\right)x_1^2 + \left(\frac{V}{2}-m_2\right)x_2^2 + \cdots + \left(\frac{V}{2}-m_{N+1}\right)x_{N+1}^2\\
&\quad + V(x_1x_2 + x_1x_3 + \cdots + x_1x_{N+1})\\
&\quad + (V-2m_2)(x_2x_3 + \cdots + x_2x_{N+1}) + \cdots + (V-2m_N)x_Nx_{N+1}\\
&= \left(\frac{V}{2}\right)\left(\sum_{i=1}^{N+1}x_i\right)^2 - m_2\left(\sum_{i=2}^{N+1}x_i\right)^2 - (m_3 - m_2)\left(\sum_{i=3}^{N+1}x_i\right)^2\\
&\quad - \cdots - (m_{N+1} - m_N)x_{N+1}^2\\
&\leq 0
\end{aligned}
\tag{7.4.3}
$$

for $x \in X^{N+1}$ since $\sum_{i=1}^{N+1} x_i = 0$. Thus $(p^* - p) \cdot A(p - p^*) \geq 0$ for all $p \in \Delta^{N+1}$. Furthermore, $(p^* - p) \cdot Ap^* \geq 0$ since p^* is a NE. Thus $(p^* - p) \cdot Ap \geq 0$ for all $p \in \Delta^{N+1}$.

Now suppose that $(p^* - p) \cdot Ap^* = 0$ for some $p = p^* + x$. Then $\text{supp}(p) \subset \{e_i \mid e_i Ap^* = p^* \cdot Ap^*\}$. If $m_i = m_{i+1}$, then $p_i^* = 0$ since $W_{i+1} + m_i = W_{i+1} + m_{i+1} \geq 0$ in the backward induction process. Furthermore, if $e_i \cdot Ap^* = p^* \cdot Ap^*$, then $p_i^* = p_{i+1}^* = 0$ (otherwise, $e_{i+1} \cdot Ap^* > e_i \cdot Ap^* = p^* \cdot Ap^*$ contradicts the fact p^* is a NE). Thus $m_i = m_{i+1}$ implies that either $x_i = 0$ or $x_i + x_{i+1} \geq 0$. In either case, $(p^* - p) \cdot Ap > 0$ from (7.4.3) unless $p = p^*$. Thus p^* is an ESS that is globally asymptotically stable by theorem 2.7.4 in chapter 2.

To show $-m_i \leq W_i \leq (V/2) - m_i$ by backward induction on i, consider the following two cases: If $W_{i+1} + m_i \geq 0$, then $W_i = W_{i+1}$ and so $-m_i \leq W_{i+1} = W_i \leq (V/2) - m_{i+1} \leq (V/2) - m_i$. On the other hand, if $W_{i+1} + m_i <$

0, then $p_i^* > 0$ and the expected payoff W_i is the value obtained by multiplying either row of the 2×2 truncated payoff matrix with the behavior strategy

$$\left(\frac{p_i^*}{p_i^* + p_{i+1}^* + \cdots + p_{N+1}^*}, \frac{p_{i+1}^* + \cdots + p_{N+1}^*}{p_i^* + p_{i+1}^* + \cdots + p_{N+1}^*} \right).$$

From the first row, we have

$$W_i = \left(\frac{V}{2} - m_i \right) \frac{p_i^*}{p_i^* + p_{i+1}^* + \cdots + p_{N+1}^*} - m_i \frac{p_{i+1}^* + \cdots + p_{N+1}^*}{p_i^* + p_{i+1}^* + \cdots + p_{N+1}^*}.$$

In particular, $-m_i \leq W_i \leq (\frac{V}{2} - m_i)$. Similarly, from the second row,

$$W_i = (V - m_i) \frac{p_i^*}{p_i^* + p_{i+1}^* + \cdots + p_{N+1}^*} + W_{i+1} \frac{p_{i+1}^* + \cdots + p_{N+1}^*}{p_i^* + p_{i+1}^* + \cdots + p_{N+1}^*}$$

$$= (V - m_i - W_{i+1}) \frac{p_i^*}{p_i^* + p_{i+1}^* + \cdots + p_{N+1}^*} + W_{i+1},$$

and so $W_i > W_{i+1}$ since $W_{i+1} + m_i < 0$.   ■

Example 7.4.2   (Discrete War of Attrition with linear cost)   Although the calculation of the ESS solution p^* of any Discrete War of Attrition is theoretically straightforward by applying the backward induction formula as outlined above for $N = 3$, its analytic expression as a function of the costs m_i is quite complicated in practice, especially as N increases. In an attempt to simplify the analysis, suppose that the possible stopping times are integer multiples, $0 \leq i \leq N+1$, of a single time unit and that the cost of waiting each time unit is c. That is, costs $m_i = c(i - 1)$ are a linear function of stopping time i.

When $c = 0$, we have "costless" waiting, in which case, from theorem 7.4.1, the solution is to Always Remain. The intuition here is that since there is no cost in waiting, the best strategy is to wait as long as possible in the hope your opponent will leave first.

When c is positive, the incentive to outwait your opponent is counteracted by the increasing cost of waiting and so one expects a mixed ESS. To examine this intuition, fix V and take parameters so that $Nc = V$. This represents the time interval $[0, V]$ partitioned into N equal subintervals each of cost c. Then $W_{N+1} + m_i = (V/2) - V + V(i - 1)/N \geq 0$ if and only if $i \geq (N/2) + 1$. By theorem 7.4.1, $p_i^* = 0$ for $(N/2) + 1 \leq i \leq N$, and so there is a gap in the support of p^*. On the other hand, it can be shown $p_i^* > 0$ for $0 \leq i \leq (N/2)$ and for $i = N+1$, although the analytic

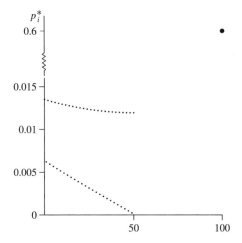

Figure 7.4.2
ESS for the Discrete War of Attrition when $N = V = 100$ (and $c = 1$) in example 7.4.2.

expression for p_i^* continues to be elusive even in this simplified situation. A typical pattern for p_i^* is shown in figure 7.4.2 when $N = V = 100$. The most obvious features of this solution are that the weight $p_{101}^* \simeq 0.6$ on Always Remain is large, that even (and odd) stopping times are monotonically decreasing for $0 \leq i \leq 50$, and that these alternate between high and low values.

7.4.2 The Continuous War of Attrition

The evolutionary games of this section are important elementary models of strategic interactions based on a continuum of pure strategies. However, our only interest in them for this book is their connection to extensive form games—especially in comparison to the N-stage models of sections 7.4.1 and 7.4.3. For this reason the necessary properties are often stated with minimal, if any, indication of their proofs (see the references given in the Notes for more details).

The classic Continuous War of Attrition with infinite time horizon (i.e., $t \in [0, \infty)$) over a resource of value V associates a cost t to remaining t units of time. Let p^* be the strategy with probability density function $p^*(t) = e^{-(t/V)}/V$ that gives the probability $p^*(t)\delta t$ an individual using p^* is prepared to wait between t and $t + \delta t$ time units.[21] This negative exponential density function $e^{-(t/V)}/V$ with rate V comes

---

21. It is possible to model this distribution with an infinite number of individuals who all use some pure strategy m that is prepared to stay exactly m time units.

from the Poisson process based on a constant probability V of leaving per unit time. If m is the pure strategy that is prepared to remain exactly m time units, then the resource is never split when p^* interacts with m since the event that both players leave at the same time (i.e., at time m) has probability zero. Then, from (7.4.1),

$$
\begin{aligned}
\pi(m, p^*) &= \int_0^m (V - t)p^*(t)\, dt + \int_m^\infty (-m)p^*(t)\, dt \\
&= [te^{-(t/V)}]_0^m + [me^{-(t/V)}]_m^\infty \qquad\qquad (7.4.4) \\
&= 0
\end{aligned}
$$

for all m and so $\pi(p, p^*) = 0$ for all probability density functions $p(t)$. Thus p^* is a NE. Another calculation involving similar integrals shows that $\pi(p^*, p) > \pi(p, p)$ if $p \neq p^*$ (i.e., p^* is an ESS for this infinite-dimensional space of probability distributions). In fact it is well known that p^* is the only ESS.

The finite time horizon game is more clearly associated to the Discrete War of Attrition. With the continuum of possible stopping times t corresponding to any element of the bounded interval $[0, V]$,[22] the unique ESS is the distribution

$$
p^*(t) = \begin{cases}
\frac{1}{V}e^{-(t/V)} & \text{if } t \leq \frac{V}{2}, \\
0 & \text{if } \frac{V}{2} < t < V, \\
e^{-1/2}\delta_V & \text{if } t = V,
\end{cases} \qquad\qquad (7.4.5)
$$

where δ_V is the Dirac delta function with weight 1 at V. That is, the solution for this game is to play the Poisson process, with probability of leaving V per unit time, on the first half of the time interval. Players who do not leave by time $V/2$, which occurs with probability $1 - \int_0^{V/2} e^{-(t/V)}\, dt = e^{-1/2}$, remain until the end. The expected payoff at equilibrium is again 0 since $\pi(m, p^*) = 0$ for any pure strategy m in the support of p^* (i.e., $p^*(m) \neq 0$). There are obvious similarities between the graph of (7.4.5) given in figure 7.4.3 and the solution to the Discrete War of Attrition depicted in figure 7.4.2 of example 7.4.2. Both solutions have a gap in their support for $V/2 < t < V$ and put over half their weight ($e^{-1/2} \simeq 0.607$) on Always Remain. One notable difference, however, is the alternating between high and low values in the discrete solution versus the monotonic decrease of $p^*(t)$ for $0 \leq t \leq \frac{V}{2}$ in the continuous model.

---

22. If instead $t \in [0, V)$, then there is no ESS since it always pays to wait a little longer.

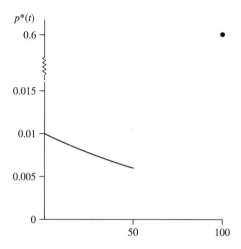

Figure 7.4.3
ESS for the Continuous War of Attrition with finite time horizon.

7.4.3 The Discrete War of Aggression

In this section we alter the Discrete War of Attrition, where the last player to leave obtains the resource, to a situation where it is the first player to leave (which is the "aggressive" behavior) who obtains the resource of value V. Furthermore, if both players attempt to leave at the same stage, a fight ensues with an associated cost C.[23] For instance, the One-Stage Discrete War of Aggression is the Hawk-Dove Game with payoff matrix $\begin{bmatrix} (V/2)-C & V \\ 0 & V/2 \end{bmatrix}$. For this reason we denote the strategies at each stage as H (aggressive) and D (display).

At each stage of the *N-Stage War of Aggression*, players either escalate or display. The game ends at the first stage where at least one player escalates or else at stage N if neither player ever escalates. Now the $N+1$ pure strategies $\{H, DH, \ldots, D \cdots DH, D \cdots DD\}$ indicate the number of stages the player is prepared to display. For each stage that both players display, they incur a nonnegative cost. Let m_i be the total cost to each player if neither escalates before stage i (we again assume $m_1 = 0$). The player who escalates first receives the resource unless both players escalate at the same stage (in which case they split the resource and incur a positive cost C of fighting) or both display for all N stages (and split the resource).

---

23. A cost of fighting can also be incorporated into the Discrete War of Attrition without changing the backward induction approach significantly.

Common sense may suggest the aggressive strategy "play H as soon as possible" should be the equilibrium. This is indeed the case if the cost of fighting is small enough. However, sufficiently large C acts as a deterrence to immediate aggression just as it leads to mixed-strategy equilibria in the One-Stage Hawk-Dove Game (see theorem 7.4.3 below).

$$
\begin{array}{c}
\quad\quad H \quad\quad\quad DH \quad\quad\quad DDH \quad\quad \cdots \quad\quad D\cdots D \\
\begin{array}{c} H \\ DH \\ DDH \\ \vdots \\ D\cdots D \end{array}
\left[
\begin{array}{ccccc}
\frac{V}{2}-C & V & V & \cdots & V \\
0 & \frac{V}{2}-C-m_2 & V-m_2 & \cdots & V-m_2 \\
0 & -m_2 & \frac{V}{2}-C-m_3 & \cdots & V-m_3 \\
\vdots & \vdots & \vdots & & \vdots \\
0 & -m_2 & -m_3 & \cdots & \frac{V}{2}-C-m_{N+1}
\end{array}
\right].
\end{array}
$$

$$(7.4.6)$$

The payoff matrix (7.4.6) for the Discrete War of Aggression is closely related to that of the Discrete War of Attrition (7.4.2). Specifically, except for the diagonal elements that include the cost of fighting, these payoff matrices are transposes of each other. If p^* is a NE of the N-Stage Discrete War of Aggression, it is not difficult to show[24] from (7.4.3) that $(p^* - p) \cdot Ap > 0$ for all $p \neq p^*$ in Δ^{N+1}. Thus there is a unique NE. Moreover p^* must be given by the backward induction procedure, and it is a globally asymptotically stable ESS.

If $(V/2) \geq C$, then H weakly dominates all other strategies, and so this is the ESS. On the other hand, if $(V/2) < C$, let $W_{N+1} = (V/2) - C - m_{N+1}$ and W_i be the expected payoff at the ith stage of the backward induction procedure. It is straightforward to show that $V - m_i > W_{i+1}$, and since $-m_i > (V/2) - C - m_i$, p^* is a completely mixed ESS. The following theorem summarizes these results:

Theorem 7.4.3   *For the N-Stage Discrete War of Aggression, there is a unique NE p^* in the reduced-strategy normal form. This is a globally asymptotically stable ESS that is given by the backward induction procedure. If $(V/2) < C$, p^* is in the interior of Δ^{N+1}. Otherwise, p^* is the pure strategy H.*

In principle, the interior ESS p^* can be determined recursively when $(V/2) < C$ by the conditions $e_i \cdot Ap^* = e_{i+1} Ap^*$ for all $1 \leq i \leq N$. These equations simplify considerably when $m_i = c(i - 1)$, which models a

---

24. Specifically, $x \cdot Ax$ is strictly negative if $x \neq 0$ since the diagonal terms here contribute the extra term $-C(x_1^2 + \cdots + x_{N+1}^2)$ to (7.4.3).

situation where players may escalate at integer multiples of a fixed unit of time and c is a nonnegative constant that is the cost of waiting one time unit (see example 7.4.2 in section 7.4.1).

For instance, if $c = 0$, then $[(V/2) - C]p_i^* + Vp_{i+1}^* = [(V/2) - C]p_{i+1}^*$. Thus $p_i^* = \lambda p_{i+1}^*$ where $0 < \lambda \equiv [C - (V/2)]/[C + (V/2)] < 1$. That is, $p_i^* = k\lambda^i$ where $\frac{1}{k} = \sum_{i=1}^{N+1} \lambda^i = \lambda(1 - \lambda^{N+1})/(1 - \lambda)$ since $p^* \in \Delta^{N+1}$. This geometric series is the discrete version of the negative exponential distribution for the Continuous War of Attrition with infinite time horizon in section 7.4.2. On the other hand, when c is positive, then $p_i^* = p_{i+1}^*/\lambda + \delta(p_{i+1}^* + \cdots + p_{N+1}^*)/[C - (V/2)]$. As $N \to \infty$, it can be shown that p_i^* again approaches a geometric series but now of the form $k\alpha^i$ for some $0 < \alpha < \lambda$. That is, in either case, p_i^* is a discrete form of the negative exponential distribution that models a Poisson process for the ESS of the Continuous War of Attrition with infinite time horizon.[25]

7.5 The Finitely Repeated Prisoner's Dilemma Game

The infinitely repeated Prisoner's Dilemma Game is probably the most studied iterated game. The overwhelming application of evolutionary game theory to this game has been an effort to explain the prevalence of cooperation that typically appears in real-life situations (and in experimental results) that are modeled on the Prisoner's Dilemma. One particular strategy that has received a great deal of attention is Tit-for-Tat (TFT), the strategy that one initially cooperates and thereafter plays what the opponent played at the previous stage. Individuals who use TFT mutually cooperate and attempt to maintain this outcome by immediately punishing those opponents who defect at the previous stage.

Here we only treat the case where the (one-shot) Prisoner's Dilemma Game is repeated exactly N times. This is an N-stage simultaneity game Γ where both players choose between Cooperate and Defect at each stage based on their a priori knowledge of N and all decisions taken at all previous stages. The central message of this section is that evolutionary game theory does not support the emergence of cooperative behavior, such as TFT, in the N-Stage Prisoner's Dilemma Game.

Remark 7.5.1 Our analysis will not rely on the symmetry of the game as all results are developed with the game treated as a two-player extensive

---

25. In the Continuous War of Aggression modeled by the appropriate changes to (7.4.1), the only ESS is to "play H immediately."

form game.[26] Of course, these results remain true when we restrict to the symmetric extensive form game. Moreover all our results are also valid when a nonnegative discount factor (which may depend on the stage) is introduced, even though we assume for simplicity a discount factor of 0 in the proofs (i.e., payoffs obtained at later stages of the repeated game have the same value as those at earlier stages). A remarkable aspect of these proofs is that they use radically different techniques from those used previously in the book. Specifically, for those results concerning dynamical systems, there is no mention of Lyapunov function or linearization methods or of induced subgame dynamic on the Wright manifold, and the like. Furthermore geometric intuition is of little use here for a large number of stages since the strategy space becomes very large (for the normal form of the N-Stage Prisoner's Dilemma Game, there are $2^{(4^N-1)/3}$ pure strategies). Modifications of these new techniques will reappear in the dynamic analysis of perfect information games in chapter 8.

The only NE outcome of the N-Stage Prisoner's Dilemma Game is mutual defection at each of the game's N stages (i.e., every NE places probability 1 on the path that defects at each stage). The following proof[27] of this well-known fact is typical of many of the proofs in this section in that it emphasizes properties of the backward induction process through the extensive form structure of Γ.

Suppose that (p^*, q^*) is a NE whose outcome is not mutual defection. Then there is some subgame Γ_{u_0} with root $u_0 = \{x\}$ at stage ℓ such that

i. u_0 is reachable under (p^*, q^*).

ii. (p^*, q^*) Defects at every reachable information set in Γ_{u_0} at a stage later than ℓ.

iii. Either p^* or q^* does not always Defect in Γ_{u_0}.[28]

Without loss of generality, p^* does not always Defect at u_0. Let α be the probability that p^* Cooperates at x times the probability $\gamma(x, (p^*, q^*))$ that x is reached. Let p be the same strategy for player one as p^* except that, at each player one information set in Γ_{u_0}, p chooses Defect. From the

26. However, we will use notation more appropriate for a symmetric normal form game (e.g., $\pi(e, f)$ for the payoff to e in a contest against f) than for a bimatrix game (e.g., where $\pi_1(e, f)$ is more precise).

27. Other methods of proof can be found in the references given in the Notes.

28. That is, either p^* does not always Defect at u_0 or q^* does not always Defect at the information set v_0 of player two that immediately follows u_0.

one-shot Prisoner's Dilemma Game payoff matrix A given by

$$\begin{array}{c} C \\ D \end{array}\begin{bmatrix} R & S \\ T & P \end{bmatrix},$$

we have $\pi(p, q^*) - \pi(p^*, q^*) = \alpha(D-C) \cdot Ab_2^{v_0}(q^*) + \sum_{v_0 \prec v}(\gamma(v, (p, q^*)) \times [D \cdot Ab_2^v(q^*)] - [\gamma(v, (p^*, q^*))[D \cdot AD])$, where $b_2^v(q^*)$ is the behavior strategy of player two induced by q^* at his information set v in Γ_{u_0}. Since $(D - C) \cdot Ab_2^{v_0}(q^*) \geq \min\{T - R, P - S\} > 0$ and $D \cdot Ab_2^v(q^*) \geq D \cdot AD$, $\pi(p, q^*) > \pi(p^*, q^*)$, which contradicts p^* being a NE.

Notice that the crucial inequalities above only depend on the facts that D strictly dominates C (i.e., $T > R$ and $P > S$) in the one-shot Prisoner's Dilemma Game and that $T \geq P$. It turns out that all the results in this section only require these conditions. Thus, for us, a Prisoner's Dilemma Game will mean a two-strategy game with payoffs satisfying[29]

$$T > R, \quad P > S, \quad \text{and} \quad T \geq P. \tag{7.5.1}$$

That is, we do not need the full force of the usual Prisoner's Dilemma Game assumptions that $T > R > P > S$ or further ones such as $2R > T + S > 2P$ that are often assumed for the infinitely repeated game.

Remark 7.5.2 The results of this section are not true for all games in the Prisoner's Dilemma Class of chapter 2.2. To see this, consider the NE structure of the reduced-strategy normal form of the two-stage game that has 8×8 payoff matrix[30]

$$\begin{bmatrix} 2R & 2R & R+S & R+S & R+S & 2S & R+S & 2S \\ 2R & 2R & R+S & R+S & S+T & S+P & S+T & S+P \\ R+T & R+T & R+P & R+P & R+S & 2S & R+S & 2S \\ R+T & R+T & R+P & R+P & S+T & S+P & S+T & S+P \\ R+T & S+T & R+T & S+T & R+P & R+P & S+P & S+P \\ 2T & T+P & 2T & T+P & R+P & R+P & S+P & S+P \\ R+T & S+T & R+T & S+T & T+P & T+P & 2P & 2P \\ 2T & T+P & 2T & T+P & T+P & T+P & 2P & 2P \end{bmatrix}.$$

$$\tag{7.5.2}$$

---

29. These conditions imply that the payoffs of the only NE of the one-shot Prisoner's Dilemma Game is its "minmax" payoff $\min_{f_j \in S}(\max_{e_i \in S} \pi_1(e_i, f_j))$. The results of this section generalize to finitely repeated two-player games whose only NE is strictly dominant and has payoff equal to this minmax payoff.

30. Many of the specific examples in this section are based on the two-stage game for which this payoff matrix proves useful.

Here the pure strategies are ordered as

$[C; CC], [C; CD], [C; DC], [C; DD], [D; CC], [D; DC]; [D; CD], [D; DD],$

where $[\alpha; \beta\gamma]$ is the strategy "play α at stage one and, at stage two, play β if the opponent played C at stage one and γ if the opponent played D at stage one."

It is easy to show that the strategies $[C; DC]$ and $[D; DD]$ are NE for the two-stage game based on the Prisoner's Dilemma Class Game with payoff matrix $\begin{bmatrix} 0 & 0 \\ 1 & 3 \end{bmatrix}$ (i.e., with $R = S = 0, T = 1, P = 3$). Thus not all NE outcomes are mutual defection. Moreover the two NE $[C; DC]$ and $[D; DD]$ cannot be distinguished on dynamic grounds. For instance, both are stable but not asymptotically stable rest points for the replicator dynamic (e.g., for $[C; DC]$, the center manifold is the entire edge $\Delta(\{[C; DC], [C; DD]\})$ which are all rest points of the dynamic).

For the remainder of this section, we consider only N-Stage Prisoner's Dilemma Games that satisfy condition (7.5.1) and so have mutual defection as their only NE outcome. Thus, by the Folk Theorem of Evolutionary Game Theory, mutually cooperative behavior such as TFT cannot emerge in the long run from the dynamic perspective of evolutionary game theory unless interior trajectories exist that maintain at least some level of cooperation as they evolve and, in particular, do not converge. One reason to hope this might be the case is that the NE outcome is highly nonpervasive since there are many information sets that are not reached. In particular, equilibrium selection via asymptotic stability as developed in section 7.3 does not apply. However, in technical terms, the central message of this section is that all interior trajectories of the standard dynamics of evolutionary game theory (replicator, monotone selection, best response, and fictitious play) for the N-Stage Prisoner's Dilemma Game evolve to the NE set, G^*, in the game's normal form. Since G^* is the connected component containing the subgame perfect NE pure strategy where both players always defect at all their decision points, the dynamic analysis selects mutual defection.

7.5.1   *The Replicator and Monotone Selection Dynamics*

The main result of this section is the following theorem whose lengthy proof comprises all of appendix A.

Theorem 7.5.3 *Every interior trajectory of a uniformly monotone selection dynamic converges to a single NE point (of mutual defection) in the normal form of the N-Stage Prisoner's Dilemma Game (with symmetry ignored).*

The proof of theorem 7.5.3 actually shows that trajectories in the interior of the boundary face $\Delta(\tilde{S})$ also converge to a NE point if, for any $e \in \tilde{S}$ we also have $e' \in \tilde{S}$ where e' is the same strategy as e except possibly at information sets in the last k stages where it unconditionally Defects (see definition 7.6.1 in appendix A). By restricting consideration to a small subset of pure strategies that includes TFT, this generalization allows a more careful examination of why cooperative behavior fails to emerge. For instance, in the Six-Stage Prisoner's Dilemma Game (with 2^{1365} pure strategies), suppose that $\tilde{S}$ consists of the seven pure strategies $e_0 \equiv TFT, e_1, \ldots, e_6$, where e_i plays TFT for the first $6 - i$ stages after which it unconditionally Defects.[31] Then any trajectory that is initially in the interior of $\Delta(\tilde{S})$ converges to a single NE point that must be the subgame perfect NE of Always Defect since it is the only NE point in $\Delta(\tilde{S})$. Computer simulations of the replicator dynamic for this example confirm this result where a clear pattern in the transient nature of the other six strategies is also apparent (see Notes). Specifically, if all seven strategies are initially given equal probability, each pure strategy in turn starting with TFT has an interval when it does well compared to the others. It is only after $p_5(t)$ is close to 1 that $p_6(t)$ can be observed above 0 after which it rapidly forces all other frequencies to zero. Such behavior is also consistent with "end effects" reported in experimental work where a tendency toward mutual defection is observed in the last stages, and this becomes more pronounced as the subjects gain experience.

On the other hand, convergence is not guaranteed for other subsets of the strategy space. For example, for the symmetric Two-Stage Prisoner's Dilemma Game, the replicator dynamic restricted to $\Delta(\{[C; DD], [D; DC], [D; CD]\})$ is given through the payoff matrix

$$\begin{bmatrix} R + P & S + P & S + T \\ T + P & R + P & S + P \\ S + T & T + P & 2P \end{bmatrix}.$$

When $R + P > S + T > 2P$, we have a generalized RSP Game (see section 2.6.1) which has periodic orbits surrounding an interior stable rest point for certain values of the payoffs satisfying our conditions (7.5.1) on the one-shot Prisoner's Dilemma Game.

---

31. In particular, e_6 is Always Defect.

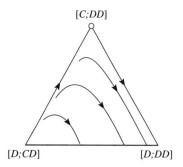

Figure 7.5.1
Replicator dynamic on a face of the Two-Stage Prisoner's Dilemma Game (with $S + T = 2P$).

Remark 7.5.4 Theorem 7.5.3 does not show that every NE point is stable or that the NE set is asymptotically stable. For instance, for the reduced-strategy normal form of the Two-Stage Prisoner's Dilemma Game with $S + T = 2P$, the NE set is the entire edge $\Delta(\{[D; CD], [D; DD]\})$. However, $[C; DD]$ is an alternative best reply to $[D; CD]$ that can invade $[D; CD]$ since $R + P > S + T$. The dynamics on $\Delta(\{[C; DD], [D; CD], [D; DD]\})$ are given in figure 7.5.1, and they clearly illustrate the first statement of this remark.[32] On the other hand, the subgame perfect NE point $[D; DD]$ is stable since its center manifold is the edge $\Delta(\{[D; CD], [D; DD]\})$ which consists entirely of rest points (this stability is also clear from figure 7.5.1). In fact every NE point except $[D; CD]$ is stable by the same argument.

7.5.2   The Best Response Dynamic and Fictitious Play

Our first result, theorem 7.5.5, that the NE set G^* is the maximal attractor of the (bimatrix) best response dynamic, combines with proposition 7.7.1 in appendix B to show that G^* is globally asymptotically stable. Thus, although every trajectory of the best response dynamic does not converge to a single NE point (see theorem 7.5.8 below), the NE outcome is still selected on dynamic grounds since every trajectory does converge

---

32. In chapter 8 the weaker condition of interior (asymptotic) stability (see definition 8.2.1) is of considerable importance. By continuity of the trajectories as a function of initial conditions, interior trajectories that start sufficiently close to $[D, CD]$ also initially diverge from the NE set. Thus theorem 7.5.3 has little to say about the dynamic stability of the NE outcome with respect to interior trajectories either.

to G^* (corollary 7.5.7 below) and, if it is initially sufficiently close to G^*, stays close.

The *maximal attractor*, M, of the best response dynamic is defined by

$$M \equiv \bigcap_{t \geq 0} F^t(\Delta),$$

where $F^t(\Delta) = \{p(t) \mid p(0) \in \Delta\}$ is the set of all points in the strategy space Δ that are time t along some best response trajectory that starts in Δ. In other words, M consists of all points in Δ that can be continued backward for any finite amount of time.[33] In particular, M is an invariant set (both forward and backward in time) for the best response dynamic and any such invariant set is contained in M. For this reason M is also called the *maximal invariant set* or, due to proposition 7.7.1, the *global attractor*.

In fact the maximal attractor is defined, and proposition 7.7.1 is also true for any autonomous dynamical system defined on a compact domain (e.g., the replicator dynamic on Δ). However, for the replicator dynamic, every trajectory can be extended backward in time (the trajectory $p(-t) \equiv \tilde{p}(t)$ for $t > 0$, where $\tilde{p}(t)$ is a trajectory of the replicator dynamic with respect to the game with payoffs the negative of the original payoffs, extends trajectories to negative times for the original payoff matrix). Thus the maximal attractor for the replicator dynamic is all of Δ, which is clearly globally asymptotically stable. That is, the theory does not tell us anything new about the replicator dynamic.

Theorem 7.5.5 *The NE set for the N-Stage Prisoner's Dilemma Game with cumulative payoffs is the maximal attractor of the bimatrix best response dynamic.*

Proof Suppose that $(p(t), q(t))$ is a complete best-response trajectory (i.e., $p(t)$ and $q(t)$ are defined for all positive and negative time). These *complete orbits* are clearly contained in M, and in fact M is the union of the set of all points on these complete orbits. Since $\text{supp}(p(t_1)) \subset \text{supp}(p(t_2))$ whenever $t_1 \leq t_2$, there is a t_0 such that $\text{supp}(p(t)) = \text{supp}(p(t_0))$ and $\text{supp}(q(t)) = \text{supp}(q(t_0))$ for all $t \leq t_0$. By lemma 7.5.6 below, if e_i and f_j are pure strategies in the supports of $p(t_0)$ and $q(t_0)$ respectively, then e_i and f_j mutually defect (at each of the N stages).

---

33. In fact $p \in M$ if and only if there is a best response trajectory $p(t)$ in Δ that is defined for all positive and negative t and satisfies $p(0) = p$.

Thus $T_0 > -\infty$, where

$$T_0 \equiv \sup \left\{ \begin{array}{l} t \mid e_i \text{ and } f_j \text{ mutually defect for all } e_i \in \text{supp}(p(t)) \\ \quad \text{and } f_j \in \text{supp}(q(t)) \end{array} \right\}.$$

We want to show that $T_0 = \infty$. If $T_0 < \infty$, consider an e_{i_0} that does not always defect against every $f_j \in \text{supp}(q(t))$. In particular, $p_{i_0}(T_0) = 0$. By the same method of proof as in the following lemma, we can show that e_{i_0} is not a best response to $q(T_0)$. Thus $e_i \in BR(q(T_0))$ if and only if e_i always defects against every $f_j \in \text{supp}(q(t))$. By upper semicontinuity of the best reply correspondence, $p_{i_0}(t) = 0$ for all $T_0 \leq t \leq T_0 + \varepsilon_i$ where $\varepsilon_i > 0$. Applying this to all such e_{i_0} (and f_{j_0} of player two), we obtain the contradiction that $T_0 \geq T_0 + \varepsilon$ for some positive ε.

Finally, we show that all $(p(t), q(t))$ are NE for all t. Otherwise, without loss of generality, there is some outcome path against an $f_j \in \text{supp}(q(t))$ that leads to a higher payoff than mutual defection. This contradicts the fact that $T_0 = \infty$. ∎

Lemma 7.5.6 *Suppose that $(p(t), q(t))$ is a complete best response trajectory such that $\text{supp}(p(t)) = \text{supp}(p(t_0))$ and $\text{supp}(q(t)) = \text{supp}(q(t_0))$ for all $t \leq t_0$. If e_i and f_j are pure strategies in the supports of $p(t_0)$ and $q(t_0)$ respectively, then e_i and f_j mutually defect (at each of the N stages).*

Proof If this were not true, let u be a last information set that is relevant for some such e_i and f_j at which cooperation occurs. In particular, e_i and f_j mutually defect at every information set following u. Without loss of generality, u is an information set of player one. Let e_i' be the same pure strategy as e_i except that it defects at u and at any player one information set following u. Then, by (7.5.1), for all $f_j \in \text{supp}(q(t_0))$, $\pi(e_i, f_j) = \pi(e_i', f_j)$ if u is not relevant for (e_i, f_j) and $\pi(e_i, f_j) < \pi(e_i', f_j)$ otherwise. Thus $e_i \notin BR(q(t))$ for all $t \leq t_0$, and so $\dot{p}_i = -p_i$ for $t \leq t_0$. If $p_i(t_0) > 0$, then $p_i(t) = ce^{-t}$ for some $c > 0$, and so $\lim_{t \to -\infty} p_i(t) = \infty$. This is impossible since $(p(t), q(t))$ is a complete best response trajectory and so cannot leave the strategy simplex Δ in finite time. Thus $p_i(t_0) = 0$ and so $e_i \notin \text{supp}(p(t))$ for all $t \leq t_0$ (a contradiction). ∎

Corollary 7.5.7 *Every best response trajectory for the N-Stage Prisoner's Dilemma Game converges to the NE set G^* (i.e., to the NE outcome of mutual defection at all N stages).*

Although theorem 7.5.3 asserts that every interior trajectory of the replicator dynamic converges to a single NE point, notice that theorem 7.5.5 and corollary 7.5.7 do not assert that every bimatrix best response trajectory converges to a NE. For the one-stage game, (D, D) is clearly the unique limit point for all these trajectories. However, for $N > 1$, the NE set is a convex set consisting of more than one point, and so there are best response trajectories that are initially in this set which do not converge to a single NE point. Theorem 7.5.8 summarizes known results about convergence under the best response dynamic to the subgame perfect pure strategy NE of Always Defect for N-stage games.

Theorem 7.5.8 *Consider the reduced-strategy normal form of the N-Stage Prisoner's Dilemma Game, and let the subgame perfect equilibrium strategy of Always Defect refer to the NE point that Defects at all relevant information sets. For $N = 2$, all best response trajectories that start in the interior of the strategy space converge to Always Defect. For $N > 2$, there are payoff choices for which a nonempty open set of initial conditions (and so some interior trajectories) does not converge to Always Defect.*

Proof For the Two-Stage Prisoner's Dilemma Game, suppose that $(p(t), q(t))$ is a best response trajectory in the interior of $\Delta^8 \times \Delta^8$. Then p_C^1, p_D^1, q_C^1, and q_D^1 are all positive.[34] From the 8×8 payoff matrix with pure strategies ordered as for (7.5.2), $BR(p(t)) \subset \Delta(\{f_4, f_8\})$ and $BR(q(t)) \subset \Delta(\{e_4, e_8\})$ for all $t \geq 0$. Since $f_4 \notin BR(\Delta(\{e_4, e_8\}))$, it is clear from the construction of best response trajectories that $f_8 \in BR(p(t_0))$ implies that $f_8 = BR(p(t))$ for all $t > t_0$, and so $q(t)$ converges to f_8. On the other hand, if $f_4 = BR(p(t))$ for all $t > 0$, then $q(t)$ converges to f_4. By the analogous argument for player one, we have that $(p(t), q(t))$ converges to a single point in $\{(e_4, f_4), (e_4, f_8), (e_8, f_4), (e_8, f_8)\}$. By the Folk Theorem of Evolutionary Game Theory, $(p(t), q(t))$ converges to the subgame perfect NE (e_8, f_8) since this is the only NE in this set.

To show the statements concerning games with $N > 2$, it is enough to consider the symmetric Three-Stage Prisoner's Dilemma Game. Suppose $S + T \leq 2P$. Consider the pure strategy $e \equiv [D; CD; DDDD]$ that always Defects in the first and last stage but Cooperates at stage 2 if and only if the opponent Cooperates at stage 1. This is a symmetric NE since $\pi(e, e) = 3P$, $\pi_1([D; **; ****], e) \leq P + \max\{S, P\} + \max\{S, P\} \leq 3P$ and $\pi([C; **; ****], e) \leq S + \max\{R, T\} + \max\{S, P\} \leq S + T + P \leq 3P$ where each asterisk $(*)$ refers to either C or D.

---

34. Recall that (p_C^1, p_D^1) is the local behavior strategy at the stage 1 information set of player one, and so on.

Let $e' \equiv [C; *C; DDDD]$. Then $\pi(e, e') = T + R + T = 2T + R$ and $\pi([D; DD; DDDD], e') = T + T + P = 2T + P$. For any completely mixed strategy p and ε sufficiently small, our assumption that $S + T < 2P$ implies that e is the unique best response to $BR(p(\varepsilon))$ where $p(\varepsilon) \equiv [(1 - \varepsilon)e + \varepsilon e' + \varepsilon^2 p]/(1 + \varepsilon^2)$.[35] To see this, use the facts that $S + T + P \leq 3P$ and $2T + P \leq 2T + R$ together with the following five payoff calculations:

1. Any element of $BR(p(\varepsilon))$ in the reduced-strategy normal form must always Defect at stage 3 since $p(\varepsilon)$ is interior.

2. $\pi(e, p(\varepsilon)) = [(1 - \varepsilon)3P + \varepsilon(2T + R) + \varepsilon^2 \pi(e, p)]/(1 + \varepsilon^2)$.

3. $\pi([C; **; DDDD], p(\varepsilon)) \leq [(1 - \varepsilon)(S + T + P) + \varepsilon(*) + \varepsilon^2 *]/(1 + \varepsilon^2)$.

4. $\pi([D; *C; DDDD], p(\varepsilon)) = [(1 - \varepsilon)(P + S + P) + \varepsilon(*) + \varepsilon^2 *]/(1 + \varepsilon^2)$.

5. $\pi([D; DD; DDDD], p(\varepsilon)) = [(1 - \varepsilon)(3P) + \varepsilon(2T + P) + \varepsilon^2 *]/(1 + \varepsilon^2)$.

Thus, for sufficiently small ε, e is a best response to all p in the sector formed by taking line segments joining these $p(\varepsilon)$ to e, and so these segments are best response trajectories that all converge to e. ∎

Remark 7.5.9   The preceding proof also shows properties of certain trajectories of the symmetric Two-Stage Prisoner's Dilemma Game that are initially on the boundary. For instance, every best response trajectory converges to Always Defect in the reduced-strategy normal form if $p_C^1(t) > 0$ for some t (i.e., if there is some cooperation at stage 1 at some time). The reason for this is that p_D^1 cannot be 0 for all t since, if it were, then the best response trajectory would converge to $\Delta (\{e_3, e_4\})$ as $\{e_1, e_2\} \notin BR(p(t))$. However, near this face, e_3 and e_4 are not best replies—a contradiction. On the other hand, if $p_C^1(0) = 0$ and $\pi(e_8, p(0)) \geq \pi(e_4, p(0))$, then there is a best response trajectory whose ω-limit set is all of G^*.

Part of the following result is a consequence of the general statement of proposition 7.7.2 in appendix B combined with theorem 7.5.5. However, we give an independent proof here for two reasons. One is that the proof of proposition 7.7.2 is not provided in appendix B. The other is that the method presented here is needed in chapter 8.

---

35. This shows, in particular, that e is a *perfect* NE since there are completely mixed strategies arbitrarily close to e for which e is a best response.

Theorem 7.5.10   *Suppose that $(p(t), q(t))$ for $t = 1, 2, \ldots$ is a fictitious play trajectory of the N-Stage Prisoner's Dilemma Game for which the best reply at each discrete time is taken to be a pure strategy. Then this trajectory converges to the NE set in such a way that the sequence of best replies converges in a finite amount of time to the set of pure strategies that mutually defect at all N stages.*

Proof   The fictitious play trajectory under consideration is of the form

$$p(m + 1) = \frac{1}{m}\left(p(1) + \sum_{k=2}^{m} e_k \right),$$

$$q(m + 1) = \frac{1}{m}\left(q(1) + \sum_{k=2}^{m} f_k \right),$$

(7.5.3)

where e_k and f_k are pure best replies to $q(k - 1)$ and $p(k - 1)$ respectively. Call a subgame Γ_u *reachable infinitely often by the sequence* $\{e_2, f_2, e_3, f_3, \ldots\}$ if, for all $n > 1$, e_i against f_j reaches $u = \{x\}$ for some $i, j \geq n$.

We will prove the following statement by induction on ℓ. For some m, e_i against f_j mutually defect in all subgames at stage ℓ that are reachable infinitely often by $\{e_2, f_2, e_3, f_3, \ldots\}$ for all $i, j \geq m$. Once this is proved, we have that the strategy induced by $(p(k), q(k))$ in all these subgames Γ_u converges to the set of strategies that mutually defect in Γ_u since, by (7.5.3), $p(k + 1) = (p(1) + \sum_{i=2}^{m} e_i)/k + (\sum_{i=m+1}^{k} e_i)/k$ converges to $(\sum_{i=m+1}^{k} e_i)/(k - m)$ which satisfies this property as does $\lim_{k \to \infty} q(k + 1)$.

If the induction statement is not true when $\ell = N$, then without loss of generality, there is a singleton information set $u_0 = \{x\}$ at stage N and a sequence e_{i_n} and f_{j_n} that reach u_0 such that $1 < j_1 < i_1 < \cdots < j_n < i_n < \cdots$ and e_{i_n} Cooperates against f_{j_n} at stage N for all n. Let e'_{i_n} be the same pure strategy as e_{i_n} except that it Defects at u. Then

$$\pi(e'_{i_n}, q(i_n - 1)) - \pi(e_{i_n}, q(i_n - 1)) = \gamma(x, i_n)\left[(D - C) \cdot Ab_2^{v_0}(i_n) \right] < 0,$$

where the probability that u_0 is reached under $(e_{i_n}, q(i_n - 1))$, $\gamma(x, i_n)$, is positive since u_0 is relevant for e_{i_n} and $f_{j_n - 1}$ and $b_2^{v_0}(i_n)$ is the behavior strategy induced by $q(i_n - 1)$ at the only player two information set v_0 satisfying $v_0 \succ u_0$. Thus e_{i_n} is not a best reply to $q(i_n - 1)$.

Assume that the statement is true for stage $\ell + 1$ where the required m is $m_{\ell+1}$. We will now show that there is some $m_\ell > m_{\ell+1}$ such that

e_i must Defect against f_j at stage ℓ for all $i, j \geq m_\ell$. If this were not the case, then without loss of generality, there is a singleton information set $u_0 = \{x\}$ at stage ℓ and a sequence e_{i_n} and f_{j_n} that reach u_0 such that $m_{\ell+1} < j_1 < i_1 < \cdots < j_n < i_n < \cdots$ and e_{i_n} Cooperates against f_{j_n} at stage ℓ for all n. Let e'_{i_n} be the same pure strategy as e_{i_n} except that it Defects at all player one information sets in Γ_{u_0}. With $\gamma'(v, i_n)$ the probability that Γ_u is reached under $(e'_{i_n}, q(i_n - 1))$ where u is the player one information set immediately preceding v, and so on, we now have $\pi(e'_{i_n}, q(i_n - 1)) - \pi(e_{i_n}, q(i_n - 1))$ equal to

$$\gamma(x, i_n)\left[(D - C) \cdot Ab_2^{v_0}(i_n)\right] + \sum_{v \succ v_0} \gamma'(v, i_n)\left[D \cdot Ab_2^v(i_n)\right]$$

$$- \sum_{v \succ v_0} \gamma(v, i_n)\left[b_1^u(p(i_n - 1)) \cdot Ab_2^v(i_n)\right].$$

(7.5.4)

Since $(p(i_n - 1), q(i_n - 1))$ converges to the set of strategies that mutually defect at all reachable subgames after stage ℓ, the last summation converges to $-\sum_{v \succ v_0} \gamma(v, i_n)D \cdot AD = -\gamma(v_0, i_n)D \cdot AD$. Since $D \cdot Ab_2^v(i_n) \geq D \cdot AD$, (7.5.4) is positive for n sufficiently large. That is, e_{i_n} is not a best reply to $q(i_n - 1)$.

Thus, there is some m such that $\{e_m, f_m, e_{m+1}, f_{m+1}, \ldots\}$ mutually defects at all N stages. Also $(p(k), q(k))$ converges to the set of strategies that mutually Defect in Γ (i.e., to the NE outcome path). If (p^*, q^*) is an ω-limit point of $(p(k), q(k))$ that is not a NE, then without loss of generality, there is a pure strategy e of player one such that $\pi(p^*, q^*) < \pi(e, q^*)$. Thus (e, q^*) does not mutually defect at all N stages and so e_{k+1} is not a best reply to $q(k)$ for all k sufficiently large.   ∎

7.6   Appendix A: Proof of Theorem 7.5.3

The proof below of theorem 7.5.3 relies on the following theory; namely definitions 7.6.1 and 7.6.2 as well as lemma 7.6.3.

Definition 7.6.1   Order the $2(1 + 4 + 16 + \cdots + 2^{2(N-1)}) = 2(4^N - 1)/3 \equiv M$ *information sets of the N-Stage Prisoner's Dilemma Game as* $u_1 \succ u_2 \succ \cdots \succ u_M$ *where* $u_i \succ u_j$ *implies that either* u_i *is at a latter stage than* u_j *or they are at the same stage, in which case either they are both information sets of the same player or* u_i *is an information set of player two.*[36] *For each pure*

---

36. This complete ordering of the information sets is consistent with the partial order introduced in chapter 6.1 through perfect recall. That is, if $u \prec v$ for the partial order, then $v \succ u$ according to definition 7.6.1.

strategy e_i of player one and any $1 \le k \le M$, let e_i^k be the same strategy as e_i except that e_i^k chooses Defection at all decision points of player one among $u_1, \ldots, u_k$. Similarly f_j^k is defined by considering player two's decision points among $u_1, \ldots, u_k$.

Until the proof is complete, consider a fixed initial state $(p(0), q(0))$ in the interior of $\Delta(S) \times \Delta(S)$. In particular, the sets E_1, E_2, F_1, and F_2 and the game Γ' defined below depend on this initial point and the given uniformly monotone selection dynamic.

Definition 7.6.2   *Let E be the subset $\{e_i \mid \int_0^\infty p_i(t) = \infty\}$ of pure strategies of player one and F the subset $\{f_j \mid \int_0^\infty q_j(t)\, dt = \infty\}$ of pure strategies of player two. Notice that these improper integrals in the definition of E and F are well defined as extended positive real numbers (i.e., either ∞ or a positive real number) since, for example, $p_i(t)$ is a continuous positive function for $t \ge 0$.*

Lemma 7.6.3   *If $e_i \in E$ and $k \in \{1, \ldots, M\}$, the following three statements are true:*

i. $\lim_{t \to \infty} p_i^k(t)/p_i(t) = L^k$ exists as a positive extended real number.

ii. If L^k is finite, then $\pi(e_i, f_j) = \pi(e_i^k, f_j)$ for all $f_j \in F$.

iii. $e_i^k \in E$.

The analogous statements also hold for player two pure strategies $f_j \in F$.

Proof of Lemma 7.6.3

The proof is by induction on k. Let $e_i \in E$. The three statements are trivially true for $k = 1$ since $e_i^1 = e_i$ as u_1 is an information set of player two. We thus start at the smallest value of k such that u_k is an information set of player one. For any $T > 0$,

$$\ln \frac{p_i^k(T)}{p_i(T)} - \ln \frac{p_i^k(0)}{p_i(0)} = \int_0^T \frac{d}{dt} \left(\ln \left(\frac{p_i^k(t)}{p_i(t)} \right) \right) dt$$

$$= \int_0^T \left(\frac{\dot{p}_i^k(t)}{p_i^k(t)} - \frac{\dot{p}_i(t)}{p_i(t)} \right) dt. \tag{7.6.1}$$

Thus $\lim_{T \to \infty} \ln p_i^k(T)/p_i(T)$ exists as an extended nonnegative real number since $\pi(e_i^k, f_j) \ge \pi(e_i, f_j)$ for all $f_j \in \Delta(S)$ (i.e., D does strictly better than C at the last stage) implies, by payoff monotonicity, $[(\dot{p}_i^k(t)/p_i^k(t)) - (\dot{p}_i(t)/p_i(t))]$ is continuous and nonnegative for all t.

Furthermore $\lim_{t\to\infty} p_i^k(t)/p_i(t) = L^k$, where L^k is either a positive real number or ∞. Also $\int_0^\infty p_i^k(t)\,dt = \int_0^\infty [p_i^k(t)/p_i(t)]p_i(t)\,dt = \infty$ since $e_i \in E$ and so $e_i^k \in E$. By uniform monotonicity, for some $K > 1$,

$$
\int_0^T \frac{d}{dt}\left(\ln\left(\frac{p_i^k(t)}{p_i(t)}\right)\right)dt = \int_0^T \left(\frac{\dot{p}_i^k(t)}{p_i^k(t)} - \frac{\dot{p}_i(t)}{p_i(t)}\right)dt
$$

$$
\geq \int_0^T \frac{1}{K}\left(\pi\left(e_i^k, q(t)\right) - \pi(e_i, q(t))\right)dt
$$

$$
= \frac{1}{K}\int_0^T \sum_{f_j \in F} q_j(t)\left(\pi\left(e_i^k, f_j\right) - \pi(e_i, f_j)\right)dt
$$

$$
+ \frac{1}{K}\int_0^T \sum_{f_j \notin F} q_j(t)\left(\pi\left(e_i^k, f_j\right) - \pi(e_i, f_j)\right)dt.
$$

If L^k is finite, then $\pi(e_i^k, f_j) = \pi(e_i, f_j)$ for any $f_j \in F$. This completes the proof of the three statements (and the analogous ones for player two) for all $1 \leq k \leq 4^{N-1}$ that correspond to the information sets of player one at the last stage.

Assume that the three statements and the analogous ones for player two are true for some k with $1 \leq k < M$. Let $e_i \in E$. To show the statement for $k+1$, we first show that $\lim_{t\to\infty} p_i^{k+1}(t)/p_i^k(t)$ exists as a positive extended real number L_k^{k+1}. First, let us show $\int_0^\infty[(\dot{p}_i^{k+1}(t)/p_i^{k+1}(t)) - (\dot{p}_i^k(t)/p_i^k(t))]\,dt$ exists as a real number or as $+\infty$. Since the integrand is continuous, this amounts to showing $\int_0^\infty \min\{[(\dot{p}_i^{k+1}(t)/p_i^{k+1}(t)) - (\dot{p}_i^k(t)/p_i^k(t))], 0\}\,dt > -\infty$. By uniform monotonicity,

$$
\int_0^\infty \min\left\{\left(\frac{\dot{p}_i^{k+1}(t)}{p_i^{k+1}(t)} - \frac{\dot{p}_i^k(t)}{p_i^k(t)}\right), 0\right\}dt
$$

$$
\geq \int_0^\infty \min\{K\left(\pi(e_i^{k+1}, q(t)) - \pi(e_i^k, q(t))\right), 0\}\,dt
$$

$$
\geq K\int_0^\infty \min\left\{\sum_{f_j \in F} q_j(t)\left(\pi(e_i^{k+1}, f_j) - \pi(e_i^k, f_j)\right), 0\right\}dt
$$

$$
\quad (7.6.2)
$$

$$
+ K\int_0^\infty \min\left\{\sum_{f_j \notin F} q_j(t)\left(\pi(e_i^{k+1}, f_j) - \pi(e_i^k, f_j)\right), 0\right\}dt.
$$

The analogue of (7.6.1) is now

$$\int_0^T \sum_{f_j \in F_2} q_j(t)\left(\pi\big(e_i^{k+1}, f_j\big) - \pi\big(e_i^k, f_j\big)\right) dt$$

$$+ \int_0^T \sum_{f_j \notin F_2} q_j(t)\left(\pi\big(e_i^{k+1}, f_j\big) - \pi\big(e_i^k, f_j\big)\right) dt. \tag{7.6.3}$$

If $\pi(e_i^{k+1}, f_j) \geq \pi(e_i^k, f_j)$ for all $f_j \in F$, we are done. If $\pi(e_i^{k+1}, f_{j'}) < \pi(e_i^k, f_{j'})$ for some $f_{j'} \in F$, then the outcome path of e_i^k matched against $f_{j'}$ reaches u_{k+1} which must be a decision node of player one and e_i^k must choose Defection there. Hence $\pi(e_i^{k+1}, f_{j'}^k) > \pi(e_i^k, f_{j'}^k)$. Moreover $f_{j'}$ does not Defect against e_i^k at all its decision points reached along this path (or else the domination of D over C implies $\pi(e_i^{k+1}, f_{j'}) > \pi(e_i^k, f_{j'})$).[37] Thus $\pi(f_{j'}^k, e_i^k) > \pi(f_{j'}, e_i^k)$. Since $e_i^k \in E$ and $f_{j'} \in F$, by induction on part ii of the lemma applied to player two, $\lim_{t\to\infty} q_{j'}^k/q_{j'} = \infty$. Thus, for t sufficiently large, $q_{j'}^k(t)(\pi(e_i^{k+1}, f_{j'}^k) - \pi(e_i^k, f_{j'}^k))$ dominates $q_{j'}(t)(\pi(e_i^{k+1}, f_{j'}) - \pi(e_i^k, f_{j'}))$ in equation (7.6.2), and so the integral $\int_0^\infty \min\{\sum_{f_j \in F} q_j(t)(\pi(e_i^{k+1}, f_j) - \pi(e_i^k, f_j)), 0\} dt$ is finite since the dominating term is positive.

By the same method applied to the upper bound (i.e., using $1/K$ in uniform monotonicity) for $\int_0^\infty [(\dot{p}_i^{k+1}(t)/p_i^{k+1}(t)) - (\dot{p}_i^k(t)/p_i^k(t))] dt$, we see that this integral is infinite if and only if $\pi(e_i^{k+1}, f_{j'}) < \pi(e_i^k, f_{j'})$. That is, L_k^{k+1} exists and is finite if and only if $\pi(e_i^{k+1}, f_j) = \pi(e_i^k, f_j)$ for all $f_j \in F$. Since $L^{k+1} = L_k^{k+1}L^k$, parts i, ii, and iii are true for $k+1$ and this completes the proof by induction. ∎

Proof of Theorem 7.5.3

Since $\lim_{t\to\infty} p_i(t) = 0$ for all $e_i \notin E$, $\limsup_{t\to\infty} p_i(t) > 0$ for some $e_i \in E$, say e_1. By lemma 7.6.3i, $L^M = \lim_{t\to\infty} p_i^M(t)/p_1(t)$ exists. Furthermore, since $\lim p_1(t) \neq 0$, L^M is finite, lemma 7.6.3ii implies that $\pi(e_1, f_j) = \pi(e_1^M, f_j)$ for all $f_j \in F$.

Repeating the argument above for all $e_i \in E$ with $\limsup_{t\to\infty} p_i(t) > 0$, we obtain $\pi(e_i, f_j) = \pi(e_i^M, f_j) = \pi(e_1^M, f_j) = \pi(e_1, f_j)$ for all $f_j \in F$. It is clear from the proof of lemma 7.6.3 that $\lim_{t\to\infty} p_i(t)/p_1(t) = L_i$ exists and is finite for all $e_i \in E$. Thus $p_i(t)$ converges to $L_i/(\sum_{e_{i'} \in E_1} L_{i'})$ for all such $e_i \in E$ and to 0 otherwise. That is, $p(t)$ converges to a point in $\Delta(S)$.

---

37. This is where we need all the conditions (7.5.1).

The proof of the theorem is completed by showing $q(t)$ also converges using the same method applied with E and F interchanged.   ∎

7.7 Appendix B: Maximal Attractor

Although the maximal attractor is defined for any differential inclusion $\dot{x} = F(x)$ where $F(x)$ is an upper semicontinuous set-valued map with compact domain X and each $F(x)$ is a convex compact set, we will restrict our discussion here to the differential inclusion $\dot{x} = BR(x) - x$ that corresponds to the best response dynamic of two-player evolutionary game theory with state space $X \equiv \Delta$. Let $F^t(x)$ be the set of all points $y \in X$ such that there is a best response trajectory $x(\cdot)$ such that $x(0) = x$ and $x(t) = y$. For the best response dynamic, $F^t(x)$ may be multiple valued since there is more than one best response trajectory for a given initial point.

The *maximal attractor*, M, is given by

$$M \equiv \bigcap_{t \geq 0} F^t(X),$$

where $F^t(X) = \{x(t) \mid x \in X\}$ is the set of all points in X that are time t along some trajectory that starts in X. In other words, M consists of all points in X that can be continued backward for any finite amount of time.[38] In particular, M is an invariant set (both forward and backward in time) for the dynamics and any such invariant set is contained in M (i.e., M is the *maximal invariant set* which is just another name for maximal attractor).

Proposition 7.7.1 *The maximal attractor (of the best response dynamic) is globally asymptotically stable.*

Proof For any $x \in X$, the ω-limit set Ω of x is an invariant set (both forward and backward) since every $y \in \Omega$ can be continued backward. Thus $\Omega \subset M$ and so M is globally asymptotically stable if it is Lyapunov stable. We will first show that M is closed.

Suppose that x_n is a sequence of points in M that converges to x and that $T > 0$. Then there is a sequence of trajectories of the best response dynamic defined for all $t \in [-T, 0]$ (i.e., absolutely continuous functions $[-T, 0] \to X$ whose derivatives are Lebesgue integrable functions that are defined almost everywhere and satisfy $\dot{x} = F(x)$) that are at x_n at $t = 0$. By the compactness of X and the upper semicontinuity of

---

38. In fact $x \in M$ if and only if there is a dynamic trajectory $x(t)$ in X that is defined for all positive and negative t and satisfies $x(0) = x$.

the differential inclusion, there is a subsequence of these continuous functions that converge uniformly to an absolutely continuous function $[-T, 0] \to X$. This limiting function defines a best-response trajectory that is at x at $t = 0$. Since T is arbitrary, $x \in M$.

Now suppose that M is not Lyapunov stable. Then there exists a neighborhood U of M and sequences of $x_n \in U$ whose distance to M decreases to 0 and positive t_n such that $x_n(t_n) \notin U$. By compactness, there is a subsequence (which we again denote x_n) that converges to an $x \in M$ such that $x_n(t_n)$ converges to a $y \notin U$. If these t_n are bounded (with accumulation point T), the argument in the preceding paragraph ensures there is a best response trajectory that is at x at $t = 0$ and at y at time T. Since M is forward invariant, $y \in M$. On the other hand, if a sequence of t_n increases to ∞, the same argument shows there is a best response trajectory for $t \in [-T, 0]$ that is at y at time 0 for all $T > 0$. Thus, in either case, we contradict the assumption that $y \notin U$. ∎

It can be shown that the "tail end" of any fictitious play trajectory is uniformly close to a best response trajectory over compact time intervals. The following result, whose proof is not given here, follows from this combined with the methods in the above proof.

Proposition 7.7.2 *The set of ω-limit points of any fictitious play trajectory is an invariant set for the best response dynamic (i.e., it consists of complete orbits of the best response dynamic). In particular, all ω-limit points of fictitious play trajectories are contained in the maximal attractor of the best response dynamic.*

7.8 Notes

The terminology "(symmetric) simultaneity game" is not standard in the literature. For instance, what we call a (symmetric) simultaneity game is also referred to as an almost perfect information game (Cressman 1997b) and as a perfect information game with simultaneous moves (Osborne and Rubinstein 1994). (The latter reference is an excellent one for the static concept of backward induction.) However, the idea of simultaneous move games is present already in von Neumann and Morgenstern (1944).[39] Van Damme (1991) used the game of figure 7.1.1a

---

39. Our simultaneity games are perhaps closer to the original formulation of an extensive form game in this reference than in the formulation by Kuhn (1953) in that all decision points in a given simultaneity game have exactly the same number of vertices preceding it. This property, which implies a "rank" structure can be imposed, is not true for the extensive form games as defined in chapter 6 as pointed out by Kuhn (1953; see also Ritzberger 1999).

as an elementary counterexample to the assertion in Selten (1983) that backward induction on the ESS structure of the subgames and their truncations produced ESSs. The dynamic analysis of the elementary examples in section 7.1 is from Cressman (1997b) where much of the theory in section 7.3 is developed.

The Two-Stage Hawk-Dove Game of section 7.2.1 is analyzed in Cressman (1995) with the simulations reported in remark 7.2.2 taken from Cannings and Whittaker (1991). Sections 7.2.2 (symmetric signaling games)[40] and 7.2.3 (cheap talk games) follow the respective approaches of Kim (1995) and Schlag (1993) where the missing proofs can be found (see also Weibull 1995). The handicap principle of section 7.2.2 is a well-documented phenomenon exhibited in biological species (Zahavi and Zahavi 1997). Most of the results in section 7.4 are contained in Bishop and Cannings (1978) who describe the backward induction procedure in section 7.4.1 without explicit reference to the game's extensive form and also analyze the Continuous War of Attrition. More recently Oechssler and Riedel (2001) have analyzed stability of the replicator dynamic when there is a continuum of pure strategies.

There are numerous books (e.g., Axelrod 1980; Sigmund 1993) as well as countless journal articles based wholly or in part on the Prisoner's Dilemma Game of section 7.5. The analysis of the replicator dynamic in section 7.5.1 is based on Cressman (1996a) although the Two-Stage Game is also done in Nachbar (1990) and the simulations are from Nachbar (1992). Selten and Stoecker (1986) observe the "end effects" phenomenon in experiments. Section 7.5.2 is based on unpublished joint work with Josef Hofbauer and Karl Schlag. The concept of the maximal attractor as used in the proof of proposition 7.7.1 is from Hofbauer (personal communication). Proposition 7.7.2 is proved by Hofbauer (1995a). A good reference for the general theory of differential inclusions is Aubin (1991).

---

40. A "signaling game" for economic game theorists (e.g., Osborne and Rubinstein 1994) usually refers to a two-player game (where player one is the sender and player two is the receiver) with a different extensive form structure than in section 7.2.2. Our form is typical of biological game theorists (e.g., Kim 1995; Hurd and Enquist 1998). To avoid confusion, the phrase "symmetric signaling game" is used instead.

8   Perfect Information Games

A (two-player) *perfect information game* is a two-player extensive form game where all player decision points are singleton information sets. That is, each player, when making a decision, is perfectly informed of all previous decisions (either by players or by nature) in the game tree. Clearly, perfect information games satisfy the weaker assumption of perfect recall whereby only those previous decisions taken by the same player are known. The condition satisfied by the simultaneity games of chapter 7 is intermediate in that each player, when making a decision, is perfectly informed of all previous decisions at earlier stages in the game tree.

Every perfect information game has at least one pure strategy NE; namely a subgame perfect NE that takes a pure behavior strategy best reply at each player decision point in the backward induction process. As shown in the following theorem (proved in appendix A), any other NE component contains a pure strategy NE as well. However, many game theorists argue that non–subgame perfect NEs should be discarded as rational solutions to perfect information games. Throughout this chapter, we examine this question from a dynamic perspective.

Theorem 8.0.1   *Every NE component G in the normal form of a perfect information game Γ contains a pure strategy pair. There is only one subgame perfect NE component.*[1]

We are primarily concerned with the dynamic stability of NE and their components in this chapter. Most of our results apply only to the subclass of perfect information games in which no relevant payoff ties emerge

---

1. Throughout this chapter (cf. theorem 7.0.1) a *subgame perfect NE component* is a NE component that contains a pure strategy pair whose realization equivalent behavior strategy is subgame perfect. By the proof of the first statement of the theorem, every mixed subgame perfect NE is realization equivalent to a NE in a subgame perfect NE component.

through any backward induction process based on pure behavior strategies. The following definition makes this precise and consequences for the NE structure are given immediately afterward.

Definition 8.0.2   *An extensive form game Γ is generic if no two pure strategy pairs that yield different outcomes have the same payoff for one of the players. For extensive form games with no moves by nature, this is equivalent to the property that no two endpoints have the same payoff for one of the players, in which case we also say Γ has distinct payoffs.*[2]

Theorem 8.0.3   *Each NE component G of a generic perfect information game Γ is a convex set that consists of a pure strategy NE together with all other NE with the same equilibrium outcome.[3] There is only one subgame perfect NE outcome.*

Proof   Suppose that $(p^*, q^*) \in G$ is a NE whose outcome is not the same as some pure strategy pair. Let u be a last decision point reached by (p^*, q^*) where one of the players (e.g., player one) does not choose a pure behavior strategy. Let p' be the same strategy as p^* except that at u, p' chooses the pure strategy that leads to the highest payoff to player one among those outcomes in the subgame Γ_u reached by (p^*, q^*) (this choice is unique since Γ is generic). Then player one receives a higher payoff playing p' against q^* than by playing p^*, which contradicts (p^*, q^*) being a NE.

By the connectivity of G, if $(p, q) \in G$, then there is a continuous curve of NE in $\Delta_1 \times \Delta_2$ that connects (p^*, q^*) to (p, q). Each NE on this curve generates the same outcome as some pure strategy pair, and by continuity, all $(p, q) \in G$ generate the same outcome as (p^*, q^*). Conversely, if (p, q) is a NE that generates the same outcome as (p^*, q^*), then so does any convex combination $(p_\lambda, q_\lambda) \equiv (\lambda p + (1-\lambda)p^*, \lambda q + (1-\lambda)q^*)$ for $0 \leq \lambda \leq 1$. (In fact, if (p, q) and (p', q') generate the same outcome, then so does $(\lambda p + (1-\lambda)p', q)$ and $(p, \lambda q + (1-\lambda)q')$.) Since each (p_λ, q_λ) is a NE (e.g., $p_0 \cdot Aq_\lambda = \lambda p_0 \cdot Aq + (1-\lambda)p_0 \cdot Aq^* \leq \lambda p \cdot Aq + (1-\lambda)p^* \cdot Aq^* = p^* \cdot Aq^* = p_\lambda \cdot Aq_\lambda$ for all $p_0 \in \Delta_1$), $(p, q) \in G$. This also shows G is convex.

By theorem 8.0.1, G contains at least one pure strategy NE. The uniqueness of the subgame perfect NE outcome then follows from theorem 8.0.1 and the first statement of theorem 8.0.3.   ∎

---

2. The property described in this definition is generic in the following sense. Given the tree of a two-player extensive form game, the set of all possible payoff assignments at the $|Z|$ terminal nodes (i.e., endpoints) for which Γ is generic is a set whose complement in $\mathbf{R}^{2|Z|}$ is a closed set with Lebesgue measure zero.

3. There may be more than one pure strategy in G.

The basic question of this chapter is whether there are dynamic grounds on which to select among the NE components of generic perfect information games. Special attention with respect to this question is paid to the unique subgame perfect NE component. We return to the general question in section 8.2 after considering it first for the elementary games of section 8.1.

8.1 Elementary Perfect Information Games

The simplest two-player extensive form game with a nontrivial strategy set for both players is the perfect information game of figure 8.1.1 which has strategies L (left) or R (right) for player one at information set u and ℓ (left) or r (right) at information set v for player two. The payoffs indicated in figure 8.1.1 are those for example 8.1.3 below. The normal form of any game with this tree structure (which also equals its reduced-strategy normal form) belongs to the six cases of two-strategy bimatrix games classified in chapter 3.3.2 where they were called "degenerate."

The following three specific games will be referred to later in this chapter for illustrative purposes and so are briefly reintroduced here.

Example 8.1.1 (A nongeneric perfect information game) Replace the payoffs in figure 8.1.1 by nongeneric ones corresponding to the payoff matrix

$$\begin{array}{c} & \ell & r \\ L & \begin{bmatrix} 0,0 & 0,0 \\ -1,0 & 1,0 \end{bmatrix} \\ R \end{array}.$$

This game has a single NE component (see figure 3.3.9 in chapter 3.3.2) that connects the two pure subgame perfect NE strategies (L, ℓ) and (R, r). This shows that more than one subgame perfect NE outcome is possible when the game is not generic (cf. theorem 8.0.3).

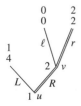

Figure 8.1.1
Elementary perfect information game of example 8.1.3.

Examples 8.1.2 and 8.1.3 are the generic perfect information games which, as mentioned in chapter 3.3.2, are the most interesting degenerate two-strategy bimatrix games. Notice that the strategies of players one and two in these two examples are no longer labeled L, R and ℓ, r respectively. The change in notation reflects their more traditional labels.

Example 8.1.2   (The Centipede Game of Length Two)   Centipede Games of arbitrary length are considered in section 8.3 below where the reason for the name "centipede" becomes readily apparent (see figure 8.3.1 in section 8.3 where the alternatives at each player decision point are "Across" and "Down"). Here we consider the Centipede Game of Length Two with payoff matrix

$$
\begin{array}{c c}
 & \begin{array}{c c} d & \quad a \end{array} \\
\begin{array}{c} D \\ A \end{array} & \left[\begin{array}{c c} 0,0 & \ 0,0 \\ -1,3 & \ 2,2 \end{array} \right]
\end{array} .
$$

This game has certain similarities with the (Finitely Repeated) Prisoner's Dilemma Game in that its single NE component[4] $G^* = \{(D, q) \mid \frac{2}{3} \leq q_d \leq 1\}$ is subgame perfect but both players would prefer a different outcome; namely (A, a). Another similarity is that evolutionary dynamics select only the subgame perfect outcome since all interior trajectories evolve to G^* (see figure 3.3.5 in chapter 3.3.2).

Example 8.1.3   (The Chain-Store Game)   Perhaps the most interesting elementary perfect information game is the one given in figure 8.1.1. First, it is the only one that has more than one NE component. From the payoff matrix[5]

$$
\begin{array}{c c}
 & \begin{array}{c c} R & \quad A \end{array} \\
\begin{array}{c} N \\ E \end{array} & \left[\begin{array}{c c} 1,4 & \ 1,4 \\ 0,0 & \ 2,2 \end{array} \right]
\end{array} .
$$

we see that $(E, A)^*$ and (N, R) are both pure strategy Nash equilibria,

---

4. Although the notation (D, q) is a bit odd as it mixes the label for an alternative D with elements of a strategy space $q \in \Delta^2$, it should not cause the reader confusion. Of course, D is identified with $\{p \mid p_D = 1\}$.

5. The choices of player one are now labeled N (not enter) and E (enter) while those of player two are R (retaliate) and A (acquiesce). In figure 8.1.1 these correspond to the choices $L, R, \ell,$ and r respectively.

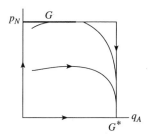

Figure 8.1.2
Replicator dynamic trajectories for the Chain-Store Game.

the former (distinguished by an asterisk) is subgame perfect and strict. The latter is contained in the connected NE component $G = \{(N, q) \mid \frac{1}{2} \leq q_R \leq 1\}$.

As mentioned in the Introduction (chapter 1.1), another reason for interest in this game is that it is often used to model a potential entrant (player one) into a market controlled by a monopolist (player two). Player one chooses whether or not to enter the market. If he chooses to enter, then player two (the monopolist) chooses either to retaliate or to acquiesce. The monopolist prefers the NE outcome corresponding to (N, R) with payoff 4 since this implies no competition (i.e., player one chooses N). On the other hand, one questions whether such a NE can be maintained from the extensive form since it involves the "threat" by the monopolist to play R if there is competition even though he would be better off in this case to play A. There is some dynamic justification for either NE outcome in that all interior trajectories of a monotone selection dynamic converge either to $G^* = \{(E, A)^*\}$ or to a unique point in G. This is clear from figure 8.1.2 which is also figure 3.3.6 in chapter 3.3.2.

We will be particularly interested in equilibrium selection via the concept of interior asymptotic stability defined in the following section. Further inspection of all the figures in chapter 3.3.2 that are relevant for the six "degenerate cases" shows this method selects the subgame perfect NE outcome in all generic elementary perfect information games. This is summarized in the following theorem:

Theorem 8.1.4 *Suppose that Γ is an elementary perfect information game (i.e., it has the tree structure of figure 8.1.1). The subgame perfect NE* *component[6] of Γ is the unique interior asymptotically stable set of NE under any monotone selection dynamic. If Γ is generic, every pure strategy NE of Γ is stable under any monotone selection dynamic, and the subgame perfect NE strategy is globally interior asymptotically stable for the best response dynamic.*

8.2   Equilibrium Selection: Dynamic Approach

Perfect information games may have many more than two NE outcomes as their game tree becomes more complicated than figure 8.1.1. Furthermore the NE components are often sets of NE points (especially if the NE outcome is not pervasive). Our preferred method of equilibrium selection is through asymptotic stability under, say, the replicator dynamic. By theorem 3.2.1 in chapter 3, we know a NE component is asymptotically stable for two-player games if and only if it is an SESet. However, SESets often do not exist for interesting two-player extensive form games such as the three examples in the previous section.[7] Thus, if the subgame perfect NE component G^* of a generic perfect information game is not a union of faces, it cannot be asymptotically stable since all points with the same outcome as a pure strategy in G^* are rest points of the dynamic and so trajectories that start at arbitrarily close non-NE points on this face do not converge to this NE component. In particular, the only NE component of the three examples in section 8.1 that is asymptotically stable is G^* in the Chain-Store Game.

Thus, although asymptotically stable sets exist[8] in general since the entire space $\Delta(S_1) \times \Delta(S_2)$ is of this type, the condition of asymptotic stability is too strong for extensive form games to select NE outcomes. We therefore weaken our dynamic criteria for equilibrium selection by considering only interior trajectories as in the following definition. Although it is written explicitly for monotone selection dynamics, the stability concepts introduced there also apply to the other standard dynamics of evolutionary game theory.

---

6. For nongeneric elementary perfect information games, the subgame perfect NE component of Γ is still unique even though it may contain more than one equilibrium outcome.

7. The Finitely Repeated Prisoner's Dilemma Game (with symmetry ignored) of chapter 7.5 often has no SESet either (e.g., under the condition $T + S > 2P$).

8. The proof of theorem 8.2.6 below shows a unique minimal asymptotically stable set under the replicator dynamic exists for every generic perfect information game. Dynamic stability with respect to monotone selection dynamics was not considered in chapter 7.5 (see remark 7.5.4). Instead, the main emphasis was on a different aspect of the Fundamental Theorem of Evolutionary Game Theory; namely convergence to NE of interior trajectories.

Definition 8.2.1 *Let G be a closed set in $\Delta(S_1) \times \Delta(S_2)$. Then*

(i) G is called interior stable *under a monotone selection dynamic if, for every neighborhood O of G, there is another neighborhood U of G such that the trajectory of any initial point in U intersected with the interior of $\Delta(S_1) \times \Delta(S_2)$ remains inside O. The strategy pair (p, q) is called* interior stable *if $\{(p, q)\}$ is interior stable.*

(ii) G is called interior attracting *if G is contained in an open set O such that every trajectory with initial point in O and also in the interior of $\Delta(S_1) \times \Delta(S_2)$ converges to G (i.e., all ω-limits are in G). G is called* globally interior attracting *if all ω-limits of trajectories starting in the interior of $\Delta(S_1) \times \Delta(S_2)$ are in G.*

(iii) G is called interior asymptotically stable *if it is interior attracting and stable. It is* globally interior asymptotically stable *if it is globally interior attracting and stable.*

This definition parallels definition 2.6.2 from chapter 2. In fact a closed set G is interior stable if and only if it is stable according to definition 2.6.2 applied to two-player games.[9] As argued in chapter 2, stability is important when perturbations are introduced into the dynamical system. By theorem 8.2.2 below, if an interior trajectory of a uniformly monotone selection dynamic converges to a stable point in a NE component G of a generic perfect information game Γ, then a single perturbation (i.e., a discontinuity in this trajectory) that is sufficiently small will result in new initial conditions of the dynamical system from which the trajectory will also converge to a NE in G. Since every NE outcome in G is the same for Γ, we expect to observe this outcome in the long run if the population starts near a stable point and there are only a finite number of small perturbations.

On the other hand, it is intuitively clear from figure 8.1.2 that a stable point in the non–subgame perfect NE component cannot withstand infinitely repeated perturbations for the Chain-Store Game. Here these perturbations can gradually shift interior trajectories to the right until q_A is near $\frac{1}{2}$ from where an additional perturbation pushing q_A past $\frac{1}{2}$ will

---

9. The "if" direction is true by definition. The converse follows from the continuous dependence of the trajectories of a monotone selection dynamic on their initial points. That is, two trajectories will remain close over any finite time interval if their initial points are sufficiently close. Thus, if a boundary trajectory initially close to G did not stay close, then an interior trajectory arbitrarily close initially would also evolve outside a small neighborhood of G.

lead the trajectory to the subgame perfect NE component $G^* = \{(E, A)\}$. For this reason the solution concept of asymptotic stability is often used for equilibrium selection since an asymptotically stable set will withstand repeated random perturbations in the dynamical system if the associated discontinuities are sufficiently rare that selection via the replicator dynamic comes close to converging between successive perturbations.

In this section we analyze primarily the slightly weaker solution concept of interior asymptotic stability that will withstand rare perturbations whose discontinuities lead to interior initial conditions. Equilibria selected based on interior trajectories as in definition 8.2.1 often differ from those selected based on all trajectories. For instance, examples 8.1.1 and 8.1.2 in the previous section do not have an attracting set of NE, but the subgame perfect NE component is interior attracting as well as interior asymptotically stable.[10]

8.2.1   The Replicator and Monotone Selection Dynamics

Equilibrium selection via these dynamics for perfect information games is built on three main results starting with convergence (theorem 8.2.2) and stability (theorem 8.2.4). Each is important in its own right since neither is true for arbitrary extensive form games. They are used together to prove the central result on interior attracting and asymptotically stable sets (theorem 8.2.6).

Theorem 8.2.2   *Suppose that Γ is a generic perfect information game. Every interior trajectory of a uniformly monotone selection dynamic converges to a NE point of the game's normal form.*

The technical proof of theorem 8.2.2, given in appendix A (see definition 8.5.1 and lemma 8.5.2 there), closely parallels the steps in the proof of theorem 7.5.3 in chapter 7.5.1 for the Finitely Repeated Prisoner's Dilemma Game. One new aspect of the proof is of independent interest, and so it is described here in the main text. Given a fixed initial point $(p(0), q(0))$ in the interior of $\Delta(S_1) \times \Delta(S_2)$, it is sufficient to consider those paths in Γ that are played most frequently (according to the following definition) by the population along the trajectory, thus yielding a new generic perfect information game Γ'.

---

10. Similarly, for the Two-Stage Prisoner's Dilemma Game with $T + S > 2P$, the NE component is interior asymptotically stable but not asymptotically stable.

Definition 8.2.3 *Let E and F be the subsets of $S_1 = \{e_1, e_2, \ldots, e_m\}$ and $S_2 = \{f_1, f_2, \ldots, f_n\}$ given by $E = \{e_i \mid \int_0^\infty p_i(t) = \infty\}$ and $F = \{f_j \mid \int_0^\infty q_j(t)dt = \infty\}$.[11] Let Γ' be the extensive form game generated by E and F. That is, the tree of Γ' is the subtree of Γ (with the same root as that of Γ) whose endpoints are precisely those reached by some pure strategy pair (e_i, f_j) where $e_i \in E$ and $f_j \in F$. The pure strategies of Γ' include all e_i and f_j with $e_i \in E$ and $f_j \in F$ when these strategies are restricted to the decision points of Γ'.*

Γ' is a two-player extensive form game with perfect information. Since Γ is generic, Γ' has a unique subgame perfect NE that may well differ from that of Γ.[12] The remainder of the proof in appendix A then shows that the trajectory converges to a single point whose outcome is obtained by applying backward induction to the game Γ'.

Now that we know from theorem 8.2.2 that each interior trajectory converges to a NE, the remainder of this section examines which NE outcome is expected in the limit. First, we consider the stability of NE points.

Theorem 8.2.4 *Let Γ be a generic perfect information game. Any NE that is in the interior of the NE set of Γ relative to the set of rest points of the replicator dynamic (i.e., there is a neighborhood U of this NE such that the only rest points in U are NE) is stable for any monotone selection dynamic.[13] Moreover a pure strategy pair is a NE if and only if it is stable.*

Proof Let (p^*, q^*) be a NE that is in the interior of the NE set of Γ relative to the set of rest points. Let H be the face of $\Delta(S_1) \times \Delta(S_2)$ that contains any pure strategy (e, f) whose outcome is the same as that of (p^*, q^*). H is a set of rest points consisting of all (mixed) strategies with the same outcome as that of (p^*, q^*). Suppose that e_1 is a pure best reply for player one to q^*. We claim that $(e_1, q^*) \in H$. If not, then there exists an f_j such that $q_j^* > 0$ and e_1 against f_j does not yield the same outcome as (p^*, q^*). Since $\pi_1(e_1, q^*) = \pi_1(p^*, q^*)$ and Γ is generic, there is such an f_j that satisfies $\pi_1(e_1, f_j) > \pi_1(p^*, q^*) = \pi_1(p^*, q_\lambda)$ for all $q_\lambda \equiv \lambda f_j + (1 - \lambda)q^*$

---

11. Note that the improper integral in the definition of E (and of F) is well defined as an extended positive real number (i.e., either ∞ or a positive real number) since $p_i(t)$ is a continuous positive function for $t \geq 0$. Also note that the sets E and F as well as the game Γ' depend on the initial point $(p(0), q(0))$ of the uniformly monotone selection dynamic.
12. For example, for any initial state from which the trajectory in figure 8.1.2 leads to G, the tree of Γ' cannot contain the alternative where player two chooses A at his information set.
13. Recall that the set of rest points of the replicator dynamic is the same as the set of rest points of any monotone selection dynamic.

where $0 \leq \lambda \leq 1$. Thus (p^*, q_λ) is a rest point in H but is not a NE if $\lambda > 0$. Since such (p^*, q_λ) can be chosen arbitrarily close to (p^*, q^*), (p^*, q^*) is not in the interior of the NE set of Γ relative to the set of rest points. By contradiction, $(e_1, q^*) \in H$.

By the same argument applied to the best replies of player two, $H = \Delta(\tilde{S}_1) \times \Delta(\tilde{S}_2)$, where $\tilde{S}_1 = \{e_i \mid e_i \text{ is a best reply to } q^*\}$ and $\tilde{S}_2 = \{f_j \mid f_j \text{ is a best reply to } p^*\}$. The stability of a monotone selection dynamic at a NE (p^*, q^*) is determined by analyzing its stability restricted to the face $\Delta(\tilde{S}_1) \times \Delta(\tilde{S}_2)$ of its best replies since the eigenvalues of the linearized dynamic associated with eigenvectors outside this invariant face are negative. Since, in our case, $\Delta(\tilde{S}_1) \times \Delta(\tilde{S}_2)$ is a set of rest points, H is the center manifold at (p^*, q^*) for the monotone selection dynamic, and so (p^*, q^*) is stable.

Now suppose that (e_1, f_1) is a pure strategy NE. We will prove that it is stable by showing that each rest point sufficiently close to it is also a NE. Since Γ is generic, every rest point (p, q) close to (e_1, f_1) has the same outcome as (e_1, f_1). Suppose that (p, q) is not a NE. Without loss of generality, $\pi_1(e_i, q) > \pi_1(p, q) = \pi_1(e_1, f_1)$ for some $e_i \in S_1$. For q sufficiently close to f_1, this implies $\pi_1(e_i, f_1) = \pi_1(e_1, f_1)$ since (e_1, f_1) is a NE. Thus (e_i, f_1), (e_1, f_1), (p, q) and (e_i, q) all have the same outcome, and so we have the contradiction that $\pi_1(e_i, q) = \pi_1(p, q)$. Conversely, stable strategy pairs are NE for any monotone selection dynamic by the Folk Theorem of Evolutionary Game Theory.   ∎

Remark 8.2.5   It is an open problem whether theorem 8.2.2 remains true for those perfect information games Γ that are not generic (even if there are no moves by nature).[14] In a nongeneric Γ, NE need not generate a pure strategy equilibrium outcome as seen by example 8.1.1 in section 8.1. Furthermore such NE are not always stable for a monotone selection dynamic even though they are in the interior of the NE set relative to the set of rest points (cf. theorem 8.2.4).

The following theorem gives the central result, together with its immediate consequences, that the subgame perfect equilibrium (e_B, f_B) is contained in any interior attracting or interior asymptotically stable set. The main step in the proof given in appendix B is to show that it is always possible to find an interior trajectory initially close to any NE

---

14. Theorem 8.2.2 is, however, true for all elementary perfect information games with game tree given in figure 8.1.1 of section 8.1. In particular, it is true for the only nongeneric case, example 8.1.1, summarized briefly there.

component other than the one containing the subgame perfect equilibrium whose unique limit point coincides with the choices of (e_B, f_B) further along the backward induction process than initially. Heuristically the population evolving along such trajectories does not forget previous steps in the backward induction process.

Theorem 8.2.6   *Every generic perfect information game, Γ, has a unique minimal interior attracting set (which must be a set of NE strategy pairs) and a unique minimal interior asymptotically stable set for any uniformly monotone selection dynamic. Both of these sets contain the subgame perfect equilibrium along with its NE component, G^*. If G is an interior asymptotically stable set such that each element of G yields the same outcome in Γ, then $G = G^*$.*

By theorem 8.1.4 the subgame perfect NE component is the unique minimal interior attracting set and the unique minimal interior asymptotically stable set for any elementary perfect information game with the tree structure of figure 8.1.1. For the Chain-Store Game, another interesting interior asymptotically stable set is the NE set together with the complete trajectory that evolves from its α-limit at the only unstable NE point to $(E, A)^*$.

Through the concepts of either interior attracting or interior asymptotic stability, theorem 8.2.6 provides a dynamic justification for including the subgame perfect equilibrium outcome in any solution, although alternative NE outcomes might also be selected in this manner. At this point theorem 8.2.6 leaves open the intriguing possibility that the subgame perfect NE component G^* is the unique minimal set that satisfies one (or both) of these concepts for all generic perfect information games. Such a result would provide a dynamic justification for selecting only the backward induction solution. Unfortunately, the following example shows this result is not true:[15]

Example 8.2.7   (The perfect information game Γ of figure 8.2.1)   In figure 8.2.1, dashed lines indicate the subgame perfect choices at each decision point. The normal form of Γ is

	$L\ell$	Lm	Lr	$R\ell$	Rm	Rr
T	2, 3	2, 3	2, 3	−2, −2	−2, −2	−2, −2
B	0, 2	1, 0	3, 1	0, 2	1, 0	3, 1

---

15. This example is probably the most elementary generic perfect information game where the subgame perfect component is not the sole NE selected on dynamic grounds. Another example with only two actions at each decision point is given in section 8.3.2.

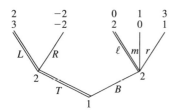

Figure 8.2.1
Elementary game with three actions at a decision point.

First consider the generic perfect information game formed by deleting action R for player two in figure 8.2.1. Then (T, ℓ) is the subgame perfect equilibrium with the corresponding NE component $G^* = \{(T, q) \mid$
$q_m + 3q_r \leq 2\}$. Consider the boundary NE $z = (T, (0, \frac{1}{2}, \frac{1}{2})) \in G^*$. On the
face $\Delta(\{T, B\}) \times \Delta(\{m, r\})$, the normal form is that of the Chain-Store
Game, and so there are trajectories on this face starting close to z that converge to (B, r). Consequently there is an interior trajectory $(p(t), q(t))$
for this game that starts close to z and evolves arbitrarily close to (B, r).
That is, G^* is not interior asymptotically stable. On the other hand, G^*
is interior attracting since G^* is the unique NE outcome.

The full game in figure 8.2.1 shows the subgame perfect NE component is not necessarily interior attracting either. Now $(T, L\ell)$ is the
subgame perfect equilibrium with the corresponding NE component
$G^* = \{(T, q) \mid q_{L\ell} + q_{Lm} + q_{Lr} = 1, q_{Lm} + 3q_{Lr} \leq 2\}$. $(B, R\ell)$ is the only
other NE in pure strategies (with the corresponding NE component
$G = \{(B, q) \mid q_{L\ell} + q_{R\ell} = 1, \frac{1}{2} \leq q_{R\ell} \leq 2\}$). From above, there are trajectories on the face $\Delta\{T, B\} \times \Delta\{Lm, Lr\}$ starting close to the NE $z =$
$(T, (0, \frac{1}{2}, \frac{1}{2}, 0, 0, 0)) \in G^*$ that converge to (B, Lr). Consequently there is
a trajectory $(p(t), q(t))$ in the interior of the face $\Delta\{T, B\} \times \Delta\{Lm, Lr, R\ell\}$
that starts close to z and a time $t' \geq 0$ such that $q_{Lr}(t') > \frac{1}{2}$. Since Lr
weakly dominates Lm, it follows that $q_{Lr}(t) > q_{Lm}(t)$ for all $t \geq t'$. This
implies that $\dot{p}_B(t) > 0$ for all $t \geq t'$ and that consequently the trajectory $(p(t), q(t))$ converges to the NE $(B, R\ell)$. Since $(B, R\ell)$ is stable by
theorem 8.2.4, there are interior trajectories for Γ that start near G^* and
converge to the NE component of $(B, R\ell)$. Thus G^* is not asymptotically
stable since any interior attracting set must contain the (unconnected)
set of all NE in this example.

Example 8.2.7 illustrates that there are perfect information games for
which G^* is neither interior asymptotically stable nor interior attracting.

The intuition behind this particular counterexample is that starting at the subgame perfect equilibrium $(T, L\ell)$, repeated perturbations in player two's strategy are not selected against (informally, strategies Lm and Lr can enter unpunished) until there may be essentially no individuals using strategy $L\ell$ and a critical mixture of Lm and Lr. At this point selection alone will drive the dynamical system toward (B, Lr). As the system moves far enough away from player one using T, player two has an incentive to use L after seeing B no matter what choice is made after T. If, in this situation, $R\ell$ is much more prevalent than $L\ell$ initially, evolution may maintain this prevalence and thus lead the population to a NE component that does not contain the subgame perfect equilibrium.[16] That is, although $L\ell$ is a weakly dominant strategy for player two, its frequency in this situation is too low to stop $R\ell$ from growing substantially.

Although there is no known criterion completely characterizing those generic perfect information games where G^* is the unique minimal interior asymptotically stable set, there are some partial results in this direction. One result, a corollary of theorem 8.2.6 that can also be shown directly, is that the only possible SESet of Γ is the subgame perfect NE component. Furthermore a pervasive NE for generic perfect information games Γ is automatically a subgame perfect equilibrium that is strict (in particular, it is a singleton SESet) and so asymptotically stable (e.g., the Chain-Store Game of section 8.1). Of course, of more interest are the nonpervasive NE. The following theorem provides a large class of generic perfect information games where G^* is the unique minimal interior asymptotically stable set, even though it is not an SESet. Given that three alternatives at a decision point off the equilibrium path can disrupt stability (example 8.2.7 above), it is not surprising we require certain decision points to have at most two alternatives.

Theorem 8.2.8 *Let Γ be a generic perfect information game, and consider all player decision points X that are not reached by the subgame perfect equilibrium outcome. For each $x \in X$, let $u(x)$ be the last decision point that comes before x and is reached by the subgame perfect equilibrium outcome. This is a player decision point. Assume that there is at most one $x \in X$ for which $u(x)$ is a decision point u of the other player and that u, if it exists, has exactly two*

---

16. The same final phenomenon occurs in the Chain-Store Game for those trajectories that converge to G in figure 8.1.2.

alternatives.[17] Then the subgame perfect NE component, G^*, is the unique minimal interior asymptotically stable set for any uniformly monotone selection dynamic.

Proof Suppose that Γ has no decision point of the player who is not the player to first deviate from the subgame perfect equilibrium outcome to reach this decision point.[18] Let G^* be the set of strategy pairs whose outcome is the same as the subgame perfect NE outcome. Since Γ is generic, any best reply pair to any point in G^* must also follow the subgame perfect equilibrium outcome. That is, G^* is the subgame perfect NE component and an SESet. In fact, in the reduced-strategy normal form, G^* is a singleton set consisting of the subgame perfect equilibrium and so is a strict NE. In any case, G^* is asymptotically stable.

Now suppose that u is the only decision point of the player who is not the player to first deviate from the subgame perfect equilibrium outcome to reach this decision point. Without loss of generality, u is a decision point of player two. In the reduced-strategy normal form, the best replies at every point in G^* are contained in the following two-dimensional face spanned by two pure strategies for each player. One pure strategy for each player is the unique subgame perfect NE. The other pure strategy of player one differs from his subgame perfect alternative only at his deviation decision point which leads to u where the alternative leading to this deviation is chosen. The other pure strategy of player two differs from his subgame perfect alternative only at u where it takes the only other possible alternative (recall u has exactly two alternatives). On this two-dimensional face, either G^* is an SESet or we have the Centipede Game of Length Two. In either case each point of G^* is stable, and so by theorem 8.2.2, G^* is interior asymptotically stable. ■

8.2.2   *Fictitious Play and Best Response Dynamic*

We begin this section by first considering convergence of fictitious play and best response trajectories for generic perfect information games. In section 8.2.1 the proof of convergence under uniformly monotone selection dynamics closely follows the steps used in chapter 7.5.1 for the

---

17. We rephrase the first assumption to state that there is at most one decision point u of the player who is not the player to first deviate from the subgame perfect equilibrium outcome to reach this decision point. The elementary perfect information games of section 8.1 satisfy both assumptions, whereas example 8.2.7 has three alternatives at u.

18. This also includes the case where Γ has no player decision points off the subgame perfect equilibrium outcome.

Finitely Repeated Prisoner's Dilemma Game. One might expect the convergence issue here to also parallel chapter 7.5.2 (see corollary 7.5.7 and theorem 7.5.10 there). Theorem 8.2.9 confirms our intuition for fictitious play trajectories. Somewhat surprisingly, convergence of best response trajectories remains an open problem—even in the case where there is a unique NE component (see section 8.3). On the other hand, theorem 8.2.10 concerning dynamic stability of the best response trajectories is the analogue to theorem 8.2.8.

Theorem 8.2.9 *Suppose that $(p(t), q(t))$ for $t = 1, 2, \ldots$ is a fictitious play trajectory for a generic perfect information game Γ for which the best reply at each discrete time is taken to be a pure strategy. Then this trajectory converges to the NE set in such a way that the sequence of best replies converges in a finite amount of time to a set of pure strategy pairs that all yield the same outcome.*

Proof The fictitious play trajectory under consideration is of the form

$$
p(m + 1) = \frac{1}{m} \left(p(1) + \sum_{t=2}^{m} e_t \right),
$$

$$
\tag{8.2.1}
$$

$$
q(m + 1) = \frac{1}{m} \left(q(1) + \sum_{t=2}^{m} f_t \right),
$$

where e_t and f_t are pure best replies to $q(t - 1)$ and $p(t - 1)$ respectively. We say a vertex x is *reached infinitely often* by the sequence $\{e_2, f_2, e_3, f_3, \ldots\}$ if, for all $n \in \mathbf{N}$, there exist $i, j \geq n$ such that (e_i, f_j) reaches x. Let Γ' be the extensive form game whose tree consists of those vertices of Γ that are reached infinitely often by $\{e_2, f_2, e_3, f_3, \ldots\}$. We claim that for n sufficiently large, (e_i, f_j) yields the same outcome for all $i, j \geq n$; namely the subgame perfect outcome of Γ'.[19] The proof is by induction on the decision points v_k in Γ' that are ordered as in definition 8.5.1 of appendix A.

There is nothing to prove when $k = 1$ if v_1 is a decision point of nature.[20] Without loss of generality, we may assume that v_1 is a decision point of player one. Suppose that there is no $n_1 \in \mathbf{N}$ such that (e_i, f_j) chooses the subgame perfect alternative at v_1 in Γ' for all $i, j \geq n_1$.

---

19. The proof shows that the tree for Γ' consists precisely of those vertices that are reached by (e_i, f_j) for all $i, j \geq n$.

20. If a final decision point in an extensive form game is a move by nature, it can be replaced by an endpoint with the appropriate truncated payoffs without effecting the dynamic analysis.

We may also assume that (e_i, f_j) does not reach any player decision point in Γ following v_1 for all $i, j \geq n_1$. Then there is a subsequence e_{i_n} and f_{j_n} that reaches v_1 such that e_{i_n} does not choose the subgame perfect alternative at v_1 in Γ'. Let e'_{i_n} be the same pure strategy as e_{i_n} except that it chooses the subgame perfect alternative at v_1. Then $\pi_1(e_{i_n}, f_t) \leq \pi_1(e'_{i_n}, f_t)$ for all $t \geq n_1$ and $\pi_1(e_{i_n}, f_{j_n}) < \pi_1(e'_{i_n}, f_{j_n})$ for all n. Since $\pi_1(e, q(t)) - \pi_1(e, \sum_{i=n_1+1}^{t} f_i/(t - n_1))$ converges to zero for every $e \in S_1$ as t increases; eventually $\pi_1(e_{i_n}, q(i_n - 1)) < \pi_1(e'_{i_n}, q(i_n - 1))$ which contradicts the fact that $e_{i_n} \in BR(q(i_n - 1))$.

Now suppose, for all $i, j \geq n_\ell$, that (e_i, f_j) chooses the subgame perfect alternative with respect to Γ' at all its reachable player decision points among $\{v_1, \ldots, v_\ell\}$ and does not reach any decision points of Γ following these, while at the same time there is no $n_{\ell+1}$ such that (e_i, f_j) chooses the subgame perfect alternative at $v_{\ell+1}$ in Γ' for all $i, j \geq n_{\ell+1}$. The same argument as in the preceding paragraph shows that eventually (e_{t+1}, f_{t+1}) is not a best reply to $(p(t), q(t))$.

If (p^*, q^*) is an ω-limit of the fictitious play trajectory, then (p^*, q^*), (e_t, q^*), (p^*, f_t), and (e_t, f_t) all yield the same outcome for t sufficiently large by the proof so far. If (p^*, q^*) is not a NE, without loss of generality, there is a pure strategy e of player one such that $\pi_1(p^*, q^*) < \pi_1(e, q^*)$, and so (e, q^*) yields a different outcome. Since Γ is generic, e_{t+1} is not a best reply to $q(t)$ for sufficiently large t.   ■

Theorem 8.2.10 *Suppose that Γ is a generic perfect information game in which there is at most one decision point u of the player who is not the player to first deviate from the subgame perfect equilibrium outcome to reach this decision point. Then the subgame perfect NE component, G^*, is asymptotically stable for the fictitious play and best response dynamics.*

Proof   Without loss of generality, suppose that u is a decision point of player one. From the proof of theorem 8.2.8, either G^* is an SESet or the set of best replies to every point in G^* in the reduced-strategy normal form is contained in a face that is spanned by two pure strategies of player one and by those pure strategies of player two that only differ from the subgame perfect equilibrium at u.[21] In this face, the situation is as in figure 8.2.1 with action R deleted for player two and possibly more than three alternatives at his other information set. It is straightforward to show that G^* is asymptotically stable on this face by using the fact the

---

21. In the proof of theorem 8.2.8 there were at most two alternatives at u. Here the number of alternatives at u is immaterial to asymptotic stability.

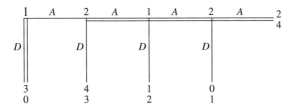

Figure 8.2.2
Perfect information game that shows instability under the best response dynamic.

frequency of the subgame perfect action of player two is always increasing. By upper semicontinuity of the best reply correspondence, G^* is asymptotically stable for the full game Γ. ∎

As mentioned in the preceding proof, in contrast to theorem 8.2.8, there is no restriction on the number of alternatives at the one decision point u of the player who is not the player to first deviate from the subgame perfect equilibrium outcome to reach this decision point. For instance, in example 8.2.7, the subgame perfect NE component is globally interior asymptotically stable under the best response dynamic. The following example is probably the simplest to show the subgame perfect NE component is not interior asymptotically stable for all generic perfect information games. It has two decision points of player two off the subgame perfect equilibrium path that follow a deviation by player one.

Example 8.2.11 (The perfect information game of figure 8.2.2) The reduced-strategy normal form of figure 8.2.2 has subgame perfect NE component $G^* = \{(D, q) \mid 3q_D \leq 2, 4q_D + 2q_{AA} \leq 3\}$ and one other NE component $G = \{(\lambda AD + (1 - \lambda)AA, D) \mid \lambda \geq \frac{1}{2}\}$. The set $\{(p, q) \mid p_{AD} > p_{AA}, q_D > \frac{2}{3}, q_{AD} > q_{AA}\}$ is arbitrarily close to the NE $(D, (\frac{2}{3}, \frac{1}{3}, 0))$ and is forward invariant since, in this set, $BR(q) = e_{AD}$ and $BR(p) = f_D$. Thus there are best response and fictitious play trajectories[22] that start arbitrarily close to G^* that converge to $(AD, D) \in G$. That is, G^* is not asymptotically stable.

Similarly the set $\{(p, q) \mid p_{AA} > p_{AD}, q_{AA} > q_{AD}\}$ is arbitrarily close to G and is forward invariant since, in this set, $BR(q) = \Delta(\{e_D, e_{AA}\})$

---

22. The best replies at all but a finite number of points along the trajectories referred to in this example are unique. This implies that there is only one possible best response trajectory for a given initial point in this set.

and $BR(p) = f_{AA}$. From this it easily follows that there are trajectories that start arbitrarily close to G that converge to $(D, AA) \in G^*$. These can be pieced together with one trajectory in each of the NE components to form a heteroclinic cycle of four best response trajectories.

8.2.3   Behavior Strategy Fictitious Play

The classical fictitious play process (8.2.1) in the preceding section is based on the game's normal form. At each stage the two players update their current belief of the (normal form) strategy combination in use by the other player. In this section we consider two other fictitious play processes where players update their current belief of the behavior strategy combination in use by the other player. The two processes differ in whether or not local behavior strategies are updated at information sets that are not reached by current best replies.

In the first scenario, called *fictitious play under empirical best replies*,[23] beliefs are only updated at information sets that are reached by the current best reply. Thus, if (b_1, b_2) is a best reply to the current beliefs $(b_1(m), b_2(m))$, then the updated beliefs are given by

$$
b_1^u(m+1) = \begin{cases} \dfrac{m}{m+1} b_1^u(m) + \dfrac{1}{m+1} b_1^u & \text{if } (b_1, b_2) \text{ reaches } u, \\[2mm] b_1^u(m) & \text{if } (b_1, b_2) \text{ does not reach } u, \end{cases}
$$

$$ \text{(8.2.2)} $$

$$
b_2^v(m+1) = \begin{cases} \dfrac{m}{m+1} b_2^v(m) + \dfrac{1}{m+1} b_2^v & \text{if } (b_1, b_2) \text{ reaches } v, \\[2mm] b_2^v(m) & \text{if } (b_1, b_2) \text{ does not reach } v, \end{cases}
$$

at information sets u and v for players one and two respectively.

Theorem 8.2.12   *Suppose that $(b_1(m), b_2(m))$ for $m = 1, 2, \ldots$ is a fictitious play trajectory under empirical best replies for a generic perfect information game Γ. The trajectory converges to the NE set in such a way that the sequence of best replies converges in a finite amount of time to a set of strategy pairs that all yield the same NE outcome. Each pure strategy NE is stable.*

---

23. One justification for this process is the assumption that players use empirical frequencies of local behavior strategies used in past plays of best reply pairs to form current beliefs. If the current best reply does not reach a particular information set, then these empirical frequencies do not change there.

Proof Let Γ' be the game with tree generated by the sequence of empirical best replies (i.e., decision points in Γ' are reached infinitely often by the sequence of outcomes of these best reply pairs). If Γ' has more than one pure strategy outcome, then, without loss of generality, there is an information set u of player one that has at least two alternatives in Γ', but all player decision points v in Γ' following u have only one alternative. By (8.2.2), $b_1^v(m)$ converges to this unique alternative for all such v. Since Γ' is generic, only one choice at u leads to the highest payoff in Γ', and so, for all m sufficiently large, the best reply at u must choose this action. That is, after a finite amount of time, all best reply strategy pairs yield the same NE outcome. The proof that all ω-limit points of the trajectory are NE follows a standard argument such as in the proof of theorem 8.2.9.

Suppose that (b_1^*, b_2^*) is a pure strategy NE (written as a pure behavioral strategy pair). Since Γ is generic, b_1^{*u} is the unique best reply to b_2^* at all player one information sets u reached by this NE and so also in a neighborhood of b_2^*. Thus $b_1^u(m+1)$ either equals $b_1^u(m)$ or is closer to b_1^{*u}. In either case, if initial beliefs are sufficiently close to (b_1^*, b_2^*), the sequences of current beliefs (8.2.2) will stay close (and actually converge at all information sets reachable by (b_1^*, b_2^*)). In particular, (b_1^*, b_2^*) is stable. ∎

In the second scenario,[24] called *fictitious play under sequential best replies*, beliefs are updated by best replies to the other player (i.e., behavior strategy combinations corresponding to normal form best replies) that are also conditional best replies at all information sets that are reached by the current beliefs (rather than by the current best replies) of both players. That is, player one updates with best replies that are subgame perfect for the one-player game with tree generated by the current beliefs and payoffs formed by replacing player two with moves by nature whose probability assignment ρ is specified by player one's current beliefs. Since current beliefs for interior fictitious play trajectories reach every information set in Γ, if b_1^u is the local behavior strategy for this subgame

---

24. A third scenario is also possible. In *fictitious play under local best replies*, beliefs are updated by a local best reply (b_1, b_2) to the current beliefs $(b_1(m), b_2(m))$ where b_1^u is a local best reply at information set u for player one to the current beliefs at all other information sets (including his own) and similarly for player two. Theorem 8.2.13 remains valid in this scenario. For (N-player) extensive form games that have at most one decision point for each player along every path, the fictitious play trajectories under sequential and local best replies are identical. However, if one player has two decision points on the same path, local best replies are best replies to the agent normal form of Γ and need not be best replies to the game's normal form.

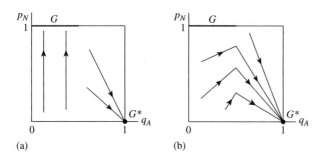

Figure 8.2.3
Trajectories for the Chain-Store Game under (a) empirical fictitious play and (b) sequential fictitious play.

perfect best reply, then the updated beliefs are given by

$$
\begin{aligned}
b_1^u(m+1) &= \frac{m}{m+1} b_1^u(m) + \frac{1}{m+1} b_1^u, \\
b_2^v(m+1) &= \frac{m}{m+1} b_2^v(m) + \frac{1}{m+1} b_2^v,
\end{aligned}
\tag{8.2.3}
$$

at all information sets u and v for players one and two respectively for a perfect information game.

The Chain-Store Game already shows the difference between empirical and sequential best replies. In figure 8.2.3b sequential and normal form fictitious play trajectories are identical (cf. figure 3.3.6 in chapter 3.3.2). However, empirical fictitious play trajectories (figure 8.2.3a) converge to the other NE component whenever $q_A < \frac{1}{2}$ since best replies never reach the decision point of player two in these circumstances.

Theorem 8.2.13   *Suppose that $(b_1(m), b_2(m))$ for $m = 1, 2, \dots$ is an interior fictitious play trajectory under sequential best reply for a generic perfect information game Γ. The trajectory converges to the subgame perfect NE in such a way that the sequence of best responses converges in a finite amount of time to the subgame perfect NE.*

Proof   Let (b_1^*, b_2^*) be the subgame perfect NE written as a pure behavioral strategy pair. By (8.2.3), at every terminal decision point of player one, $b_1^u(m) \to b_1^{*u}$ since b_1^{*u} is the local best reply for all m. Thus, for all m sufficiently large, b_i^* is the unique local best reply at all player i decision points v that are immediately preceding a terminal decision point and so $b_i^v(m) \to b_i^{v*}$. The remainder of the proof is a straightforward continuation of this backward induction argument.   ∎

Remark 8.2.14 As mentioned in chapter 2, there are typically many fictitious play and best response trajectories for the same initial conditions, especially for extensive form games where pure strategy best replies may have many unreached information sets. One possibility is to choose a sequential best reply as described above. With this choice, one might expect interior fictitious play trajectories (8.2.1) of section 8.2.2, which are based on the game's normal form, to all converge to the subgame perfect equilibrium as in theorem 8.2.13. However, example 8.2.11 in section 8.2.2 shows this is not the case since the two complete trajectories described that join the two NE components in either direction are actually sequential best reply trajectories.

8.3   The Centipede Game

A Centipede Game of length N (cf. figure 8.3.1) is a two-player perfect information game with N decision points, each of which consists of two alternatives, Across or Down. Decisions alternate between player one and two (in particular, there are no moves by nature) until someone plays D, say at the ith decision point, when the game ends with payoffs a_i and b_i to player one and two respectively. If A is chosen at all N decision points, the respective payoffs are a_{N+1} and b_{N+1}. We assume $a_1 > a_2, b_2 > b_3, a_3 > a_4, \ldots$ and either $b_N > b_{N+1}$ if N is even or $a_N > a_{N+1}$ if N is odd.

These conditions on the payoffs imply that the subgame perfect NE has both players choosing D at all their decision points and that this is the only equilibrium outcome. For instance, if player one at a NE (p^*, q^*) chooses A at the initial decision point with positive probability, then this NE must induce a NE in the subgame Γ_u where u is the second decision point. By induction, this NE must induce player two to always choose

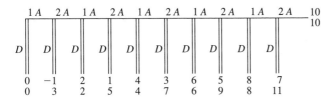

Figure 8.3.1
Centipede Game of Length Ten.

D at u. That is, since $a_1 > a_2$,

$$\pi_1(p^*, q^*) = \pi_1(p^*, D)$$
$$< \pi_1(D, D)$$
$$= \pi_1(D, q^*),$$

and so (p^*, q^*) is not a NE. Thus the NE component, G^*, consists of all strategy pairs (D, q) where $a_1 \geq \pi_1(p, q)$ for all $p \in \Delta^{\lfloor (N+1)/2 \rfloor}$.[25]

Centipede Games provide a large class of perfect information games with long chains of decision points that are often used in the literature to test theories that predict behavior when equilibrium outcome(s) have many unreached decision points. Sections 8.3.1 and 8.3.2 consider this question from the dynamic perspective. It turns out that the assumption of generic payoffs is no longer needed. For instance, every interior trajectory of the replicator dynamic converges to a NE point for any Centipede Game of length N (see example 9.2.7 in chapter 9). Of course, if the game is generic, this also follows from theorem 8.2.2.

The analysis of this section is unaffected by adding the further conditions

$$a_{k+2} > a_k,$$

$$b_{k+2} > b_k,$$

satisfied by a typical Centipede Game such as in Figure 8.3.1. Then, at each decision point $i < N-1$, both players would prefer the game go at least two more moves. The only pure strategy NE is (D, D). These games are then similar to the Finitely Repeated Prisoner's Dilemma Games that have a single NE component whose outcome does not yield the most preferred payoff for either player.

8.3.1   Centipede Games of Lengths Two and Three

Stability results for the replicator dynamic follow directly from the theory developed in section 8.2 applied to these games. In particular, when $N \leq 3$, G^* is globally interior asymptotically stable for any uniformly monotone selection dynamic by theorems 8.2.2 and 8.2.8.

All fictitious play and best response trajectories when $N = 2$, except those that start in G^*, converge to (D, D). Although interior convergence

---

25. $\lfloor \cdot \rfloor$ is the *greatest integer function*. Thus $\lfloor (N+1)/2 \rfloor$ is $N/2$ if N is even and $(N+1)/2$ if N is odd.

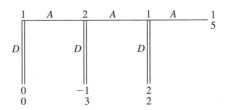

Figure 8.3.2
Centipede Game of Length Three.

to (D, D) is no longer guaranteed for $N = 3$, we have the following analogue of theorems 7.5.5 and 7.5.8 in chapter 7.5.2:

Theorem 8.3.1 *The NE set G^* for a Centipede Game of length at most three is the maximal attractor of the best response dynamic. That is, all best response trajectories and fictitious play trajectories converge to G^* which is globally asymptotically stable.[26] Almost all best response trajectories converge to (D, D). Specifically, all interior best response trajectories when $N = 2$ and also for $N = 3$, except those initially in a two-dimensional rectangle of measure zero intersecting $\Delta^3 \times \Delta^2$, evolve to (D, D).*

Proof The proof for the Centipede Game of Length Three is based on Figure 8.3.2[27] whose reduced-strategy normal form payoff matrix is

$$
\begin{array}{c c}
 & \begin{array}{c c} D & \quad A \end{array} \\
\begin{array}{c} D \\ AD \\ AA \end{array} &
\left[\begin{array}{c c} 0,0 & 0,0 \\ -1,3 & 2,2 \\ -1,3 & 1,5 \end{array} \right] .
\end{array}
\tag{8.3.1}
$$

The proof for general Centipede Games of Length Three is a straightforward generalization. Since

$$
BR(q) = \begin{cases} e_D & \text{if } q_D > \frac{2}{3}, \\ e_{AD} & \text{if } q_D < \frac{2}{3}, \end{cases}
$$

e_{AA} is never a best reply, and so $p_{AA}(t) = 0$ for any complete best response trajectory $(p(t), q(t))$.[28] Thus the maximal attractor for any

---

26. Asymptotic stability of G^* also follows from theorem 8.2.10.
27. This game is simply the truncation of figure 8.3.1 at length three with respect to alternative D for player two at his second decision point.
28. If $p_{AA}(t_0) > 0$, then $p_{AA}(t) > 1$ for some $t \leq t_0$ since $\dot{p}_{AA} = -p_{AA}$ for all $t \in \mathbf{R}$.

Centipede Game of Length Three is contained in the face $\Delta(\{D, AD\}) \times \Delta(\{D, A\})$ where we have the Centipede Game of Length Two. Thus the maximal attractor is G^*. The statements when $N = 2$ follow from the discussion above.

From (8.3.1),

$$BR(q) = \begin{cases} e_D & \text{if } q_D > \frac{2}{3}, \\ e_{AD} & \text{if } q_D < \frac{2}{3}, \end{cases}$$

and

$$BR(p) = \begin{cases} f_D & \text{if } p_{AD} > 2p_{AA}, \\ f_A & \text{if } p_{AD} < 2p_{AA}. \end{cases}$$

Any line segment from a point in the rectangle $\{(p, q) \mid q_D > \frac{2}{3}, p_{AD} = 2p_{AA}\}$ to a point in $G^* = \{(D, q) \mid q_D \geq \frac{2}{3}\}$ is a best response trajectory and so interior trajectories need not converge to (D, D).[29] On the other hand, any initial point (p, q) that is not in the closure of this rectangle does converge to (D, D).   ■

Remark 8.3.2   In Figure 8.3.2 replace the final decision point of player one by a decision point of a third player, and suppose that the payoff c_i to player three equals the payoff a_i to player one at each endpoint.[30] Again, there is a unique NE component G^*, and it contains the subgame perfect NE where all three players choose D. Moreover $(D, \frac{1}{2}D + \frac{1}{2}A, A)$ is a boundary NE in G^*, and on the face $\Delta\{D, A\} \times \Delta\{D, A\} \times \Delta\{A\}$ we have the Chain-Store Game between players one and two. Thus, on this face, there are trajectories of any uniformly monotone selection dynamic that start near G^* but evolve to (A, A, A). That is, G^* is not interior asymptotically stable.

8.3.2   Centipede Games of Length $N \geq 4$

As mentioned previously, convergence of all interior best response trajectories to the NE set is an open problem for generic perfect information

---

29. We do not need to take line segments here. For any closed interval contained in G^*, there is a best response trajectory with initial point in this rectangle that has this interval as its set of limit points.

30. The normal form of this altered game is the agent normal form of figure 8.3.2. The discussion here shows there can be qualitative differences between the dynamic stability of normal form and agent normal form games. It should also be noted that, as a three-player game, this example no longer satisfies the conditions of theorem 8.2.8.

games. Actually this result has not even been shown for all Centipede Games of arbitrary length (see Notes). In this section we will show that G^* is neither interior asymptotically stable for the replicator dynamic nor the maximal attractor for the best response dynamic when $N = 4$, the shortest Centipede Game that does not satisfy the conditions of theorems 8.2.8 or 8.2.10. Standard arguments then extend these same conclusions to Centipede Games of Length $N > 4$.

Suppose that figure 8.3.1 is truncated at the third decision point of player one by taking alternative D there. The resultant game is given in figure 8.3.3.

In the reduced-strategy normal form, $G^* = \{(D, q) \in \Delta^3 \times \Delta^3 \mid \max(2q_{AD} + 2q_{AA}, q_{AD} + 4q_{AA}) \le q_D\}$. In particular, $(D, (\frac{4}{5}, 0, \frac{1}{5}))$ is a point in G^*. On the face $\Delta(\{D, AA\}) \times \Delta(\{D, AA\})$, we have qualitatively the Chain-Store Game of example 8.1.3 where there exist trajectories starting close to this NE that evolve to (AA, AA). By techniques that are now familiar (e.g., example 8.2.7 and the proof of theorem 8.2.6), G^* is neither stable nor interior asymptotically stable under any uniformly monotone selection dynamic.

Furthermore $(p(t), q(t)) = ((1 - t, 0, t), (\frac{4}{5}(1 - t), t, \frac{1}{5}(1 - t))$ is the direction of a best response trajectory for $0 \le t \le \frac{1}{6}$, since $e_{AA} = BR(q(t))$ and $f_{AD} = BR(p(t))$ for all $0 < t < \frac{1}{6}$. This trajectory, initially at the NE point $(D, (\frac{4}{5}, 0, \frac{1}{5}))$, leads away from G^*. Thus G^* is not the maximal attractor and, in particular, is not (interior) asymptotically stable for the fictitious play or best response dynamics.

The intuition behind the stability differences between Centipede Games of lengths three and four is interesting. In the Centipede Game of Length Three, starting at the subgame perfect equilibrium, perturbations in the strategy of player two that move this population toward A can enter unpunished (i.e., without changing the best reply for player one and hence not changing the outcome). Once sufficiently many of the players in population two play A, the best response of player one is

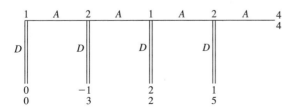

Figure 8.3.3
Centipede Game of Length Four.

to play AD. However, this gives an incentive to player two to go back to playing D. Thus the proportion of population two who play A is held bounded. This is different in the Centipede Game of Length Four. Initially the strategy AA of player two can enter unpunished. Once sufficiently many are in, the best response for player one is to play AA which gives more incentive for player two to play A at his initial decision point. Thus the entry of AA in population one cannot be prevented in the short run and the NE component fails to be stable.

8.4   Extensive Form Bandits
Coauthor: Karl H. Schlag[31]

An *extensive form bandit* is a one-player perfect information game. That is, in his game against nature, the player knows at each of his decision points all of the previous moves by nature. Multi-armed bandits in chapter 2.10 and parallel bandits in chapter 4.6.2 are then the special extensive form bandits that either have no moves by nature or whose only move by nature is the initial move, respectively. As in chapter 4.6.2, realized payoffs at each endpoint $z \in Z$ are drawn at random from a discrete probability distribution P^z with support contained in $[\alpha, \omega]$ and expected value π_z. Let S be the set of pure strategies for this extensive form bandit (i.e., $e \in S$ specifies a choice e_k at each player decision point k).[32] Recall, from chapter 4.6.2, that $\gamma(z, e)$ is the probability endpoint $z \in Z$ is reached if strategy e is used and $\pi_e = \sum_{z \in Z} \gamma(z, e)\pi_z$ is the expected payoff of strategy e. For a given one-player perfect information game with extensive form Γ, the set of all such extensive form bandits is denoted by $EB(\Gamma, [\alpha, \omega])$.

A major difference between extensive form bandits that involve sequential decisions and the special cases considered in chapters 2.10 and 4.6.2 is that now the player's action at one decision affects whether or not subsequent player decisions are reached in the extensive form. *Play in a given round is still a single path in Γ to an endpoint z and so can be identified with z. However, the play z now consists of all player decisions k and actions e_k chosen on the path to z. We say that endpoint*

---

31. This section and chapter 4.6.2 on parallel bandits were written jointly by myself and Karl H. Schlag, Economics Department, European University Institute, 50016 San Domenico di Fiesole, Italy.

32. For notational convenience, we reserve the letter k for a player decision point, and so, for example, e_k is the action specified by pure strategy e at k. The notation e_i stands for the ith pure strategy in S, and so e_{i_k} is the action specified by e_i at k.

z is *reachable* by strategy e if $\gamma(z, e) > 0$ and that decision k is *reachable* if some endpoint z following k is reachable; otherwise, z (and k) is *unreachable*. Furthermore we say that two strategies e and e' *yield the same play* if $\gamma(\cdot, e) \equiv \gamma(\cdot, e')$; otherwise, they *yield different play*. In chapters 2.10 and 4.6.2 all endpoints are reachable, and so two strategies that yield the same play are identical. However, in general (see section 8.4.1 for an explicit example), two strategies that yield the same play may differ at decisions that are unreachable by them.[33]

Thus, in our search for characteristics of good behavioral rules similar to those in theorem 4.6.3 for parallel bandits, we no longer expect a unique best strategy. Instead, in this general setting, we restrict attention primarily to extensive form bandits B with a *unique optimal outcome* (i.e., the set of best strategies all yield the same play). We call F a *good behavioral rule (for an extensive form bandit B)* if the set of best strategies is the only asymptotically stable set of strategies that yield the same play. Also the concept of playwise imitation must be handled more carefully when there are sequential decisions. In the remainder of the section, we develop this concept, derive characteristics (some of which are necessary and some of which are sufficient) summarized in theorem 8.4.1 below of good behavioral rules that are playwise imitative, and provide a general class of such rules regardless of the specific extensive form bandit.

Recall, from chapter 4.6.2, that a behavioral rule $F = F(e, z, x, w, y)_{e'}$ is a map that specifies the probability of choosing strategy e' in the next round if one's own last strategy is e with experienced play z and payoff x and the sampled play is w with payoff y. Imitation of sampled action(s) can be divided into two types, namely those that yield different play and those that yield the same play. The former results in a *change of play* and the latter in a *change of memory*. It is natural to restrict changes in play to those that make the sampled endpoint reachable under the revised strategy and so we call a behavioral rule F *playwise imitative* if

1. any change of play occurs through adopting all sampled actions, and

2. change of memory occurs when no sampled actions are adopted at decision points reachable by own current strategy but some or all sampled actions are adopted at decisions that are currently unreachable.

---

33. This is related to the difference between the standard and reduced normal forms of an extensive form game (see chapter 6.2). A natural question at this point is why the reduced-strategy normal form is not used here. The problems with this approach are illustrated by our analysis of the Centipede Bandit in section 8.4.1 (see theorem 8.4.3).

Formally, if $e \neq e'$, then $F(e, z, x, w, y)_{e'} > 0$ implies that either there is a change in play (see point 1 above) in which case $e' = e \backslash w$ yields a different play than e^{34} or there is a change in memory (see point 2 above) in which case $e'_k = e_k$ whenever decision k is reachable by e (i.e., e and e' yield the same play) and $e'_k = (e \backslash w)_k$ whenever $e'_k \neq e_k$.

Let $Fp(e, w)$ be the probability of changing play from e after sampling w and $Fm(e, w)$ be the probability of changing memory in these circumstances. Then $F(e, w) = Fp(e, w) + Fm(e, w)$ is the probability of changing strategy after sampling w. Furthermore let $Fp(e, e') = \sum_{w \in Z} \gamma(w, e') Fp(e, w)$ be the probability of changing play from e if the sampled individual is using strategy e' and $Fp(e, e', e'')$ of changing play to e'' in these circumstances. Similarly the notation $Fm(e, e')$, $F(e, e')$, and so on, denote the obvious probabilities. As in (4.6.1), for any behavioral rule,

$$p'_e = p_e + \sum_{e', e'' \in S} p_{e'} p_{e''} F(e', e'', e) - \sum_{e' \in S} p_e p_{e'} F(e, e'). \tag{8.4.1}$$

It turns out that the initial analysis of good behavioral rules is independent of changing memory (see theorem 8.4.1 below), and so Fm receives little attention in this section. However, Fm does affect convergence properties for interior trajectories in section 8.4.1 (see the discussion following theorem 8.4.6).

Suppose that under a playwise imitative rule F, Δ_0 is an asymptotically stable set of strategies, all of which yield the same play, and that e is a pure strategy in Δ_0. To obtain conditions for asymptotic stability similar to those given in theorem 4.6.3 for parallel bandits, consider deviations from e at exactly one player decision k. Given a strategy e, let $e \backslash a^k$ be the same strategy except that it specifies an action a different from e_k at decision k. Since F is playwise imitative, $Fm(e \backslash a^k, e) = 0 = Fm(e, e \backslash a^k)$. Thus $F(e \backslash a^k, e) = Fp(e \backslash a^k, e) = Fp(e \backslash a^k, e, e)$ and $F(e, e \backslash a^k) = Fp(e, e \backslash a^k) = Fp(e, e \backslash a^k, e \backslash a^k)$ (in particular, these expressions are all 0 if decision k is unreachable by e). Thus $\Delta(\{e, e \backslash a^k\})$ is invariant under F, and there can be no change of memory when the initial state $p \in \Delta(\{e, e \backslash a^k\})$. From (8.4.1),

$$p'_e = p_e + p_e p_{e \backslash a^k} (F(e \backslash a^k, e) - F(e, e \backslash a^k))$$

on this invariant set. In particular, by asymptotic stability of

---

34. Recall from chapter 4.6.2 that $e \backslash w$ is the same strategy as e except that at any decision point on the path to w, it prescribes the action leading to w.

Δ_0, $Fp(e\backslash a^k, e) > Fp(e, e\backslash a^k)$ must hold whenever $e \in \Delta_0$ and $e\backslash a^k \notin \Delta_0$. This proves part i of the following theorem:

Theorem 8.4.1 *Suppose that F is a playwise imitative rule for an extensive form bandit B with a unique optimal outcome.*

i. If the set of best strategies of B is asymptotically stable under F, then $Fp(e^*\backslash a^k, e^*) > Fp(e^*, e^*\backslash a^k)$ whenever $e^* \in \arg\max\{\pi_e\}$ and $\pi_{e^*} > \pi_{e^*\backslash a^k}$.

ii. If $e^* \in \arg\max\{\pi_e\}$ and

$$Fp(e, e^*) > Fp(e^*, e) \quad \text{for all } e \text{ that yield different play than } e^*, \quad (8.4.2)$$

then e^* is Lyapunov stable under F. If (8.4.2) holds for any $e^* \in \arg\max\{\pi_e\}$, then the set of best strategies $\Delta\{\arg\max\{\pi_e\}\}$ of B is asymptotically stable under F.

iii. If F satisfies

$$Fp(e\backslash a^k, e) > Fp(e, e\backslash a^k) \quad \text{whenever } \pi_e > \pi_{e\backslash a^k}, \quad (8.4.3)$$

then $\Delta\{\arg\max\{\pi_e\}\}$ is the only possible asymptotically stable set of strategies that all yield the same play. Thus F is a good behavioral rule for B if F satisfies (8.4.2) and (8.4.3).

Proof (ii) Suppose that $e^* \in \arg\max\{\pi_e\}$ and that F is playwise imitative. We will show that e^* is Lyapunov stable by linearizing the dynamic (8.4.1) about $p_{e^*} = 1$. Since, for any other strategy e, only those interaction terms in this dynamic that involve e^* are relevant, the linearization has entry in row e and column e' given by

$$\begin{cases} 1 + F(e^*, e, e) - F(e, e^*) & \text{if } e = e', \\ F(e^*, e', e) + F(e', e^*, e) & \text{if } e \neq e', \end{cases}$$

where $F(e^*, e', e)$ is the probability of changing to strategy e if own strategy is e^* and sampled individual is using strategy e', and so on.

Partition the pure strategies in S into sets S_i as follows, and then order the strategies with e after e' if $e' \in S_i$ and $e \in \bigcup_{j>i} S_j$. Let S_i be the set of all pure strategies that differ from e^* at exactly i decision points reachable by e^*. For instance, S_0 is the set of all strategies that yield the same play as e^*. Since F is playwise imitative, $F(e^*, e) = F(e, e^*) = 0$ for all $e \in S_0$. Similarly, if $e \in S_j$ and $e' \in S_i$ with $j > i$, then $F(e^*, e', e) = F(e', e^*, e) = 0$. Thus, with this ordering of strategies, the linearization is upper block diagonal (i.e., the interactions between strategies in each S_i form a block, L_i, on the main diagonal and below this block all entries are 0). In particular, the block L_0 is the identity matrix.

Thus an application of center manifold theory for discrete dynamical systems shows e^* is Lyapunov stable (and is asymptotically stable if it is the unique best strategy) if all the eigenvalues of each of the blocks L_i with $i \geq 1$ have modulus less than 1. The reason for this is that the center manifold at such an e^* is then S_0, and each point on this manifold is a rest point of the dynamic since F is playwise imitative.

Let $i \geq 1$, and suppose that $e, e' \in S_i$. Since e and e' agree with e^* at the same number of e^*-reachable decision points and F is playwise imitating, all changes under consideration that result in a strategy in S_i must be a change in play. Thus $F(e', e^*, e) = 0$ and $F(e^*, e', e) = Fp(e^*, e', e)$, and the entry in row e and column e' of the block L_i is actually

$$\begin{cases} 1 + Fp(e^*, e, e) - F(e, e^*) & \text{if } e = e', \\ Fp(e^*, e', e) & \text{if } e \neq e'. \end{cases}$$

Then Gerschgorin's (column sum) theorem[35] guarantees that all eigenvalues of L_i have modulus less than 1. To see this, recall that every eigenvalue of an $n \times n$ matrix with entries a_{ij} lies in

$$\bigcup_j \left\{ \lambda : |\lambda - a_{jj}| \leq \sum_{i:i \neq j} |a_{ij}| \right\}.$$

In particular, $|\lambda| \leq \max_j \sum_i \{|a_{ij}| : 1 \leq i \leq n\}$. For L_i, since all entries are nonnegative, the sum for the column corresponding to e' is $1 + \sum_{e \in S_i} Fp(e^*, e', e) - F(e', e^*)$, and this satisfies

$$1 + \sum_{e \in S_i} Fp(e^*, e', e) - F(e', e^*) \leq 1 + Fp(e^*, e') - Fp(e', e^*).$$

By (8.4.2), $0 \leq 1 + Fp(e^*, e') - Fp(e', e^*) < 1$, and so e^* is Lyapunov stable.

To prove that the set of optimal (mixed) strategies $\Delta\{\arg\max\{\pi_e\}\}$ is asymptotically stable for any extensive form bandit with a unique optimal outcome under an F that satisfies (8.4.2) for all optimal pure strategies e^*, we will first show that each $p^* \in \Delta\{\arg\max\{\pi_e\}\}$ is Lyapunov stable. Suppose that p^* is the convex combination $\sum_\ell \alpha_\ell e_\ell$. Then $e_\ell \in \arg\max\{\pi_e\}$ whenever $\alpha_\ell > 0$, and each such e_ℓ agrees with p^* at all

---

35. The Perron-Frobenius theorem for nonnegative matrices is also applicable here to conclude $|\lambda| \leq \max_j \sum_i \{|a_{ij}| : 1 \leq i \leq n\}$. See Notes for references to these two theorems in matrix algebra as well as to center manifold theory as it applies to discrete dynamical systems.

e_ℓ reachable decision points. Thus the linearization about p^* using the same ordering of pure strategies as above remains upper block diagonal with L_0 the identity matrix. For $i \geq 1$, the entry in row e and column e' of the block L_i becomes

$$\begin{cases} 1 + \sum_\ell \alpha_\ell (Fp(e_\ell, e, e) - F(e, e_\ell)) & \text{if } e = e', \\ \sum_\ell \alpha_\ell Fp(e_\ell, e', e) & \text{if } e \neq e'. \end{cases}$$

Lyapunov stability of p^* again follows from Gerschgorin's theorem.

Furthermore, since the center manifold at each $p^* \in \Delta\{\arg\max\{\pi_e\}\}$ is $\Delta\{\arg\max\{\pi_e\}\}$, each trajectory of the dynamic that starts sufficiently close to $\Delta\{\arg\max\{\pi_e\}\}$ converges to this set. Asymptotic stability of $\Delta\{\arg\max\{\pi_e\}\}$ now follows from its compactness.

(iii) Suppose that Δ_0 is an asymptotically stable set of strategies that all yield the same play. Each point in Δ_0 is a rest point of the dynamic since F is playwise imitative. Thus Δ_0 must contain $\{e_i \in S \mid p_i > 0$ for some $p \in \Delta_0\}$. In particular, if there is a suboptimal mixed strategy in Δ_0, then there is a suboptimal pure strategy $e \in \Delta_0$ as well, and so there is some decision k with action a^k such that $\pi_e < \pi_{e \backslash a^k}$. Since $\Delta\{e, e \backslash a^k\}$ is invariant under F and all changes in strategy result from a change in play for any state in $\Delta\{e, e \backslash a^k\}$, there are initial points p arbitrarily close to e that converge to $e \backslash a^k$ by (8.4.3). Since e and $e \backslash a^k$ do not yield the same play, $e \backslash a^k \notin \Delta_0$. That is, Δ_0 is not asymptotically stable. ∎

By theorem 8.4.1, F is a good behavioral rule if it is playwise imitative and satisfies

$$Fp(e', e) > Fp(e, e') \qquad \text{whenever } \pi_e > \pi_{e'}. \tag{8.4.4}$$

Inequality (8.4.4) is the analogue of (4.6.2) in chapter 4.6.2 on parallel bandits.[36] We now use (8.4.4) in a similar fashion to verify several intuitive playwise imitative rules (without change of memory) are good behavioral rules.

Consider the playwise imitative rule that adopts all sampled actions with probability proportional to the sampled payoff, and does not switch otherwise (i.e., there is no change of memory). When applied to the parallel bandits of chapter 4.6.2, this is the rule F^{POR} and so we will continue to denote it as F^{POR} (with no memory switch). We will now

---

36. Notice that (8.4.4) requires these switching rates be checked for all e and e' that yield different play whereas the corresponding inequality (4.6.2) in theorem 4.6.3 for parallel bandits only required comparisons when e and e' differ at exactly one decision. The reason for this is that for parallel bandits the relevant eigenvalues automatically have moduli less than 1 whenever e and e' differ at more than one decision.

show that this intuitive rule satisfies (8.4.4). Let $F^{POR}(e, z, x, w, y)$ denote the probability of changing strategy by pasting all choices on the path to w onto strategy e if own strategy is e with play z and payoff x and sampled play is w with payoff y. By definition, if $e \neq e \backslash w$,

$$
F^{POR}(e, z, x, w, y) = \begin{cases} \dfrac{y - \alpha}{\omega - \alpha} & \text{if } \gamma(w, e) = 0, \\ 0 & \text{if } \gamma(w, e) \neq 0. \end{cases}
$$

Thus, if $e \neq e'$,

$$
\begin{aligned}
F^{POR}(e, e') &= \sum_z \gamma(z, e) \sum_x P^z(x) \sum_w \gamma(w, e') \sum_y P^w(y) F^{POR}(e, z, x, w, y) \\
&= \sum_{\{w : \gamma(w,e)=0\}} \gamma(w, e') \sum_y P^w(y) \frac{y - \alpha}{\omega - \alpha} \\
&= \sum_{\{z : \gamma(z,e)=0\}} \gamma(z, e') \frac{\pi_z - \alpha}{\omega - \alpha}.
\end{aligned}
$$

Thus, since $\gamma(z, e) = \gamma(z, e')$ if both are nonzero,

$$
\begin{aligned}
F^{POR} p(e, e') &- F^{POR} p(e', e) \\
&= \sum_{\{z : \gamma(z,e)=0\}} \gamma(z, e') \frac{\pi_z - \alpha}{\omega - \alpha} - \sum_{\{z : \gamma(z,e')=0\}} \gamma(z, e) \frac{\pi_z - \alpha}{\omega - \alpha} \\
&= \sum_z \gamma(z, e') \frac{\pi_z - \alpha}{\omega - \alpha} - \sum_z \gamma(z, e) \frac{\pi_z - \alpha}{\omega - \alpha} \\
&= \frac{\pi_{e'} - \pi_e}{\omega - \alpha}.
\end{aligned}
$$

(8.4.5)

Summarizing, we obtain that F^{POR} is a good behavioral rule in any extensive form bandit that contains a unique optimal outcome as it satisfies condition (8.4.4).

The F^{POR} rule can be generalized to find other good playwise imitative rules (without change of memory). For the parallel bandits of chapter 4.6.2, the $F^{f/POR}$ rules that used an $f(x, y)$ satisfying (4.6.5) for within-decision learning and POR for cross-decision learning satisfy (8.4.4). For general extensive form bandits, within-decision learning occurs when sampled play differs from own play for the first time at a player decision point. Likewise cross-decision learning occurs when sampled play differs from own play for the first time at a move of nature. Thus $F^{f/POR}$ for an extensive form bandit is defined as 0 if $\gamma(w, e) \neq 0$

and otherwise

$$F^{f/POR}(e, z, x, w, y) = \begin{cases} \dfrac{y - \alpha}{\omega - \alpha} & \text{if } n(z, w) = 1, \\ f(x, y) & \text{if } n(z, w) = 0, \end{cases} \quad (8.4.6)$$

where $n(z, w)$ is the indicator function that equals 1 if the first decision point at which z and w differ is a move of nature, and equals 0 if this first such decision point is a player decision point.[37] In the following we will verify that $F^{f/POR}$ satisfies (8.4.4).

First note that when $n(z, w) = 0$, $\gamma(w, e)\gamma(z, e) = 0$ if $z \neq w$. Thus the contribution to $F^{f/POR}(e, e')$ from within-decision learning is

$$\sum_{\{z, w | n(z,w)=0, \gamma(w,e)=0\}} \gamma(w, e')\gamma(z, e) \sum_x P^z(x) \sum_y P^w(y) f(x, y)$$

$$= \sum_{\{z, w | n(z,w)=0\}} \gamma(w, e')\gamma(z, e) \sum_x P^z(x) \sum_y P^w(y) f(x, y).$$

The contribution to $F^{f/POR}(e, e') - F^{f/POR}(e', e)$ from within-decision learning is then given by

$$\sum_{\{z, w | n(z,w)=0\}} \gamma(w, e')\gamma(z, e) \sum_x P^z(x) \sum_y P^w(y)(f(x, y) - f(y, x))$$

$$= \sum_{\{z, w | n(z,w)=0\}} \gamma(w, e')\gamma(z, e) \sum_x P^z(x) \sum_y P^w(y) \frac{y - x}{\omega - \alpha}$$

$$= \sum_{\{z, w | n(z,w)=0\}} \gamma(w, e')\gamma(z, e) \frac{\pi_w - \pi_z}{\omega - \alpha}.$$

On the other hand, a calculation similar to the one above for F^{POR} shows the contribution from cross-decision learning is $\sum_{\{z, w | n(z,w)=1\}} \gamma(w, e') \times \gamma(z, e)(\pi_w - \pi_z)/(\omega - \alpha)$. In total, we have

$$F^{f/POR}(e, e') - F^{f/POR}(e', e) = \sum_z \sum_w \gamma(w, e')\gamma(z, e) \frac{\pi_w - \pi_z}{\omega - \alpha}$$

$$= \frac{\pi_{e'} - \pi_e}{\omega - \alpha}$$

$$= F^{POR}(e, e') - F^{POR}(e', e),$$

which satisfies (8.4.4).

---

37. Notice that the choice of f in (8.4.6) can only depend on the unordered pair $\{z, w\}$. In particular, it is independent of e.

To conclude this section, notice that the sufficient conditions (8.4.2) and (8.4.3) for a good behavioral rule stated in theorem 8.4.1 only refer to the probabilities of changing play. Thus, any sort of change of memory added to $F^{f/POR}$ will not alter the fact that it is a good behavioral rule (for an extensive form bandit with a unique optimal outcome). In chapter 4.6.2 all the $F^{f/POR}$ rules induce the same population dynamic on a given parallel bandit that is automatically subbandit monotone (see (4.6.4)) for all parallel bandits. In particular, the set of best strategies is globally asymptotically stable whether or not the parallel bandit has a unique optimal outcome. On the other hand, as illustrated in the following section, different choices of f and of change of memory have different effects on the population dynamic for general extensive form bandits. These differences have the potential to change the stability properties of their set of best strategies.

8.4.1   The Centipede Bandit

This section considers a specific extensive-form bandit illustrated in figure 8.4.1 that we call a *Centipede Bandit* because its extensive form resembles the (three-legged) Centipede Game of section 8.3.1. It is an elementary example of an extensive form bandit that is neither a multi-armed nor parallel bandit since it involves sequential player decisions separated by a move by nature. Nature moves down with probability q and across otherwise (here q is a fixed but arbitrary parameter satisfying $0 \leq q \leq 1$) after a player choice of A at decision 1. Then $Z = \{D, n, d, a\}$ is the set of endpoints and P^z has support contained in $[\alpha, \omega]$ for each $z \in Z$. For the standard normal form, $\{Dd, Da, Ad, Aa\}$ is the set of pure strategies where, for instance, Dd has the usual meaning (as in standard game theory) that player one will choose D at decision 1 and d if asked to move at decision 2. The expected payoffs of the pure strategies are

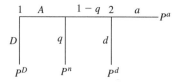

Figure 8.4.1
Extensive form of the Centipede Bandit.

then given by $\pi_{Dd} = \pi_{Da} = \pi_D$, $\pi_{Ad} = q\pi_n + (1-q)\pi_d$ and $\pi_{Aa} = q\pi_n + (1-q)\pi_a$.

The following two theorems demonstrate clearly that sequential player moves complicate the analysis of extensive form bandits. Specifically theorem 8.4.2 shows that unlike multi-armed or parallel bandits, we cannot produce behavioral rules that always select the set of best strategies. In particular, no behavioral rule can induce any of the standard dynamics of evolutionary game theory whether or not the rule is developed through the subgame structure. Theorem 8.4.3 (and its proof) shows the problems behavioral rules encounter when players have no memory of what action to adopt at decision points that are unreachable by current strategy choice.

Theorem 8.4.2 *There is no behavioral rule F for which the set of best strategies is asymptotically stable for all Centipede Bandits.*

Proof By theorem 8.4.1 and the construction of the $F^{f/\text{POR}}$ rules in the previous section, the difficulty in finding such an F must involve Centipede Bandits whose set of best strategies does not yield a unique optimal outcome. Suppose that either $F(Dd, D, x, n, y)_{Aa}$ or $F(Da, D, x, n, y)_{Aa}$ is not zero for some $x, y \in [\alpha, \omega]$.[38] There is some Centipede Bandit for which $P^D(x)P^n(y) > 0$ and for which $\Delta(\{Dd, Da, Ad\})$ is the set of best strategies. Then $\Delta(\{Dd, Da, Ad\})$ is not invariant under F and so is not asymptotically stable. Thus our F must satisfy $F(Dd, D, x, n, y)_{Aa} = F(Da, D, x, n, y)_{Aa} = F(Dd, D, x, n, y)_{Ad} = F(Da, D, x, n, y)_{Ad} = 0$ for all $x, y \in [\alpha, \omega]$. Now take a Centipede Bandit for which $q = 1$ and $\Delta(\{Ad, Aa\})$ is the set of best strategies. Since there is no change in strategy from Dd or Da to either Ad or Aa under F, $p'_D \geq p_D$, where $p_D \equiv p_{Dd} + p_{Da}$, and so $\Delta(\{Ad, Aa\})$ is not asymptotically stable. ∎

Theorem 8.4.3 *There does not exist a good playwise imitative rule for all reduced-strategy normal form Centipede Bandits for which there is a unique optimal outcome.*

Proof First, let us clarify what playwise imitative means here for the reduced-strategy normal form. There is no longer a concept corresponding to "change of memory" for the pure strategy space $\{D, Ad, Aa\}$. The

---

38. The proof can be easily revised to show the theorem remains valid when the reduced normal form (see theorem 8.4.3) with strategy space $\{D, Ad, Aa\}$ is used instead.

change of play conditions given by probabilities $F(e, z, x, w, y)_{e'}$ are all clear except when own current strategy is $e = D$ and sampled play is n. When there is a change in play in this case, the player must choose between $e' = Ad$ and $e' = Aa$ without recourse to his own memory. Intuitive choices are $F(D, n) = 0$ (i.e., don't change play unless the entire strategy is sampled) or, failing this, $F(D, n, Ad) = F(D, n, Aa)$ (i.e., since there seems to be no a priori reason to favor Ad over Aa, decide by "flipping a fair coin"). The remainder of the proof, which is quite technical and so relegated to appendix B, does not make use of either of these heuristic assumptions even though it would be considerably shortened by doing so.   ∎

The result above shows that theorem 8.4.1 does not apply to the reduced-strategy normal form of the Centipede Bandit. Because of this we assume the standard normal form for our Centipede Bandits in the remainder of this section. By theorem 8.4.2 (see also remark 8.4.5 below), even our good behavioral rules F from section 8.4 do not always learn to play the optimal outcome in all Centipede Bandits. We now take a closer look at what, if any, outcome is learned by analyzing the resultant population dynamic. Initially our analysis answers this question for arbitrary playwise imitative rules and a large class of Centipede Bandits (see theorem 8.4.4 below), but eventually we must restrict attention to certain $F^{f/POR}$ rules (see theorem 8.4.6 below).

Let us first consider the change in the frequency of strategy Dd from one round to the next. Since F is playwise imitative, these changes can only occur when strategy Dd interacts with either Ad or Aa or when strategies Ad and Da interact. An examination of these three types of interactions leads to

$$p'_{Dd} - p_{Dd} = p_{Ad}\, p_{Dd}(Fp(Ad, Dd, Dd) - Fp(Dd, Ad, Ad))$$

$$+ p_{Ad}\, p_{Da}(Fp(Ad, Da, Dd) + Fm(Da, Ad, Dd)) \qquad (8.4.7)$$

$$- p_{Aa}\, p_{Dd}(Fp(Dd, Aa, Aa) + Fp(Dd, Aa, Ad)$$

$$+ Fm(Dd, Aa, Da)).$$

Clearly, the population dynamic depends on the memory component of F. It is also readily checked, when (8.4.7) is applied to the $F^{f/POR}$ rules, that the population dynamic changes for different choices of f since each change in play involves within-decision learning (i.e., the indicator function $n(z, w)$ equals 0 in (8.4.6)). Using the analogous expression for $p'_{Da} - p_{Da}$, we find the two terms that involve change in memory disappear in the following expression:

$$p'_D - p_D \equiv p'_{Dd} - p_{Dd} + p'_{Da} - p_{Da}$$

$$= p_{Ad}\, p_{Dd}(Fp(Ad, Dd, Dd) - Fp(Dd, Ad, Ad))$$

$$+ p_{Aa}\, p_{Da}(Fp(Aa, Da, Da) - Fp(Da, Aa, Aa))$$

$$+ p_{Ad}\, p_{Da}(Fp(Ad, Da, Dd) - Fp(Da, Ad, Ad)$$

$$- Fp(Da, Ad, Aa))$$

$$+ p_{Aa}\, p_{Dd}(Fp(Aa, Dd, Da) - Fp(Dd, Aa, Aa)\qquad (8.4.8)$$

$$- Fp(Dd, Aa, Ad))$$

$$= p_{Ad}\, p_{Dd}(Fp(Ad, Dd) - Fp(Dd, Ad))$$

$$+ p_{Aa}\, p_{Da}(Fp(Aa, Da) - Fp(Da, Aa))$$

$$+ p_{Ad}\, p_{Da}(Fp(Ad, Da) - Fp(Da, Ad))$$

$$+ p_{Aa}\, p_{Dd}(Fp(Aa, Dd) - Fp(Dd, Aa)).$$

Suppose that D is either the unique best or the unique worst outcome. Then, for any playwise imitative rule F that satisfies (8.4.4), either all terms on the right-hand side of (8.4.8) are positive or all are negative respectively. That is, p_D is a Lyapunov function for the discrete-time population dynamic induced by such an F.[39] Thus p_D will converge monotonically to either 1 or 0 respectively if $0 < p_D < 1$ initially. Furthermore it is also clear that under such F, the dynamic on $\Delta(\{Ad, Aa\})$ is monotone and every point in $\Delta(\{Dd, Da\})$ is a rest point. Thus we have proved the following result:

Theorem 8.4.4 *Suppose that F is a playwise imitative rule that satisfies (8.4.4). Then, for any Centipede Bandit for which D is either the unique best or the unique worst outcome, all interior strategies converge to a single point in the set of best strategies. The set of best strategies is globally asymptotically stable. In particular, these rules learn to play the optimal outcome in all such Centipede Bandits.*

Remark 8.4.5 The following eigenvalue analysis, similar to that used in the proof of theorem 8.4.3, shows that for every good playwise imitative rule F, there is some Centipede Bandit for which Da is Lyapunov stable

---

39. To be precise, $1 - p_D$ is the Lyapunov function when D is the unique worst outcome.

under F at the same time that Ad is the unique optimal strategy. That is, F does not always learn to play the unique optimal outcome. By theorem 8.4.4, D cannot be the unique best or worst outcome in such examples. To avoid degenerate situations, suppose $\pi_{Ad} > \pi_D > \pi_{Aa}$ (i.e., nature moves down with probability q satisfying $q\pi_n + (1-q)\pi_d > \pi_D > q\pi_n + (1-q)\pi_a$) in our Centipede Bandit. In fact this Centipede Bandit will satisfy $\pi_n > \pi_D > \pi_d > \pi_a$, and the support of P^z is the same for all endpoints z.

From (8.4.1) the linearization about $p_{Da} = 1$ with the pure strategies ordered as Da, Dd, Aa, Ad produces an upper triangular matrix with diagonal entries 1, 1, $1 + Fp(Da, Aa) - Fp(Aa, Da)$, $1 + Fp(Da, Ad, Ad) - Fp(Ad, Da)$. Now $1 + Fp(Da, Aa) - Fp(Aa, Da)$ is less than one since this expression is independent of P^d and must be less than one when D is the unique optimal outcome. The only eigenvalue of interest is thus $1 + Fp(Da, Ad, Ad) - Fp(Ad, Da)$. If $p_{Da} = 1$ is Lyapunov stable for those q with $\pi_D > \pi_{Ad}$ but not for larger q with $\pi_D < \pi_{Ad}$, then $Fp(Da, Ad, Ad) - Fp(Ad, Da) = 0$ when $\pi_D = \pi_{Ad} = q\pi_n + (1-q)\pi_d$— that is, when $q/(1-q) = (\pi_D - \pi_d)/(\pi_n - \pi_D)$. Since

$$Fp(Da, Ad, Ad) - Fp(Ad, Da)$$

$$= (1-q)Fp(Da, d, Ad) - qFp(Ad(n), D, Dd)$$

$$- (1-q)Fp(Ad(d), D, Dd)$$

(where $F(Ad(d), D, Dd)$, for instance, denotes the probability of switching to Dd from Ad if own current action is d), we have

$$(\pi_n - \pi_D)(Fp(Da, d, Ad) - Fp(Ad(d), D, Dd))$$

$$= (\pi_D - \pi_d)Fp(Ad(n), D, Dd).$$

Now $Fp(Ad(n), D, Dd) \neq 0$ by our assumption that all P^z have the same support.[40] Thus $(Fp(Da, d, Ad) - Fp(Ad(d), D, Dd)) > 0$. This contradicts the Lyapunov stability of $p_{Da} = 1$ when $q = 0$.

Theorems 8.4.1 and 8.4.4 show that there are many trajectories of the population dynamic that converge to a single outcome (which may be suboptimal by remark 8.4.5). However, when D is neither the unique

---

40. The argument here is that, otherwise, $p_{Dd} = 1$ is not Lyapunov stable for other Centipede Bandits with $q = 1$ and D the unique optimal outcome. See the proof of theorem 8.4.3 in appendix B for a similar argument applied to the reduced-strategy normal form.

best nor unique worst outcome, it is unknown whether every trajectory induced by a good behavioral rule converges to a single outcome. Theorem 8.4.6 below shows convergence can be guaranteed for many of the $F^{f/POR}$ rules.

For the $F^{f/POR}$ rules, the calculation of $p'_D - p_D$ in (8.4.8) above simplifies considerably. Specifically, each of the four terms on the right-hand side of (8.4.8) involve within-decision learning. Thus, from (8.4.6), under any $F^{f/POR}$ rule each term involves $f(x, y) - f(y, x) = (y - x)/(\omega - \alpha)$, and so

$$
\begin{aligned}
p'_D - p_D &= p_{Ad} p_{Dd} \left(\frac{\pi_D - \pi_{Ad}}{\omega - \alpha} \right) + p_{Aa} p_{Da} \left(\frac{\pi_D - \pi_{Aa}}{\omega - \alpha} \right) \\
&\quad + p_{Ad} p_{Da} \left(\frac{\pi_D - \pi_{Ad}}{\omega - \alpha} \right) + p_{Aa} p_{Dd} \left(\frac{\pi_D - \pi_{Aa}}{\omega - \alpha} \right) \\
&= \frac{p_D(\pi_D - (p_{Dd}\pi_D + p_{Da}\pi_D + p_{Ad}\pi_{Ad} + p_{Aa}\pi_{Aa}))}{\omega - \alpha} \\
&\equiv \frac{p_D(\pi_D - \pi(p))}{\omega - \alpha}.
\end{aligned}
\tag{8.4.9}
$$

This makes it even more clear that whenever D is either the unique best or the unique worst outcome, all interior strategies converge to the set of best strategies. The following result considers other Centipede Bandits as well for a special class of $F^{f/POR}$ rules:

Theorem 8.4.6 *Suppose that F is an $F^{f/POR}$ rule (with or without change of memory) that satisfies*

$$
0 \le (F(Da, d) - F(Dd, a))(\pi_d - \pi_a) \le \frac{(\pi_d - \pi_a)^2}{\omega - \alpha}
\tag{8.4.10}
$$

for all Centipede Bandits.

i. If D is either the best or the worst outcome, then all interior trajectories converge to the set of best strategies.

ii. If $\min\{\pi_{Ad}, \pi_{Aa}\} < \pi_D < \max\{\pi_{Ad}, \pi_{Aa}\}$, then any interior trajectory converges either to $\arg\max\{\pi_e\}$ or to a point in $\{p : p_D = 1, \pi_D \ge p_{Dd}\pi_{Ad} + p_{Da}\pi_{Aa}\}$.

Proof (i) If D is either the unique best or the worst outcome, this is a corollary of theorem 8.4.4. If D is a best outcome, the proof there shows that p_D increases monotonically and any ω-limit point p^*

satisfies $\pi(p^*) = \pi_D = \arg\max\{\pi_e\}$. That is, p converges to the set of best strategies.[41]

(ii) Without loss of generality, assume $\pi_{Aa} < \pi_D < \pi_{Ad}$. The proof relies on the forward invariance of $\{p \mid W(p) \le 0\}$ under F and the following expressions for the population dynamic in terms of W (these facts are all shown in appendix B):[42]

$$W \equiv p_{Dd}\,p_{Aa} - p_{Da}\,p_{Ad} = p_{Dd} - p_D p_d, \tag{8.4.11}$$

$$\pi(p) = p_D\pi_D + p_A(p_d\pi_{Ad} + p_a\pi_{Aa}) - W(\pi_{Ad} - \pi_{Aa}), \tag{8.4.12}$$

$$p'_{Dd} - p_{Dd} = p_{Ad}(p_{Dd} + p_{Da})\left(\frac{\pi_D - \pi_{Ad}}{\omega - \alpha}\right) - q\,WF(Dd, n)$$
$$+ (1 - q)[p_{Ad}\,p_{Da}(Fp(Da, d, Ad) \tag{8.4.13}$$
$$+ Fm(Da, d, Dd) - p_{Aa}\,p_{Dd}\,F(Dd, a)],$$

$$p'_{Ad} - p_{Ad} = \frac{p_{Ad}(\pi_{Ad} - \pi(p))}{\omega - \alpha} + q\,WFp(Dd, n). \tag{8.4.14}$$

Analogous expressions hold for $p'_{Da} - p_{Da}$ and $p'_{Aa} - p_{Aa}$. We also need

$$p'_d - p_d \equiv (p'_{Dd} + p'_{Ad}) - (p_{Dd} + p_{Ad})$$
$$= p_{Aa}\,p_{Ad}\left(\frac{\pi_{Ad} - \pi_{Aa}}{\omega - \alpha}\right) \tag{8.4.15}$$
$$+ (1 - q) \cdot [-WF(Da, d) + p_{Dd}\,p_{Aa}(F(Da, d) - F(Dd, a))].$$

First assume that $W^t > 0$ for all t. By (8.4.14), p_{Ad} is monotonically increasing for any interior trajectory (since $\pi_{Ad} > \pi(p)$) with $\lim_{t \to \infty} p^t_{Ad} = 1$ and the proof is complete.

Now assume that there exists $t_0 \ge 0$ such that $W^{t_0} \le 0$. Then $W^t \le 0$ for all $t > t_0$, and so p_d is monotonically increasing once $t > t_0$ by (8.4.15). Let $\lambda = \lim_{t \to \infty} p^t_d$. Then $\lambda \ge p^{t_0}_d > 0$. In fact, since $\pi_{Ad} > \pi_{Aa}$ and $F(Da, d) - F(Dd, a) > 0$, (8.4.15) also implies that $W^t \to 0$ and $p^t_{Ad}\,p^t_{Aa} \to 0$ as $t \to \infty$.

---

41. Note that this set is not invariant if D is not the unique best outcome.

42. From chapter 6.3 the Wright manifold for the standard normal form of figure 8.4.1, $\{p \in \Delta^4 \mid p_{Dd}\,p_{Aa} = p_{Da}\,p_{Ad}\} = \{p \mid W(p) = 0\}$, consists of those (mixed) strategies where the player's planned action at decision 2 is independent of his choice at decision 1. This curved surface divides the tetrahedron Δ^4 into two equal parts. The invariance of $\{p \mid W(p) \le 0\}$ means an initial bias in favor of choosing A at decision 1 among those whose planned action is d at decision 2 (compared to those whose planned action is a) persists indefinitely.

Suppose $\lambda < 1$. Since $W^t \cdot p_{Ad}^t = p_{Da}^t p_{Aa}^t p_{Ad}^t - p_{Da}^t (p_{Ad}^t)^2 \to 0$, we obtain $p_{Ad}^t p_{Da}^t \to 0$, and hence $p_{Ad}^t \cdot p_a^t \to 0$ as $t \to \infty$. Since $p_a^t \geq 1 - \lambda > 0$ for all $t > t_0$, $p_{Ad}^t \to 0$ and $p_{Da}^t \to \lambda$ as $t \to \infty$. Now $\lim_{t\to\infty} W^t \to 0$ implies that $\lim_{t\to\infty} p_{Aa}^t = 0$. Consequently $\lim_{t\to\infty} p_D^t = 1$. Since $W^t \leq 0$ for all $t > t_0$, by (8.4.12),

$$\pi(p^t) \geq p_D^t \pi_D + p_A^t (p_d^t \pi_{Ad} + p_a^t \pi_{Aa}).$$

Thus, for t sufficiently large, $\pi(p^t) > \pi_D$ if $\lambda > \lambda_0$ where $\pi_D = \lambda_0 \pi_{Ad} + (1 - \lambda_0)\pi_{Aa}$, and so p_D^t is decreasing for t sufficiently large by (8.4.9). Since this contradicts $\lim_{t\to\infty} p_D^t = 1$, we have $0 \leq \lambda \leq \lambda_0$. That is, we obtain a unique limit point in $\{p : p_D = 1, \pi_D \geq p_d \pi_{Ad} + p_a \pi_{Aa}\}$ if $\lambda < 1$.

Suppose now that $\lambda = 1$. Then $\pi(p^t) > \pi_D$ for t sufficiently large as above. Thus, p_D^t is decreasing to zero which implies $p_{Ad}^t \to 1$ since $\lim_{t\to\infty} p_d^t = 1$. ∎

A natural question following theorem 8.4.6 is which, if any, $F^{f/POR}$ rules satisfy inequality (8.4.10). For those rules F with *no change of memory* (i.e., $Fm(Da, d) = Fm(Dd, a) = 0$), a calculation similar to (8.4.5), yields $F^{POR}(Da, d) - F^{POR}(Dd, a) = (\pi_d - \pi_a)/(\omega - \alpha)$ and so satisfies (8.4.10). Similarly the PRR rule (i.e., $f(x, y) = (\omega - x)/(\omega - \alpha)$ for within-decision learning satisfies (8.4.10). On the other hand, if the PIR rule is used when the action at decision 2 is sampled and own choice is D, then (8.4.10) is not satisfied for all Centipede Bandits. For instance, the Centipede Bandit may have $\pi_d > \pi_a$ at the same time that no realized payoff from P^d is higher than any x in the support of P^D whereas P^a is higher for some. Thus care must be taken to assert convergence is guaranteed when rules with no change of memory are used.

$F^{f/POR}$ rules with *maximal change of memory* (i.e., $F(Da, d) = F(Dd, a) = 1$) obviously satisfy inequality (8.4.10). These rules adopt any sampled action at decision 2 if own action is D whether play is changed or not. Besides their simplicity, there are several reasons $F^{f/POR}$ with maximal change of memory are preferred to rules with no change of memory. For instance, an eigenvalue analysis suggests the basin of attraction of the optimal strategy of the former rules is larger when $\pi_{Ad} > \pi_D > \pi_{Aa}$ and simulations indicate they also have a faster rate of convergence (see Notes).

The results of theorem 8.4.6 are closely related to the standard dynamics of evolutionary game theory applied to the agent normal form of the extensive form game given by figure 8.4.1 with expected payoffs replacing the lotteries at the endpoints. For a fixed q, this two-player game (with one move by nature) has a unique Nash equilibrium outcome when D is either the unique best or worst choice. When $\pi_{Ad} > \pi_D > \pi_{Aa}$, we have the Chain-Store Game. There are then two Nash equilibrium outcomes; namely the subgame perfect NE (A, d) and the outcome D with corresponding NE component

$$\left\{ (D, \lambda d + (1 - \lambda)a) \mid 0 \le \lambda \le \lambda_0 = \frac{\pi_D - \pi_{Aa}}{\pi_{Ad} - \pi_{Aa}} \right\}.$$

Thus theorem 8.4.6i and ii assert that all interior trajectories converge to a NE of the agent normal form and that the subgame perfect NE outcome is the only asymptotically stable set of limit points.[43] These are the same results as the standard replicator dynamic of evolutionary game theory. Heuristically each decision is eventually treated independently by the $F^{f/POR}$ rules that satisfy (8.4.10). The proof of theorem 8.4.6ii also has similarities with the replicator dynamic, giving some intuition why the optimal outcome is not always learned. First, p_D increases as long as p_d is small. From (8.4.15) the rate of change of p_d depends on how often decision 2 is reached. If p_d is small, then D is currently the best choice at decision 1. The consequent increased play of D diminishes the number of times individuals can learn that Ad is better than Aa, and eventually p_D may converge to 1. Thus play can be locked in at the second-best outcome for essentially the same reasons that the replicator dynamic applied to the Chain-Store Game may not lead to the subgame perfect NE.

8.5   Appendix A

Proof of Theorem 8.0.1

Suppose that $(p^*, q^*) \subset G$ induces a mixed behavior at some reachable player information set. Let u be the initial such information set (i.e., the induced behavior strategy at every player decision point on the path from the root to u is pure), say of player one. If $p^* \in \Delta_1$ induces b_1^u at u, then $(p^* \backslash b_1^{u'}, q^*)$ is a NE for any local behavior strategy $b_1^{u'}$ given

---

43. This last assertion follows immediately from the proof of theorem 8.4.6.

by a convex combination of the form $\sum_i \alpha_i b^u_{1i}$ where b^u_{1i} is a local pure behavior strategy in the support of b^u_1. To see this, note that $\pi_1(p, q^*) \leq \pi_1(p^*, q^*) = \sum_i \alpha_i \pi_1(p^* \backslash b^u_{1i}, q^*) = \pi_1(p^* \backslash b^{u'}_1, q^*)$ since $\pi_1(p^* \backslash b^u_1, q^*) = \pi_1(p^* \backslash b^u_{1i}, q^*)$ as (p^*, q^*) is a NE. Also $\pi_2(p^* \backslash b^{u'}_1, q) \leq \pi_2(p^* \backslash b^{u'}_1, q^*)$ since (p^*, q^*) induces a NE in each subgame Γ_v of Γ_u where v is reachable by (p^*, q^*).[44] Thus (p^*, q^*) is in the same NE component as another NE that chooses a single alternative at u and induces the same behavior strategy as (p^*, q^*) at all other player information sets. Applying this argument recursively to all reachable information sets, we see that (p^*, q^*) is in the same NE component as another NE that chooses a single alternative at all reachable player decision points of this latter NE.

Now consider a final player decision point (e.g., of player two) u that is relevant for q^* but not reachable by a mixed $(p^*, q^*) \in G$ that chooses a single alternative at all its reachable player decision points. Then $(p^*, q^* \backslash b^u_2)$ is a NE (in the same connected component) where $q^* \backslash b^u_2$ induces a pure strategy in Γ_u that leads to the smallest payoff of player one. To see this, note that $\pi_1(p, q^* \backslash b^u_2) \leq \pi_1(p, q^*) \leq \pi_1(p^*, q^*) = \pi_1(p^*, q^* \backslash b^u_2)$ and $\pi_2(p^*, q) \leq \pi_2(p^*, q^*) = \pi_2(p^*, q^* \backslash b^u_2)$. Thus there is a $(p^*, q^*) \in G$ that chooses a single alternative at all of its relevant final decision points and at all its reachable player decision points. This argument can now be repeated for next to final decision points, and so on. For instance, at a next to final decision point u (e.g., of player two) that is relevant for q^*, $(p^*, q^* \backslash b^u_2)$ is a NE where b^u_2 is a local pure behavior strategy at u such that $q^* \backslash b^u_2$ induces a pure strategy in Γ_u that leads to the smallest payoff of player one when competing against any strategy of the form $b^{u'}_2$. Thus we may assume that the NE (p^*, q^*) induces pure behavior strategies at all decision points of players one and two that are relevant for p^* and q^* respectively. Finally, it is immaterial what behavior strategies are specified at the other player decision points since they are not relevant for the NE (alternatively, we can take the reduced-strategy normal form), and so there is a pure strategy NE pair in the NE component of (p^*, q^*).

We will use induction on the number of player information sets to prove that there is only one subgame perfect NE component. The statement is obvious if there is a single player information set. If there are two or more player information sets, suppose that u is an initial one, say

---

44. Equivalently, q^* is subgame perfect in the one player subtree of Γ_u that is generated by using p^* to specify moves by nature at decision points of player one.

of player one. Note that u is reachable by any strategy. If b and b' are different pure behavior strategy combinations that are subgame perfect, by induction, the behavior strategies induced in any proper subgame following u are in the same NE component. In particular, there is a continuous curve $b(t)$ joining these two induced strategies in each such subgame.

If there are no payoff ties at u for player one when all these subgames are truncated by any $b(t)$, then b and b' must both specify the same pure behavior strategy at u; namely the one that leads to the highest payoff in the truncations. By the first statement of theorem 6.1.1, this choice at u together with $b(t)$ is a NE of Γ_u for all t. Thus b and b' restricted to Γ_u are in the same NE component of Γ_u.

If truncation with respect to $b(t_0)$ leads to a payoff tie for player one, the argument in the first paragraph of the proof shows that any convex combination of local behavior strategies at u that lead to the same payoff as $b(t_0)$ is a NE of Γ_u and so in the same NE component of Γ_u. Thus all choices of NE for Γ_u that induce any $b(t)$ are in the same NE component of Γ_u. In particular, b^u and $b^{u'}$ are in the same NE component of Γ_u.

If there is only one initial player decision point (e.g., if there are no initial moves by nature), the proof is complete. Otherwise, the argument above shows there is only one subgame perfect NE component in each subgame following an initial move by nature. These combine to form a single subgame perfect NE component of Γ.   ■

The following proof of theorem 8.2.2 relies on definition 8.5.1 and lemma 8.5.2 below. Recall that throughout this proof we consider a fixed initial state $(p(0), q(0))$ in the interior of $\Delta(S_1) \times \Delta(S_2)$ for which the sets E and F, given in definition 8.2.3, generate the perfect information game Γ'.

Definition 8.5.1   *Order the N decision points $v_1 \succ v_2 \succ \cdots \succ v_N$ of Γ' so that the following is true: v_1 is a final decision point (i.e., a decision point from which all alternatives lead to endpoints) of Γ' and $v_k \succ v_\ell$ whenever v_k follows v_ℓ along a path in Γ'. For any pure strategy e_i of Γ and any $1 \leq k \leq N$, let e_i^k be the same strategy on Γ' as that induced by e_i except that e_i^k chooses according to the subgame perfect Nash equilibrium of Γ' at all decision points of player one among $v_1, \ldots, v_k$. Similarly f_j^k is defined by considering player two's decision points among $v_1, \ldots, v_k$.*

Lemma 8.5.2 *If $e_i \in E$ and $k \in \{1, \ldots, N\}$, the following three statements are true:*

  i. $\lim_{t \to \infty} p_i^k(t)/p_i(t) = L^k$ exists as a positive extended real number.

  ii. If L^k is finite, then $\pi_1(e_i, f_{j'}) = \pi_1(e_i^k, f_{j'})$ for all $f_{j'} \in F$.

  iii. $e_i^k \in E$.

The analogous statements also hold for player two pure strategies $f_j \in F$.

Proof The proof is by induction on k. Let $e_i \in E$. For $k = 1$, $T > 0$, and our uniformly monotone selection dynamic, there is some $K \geq 1$ such that

$$\ln \frac{p_i^1(T)}{p_i(T)} - \ln \frac{p_i^1(0)}{p_i(0)} = \int_0^T \frac{d}{dt} \left(\ln \left(p_i^1(t)/p_i(t) \right) \right) dt$$

$$= \int_0^T \left(\frac{\dot{p}_i^1(t)}{p_i^1(t)} - \frac{\dot{p}_i(t)}{p_i(t)} \right) dt$$

$$\geq \int_0^T \frac{1}{K} \left[\left(\pi_1(e_i^1, q) - \pi_1(p, q) \right) - \left(\pi_1(e_i, q) - \pi_1(p, q) \right) \right] dt \qquad (8.5.1)$$

$$= \frac{1}{K} \int_0^T \pi_1 \left(e_i^1, \sum_{j=1}^n q_j(t) f_j \right) - \pi_1 \left(e_i, \sum_{j=1}^n q_j(t) f_j \right) dt$$

$$= \frac{1}{K} \int_0^T \sum_{f_j \in F} q_j(t) \left(\pi_1(e_i^1, f_j) - \pi_1(e_i, f_j) \right) dt$$

$$+ \frac{1}{K} \int_0^T \sum_{f_j \notin F} q_j(t) \left(\pi_1(e_i^1, f_j) - \pi_1(e_i, f_j) \right) dt.$$

Since v_1 is a final decision point of Γ', by the definition of e_i^1, $\pi_1(e_i^1, f_j) \geq \pi_1(e_i, f_j)$ for any $f_j \in F$. Since $\int_0^\infty q_j(t) \, dt < \infty$ if $f_j \notin F$, by (8.5.1), $\lim_{T \to \infty} (\ln p_i^1(T)/p_i(T))$ exists as an extended real number in $\mathbf{R} \cup \{\infty\}$, and so $\lim_{t \to \infty} p_i^1(t)/p_i(t) = L^1$ where L^1 is a positive real number or ∞. If L^1 is finite, then $\pi_1(e_i^1, f_j) = \pi_1(e_i, f_j)$ for all $f_j \in F$. In either case, $\int_0^\infty p_i^1(t) \, dt = \int_0^\infty [p_i^1(t)/p_i(t)] \cdot p_i(t) \, dt = \infty$ since $e_i \in E$, and this concludes the proof for $k = 1$.

Assume that the three statements and the analogous ones for player two are true for some k with $1 \leq k < N$. Let $e_i \in E$. To show the statement for $k + 1$, we first show that $\lim_{t \to \infty} p_i^{k+1}(t)/p_i^k(t)$ exists as a positive extended real number L_k^{k+1}. First, let us show $\int_0^\infty (\dot{p}_i^{k+1}(t)/p_i^{k+1}(t) - \dot{p}_i^k(t)/p_i^k(t)) \, dt$ exists as a real number or as $+\infty$. Since the integrand is continuous, this amounts to showing $\int_0^\infty \min\{(\dot{p}_i^{k+1}(t)/p_i^{k+1}(t) - \dot{p}_i^k(t)/p_i^k(t)), 0\}\, dt > -\infty$. By uniform monotonicity,

$$\int_0^\infty \min\left\{\left(\frac{\dot{p}_i^{k+1}(t)}{p_i^{k+1}(t)} - \frac{\dot{p}_i^k(t)}{p_i^k(t)}\right), 0\right\} dt$$

$$\geq K \int_0^\infty \min\left(\pi_1\left(e_i^{k+1}, q(t)\right) - \pi_1\left(e_i^k, q(t)\right), 0\right) dt$$

$$\geq K \int_0^\infty \min\left\{\sum_{f_j \in F} q_j(t)\left(\pi_1\left(e_i^{k+1}, f_j\right) - \pi_1\left(e_i^k, f_j\right)\right), 0\right\} dt \tag{8.5.2}$$

$$+ K \int_0^\infty \min\left\{\sum_{f_j \notin F} q_j(t)\left(\pi_1\left(e_i^{k+1}, f_j\right) - \pi_1\left(e_i^k, f_j\right)\right), 0\right\} dt.$$

The analogue of (8.5.1) is now

$$\int_0^T \sum_{f_j \in F} q_j(t)\left(\pi_1\left(e_i^{k+1}, f_j\right) - \pi_1\left(e_i^k, f_j\right)\right) dt$$

$$+ \int_0^T \sum_{f_j \notin F} q_j(t)\left(\pi_1\left(e_i^{k+1}, f_j\right) - \pi_1\left(e_i^k, f_j\right)\right) dt. \tag{8.5.3}$$

If $\pi_1(e_i^{k+1}, f_j) \geq \pi_1(e_i^k, f_j)$ for all $f_j \in F$, then L_k^{k+1} exists and is finite if and only if $\pi_1(e_i^{k+1}, f_j) = \pi_1(e_i^k, f_j)$ for all $f_j \in F$.

Suppose $\pi_1(e_i^{k+1}, f_{j'}) < \pi_1(e_i^k, f_{j'})$ for some $f_{j'} \in F$. Then v_{k+1} must be a decision node of player one, and it is reached by the pair $(e_i^k, f_{j'})$. Hence $\pi_1(e_i^{k+1}, f_{j'}^k) > \pi_1(e_i^k, f_{j'}^k)$. Moreover $f_{j'}$ does not choose the backward induction alternative for Γ' at all decision points $v_1, \ldots, v_k$. Since Γ' is generic, $\pi_2(e_{i'}, f_{j'}) \neq \pi_2(e_{i'}, f_{j'}^k)$ for some $e_{i'} \in E$. By the induction assumption applied to player two, $\lim_{t \to \infty} q_{j'}^k/q_{j'} = \infty$. Thus, for t sufficiently large, $q_{j'}^k(t)(\pi_1(e_i^{k+1}, f_{j'}^k) - \pi_1(e_i^k, f_{j'}^k))$ dominates $q_{j'}(t)(\pi_1(e_i^{k+1}, f_{j'}) - \pi_1(e_i^k, f_{j'}))$ in equation (8.5.2) and so the integral, $\int_0^\infty \min\{\sum_{f_j \in F} q_j(t)(\pi_1(e_i^{k+1}, f_j) - \pi_1(e_i^k, f_j)), 0\}\, dt$, is finite since the dominating term is positive.

By the same method applied to the upper bound (i.e., using $1/K$ from uniform monotonicity) for $\int_0^\infty (\dot{p}_i^{k+1}(t)/p_i^{k+1}(t) - \dot{p}_i^k(t)/p_i^k(t))\, dt$, we see that this integral is infinite if and only if $\pi_1(e_i^{k+1}, f_{j'}) < \pi_1(e_i^k, f_{j'})$ for some $f_{j'} \in F$. That is, L_k^{k+1} exists and is finite if and only if $\pi_1(e_i^{k+1}, f_j) = \pi_1(e_i^k, f_j)$ for all $f_j \in F$. Since $L^{k+1} = L_k^{k+1} L^k$, parts i, ii, and iii are true for $k+1$ and this completes the proof by induction. ∎

Proof of Theorem 8.2.2

Since $\lim_{t\to\infty} p_i(t) = 0$ for all $e_i \notin E$, $\limsup_{t\to\infty} p_i(t) > 0$ for some $e_i \in E$, say e_1. By lemma 8.5.2i, $L^N = \lim_{t\to\infty} p_1^N(t)/p_1(t)$ exists. Furthermore, since $\lim p_1(t) \neq 0$, L^N is finite. Lemma 8.5.2ii implies that $\pi_1(e_1, f_j) = \pi_1(e_1^N, f_j)$ for all $f_j \in F$.

Repeating the argument above for all $e_i \in E$ with $\limsup_{t\to\infty} p_i(t) > 0$, we obtain $\pi_1(e_i, f_j) = \pi_1(e_i^N, f_j) = \pi_1(e_1^N, f_j) = \pi_1(e_1, f_j)$ for all $f_j \in F$. It is clear from the proof of lemma 8.5.2 that $\lim_{t\to\infty} p_i(t)/p_1(t) = L_i$ exists and is finite for all $e_i \in E$. Thus $p_i(t)$ converges to $L_i/(\sum_{e_{i'} \in E} L_{i'})$ for all such $e_i \in E$ and to 0 otherwise. That is, $p(t)$ converges to a point in $\Delta(S_1)$.

The proof of the theorem is completed by showing that $q(t)$ also converges using the same method applied with E and F interchanged. ■

Proof of Theorem 8.2.6

Let G be an interior attracting set. Assume that G does not contain the subgame perfect equilibrium (e_B, f_B). From theorem 8.2.2, G contains a Nash equilibrium, say (p, q). We will first show that the Nash equilibrium component G' containing (p, q) is contained in G. Since all Nash equilibria which are in the interior of G' relative to the set of rest points (and are sufficiently close to G) must be in G by theorem 8.2.4 and the assumption of interior attraction, G contains the relative interior of G'. Moreover the fact that G is closed implies that $G' \subseteq G$.

Thus, by theorem 8.0.3, there is a pure strategy NE in G that does not yield the same outcome as (e_B, f_B). In fact we can choose such a NE $(e_1, f_1) \in G$ satisfying the following maximality condition: (e_1, f_1) is not subgame perfect at information set u but is at every other information set in Γ_u, and there is no other pure strategy NE in G that is subgame perfect in Γ_u. Note that this condition implies that u is a player decision point.

Since (e_1, f_1) is a NE, (e_1, f_1) does not reach u. Without loss of generality, assume that u is a decision point of player two. Let f_2 be the strategy of player two that is identical to f_1 except that f_2 is subgame perfect in Γ_u (i.e., f_2 chooses the subgame perfect alternative at u). Then (e_1, f_2) follows the same path as (e_1, f_1), but (e_1, f_2) is not a NE.[45]

---

45. Otherwise, $(e_1, (1-\lambda)f_1 + \lambda f_2)$ is a NE for all $0 \leq \lambda \leq 1$, and so $(e_1, f_2) \in G$, which contradicts the assumption that there is no other pure strategy NE in G that is subgame perfect in Γ_u.

Thus there is some e_2 such that $\pi_1(e_2, f_2) > \pi_1(e_1, f_2)$ since $\pi_2(e_1, f) \le \pi_2(e_1, f_1) = \pi_2(e_1, f_2)$ for all $f \in S_2$. In fact (e_2, f_2) must reach u; otherwise, $\pi_1(e_2, f_2) = \pi_1(e_2, f_1) \le \pi_1(e_1, f_1) = \pi_1(e_1, f_2)$ since (e_1, f_1) is a NE. We can even take e_2 to be subgame perfect in Γ_u.

This argument implies, by the definition of f_2 and u, that $\pi_2(e_2, f_2) > \pi_2(e_2, f_1)$ since Γ is generic. Consider trajectories on the face $\Delta(\tilde{S}_1) \times \Delta(\tilde{S}_2)$ spanned by $\tilde{S}_1 = \{e_1, e_2\}$ and $\tilde{S}_2 = \{f_1, f_2\}$. The structure of the game on this face is that of the Chain-Store Game (see example 8.1.3) which we now exploit. Specifically, let $\lambda_0 = (\pi_1(e_1, f_1) - \pi_1(e_2, f_1))/(\pi_1(e_2, f_2) - \pi_1(e_2, f_1))$ and $BR_1(q)$ be the best responses of player one to the mixed strategy q of player two. Then $BR_1(f_1) \subseteq BR_1((1 - \lambda)f_1 + \lambda f_2)$ if $\lambda \le \lambda_0$, and hence $\{(e_1, (1 - \lambda)f_1 + \lambda f_2) \mid 0 \le \lambda \le \lambda_0\}$ is a set of NE. Moreover $e_2 \in BR_1((1 - \lambda_0)f_1 + \lambda_0 f_2)$. In particular, there is a trajectory $(p(t), q(t))$ starting arbitrarily close to $(e_1, (1 - \lambda_0)f_1 + \lambda_0 f_2)$ that converges to (e_2, f_2) on this face.

The remainder of the proof that G contains (e_B, f_B) assumes the replicator dynamic (see the Notes at the end of the chapter for the general case of a uniformly monotone selection dynamic). By continuity of the trajectories, there exists a sequence of interior trajectories, whose initial points on the Wright manifold W^u converge to $(e_1, (1 - \lambda_0)f_1 + \lambda_0 f_2)$,[46] that evolves arbitrarily close to (e_2, f_2). In the subgame Γ_u, the subgame perfect NE pure strategy is stable under any monotone selection dynamic (theorem 8.2.4), and so these trajectories $(p(t), q(t))$ induce strategies in Γ_u that remain arbitrarily close to this subgame perfect NE pure strategy for all t sufficiently large (in particular, since Γ is generic, the trajectories stay away from any other NE component in Γ_u). On the other hand, $(p(t), q(t))$ converges to a NE in Γ, and since the NE component is closed, there is a NE point in G that is subgame perfect in Γ_u. Thus, by theorem 8.0.3, there is a pure strategy NE that is subgame perfect in Γ_u. This contradicts the maximality condition of (e_1, f_1) and so any interior attracting set G contains (e_B, f_B) together with G^*.

By theorem 8.2.2, interior attracting sets exist and minimal ones will contain only NE. Let G and G' be two different minimal interior attracting sets. Then $(e_B, f_B) \in G \cap G'$ and $G \cap G'$ is not interior attracting by the minimality condition. Hence, there is a trajectory starting arbitrarily close to $G \cap G'$ that converges to some $(p, q) \in (G \backslash G') \cup (G' \backslash G)$. This, however, contradicts the interior attracting property of either G or G'. Hence $G = G'$.

---

46. Since f_1 and f_2 are identical except at u, $(e_1, (1 - \lambda_0)f_1 + \lambda_0 f_2)$ is a point in the closure of W^u.

Let G be an interior asymptotically stable set. Since G is interior attracting by definition, $G^* \subseteq G$. The uniqueness of minimal interior asymptotically stable sets then follows by an argument similar to that used in the preceding paragraph. Furthermore, if each element of G yields the same outcome in Γ, then all points in G yield the subgame perfect outcome. In this case we will show that $G = G^*$. By the definition of G^*, there exists an open neighborhood U of G^* such that the only Nash equilibria contained in U are in G^*. Assume that there is some $(p, q) \in (U \cap G)\backslash G^*$. Since (p, q) is not a Nash equilibrium, without loss of generality, there is an $e_i \in \Delta(S_1)$ with $\pi_1(e_i, q) > \pi_1(p, q)$. Since any $(p, q) \in G$ is a rest point, it follows that $p_i = 0$. Thus there exists an open neighborhood V of (p, q) such that $V \cap G \subseteq \{(p, q) \mid p_i = 0\}$ and $\pi_1(e_i, q) > \pi_1(p, q)$ for all $(p, q) \in V$. By uniform monotonicity, $\dot{p}_i > 0$ for all interior trajectories in V, and so these trajectories do not stay close to G. Thus no such (p, q) exists (i.e., $(U \cap G)\backslash G^* = \emptyset$), and so $G = G^*$. ∎

8.6   Appendix B

Proof of Theorem 8.4.3

Consider the set of reduced-strategy normal form Centipede Bandits $\mathcal{B}$ for which P^z has the same support for all $z \in Z$, all π_z are different and q is arbitrary between 0 and 1. Suppose that F is a good playwise imitative rule. We will first show that $F(D, n) > 0$ for all bandits B in $\mathcal{B}$. Suppose, on the contrary, that $F(D, n) = 0$ for some such B. Then, by our assumption of common support for all P^z, $F(D, n) = 0$ for all bandits B in $\mathcal{B}$. Choose those bandits in $\mathcal{B}$ with $\pi_n > \pi_D > \pi_d > \pi_a$. Since F is playwise imitative, we need

$$F(Ad(d), D, D) > F(D, d, Ad) \tag{8.6.1}$$

when $q = 0$ since D is the unique best strategy in this case (here $F(Ad(d), D, D)$ denotes the probability of switching to D from Ad if own current action is d).

On the other hand, for q sufficiently close (but not equal) to 1, Ad is the unique best strategy. From (8.4.1), the linearization about $p_{Ad} = 1$ is

	Ad	D	Aa
Ad	1	$F(D, Ad, Ad) - F(Ad, D)$	$F(Aa, Ad, Ad) - F(Ad, Aa)$
D	0	$1 + F(Ad, D, D) - F(D, Ad)$	$F(Ad, Aa, D) + F(Aa, Ad, D)$
Aa	0	$F(D, Ad, Aa) + F(Ad, D, Aa)$	$1 + F(Ad, Aa, Aa) - F(Aa, Ad)$

The eigenvalues of this matrix are 1 (corresponding to the invariance of Δ^3) plus those of the 2×2 matrix (note that $F(Ad, D, Aa)$, $F(Ad, Aa, D)$ and $F(Aa, Ad, D)$ are all 0 since F is playwise imitative):

$$\begin{bmatrix} 1 + F(Ad, D, D) - F(D, Ad) & 0 \\ F(D, Ad, Aa) & 1 + F(Ad, Aa, Aa) - F(Aa, Ad, Ad) \end{bmatrix}.$$

(8.6.2)

The eigenvalues (i.e., the diagonal entries) must both be less than 1 so that $p_{Ad} = 1$ is asymptotically stable. In particular, $F(D, Ad) > F(Ad, D, D)$. That is,

$$q F(D, n) + (1 - q)F(D, d, Ad)$$
$$> q F(Ad(n), D, D) + (1 - q)F(Ad(d), D, D).$$

Substitution of (8.6.1) shows $F(D, n) > q F(Ad(n), D, D) \geq 0$. Thus either $F(D, n, Ad) > 0$ or $F(D, n, Aa) > 0$ (or both).

Without loss of generality, let us assume $F(D, n, Aa) > 0$ for all bandits B in $\mathcal{B}$. Now consider those B in $\mathcal{B}$ for which $\pi_d > \max\{\pi_n, \pi_a\}$ and $\pi_D = \frac{1}{2}(\pi_n + \pi_d)$. Then, for $q > \frac{1}{2}$, D is the unique best strategy, and so $p_D = 1$ must be asymptotically stable under F and $p_{Ad} = 1$ must be unstable. Similarly, for $q < \frac{1}{2}$, Ad is the unique best strategy, and the roles of D and Ad are reversed. Since matrix (8.6.2) is nonnegative, the Perron-Frobenius theorem guarantees there is a positive eigenvalue λ_1 such that $\lambda_1 \geq |\lambda_2|$ where λ_2 is the other (real) eigenvalue. Since each of the payoff entries is continuous in q (e.g., $F(D, Ad) = q F(D, n) + (1 - q)F(D, a)$), $\lambda_1 = 1$ when $q = \frac{1}{2}$. In particular, $F(Ad, D, D) - F(D, Ad) = 0$ when $q = \frac{1}{2}$. That is,

$$F(Ad(n), D, D) + F(Ad(d), D, D) = F(D, n) + F(D, d, Ad). \qquad (8.6.3)$$

The corresponding linearization about $p_D = 1$ yields the 2×2 matrix (with rows ordered as Ad and Aa)

$$\begin{bmatrix} 1 + F(D, Ad, Ad) - F(Ad, D) & F(D, Aa, Ad) \\ F(D, Ad, Aa) & 1 + F(D, Aa, Aa) - F(Aa, D) \end{bmatrix}.$$

(8.6.4)

Substitution of (8.6.3) into (8.6.4) yields, for arbitrary q,

$$\begin{bmatrix} 1 - q F(D, n, Aa) + & q F(D, n, Ad) \\ (2q - 1)[F(Ad(d), D, D) - F(D, d, Ad)] & \\ q F(D, n, Aa) & 1 + F(D, Aa, Aa) - F(Aa, D, D) \end{bmatrix}.$$

Now an eigenvalue of 1 when $q = \frac{1}{2}$ implies that

$$0 = \frac{1}{2}F(D, n, Ad) + F(D, Aa, Aa) - F(Aa, D, D)$$

$$= \frac{1}{2}F(D, n, Ad) + \frac{1}{2}F(D, n, Aa) - \frac{1}{2}F(Aa(n), D, D)$$

$$+ \frac{1}{2}F(D, a, Aa) - \frac{1}{2}F(Aa(a), D, D).$$

Thus $F(D, a, Aa) - F(Aa(a), D, D)$ does not depend on P^a (i.e., it depends only on P^D and P^n). Consider those bandits in $\mathcal{B}$ with the same P^D and P^n satisfying $\pi_d < \min\{\pi_D, \pi_a\}$. For $q = 0$, we need $F(D, a, Aa) - F(Aa(a), D, D) > 0$ when $\pi_D < \pi_a$ (or else p_{Aa} is not asymptotically stable), and we need $F(D, a, Aa) - F(Aa(a), D, D) < 0$ when $\pi_D > \pi_a$. This contradiction completes the proof. $\blacksquare$

Proof of Theorem 8.4.6

Let us first show the identities (8.4.13) to (8.4.15); the other two, (8.4.11) and (8.4.12), are left as elementary exercises.

For the $F^{f/POR}$ rules, from (8.4.7),

$$p'_{Dd} - p_{Dd} = p_{Ad}p_{Dd}(Fp(Ad, Dd, Dd) - Fp(Dd, Ad, Ad))$$

$$+ p_{Ad}p_{Da}(Fp(Ad, Da, Dd) + Fm(Da, Ad, Dd))$$

$$- p_{Aa}p_{Dd}(Fp(Dd, Aa, Aa) + Fp(Dd, Aa, Ad)$$

$$+ Fm(Dd, Aa, Da))$$

$$= p_{Ad}(p_{Dd} + p_{Da})\left(\frac{\pi_D - \pi_{Ad}}{\omega - \alpha}\right) - qWF(Dd, n, Ad)$$

$$+ (1 - q)[p_{Ad}p_{Da}(Fp(Da, d, Ad) + Fm(Da, d, Dd)$$

$$- p_{Aa}p_{Dd}F(Dd, a)].$$

In this calculation (and in the following ones), we use the facts that $Fp(Da, n, Aa) = Fp(Dd, n, Ad) = Fp(Dd, n)$ and $Fp(Da, d) = Fp(Dd, d)$ for the $F^{f/POR}$ rules. By a similar calculation, $p'_{Ad} - p_{Ad}$ is equal to

$$p_{Aa}p_{Ad}(Fp(Aa, Ad) - Fp(Ad, Aa)) + p_{Aa}p_{Dd}Fp(Dd, Aa, Ad)$$

$$+ p_{Ad}p_{Da}(Fp(Da, Ad, Ad) - Fp(Ad, Da))$$

$$+ p_{Ad}p_{Dd}(Fp(Dd, Ad, Ad) - Fp(Ad, Dd))$$

$$= \frac{p_{Ad}(p_{Dd} + p_{Da})(\pi_{Ad} - \pi_D)}{\omega - \alpha} + q\,WF p(Dd, n)$$

$$+ \frac{p_{Aa}\,p_{Ad}(\pi_{Ad} - \pi_{Aa})}{\omega - \alpha}$$

$$= \frac{p_{Ad}(\pi_{Ad} - \pi(p))}{\omega - \alpha} + q\,WF p(Dd, n).$$

Analogous expressions hold for $p'_{Da} - p_{Da}$ and $p'_{Aa} - p_{Aa}$. Consequently

$$p'_d - p_d = p_{Ad}\left(\frac{\pi_{Ad} - \pi(p)}{\omega - \alpha}\right) + q\,WF p(Dd, n)$$

$$+ p_{Ad}\,p_D\left(\frac{\pi_D - \pi_{Ad}}{\omega - \alpha}\right) - q\,WF p(Dd, n)$$

$$+ (1 - q)[p_{Da}\,p_{Ad}\,F(Da, d) - p_{Dd}\,p_{Aa}\,F(Dd, a)]$$

$$= p_{Aa}\,p_{Ad}\left(\frac{\pi_{Ad} - \pi_{Aa}}{\omega - \alpha}\right)$$

$$+ (1 - q)[p_{Da}\,p_{Ad}\,F(Da, d) - p_{Dd}\,p_{Aa}\,F(Dd, a)].$$

The proof is completed by showing that $\pi_{Aa} < \pi_D < \pi_{Ad}$ implies the forward invariance of $\{p \mid W(p) \leq 0\}$. When $W \leq 0$, we have

$$W' - W = p'_{Dd} - p'_D p'_d - (p_{Dd} - p_D p_d)$$

$$= p'_{Dd} - p_{Dd} - (p'_D - p_D)p_d - p'_D(p'_d - p_d)$$

$$= p_{Dd}\,p_{Ad}\left(\frac{\pi_D - \pi_{Ad}}{\omega - \alpha}\right) + p_{Da}\,p_{Ad}\left(\frac{\pi_D - \pi_{Ad}}{\omega - \alpha}\right)$$

$$+ p_{Da}\,p_{Ad}[q\,F p(Da, Ad, Aa) + (1 - q)F(Da, d)]$$

$$- p_{Dd}\,p_{Aa}[q\,F p(Dd, Aa, Ad) + (1 - q)F(Dd, a)]$$

$$- p_D\left(\frac{\pi_D - \pi(p)}{\omega - \alpha}\right)p_d - p'_D\,p_{Aa}\,p_{Ad}\left(\frac{\pi_{Ad} - \pi_{Aa}}{\omega - \alpha}\right)$$

$$- p'_D(1 - q)[-WF(Da, d) + p_{Dd}\,p_{Au}(F(Da, d) - F(Dd, u))]$$

$$= -W[q\,F(Dd, n) + (1 - q)(1 - p'_D)F(Da, d)]$$

$$+ p_D\,p_d\left(\frac{\pi(p) - \pi_{Ad}}{\omega - \alpha}\right)$$

$$- p_{Dd}\,p_D\left(\frac{\pi_D - \pi_{Ad}}{\omega - \alpha}\right) - p'_D\,p_{Aa}\,p_{Ad}\left(\frac{\pi_{Ad} - \pi_{Aa}}{\omega - \alpha}\right)$$

$$+ (1 - q)p_{Dd}\,p_{Aa}[F(Da, d) - F(Dd, a)](1 - p'_D)$$

$$\leq -W + p_{Dd}\left(\frac{\pi(p) - \pi_{Ad}}{\omega - \alpha}\right) - p_{Dd}\,p_D\left(\frac{\pi_D - \pi_{Ad}}{\omega - \alpha}\right)$$

$$- p'_D p_{Aa}\,p_{Ad}\left(\frac{\pi_{Ad} - \pi_{Aa}}{\omega - \alpha}\right) + (1-q)\,p_{Dd}\,p_{Aa}[F(Da, d)$$

$$- F(Dd, a)](1 - p'_D)$$

$$\leq -W + \frac{p_{Dd}}{\omega - \alpha}[p_D\pi_D + p_{Ad}\pi_{Ad} + p_{Aa}\pi_{Aa} - \pi_{Ad}$$

$$- p_D(\pi_D - \pi_{Ad})] - p'_D p_{Aa}\,p_{Ad}\left(\frac{\pi_{Ad} - \pi_{Aa}}{\omega - \alpha}\right)$$

$$+ (1-q)\,p_{Dd}\,p_{Aa}(1 - p'_D)\left(\frac{\pi_d - \pi_a}{\omega - \alpha}\right)$$

$$= -W + p_{Aa}\left(\frac{\pi_{Aa} - \pi_{Ad}}{\omega - \alpha}\right)p'_D(p_{Ad} + p_{Dd})$$

$$\leq -W.$$

Thus $W' \leq 0$ when $W \leq 0$. ∎

8.7 Notes

The dynamic analysis of this chapter extends the approach taken by Cressman and Schlag (1998a). Osborne and Rubinstein (1994) consider the static NE structure of these games in more depth—especially its relationship with the backward induction process. Their methods also include the simultaneity games of chapter 7 which they define as "extensive games with perfect information and simultaneous moves."

The Chain-Store Game of section 8.1 goes by several other names in the literature. Gale et al. (1995) considered a game, called the Ultimatum Mini Game, with the same qualitative payoff structure as the Chain-Store Game as part of their dynamic analysis of the Ultimatum Game. The payoffs in figure 8.1.1 are taken from Weibull (1995) where it is called the Entry Deterrence Game.

The proofs of the theorems in section 8.2.1 follow closely the method in Cressman and Schlag (1998a) except for the use that the present proof of theorem 8.2.6 makes of the Wright manifold for the replicator dynamic. In fact their proof (which was reported only for the replicator dynamic) extends to any uniformly monotone selection dynamic. Section 8.2.3 on behavioral strategy fictitious play is based on Canning (1992) and Hendon et al. (1996).

It is also interesting to compare the equilibrium selection techniques of section 8.2 with rationality arguments common in the literature. For instance, the game in example 8.2.7 is "belief consistent" according to Reny (1993) which leads to (T, Ll) being the only rational decision. At the same time, this subgame perfect equilibrium outcome is the unique prediction when the stochastic evolutionary model of Nöldeke and Samuelson (1993) (which is based on myopic best responses) is applied to this game. These results contrast with our finding that this G^* cannot be selected through dynamic stability arguments based on monotone selection. On the other hand, our methods select the subgame perfect NE component for the Centipede Game of Length Three in section 8.3.1 whereas rationality arguments are less conclusive here (cf. Reny 1993).

The explicit Centipede Game of figure 8.3.1 in section 8.3 is taken from Rosenthal (1981). Ponti (2000) has done extensive computer simulations of monotone selection dynamics for Centipede Games that indicate repeated perturbations near the boundary can affect the asymptotic stability even for games of length three. The material on fictitious play and the best response dynamic in this section is based on unpublished joint work with Josef Hofbauer and Karl Schlag where convergence of all interior best response trajectories for Centipede Games of Lengths $N = 4$ and $N = 5$ is shown.

Section 8.4 follows more recent work by Cressman and Schlag (1998b). The theory from matrix algebra used in the proof of theorem 8.4.1 is in standard texts (e.g., Horn and Johnson 1985) and center manifold theory for discrete dynamical systems in Wiggins (1990). Comparisons of the $F^{f/POR}$ rules with (maximal) change of memory to those without was carried out by Cressman and Schlag (1998b) for the Centipede Bandit.

This chapter develops a general theory of subgame monotone trajectories for an N-player extensive form game Γ with perfect recall. After monotone trajectories are defined in section 9.1 through the game's normal form, the parallel theory of subgame monotonicity based directly on the game's extensive form is introduced in section 9.2. Here and in section 9.3, the theory is connected to the concepts of the Wright manifold and the backward induction process, both of which have been used throughout the book. The discussion (section 9.4) includes a brief overview of the book from this new perspective.

9.1   Monotone Trajectories

Suppose that Γ is an N-player extensive form game of perfect recall. Recall the notation from chapter 6; $e_{n,i}$ denotes the ith pure strategy of player $n \in \{1, \ldots, N\}$, mixed strategies of player n are probability vectors $p_n \in \Delta_n$ whose ith component $p_{n,i}$ specifies the probability strategy $e_{n,i}$ is used.[1] The strategy space for Γ is then $\Delta = \times_{n=1}^{N} \Delta_n = \{p = (p_1, \ldots, p_N) \mid p_n \in \Delta_n\}$. A pure strategy e is an element of Δ such that all its components are pure behavior strategies. The payoff function

$$\pi_n : \Delta_n \times \Delta \to R$$

is the standard extension to mixed strategies in Δ_n of the expected payoff $\pi_n(e_{n,i}, p)$ to pure strategy $e_{n,i}$ when the other $N-1$ players are using mixed strategies $p_1, \ldots, p_{n-1}, p_{n+1}, \ldots, p_N$.

Although our main interest is in the analysis of trajectories through the subgame structure of Γ (starting with definition 9.2.1 below), we begin by introducing monotonicity for Γ irrespective of these subgames.

---

1. Care must be taken to distinguish the vector $p_n \in \Delta_n$ from p_n as the nth component of $p \in \Delta$ in chapter 2.

Definition 9.1.1   *An* interior trajectory *C for* Γ *is a curve* $p(t)$ *in the interior of* Δ *for all* $t \geq 0$ *that is continuously differentiable with respect to the time parameter* t.[2] *The explicit dependence of* p *on* t *is often suppressed.*

The interior trajectory, C, is called monotone with respect to Γ *if it satisfies, for all* $t \geq 0$ *and for all possible pairs* (n, i) *and* (n, j),

$$\frac{\dot{p}_{n,i}}{p_{n,i}} > \frac{\dot{p}_{n,j}}{p_{n,j}} \quad \text{if and only if} \quad \pi_n(e_{n,i}, p) > \pi_n(e_{n,j}, p). \tag{9.1.1}$$

If there is a sequence of times t_M *increasing to infinity such that* $p(t_M)$ *converges to* p^*, *then* p^* *is called an* ω-limit point *of C. Let* Ω *be the set of* ω-limit points of C which is nonempty by the compactness of Δ. C is called ω-monotone with respect to Γ at $p^* \in \Omega$ if, for all sequences $p(t_M)$ converging to p^* with t_M increasing to ∞, $\lim_{M \to \infty} \dot{p}_{n,i}/p_{n,i}$ exists for all (n, i) and these limits satisfy (9.1.1) above. C is ω-monotone with respect to Γ if it is monotone with respect to Γ and ω-monotone at all $p^* \in \Omega$.*

The definition parallels that of a monotone selection dynamic given in definitions 2.3.1 and 2.3.2 of chapter 2 (see also the analogous development in chapter 3.5 for bimatrix games) except that here the concept is applied to a single trajectory as opposed to the entire vector field. In particular, (9.1.1) implies the intuitive notion of monotonicity; namely that strategies with higher payoffs increase in relative frequency for each player.[3] The stronger concept of ω-monotonicity insists that this intuition carry over to all limit points of the trajectory as well.

It is straightforward to verify that every interior trajectory of a smooth monotone selection dynamic on Δ is ω-monotone with respect to Γ. However, not all monotone trajectories are given as trajectories of some monotone selection dynamic. For instance, a monotone trajectory can intersect itself transversely (i.e., with different tangent lines at the point of intersection) and so the flow need not be given by a single vector field. The following example illustrates another difference between monotone and ω-monotone trajectories.

---

2. To emphasize these trajectories are required to be continuously differentiable, we often describe them as smooth interior trajectories even though "smooth" may suggest infinitely often differentiable to some readers.

3. To see this, recall from chapter 2.3, that

$$\frac{d}{dt}\left(\frac{p_{n,i}}{p_{n,j}}\right) = \frac{p_{n,i}}{p_{n,j}}\left(\frac{\dot{p}_{n,i}}{p_{n,i}} - \frac{\dot{p}_{n,j}}{p_{n,j}}\right)$$

(i.e., $p_{n,i}/p_{n,j}$ is increasing if and only if $\dot{p}_{n,i}/p_{n,i} > \dot{p}_{n,j}/p_{n,j}$).

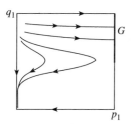

Figure 9.1.1
Replicatorlike trajectories for the Chain-Store Game.

Example 9.1.2 (The Chain-Store Game)   Consider the game player two plays against nature in the subgame Γ_v of the two-player Chain-Store Game (figure 8.1.1 of chapter 8.1) with bimatrix

$$\begin{bmatrix} 1,4 & 1,4 \\ 0,0 & 2,2 \end{bmatrix}.$$
(9.1.2)

As a single-player game against nature, q_1 must converge to 0 for any interior trajectory of a monotone selection dynamic since the second strategy always receives the higher payoff.[4] On the other hand, by definition 9.1.1, monotonicity holds if condition (9.1.1) is satisfied for $n = 2$.[5]

The replicator dynamic of the Chain-Store Game for player two is

$$\dot{q}_1 = -2(1 - p_1)q_1(1 - q_1).$$

Any trajectory of this dynamic in the interior of Δ^2 will be monotone for any choice of smooth function $p_1(t)$ satisfying $0 \le p_1(t) < 1$ for all $t \ge 0$. If $p_1(t)$ converges to 1 sufficiently quickly, then q_1 may not converge to 0 (as it must for any monotone selection dynamic). This possibility is precisely what occurs in figure 9.1.1 when, in the two-player game, the trajectory approaches an ω-limit point in the NE component G.

That is, considered as a game against nature by player two, such a trajectory is monotone but not the complete trajectory of a monotone selection dynamic since it is not ω-monotone. Heuristically the trajectory has followed that of a monotone selection dynamic but has "run out of time" with evolution stopping before a NE is selected.

---

4. Note that we have adopted the standard convention of using p_1 and q_1 as the frequencies of the first strategies for players one and two respectively (rather than $p_{1,1}$ and $p_{2,1}$) since this is a two-player game.
5. For these trajectories, p_1 is evolving more quickly than in the standard replicator dynamic (cf. figure 8.1.2) which produces a much larger basin of attraction for G.

On the other hand, for ω-monotone trajectories, we have the following theorem that generalizes part ii of the Folk Theorem of Evolutionary Game Theory as stated in the Introduction (i.e., that any convergent interior trajectory must converge to a NE). Its proof is essentially the same as the original proof of part ii (see Notes). The other two parts of the Fundamental Theorem on stability of NE are not relevant in this chapter which concentrates on single trajectories.

Theorem 9.1.3 *If C is an ω-monotone trajectory with respect to Γ with unique ω-limit point p^*, then p^* is a NE.*

Proof If p^* is not a NE, we may assume without loss of generality that $\pi_1(p_1, p^*) > \pi_1(p_1^*, p^*)$ for some $p_1 \in \Delta_1$. Since the trajectory C converges, $\lim_{t \to \infty} \dot{p}_{1,i} = 0$ for all i. Therefore, if $e_{1,i}$ is in the support of p_1^* (i.e., if $p_{1,i}^* > 0$), then $\lim_{t \to \infty} \dot{p}_{1,i} / p_{1,i} = 0$. Since C is ω-monotone, $\pi_1(e_{1,i}, p^*) = \pi_1(e_{1,j}, p^*) = \pi_1(p_1^*, p^*)$ for all $e_{1,i}$ and $e_{1,j}$ in the support of p_1^*. Thus there is some pure strategy $e_{1,0}$ of player one outside the support of p_1^* satisfying $\pi_1(e_{1,0}, p^*) > \pi_1(p_1^*, p^*)$. By ω-monotonicity, $\lim_{t \to \infty} \dot{p}_{1,0} / p_{1,0} > 0$, and this implies that $\dot{p}_{1,0}$ is positive for t sufficiently large, contradicting the condition $\lim_{t \to \infty} p_{1,0}(t) = 0$.   ∎

9.2   Subgame Monotone Trajectories

We are now in a position to take into account the subgame structure of Γ. Suppose that u is an information set for Γ that consists of a single decision point and that Γ_u is a subgame of Γ with root at u (see section 6.1.2). Recall that any point p in the interior of Δ induces a point p^u in the interior of the normal form strategy simplex for Γ_u. In analogy to (6.1.1) (see also (6.3.3)), if $e_{n,i}^u$ is a pure strategy of player n for Γ_u, let the corresponding components of p_n^u be defined by[6]

$$p_{n,i}^u = \frac{\sum_j \{p_{n,j} \mid u \text{ is relevant for } e_{n,j} \text{ and } e_{n,j} \text{ restricts to } e_{n,i}^u \text{ on } \Gamma_u\}}{\sum_j \{p_{n,j} \mid u \text{ is relevant for } e_{n,j}\}}.$$

(9.2.1)

Γ can also be truncated at u by replacing the decision point u with an endpoint that has payoffs given by p^u in Γ_u. Denote this truncated game

---

6. Recall that the information set u is *relevant* for $e_{n,j}$ (or for a mixed strategy p_n with $p_{n,j} > 0$) if there is some pure strategy $e \in \Delta$ with nth component $e_{n,j}$ that reaches u.

by $\Gamma_{-u}(p^u)$. If $e_{n,i}^{-u}$ is a pure behavior strategy for player n on Γ_{-u}, then

$$p_{n,i}^{-u} = \sum \{ p_{n,i} \mid e_{n,i} \text{ restricts to } e_{n,i}^{-u} \text{ on } \Gamma_{-u} \} \tag{9.2.2}$$

defines a truncated interior point p^{-u} for Γ_{-u}. The following definition parallels definition 9.1.1 for the subgame Γ_u:

Definition 9.2.1 *Suppose that Γ_u is a subgame of Γ and $p(t)$ is an interior trajectory C for Γ. C is monotone with respect to the subgame Γ_u if*

(i) the induced trajectory p^u on Γ_u is monotone with respect to Γ_u and

(ii) the truncated trajectory p^{-u} on Γ_{-u} is monotone with respect to $\Gamma_{-u}(p^u)$.

C is called subgame monotone *if it is monotone with respect to all subgames of Γ (including Γ itself).*

C is called ω-monotone with respect to Γ_u if the induced trajectory is monotone with respect to Γ_u, the truncated trajectory is ω-monotone with respect to Γ_{-u}, and the induced trajectory is ω-monotone with respect to Γ_u at all $p^* \in \Omega$ for which u is relevant for each player n.[7] C is subgame ω-monotone *if it is ω-monotone with respect to all subgames of Γ.*

The analysis of the Chain-Store Game in example 9.1.2 shows that all its interior trajectories (with respect to the replicator dynamic) are ω-monotone with respect to Γ_v. Furthermore all interior trajectories of the replicator dynamic are automatically ω-monotone with respect to Γ. Thus these trajectories are all subgame ω-monotone. On the other hand, interior trajectories of the replicator dynamic are not subgame monotone for all extensive form games. An important illustration of this is the dynamic counterexample in chapter 4.6.1 (see also example 9.2.3 below). It was mentioned there that the most intuitive explanation of this surprising result is that trajectories off the Wright manifold are not necessarily subgame monotone.[8]

At this point we do not know if subgame monotone trajectories exist for extensive form games beyond specific elementary examples. This question can be quickly answered by taking another look, from the

---

7. That is, $\sum \{ p_{n,i}^* \mid u \text{ is relevant for } e_{n,i} \}$ is positive for all $1 \le n \le N$.

8. The preceding formal definitions of (subgame) monotone trajectories are not written explicitly for symmetric games where it is natural to call a trajectory C *symmetric* if $p(t) = q(t)$ for all $t \ge 0$. In particular, all trajectories of the symmetric replicator dynamic are symmetric if they are so at time $t = 0$. Then the condition (9.1.1) that defines (subgame) monotonicity for these symmetric trajectories need only be verified for $n = 1$ in definitions 9.1.1 and 9.2.1.

perspective of subgame monotonicity, at the theory developed in
chapter 6.3 of the replicator dynamic (6.3.2) applied to the Wright manifold. Theorem 6.3.3 there translates into the following result using the
notation of this chapter.

Theorem 9.2.2   *If Γ_u is a subgame of Γ, then*

   *i. The Wright manifold with respect to Γ_u, W^u, is invariant for the replicator
dynamic (6.3.2), and*

   ii. Any interior trajectory of (6.3.2) in W^u is ω-monotone with respect to Γ_u.

   *Moreover, parts i and ii imply that the Wright manifold, W, is invariant for
the replicator dynamic and all interior trajectories of (6.3.2) in W are subgame
ω-monotone.*

   Thus every N-player extensive form game has an ample supply of
subgame ω-monotone trajectories. The complex calculations used in
chapter 6 to prove the result above somewhat obscures the intuition behind it. The following perfect information game clarifies the method and
also illustrates the importance of subgame monotonicity in the dynamic
analysis:

Example 9.2.3   (A two-player perfect information game with three
information sets)   Consider the generic perfect information game (figure 9.2.1) that adds a disjoint information set, v_2, for player two to the
tree structure of the Chain-Store Game (figure 8.1.1). Without loss of
generality, assume $a_2 > b_2, c_2 > d_2$, and $a_1 > c_1$. Player two now has
four pure behavior strategies; namely $\ell\ell$, ℓr, $r\ell$, and rr where $\alpha\beta$ means
"play α after L and β after R." The bimatrix normal form (A, B) for the

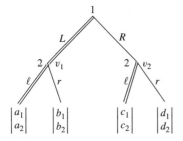

Figure 9.2.1
Extensive form of example 9.2.3.

two-player game of figure 9.2.1 is

$$
\begin{array}{c}
\quad\; \ell\ell \quad\;\; \ell r \quad\;\; r\ell \quad\;\; rr \\
\begin{array}{c} L \\ R \end{array}
\begin{bmatrix}
a_1, a_2 & a_1, a_2 & b_1, b_2 & b_1, b_2 \\
c_1, c_2 & d_1, d_2 & c_1, c_2 & d_1, d_2
\end{bmatrix}.
\end{array}
\tag{9.2.3}
$$

The frequency of individuals in population two using the dominant behavior strategy ℓ in the subgame Γ_{v_1} is $q_1 + q_2$. Subgame monotonicity implies this frequency is nondecreasing (i.e., $(\dot{q}_1 + \dot{q}_2) \geq 0$) for any subgame monotone trajectory. Substitution of the payoff entries in (9.2.3) into the bimatrix replicator dynamic (3.2.1) yields

$$
\begin{aligned}
(q_1 + q_2)^{\cdot} &= (q_1(f_1 - q) + q_2(f_2 - q)) \cdot Bp \\
&= (q_1 + q_2)(1 - (q_1 + q_2))(a_2 - b_2)p_1 \\
&\quad + (q_1 q_4 - q_2 q_3)(c_2 - d_2)p_2.
\end{aligned}
\tag{9.2.4}
$$

It is straightforward to verify that $q_1 q_4 / q_2 q_3$ is an invariant of motion for the bimatrix replicator dynamic (3.2.1) (i.e., its time derivative is zero). Furthermore, if $0 < q_1 q_4 / q_2 q_3 < 1$, there are points on the corresponding invariant surface where $\dot{q}_1 + \dot{q}_2 < 0$. Thus, in contrast to example 9.1.2, the normal-form bimatrix replicator dynamic (3.2.1) is not always monotone with respect to Γ_{v_1}. In particular, (9.2.4) is not the replicator dynamic on Γ_{v_1} for player two against nature unless $q_1 q_4 - q_2 q_3 = 0$.

It is also straightforward to verify that the invariant surface

$$
W = \{(p, q) \in \Delta^2 \times \Delta^4 \mid q_1 q_4 = q_2 q_3 \text{ and all } p_i, q_k > 0\}
\tag{9.2.5}
$$

is the Wright manifold for this example. On W, trajectories of (3.2.1) do induce trajectories on Γ_{v_1} and Γ_{v_2} that are rescaled trajectories of the replicator dynamic against nature in these subgames. Furthermore

$$
\begin{aligned}
\dot{p}_1 &= p_1(1 - p_1)[a_1(q_1 + q_2) + b_1(q_3 + q_4) \\
&\quad - c_1(q_1 + q_3) - d_1(q_2 + q_4)],
\end{aligned}
\tag{9.2.6}
$$

which is the replicator dynamic for player one against nature when figure 9.2.1 is truncated at v_1 and v_2 using q.

The observations above allow a qualitative description of all trajectories of the bimatrix replicator dynamic (3.2.1) restricted to W. On W, $q_1 + q_2$ increases and will converge to 1 unless $p_1 \longrightarrow 0$. Similarly $q_1 + q_3$ increases and will converge to 1 unless $p_2 \longrightarrow 0$. If neither p_1 nor p_2 converges to 0, then q_1 approaches 1, which implies that L eventually strictly dominates R along any interior trajectory, and so p_2 necessarily converges to 0. Thus either $p_1 \longrightarrow 0$ or $p_2 \longrightarrow 0$.

If $p_1 \longrightarrow 0$ on W, then $q_1 + q_3$ increases to 1, and on this invariant face, (9.2.3) becomes the bimatrix game

$$
\begin{array}{cc}
& \ell\ell \qquad r\ell \\
\begin{array}{c} L \\ R \end{array} &
\left[
\begin{array}{cc}
a_1, a_2 & b_1, b_2 \\
c_1, c_2 & c_1, c_2
\end{array}
\right],
\end{array}
$$

which is the truncation of figure 9.2.1 by ℓ at v_2. Since $a_1 > c_1$ and $p_1 \longrightarrow 0$, then necessarily $c_1 > b_1$. This is the Chain-Store Game (with strategies reordered) and our interior trajectory approaches a NE of the form $(R, (q_1, 0, q_3, 0))$ in the nonsubgame perfect NE component. On the other hand, if $p_1 \longrightarrow 1$, then $q_1 + q_2$ increases to 1 which means that figure 9.2.1 is truncated by ℓ at v_1. In particular, the trajectory converges to a NE of the form $(L, (q_1, q_2, 0, 0))$ in the subgame perfect NE component of this truncated game.

What is important for us is that in both cases the overall dynamic on W can be best understood by analyzing the subgame dynamic and the resultant reduction of Γ to a game with one less information set. The essential properties in this approach are the monotonicity of the overall dynamic and of the subgame dynamic. That is, the qualitative behavior above occurs for all subgame ω-monotone trajectories, and in particular, these trajectories all converge to some NE.

Actually for most nonelementary extensive form games there are interior trajectories of the replicator dynamic that are not subgame monotone. Example 9.2.3 is a straightforward example of this[9] since other invariant manifolds of (3.2.1) besides the Wright manifold have points where (9.2.4) is not monotone with respect to Γ_{v_1}. Conversely, the imitation dynamic for the example considered in section 9.3 below shows that trajectories that are subgame monotone with respect to Γ_{v_1} (and Γ_{v_2}) in example 9.2.3 need not be monotone with respect to Γ. Thus care must be taken when transferring theory developed for monotone selection dynamics to trajectories that are monotone with respect to the subgame structure of the extensive form game—especially if we only assume monotonicity with respect to a single subgame as in the following two theorems. We start by generalizing theorem 9.1.3.

---

9. A less straightforward example is the symmetric extensive form game of chapter 4.6.1.

Theorem 9.2.4 *Suppose that C is an ω-monotone trajectory with respect to Γ_u for some subgame of Γ. If C has a unique ω-limit point p^*, then p^* is a NE.*

Proof Since $p^{-u}(t)$ converges and is ω-monotone on Γ_{-u}, the limit point p^{-u*} is a NE of $\Gamma_{-u}(p^*)$ by the same method used to prove theorem 9.1.3 applied to Γ_{-u}. Also $\lim_{t\to\infty}\sum_i\{p_{n,i}\mid u$ is relevant for $e_{n,i}\}$ exists for all $1\le n\le N$.

If all these limits are positive, then $p^u(t)$ is ω-monotone with respect to Γ_u by definition 9.2.1. By theorem 9.1.3, the limit point p^{u*} is a NE. By theorem 6.1.1 in chapter 6.1.2, p^* is a NE of Γ.

Now suppose that one of the limits is zero, say $\sum\{p^*_{1,i}\mid u$ is relevant for $e_{1,i}\}=0$. To see that p^* is a NE, suppose that player n, with $n>1$, changes strategy from p^*_n. Since the play never reaches Γ_u and p^{-u*} is a NE of $\Gamma_{-u}(p^*)$, $\pi_n(p_n,p^*)\le\pi_n(p^*_n,p^*)$ for all $p_n\in\Delta^n$. Similarly, if $\pi_1(e_{1,0},p^*)>\pi_1(p^*_1,p^*)$ for some pure strategy $e_{1,0}$ of player one, then u must be relevant for $e_{1,0}$ and so $e_{1,0}$ is not in the support of p^*_1. That is, $\lim p_{1,0}(t)=0$. Since $\lim \dot p_{1,i}(t)=0$ for all $e_{1,i}$ in the support of p^*_1, $\dot p_{1,0}/p_{1,0}>0$ for all $p(t)$ in some neighborhood of p^*. Since $\dot p_{1,0}$ is positive in this neighborhood, $\lim p_{1,0}(t)$ cannot equal 0. By contradiction, we have $\pi_1(e_{1,0},p^*)\le\pi_1(p^*_1,p^*)$ for all pure strategies $e_{1,0}$ of player one. ∎

As stated at the beginning of this section, our main interest is in analyzing properties of interior trajectories for Γ by decomposing them using the subgame structure of Γ. Notice that, in the above proof of theorem 9.2.2, we could not assume $p^u(t)$ converges if, for instance, $\sum_i\{p^*_{n,i}\mid u$ is relevant for $e_{n,i}\}=0$ because the play never reaches Γ_u at p^*. On the other hand, if both $p^{-u}(t)$ and $p^u(t)$ converge in Γ_{-u} and Γ_u respectively, then one might expect $p(t)$ to also converge. This may not happen since there are often many mixed strategies in the normal form for Γ whose induced strategy in Γ_u is p^{u*} and whose truncated strategy in Γ_{-u} is p^{-u*}. However, we do have the following partial converse of theorem 9.2.4 to rebuild interior trajectories for Γ from the decomposed trajectories for Γ_u and Γ_{-u}.

Theorem 9.2.5 *Suppose that C is an ω-monotone trajectory with respect to Γ_u for some subgame of Γ. If $p^{-u}(t)$ and $p^u(t)$ converge in Γ_{-u} and Γ_u respectively, then all ω-limit points of C lie in the same NE component of Γ. In fact all ω-limit points of C describe the same behavior strategy of Γ.*

Proof Assume that $p^{-u}(t)$ converges to $p^{-u*}(t)$ and that $p^u(t)$ converges to p^{u*}. Then $\lim_{t\to\infty}\sum_i\{p_{n,i}\mid u$ is relevant for $e_{n,i}\}=\lim_{t\to\infty}\sum_i\{p^{-u}_{n,i}\mid u$

is relevant for $e_{n,i}^{-u}$} exists. Also the truncated game is the same for any ω-limit point p^* of C; namely $\Gamma_{-u}(p^*)$. The proof of theorem 9.2.4 can now be applied to show that p^* is a NE of Γ.

Furthermore, since the behavior strategy at all information sets of Γ for any point along the interior trajectory C is given through either $p^{-u}(t)$ or $p^u(t)$, the two convergence assumptions imply that each ω-limit point of C describes the same behavior strategy. In particular, all ω-limit points are in the same NE component of Γ.   ■

Theorems 9.2.4 and 9.2.5 are particularly useful for the dynamical analysis of extensive form games that have a high degree of decomposability, such as general games with perfect information that include the two elementary examples already analyzed in this chapter. For generic two-player perfect information games, theorem 8.2.2 of chapter 8.2.1 shows that every interior trajectory of a uniformly monotone selection dynamic converges to a NE whose play follows some equilibrium path. However, the methods of chapter 8 do not apply for general interior monotone trajectories where convergence remains an open problem. On the other hand, the following theorem[10] shows that the result does generalize if the trajectories are subgame ω-monotone.

Theorem 9.2.6   *If Γ is a generic N-player perfect information game and C is an interior subgame ω-monotone trajectory, then all ω-limit points of C are NE with the same equilibrium outcome.*

Proof   If Γ has only one subgame, then it has only one information set which we may assume is for player one. By our generic assumption, each choice of player one leads to a different payoff. Any ω-monotone trajectory will converge to the unique NE that has player one choosing the path that leads to the highest payoff.

Suppose that Γ has more than one subgame. Assume that the root of Γ is a decision point u of player one, and let v be an information set immediately following u. If p^* is an ω-limit point of C such that v is relevant for p_1^*, then the induced trajectory is subgame ω-monotone with respect to Γ_v, and so, by our induction assumption, all its ω-limit points are NE and follow the same equilibrium path. This is true for all information sets that immediately follow u. If no such relevant v exist for any ω-limit point p^*, then all limiting outcome paths have length 1, and so must be the same path by continuity of the trajectory.

---

10. The proof provided, by induction on the number of subgames of Γ, assumes that there are no moves by nature. It is readily extended to include generic games with moves by nature.

If at least two of these information sets are relevant for p_1^*, then eventually (i.e., for all t sufficiently large) player one will only receive a highest payoff through using a particular choice at u by our generic assumption. By monotonicity, the frequency of this choice strictly increases for all t sufficiently large, and this implies that at most one information set v_0 is relevant for p_1^*. That is, p_1^* must make the same choice at u for all ω-limit points of C. Thus all ω-limit points of C follow the same equilibrium path. Also, if p^* is not a NE for Γ, a contradiction is readily obtained. ∎

The preceding proof resembles the backward induction argument for generic perfect information games that asserts there is a unique subgame perfect NE. However, one cannot conclude from theorem 9.2.6 that all interior subgame ω-monotone trajectories approach the subgame perfect NE component. That care must be taken is already illustrated in figure 9.1.1 for the one-shot Chain-Store Game where some such trajectories approach the subgame perfect NE while others approach G.

By theorem 9.2.2, the general theory of subgame monotonicity (as summarized in theorems 9.2.4, 9.2.5, and 9.2.6) can be applied to the replicator dynamic (6.3.2) restricted to the Wright manifold. In many cases the Wright manifold can be identified with the set of behavior strategies (cf. theorems 6.3.2, 6.4.5, and 7.3.1 in chapters 6 and 7). We then have a "monotone behavior strategy dynamic," which simplifies considerably the dynamic analysis as seen in example 9.2.3. Unfortunately, we cannot expect the replicator dynamic to restrict so naturally to a behavior strategy dynamic for all extensive form games. For instance, Γ may have few, if any, subgames, in which case the Wright manifold will typically be much larger than the set of mixed representatives. Even those Γ that have a high degree of decomposability may have a large Wright manifold. The following example illustrates this latter situation.

Example 9.2.7 (Extensive form games with the tree structure of a three-legged centipede) Consider the two-player perfect information game with reduced-strategy normal form strategy simplex $\Delta = \Delta^3 \times \Delta^2$ and extensive form given in figure 9.2.2. Since neither player has a pair of independent information sets, W is all of Δ.[11] In particular, this game with general payoffs cannot have a monotone behavior strategy dynamic for

---

11. The standard normal form, with strategy simplex $\Delta = \Delta^4 \times \Delta^2$ does have a Wright manifold that is not all of Δ. This was noted in chapter 8.4.1 (see the proof of theorem 8.4.6) where the Wright manifold was needed for the analysis of population dynamics generated by good behavioral rules.

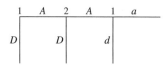

Figure 9.2.2
Extensive form of example 9.2.7.

player one at his initial information set since the frequency of the behavior strategy for choice A there, $p_{Aa} + p_{Ad}$, may be the same for two
populations that have opposite best replies.

Moreover every interior trajectory of the replicator dynamic (6.3.2) is
subgame ω-monotone for this game by theorem 9.2.2. Thus, by theorem 9.2.6, they must converge to some NE component for any generic
specification of payoffs. On the other hand, if an arbitrary monotone selection dynamic for this game is analyzed instead, its trajectories are not
necessarily subgame ω-monotone (specifically, while the induced trajectory is guaranteed to be monotone with respect to any subgame, the
truncated trajectory need not be), and so theorem 9.2.6 does not apply
and convergence remains an open problem.[12]

The convergence arguments that combine theorems 9.2.2 and 9.2.6 in
example 9.2.7 generalize to prove that every interior trajectory of the
N-player replicator dynamic (6.3.2) on the Wright manifold converges
to the set of NE for all generic perfect information games (e.g., examples 9.1.2 and 9.2.3).

We conclude this section by briefly illustrating how the theory applies
to the symmetric extensive form game Γ given in chapter 4.6.1. Its Wright
manifold is determined by considering the symmetric Rock–Scissors–
Paper subgame Γ_u on the left-hand side of figure 4.6.1. In the notation of
chapter 4.6.1, $W = \{p \in \Delta^9 \mid p_{ik} = p_i^u p_k^v\}$. This is again the set of mixed
representatives of the completely mixed behavior strategies of Γ. There
is a unique point $p^* \in W$ with $p^{u*} = p^{v*} = p_0^*$, the unique symmetric NE
of Γ_u. Since the replicator dynamic restricted to W actually induces the
replicator dynamic (2.1.2) on both Γ_u and Γ_v, every interior trajectory
on W of (6.3.2) converges to p^* (i.e., p^* is globally asymptotically stable

---

12. In this regard consider the special case where the payoffs are those of a Three-Legged
Centipede Game (see chapter 8.3.1). Here the only NE outcome is the subgame perfect
one where both players choose "Down" at all their information sets. It can then be shown
(see Notes) that each interior trajectory of any monotone selection dynamic converges to
a single ω-limit point in the corresponding NE component.

with respect to W). Thus the interior unstable NE reported in chapter 4.6.1 is forced to be a point in the four-dimensional NE set that is not on the Wright manifold. Moreover almost all trajectories near this unstable NE are not subgame monotone with respect to Γ_u.

9.3 An Imitation Example

Learning rules based on imitative behavior are commonly used to model the evolution of strategy choice for rational individuals (see chapters 2.10, 4.6.2, and 8.4). A particularly appealing rule is proportional imitation, since it leads to the replicator dynamic in normal form games (theorem 2.10.1 and definition 2.10.2).[13] For this rule each individual observes the strategy and payoff of one randomly sampled player per unit time and switches to this strategy if the observed payoff is higher than his, with probability proportional to how much higher it is.

The imitation model of this section assumes that individuals observe actions along the outcome path rather than strategy in the extensive form game of example 9.2.3. As a game against nature from the perspective of player two (i.e., when player one's strategy is fixed), we have a parallel bandit (chapter 4.6.2), whereas from player one's perspective, the game is a multi-armed bandit. The dynamic is generated by the following two-part learning rule based on proportional imitation as discussed in chapters 2.10 and 4.6.2.

1. An individual in population one observes a random interaction and, if the observed player in population one has higher payoff, switches to this strategy with probability equal to the payoff difference. This is the PIR rule of definition 2.10.2 in chapter 2.

2. An individual in population two also observes a random interaction and, if the observed player in population two has higher payoff than the individual would have in this subgame, switches to the action at the observed information set with probability equal to the payoff difference. This is essentially the PIR rule for within-decision learning of chapter 4.6.2.[14]

---

13. In fact chapter 2.10 only shows this is true for multi-armed bandits. However, it is straightforward to generalize the approach there to develop continuous-time dynamics for normal form games based on behavioral rules.

14. One technical difference is that here we assume individuals in population two know the expected payoff of their current choice in each subgame. In chapter 4.6.2 only the realized payoff in one of the subgames is known.

Recall that in figure 9.2.1 we assumed $a_2 > b_2, c_2 > d_2$ and $a_1 > c_1$. Suppose that current average strategies of the two populations are at $(p, q) \in \Delta^2 \times \Delta^4$. From a case by case calculation of the four possible outcome paths and their expected frequency of observation, the learning rule above yields the following dynamic for population two:

$$\dot{q}_1 = q_3(q_1 + q_2)(a_2 - b_2)p_1 + q_2(q_1 + q_3)(c_2 - d_2)p_2,$$

$$\dot{q}_2 = q_4(q_1 + q_2)(a_2 - b_2)p_1 - q_2(q_1 + q_3)(c_2 - d_2)p_2,$$

$$\dot{q}_3 = -q_3(q_1 + q_2)(a_2 - b_2)p_1 + q_4(q_1 + q_3)(c_2 - d_2)p_2,$$

$$\dot{q}_4 = -q_4(q_1 + q_2)(a_2 - b_2)p_1 - q_4(q_1 + q_3)(c_2 - d_2)p_2.$$

(9.3.1)

For instance, the first term on the right-hand side of $\dot{q}_1$ is the rate of change from r at v_1 and ℓ at v_2 to ℓ at v_1 and ℓ at v_2; namely the frequency of the former strategy (q_3) times the probability ℓ is observed at v_1 ($(q_1 + q_2)p_1$) times the payoff difference ($a_2 - b_2$). A similar calculation for population one leads to (9.2.6), thereby confirming the intuition that the learning rule applied to this population becomes the replicator dynamic on $\Gamma_{-u}(q)$.

This imitation dynamic on $\Delta^2 \times \Delta^4$ is quite different than the bimatrix replicator dynamic (3.2.1). First, it is not a monotone selection dynamic on the game's normal form (9.2.3) since, for example, $\dot{q}_2/q_2 = \dot{q}_3/q_3$ is not always true in (9.3.1) when $\pi_2(p, f_2) = \pi_2(p, f_3)$. Perhaps the most striking difference is that the imitation dynamic allows the emergence of pure behavior strategies f_ℓ that are currently extinct (i.e., $q_\ell = 0$). For instance, $\dot{q}_1 > 0$ if $q_1 = 0$ and $q_2 q_3 > 0$, since some ℓr and $r\ell$ strategists will switch to $\ell\ell$. Such phenomena are impossible under any smooth monotone selection dynamic. However, the interior of $\Delta^2 \times \Delta^4$ remains forward invariant under this imitation dynamic.

From (9.3.1), $\dot{q}_1 + \dot{q}_2 = (q_1 + q_2)(1 - (q_1 + q_2))(a_2 - b_2)p_1$. Comparison with (9.2.4) shows that (9.3.1) is ω-monotone with respect to Γ_{v_1} and that the imitation dynamic is just the replicator dynamic on the Wright manifold. Again, we have a well-defined dynamic for behavior strategies, this time without assuming that the expected strategy choice at v_1 is independent of the individual's choice at v_2. It is also interesting to note that in this example,

$$\frac{d}{dt}(q_1 q_4 - q_2 q_3)$$

$$= -(q_1 q_4 - q_2 q_3)[(q_1 + q_2)(a_2 - b_2)p_1 + (q_2 + q_3)(c_2 - d_2)p_2].$$

Thus the Wright manifold is again invariant for this imitation dynamic while all other trajectories approach the Wright manifold asymptotically. In particular, the qualitative description of the trajectories on W given in the dynamic analysis of example 9.2.3 now applies to all trajectories in the interior of $\Delta^2 \times \Delta^4$.

9.4 Discussion

The main purpose of this chapter is to motivate and develop a theory of subgame monotonicity as an essential tool to apply evolutionary game theory techniques to extensive form games. The nonsymmetric perfect information game example of section 9.2 (example 9.2.3) and the symmetric extensive form game of chapter 4.6.1 show that the more common assumption of monotonicity (as opposed to subgame monotonicity) is not sufficient to predict the long run evolutionary outcome. The theory of section 9.2 is motivated by these examples and is then used to develop the dynamic consequences of subgame monotonicity.

The chapter also serves as a summary of the key issues considered throughout the book. Specifically, it addresses how the extensive form structure is connected to the dynamic analysis of the extensive form game. In retrospect, this connection was built up progressively from chapter 3 to chapter 8 as the properties of the Wright manifold and/or backward induction were developed. These two central concepts of extensive form games, which are both clearly based on the extensive form structure, culminate in chapter 9 where they emerge as natural features associated with subgame monotonicity.

As stated in the Introduction, my intention in this book was to strike a middle ground between the two main groups of practitioners of evolutionary game theory; namely economic game theorists and biological game theorists. I suspect the dynamic analysis emphasized here will initially be of more interest to the former group.[15] The following concluding remarks are addressed mostly for people in this group.

For economic game theorists, evolutionary game theory has become an important equilibrium selection technique either through static

---

15. My opinion here is based on the fact that most current research on extensive form games is published in journals intended for readers with an interest in economics. However, there is some evidence this is changing (see Notes), although the evolutionary dynamics analyzed in the biological literature that are based on games with sequential decisions between interacting individuals are seldom described in explicit extensive form. It is my hope this book will help promote the use of the extensive form approach in this area.

stability concepts such as the ESS or through the dynamic stability concept of local asymptotic stability. Both approaches attempt to predict the long-run equilibrium outcome of populations where the evolution of strategy frequency depends on each strategy's current payoff. However, these techniques have had little success for general extensive form games. For example, the ESS concept for bimatrix games is identical to that of strict NE and to the local asymptotic stability of a single strategy under the bimatrix replicator dynamic. Since strict NE do not often exist in interesting extensive form games, these (single-strategy) approaches to equilibrium selection break down.

This book provides a more thorough analysis of the dynamic perspective of evolutionary game theory. Convergence and limit properties of dynamic trajectories, as suggested by the Folk Theorem of Evolutionary Game Theory (see Introduction), have been emphasized along with asymptotic stability (of single strategies and of sets of equilibria). Dynamics for an evolutionary game have been typically defined through the game's normal form. Unfortunately, as we have seen (e.g., example 9.2.3 and chapter 4.6.1), normal form evolutionary dynamics (e.g., the various versions of the replicator dynamic) are often unconnected to the structure of the game tree for many interesting extensive form games. For this reason I feel that it is essential for a dynamic theory of extensive form games to be based directly on concepts like subgame monotonicity if this theory is to become equally well accepted as an important predictor of the long-run outcome in general extensive form games. I will have achieved a main goal in writing this book if I have convinced you of the potential of this more direct approach. Chapter 9 then represents only the beginning of "evolutionary dynamics for extensive form games"—the final story is yet to be written.

9.5   Notes

Definition 9.1.1 parallels the slightly altered form of a monotone selection dynamic as given by Samuelson (1997) of the original definition by Samuelson and Zhang (1992). The proof of theorem 9.1.3 adapts the method used by Weibull (1995; see also Samuelson and Zhang 1992) for monotone selection dynamics to show a convergent interior trajectory evolves to a NE. The theory of subgame monotonicity is from Cressman (2000) as are the specific examples considered in this chapter. Ponti (2000) showed all interior trajectories of any monotone selection dynamic for an N-legged Centipede Game do converge to a single ω-limit point in the subgame perfect NE component. Learning processes based on imitation models have been studied by many researchers (e.g., Weibull 1995; Samuelson 1997; Schlag 1998; Fudenberg and Levine 1998) but typically for normal form games. Examples of evolutionary processes in the biological literature based on extensive form games (although they are rarely described explicitly as such) can be found in Bishop and Cannings (1978), Cannings and Whittaker (1991), as well as in more recent work such as Kim (1995), Hurd and Enquist (1998), Crowley (2000), and Hammerstein (2001).

Bibliography

Akin, E. 1979. *The Geometry of Population Genetics*. Lecture Notes in Biomathematics 31. Berlin: Springer-Verlag.

Akin, E. 1982. Exponential families and game dynamics. *Can. J. Math.* 34: 374–405.

Aubin, J.-P. 1991. *Viability Theory*. Boston: Birkhäuser.

Axelrod, R. 1984. *The Evolution of Cooperation*. New York: Basic Books.

Balkenborg, D. 1994. Strictness and evolutionary stability. Discussion paper 52. Hebrew University of Jerusalem Center for Rationality and Interactive Decision Theory.

Balkenborg, D., and K. H. Schlag. 2000. Evolutionarily stable sets. *Int. J. Game Theory* 29: 571–95.

Balkenborg, D., and K. H. Schlag. 2001. On the evolutionary selection of Nash equilibrium. Mimeo: University of Exeter.

Berger U. 2002. The best-response dynamics for role games. *Int. J. Game Theory* 30: 527–38.

Binmore, K. 1992. *Fun and Games*. Lexington, MA: D.C. Heath.

Binmore, K., and L. Samuelson. 2001. Evolution and mixed strategies. *Games Econ. Behav.* 34: 200–26.

Binmore, K., L. Samuelson, and R. Vaughan. 1995. Musical chairs: Modelling noisy evolution. *Games Econ. Behav.* 11: 1–35.

Bishop, D. T., and C. Cannings. 1978. A generalized war of attrition. *J. Theor. Biol.* 70: 85–124.

Bomze, I. M. 1983. Lotka-Volterra equations and replicator dynamics: A two dimensional classification. *Biol. Cybern.* 48: 201–11.

Bomze, I. M. 1995. Lotka-Volterra equation and replicator dynamics: New issues in classification. *Biol. Cybern.* 72: 447–53.

Bomze, I. M., and B. M. Pötscher. 1989. *Game Theoretical Foundations of Evolutionary Theory*. Lecture Notes in Economics and Mathematical Systems 324. Berlin: Springer-Verlag.

Brown, G. W. 1951. Iterative solutions of games by fictitious play. In *Activity Analysis of Production and Allocation*. New York: Wiley, pp. 374–76.

Bürger, R. 2000. *The Mathematical Theory of Selection, Recombination, and Mutation*. New York: Wiley.

Canning, D. 1992. Learning the subgame perfect equilibrium. Discussion paper 608. Columbia University.

Cannings, C., and J. C. Whittaker. 1991. A two-trial two-strategy conflict. *J. Theor. Biol.* 149: 281–86.

Chamberland, M., and R. Cressman. 2000. An example of dynamic (in)consistency in symmetric extensive form evolutionary games. *Games Econ. Behav.* 30: 319–26.

Cressman, R. 1992. *The Stability Concept of Evolutionary Game Theory: A Dynamic Approach*. Lecture Notes in Biomathematics 94. Berlin: Springer-Verlag.

Cressman, R. 1995. Evolutionary stability for two-stage hawk–dove games. *Rocky Mtn. J. Math.* 25: 145–55.

Cressman, R. 1996a. Evolutionary stability in the finitely repeated prisoner's dilemma game. *J. Econ. Theory* 68: 234–48.

Cressman, R. 1996b. Frequency-dependent stability for two-species interactions. *Theor. Pop. Biol.* 49: 189–210.

Cressman, R. 1997a. Local stability of smooth selection dynamics for normal form games. *Math. Soc. Sci.* 34: 1–19.

Cressman, R. 1997b. Dynamic stability in symmetric extensive form games. *Int. J. Game Theory* 26: 525–47.

Cressman, R. 1999. Natural selection as an extensive form game. In *Fields Institute Communications*, Vol. 21. Providence, RI: American Mathematical Society, pp. 119–30.

Cressman, R. 2000. Subgame monotonicity in extensive form evolutionary games. *Games Econ. Behav.* 32: 183–205.

Cressman, R., J. Garay, and J. Hofbauer. 2001. Evolutionary stability concepts for *N*-species frequency-dependent interactions. *J. Theor. Biol.* 211: 1–10.

Cressman, R., A. Gaunersdorfer, and J.-F. Wen. 2000. Evolutionary and dynamic stability in symmetric evolutionary games with two independent decisions. *Int. Game Theory Rev.* 2: 67–81.

Cressman, R., W. G. Morrison, and J.-F. Wen. 1998. On the evolutionary dynamics of crime. *Can. J. of Econ.* 31: 1101–17.

Cressman, R., and K. Schlag. 1998a. The dynamic (in)stability of backwards induction. *J. Econ. Theory* 83: 260–85.

Cressman, R., and K. Schlag. 1998b. Updating strategies through observed play— Optimization under bounded rationality. Discussion paper B-432. University of Bonn.

Crowley, P. H. 2000. Hawks, doves, and mixed-symmetry games. *J. Theor. Biol.* 204: 543–63.

Dalkey, N. 1953. Equivalence of information patterns and essentially determinate games. In H. W. Kuhn and A. W. Tucker, eds., *Contributions to the Theory of Games*, Vol. 2, Princeton: Princeton University Press, pp. 217–45.

Elmes, S., and P. J. Reny. 1994. On the strategic equivalence of extensive form games. *J. Econ. Theory* 62: 1–23.

Fisher, R. A. 1930. *The Genetical Theory of Natural Selection*. Oxford: Clarendon Press.

Foster, D., and P. Young. 1990. Stochastic evolutionary game dynamics. *J. Theor. Biol.* 38: 219–32.

Friedman, D. 1991. Evolutionary games in economics. *Econometrica* 59: 637–66.

Fudenberg, D., and D. K. Levine. 1998. *The Theory of Learning in Games*. Cambridge: MIT Press.

Gale, J., K. G. Binmore, and L. Samuelson. 1995. Learning to be imperfect: The ultimatum game. *Games Econ. Behav.* 8: 56–90.

Gaunersdorfer, A., J. Hofbauer, and K. Sigmund. 1991. On the dynamics of asymmetric games. *Theor. Pop. Biol.* 39: 345–57.

Gintis, H. 2000. *Game Theory Evolving*. Princeton: Princeton University Press.

Güth, W., R. Schmittberger, and B. Schwarze. 1982. An experimental analysis of ultimatum bargaining. *J. Econ. Behav. Org.* 3: 367–88.

Haigh, J. 1989. How large is the support of an ESS? *J. Appl. Prob.* 26: 164–70.

Hammerstein, P. 2001. Games and markets: economic behavior in humans and other animals. In R. Noë, J. A. R. A. M. van Hooff and P. Hammerstein, eds., *Economics in Nature: Social Dilemmas, Mate Choice and Biological Markets*. Cambridge: Cambridge University Press, pp. 1–19.

Harsanyi, J. C., and R. Selten. 1988. *A General Theory of Equilibrium Selection in Games*. Cambridge: MIT Press.

Helbing, D. 1992. Interrelations between stochastic equations for systems with pair interactions. *Physica A* 181: 29–52.

Hendon, E., H. J. Jacobsen, and B. Sloth. 1996. Fictitious play in extensive form games. *Games Econ. Behav.* 15: 177–202.

Hines, W. G. S. 1987. Evolutionarily stable strategies: A review of basic theory. *Theor. Pop. Biol.* 31: 195–272.

Hofbauer, J. 1995a. Stability for the best response dynamics. Mimeo. University of Vienna.

Hofbauer, J. 1995b. Imitation dynamics for games. Mimeo. University of Vienna.

Hofbauer, J. 1996. Evolutionary dynamics for bimatrix games. *J. Math. Biol.* 34: 675–88.

Hofbauer, J., and K. Sigmund. 1988. *The Theory of Evolution and Dynamical Systems*. Cambridge: Cambridge University Press.

Hofbauer, J., and K. Sigmund. 1998. *Evolutionary Games and Population Dynamics*. Cambridge: Cambridge University Press.

Horn, R. A., and C. R. Johnson. 1985. *Matrix Analysis*. Cambridge: Cambridge University Press.

Houston, A. I., and J. M. McNamara. 1999. *Models of Adaptive Behaviour*. Cambridge: Cambridge University Press.

Hurd, P. L., and M. Enquist. 1998. Conventional signalling in aggressive interactions: The importance of temporal structure. *J. Theor. Biol.* 192: 197–211.

Kandori, M., G. J. Mailath, and R. Rob. 1993. Learning, mutation, and long-run equilibria in games. *Econometrica* 61: 29–56.

Kim, Y.-G. 1995. Status signaling games in animal contests. *J. Theor. Biol.* 176: 221–31.

Kohlberg, E., and J.-F. Mertens. 1986. On the strategic stability of equilibria. *Econometrica* 54: 1003–37.

Kuhn, H. 1953. Extensive games and the problem of information. In H. Kuhn and A. Tucker, eds., *Contributions to the Theory of Games II. Annals of Mathematics* 28. Princeton: Princeton University Press, pp. 193–216.

Lessard, S. 1984. Evolutionary dynamics in frequency dependent two-phenotype models. *Theor. Pop. Biol.* 25: 210–34.

Lyubich, Y. I. 1992. *Mathematical Structures of Population Genetics.* Biomathematics, vol. 22. Berlin: Springer-Verlag.

Mailath, G. J., L. Samuelson, and J. M. Swinkels. 1993. Extensive form reasoning in normal form games. *Econometrica* 61: 273–302.

Matsui, A. 1992. Best response dynamics and socially stable strategies. *J. Econ. Theory* 57: 343–62.

Maynard Smith, J. 1974. The theory of games and the evolution of animal conflicts. *J. Theor. Biol.* 47: 209–21.

Maynard Smith, J. 1982. *Evolution and the Theory of Games.* Cambridge: Cambridge University Press.

Maynard Smith, J., and G. Price. 1973. The logic of animal conflicts. *Nature* 246: 15–18.

Mesterton-Gibbons, M. 1992. *An Introduction to Game-Theoretic Modelling.* Reading, MA: Addison-Wesley.

Mesterton-Gibbons, M. 2000. *An Introduction to Game-Theoretic Modelling,* 2nd ed. Providence RI: American Mathematical Society.

Nachbar, J. 1990. "Evolutionary" selection in games: Convergence and limit properties. *Int. J. Game Theory* 19: 59–89.

Nachbar, J. 1992. Evolution in the finitely repeated Prisoner's Dilemma. *J. Econ. Behav. Org.* 19: 307–26.

Nagylaki, T. 1992. *Introduction to Theoretical Population Genetics.* Biomathematics, vol. 21. Berlin: Springer-Verlag.

Nagylaki, T., J. Hofbauer, and P. Brunovský. 1998. Convergence of multilocus systems under weak epistasis or weak selection. *J. Math. Biol.* 38: 103–33.

Nöldecke, G., and L. Samuelson. 1993. An evolutionary analysis of backward and forward induction. *Games Econ. Behav.* 5: 425–54.

Oechssler, J., and F. Riedel. 2001. Evolutionary dynamics on infinite strategy spaces. *Econ. Theory* 17: 141–62.

Osborne, M. J., and A. Rubinstein. 1994. *A Course in Game Theory.* Cambridge: MIT Press.

Owen, G. 1995. *Game Theory,* 3rd ed. San Diego: Academic Press.

Ponti, G. 2000. Cycles of learning in the centipede game. *Games Econ. Behav.* 30: 115–41.

Reny, P. J. 1993. Common belief and the theory of games with perfect information. *J. Econ. Theory* 59: 257–74.

Ritzberger, K. 1999. Recall in extensive form games. *Int. J. Game Theory* 28: 69–87.

Ritzberger, K., and J. Weibull. 1995. Evolutionary selection in normal-form games. *Econometrica* 63: 1371–99.

Robinson, J. 1951. An iterative method of solving a game. *Ann. Math.* 54: 296–301.

Rosenthal, R. 1981. Games of perfect information, predatory pricing and the chain-store paradox. *J. Econ. Theory* 25: 92–100.

Roughgarden, J. 1979. *Theory of Population Genetics and Evolutionary Ecology: An Introduction.* New York: Macmillan.

Samuelson, L. 1991. Limit evolutionarily stable strategies in two-player, normal form games. *Games Econ. Behav.* 3: 110–28.

Samuelson, L. 1997. *Evolutionary Games and Equilibrium Selection.* Cambridge: MIT Press.

Samuelson, L., and J. Zhang. 1992. Evolutionary stability in asymmetric games. *J. Econ. Theory* 57: 363–91.

Schlag, K. H. 1993. Cheap talk and evolutionary dynamics. Discussion paper B-242. University of Bonn.

Schlag, K. H. 1997. Why imitate, and if so, how? A boundedly rational approach to multi-armed bandits. *J. Econ. Theory* 78: 130–56.

Schwalbe, U., and P. Walker. 2001. Zermelo and the early history of game theory. *Games Econ. Behav.* 34: 123–37.

Selten, R. 1975. Reexamination of the perfectness concept for equilibrium points in extensive-form games. *Int. J. Game Theory* 4: 25–55.

Selten, R. 1978. The chain-store paradox. *Theory and Decision* 9: 127–59.

Selten, R. 1980. A note on evolutionarily stable strategies in asymmetrical animal conflicts. *J. Theor. Biol.* 84: 93–101.

Selten, R. 1983. Evolutionary stability in extensive two-person games. *Math. Soc. Sci.* 5: 269–363.

Selten, R. 1995. An axiomatic theory of a risk dominance measure for bipolar games with linear incentives. *Games Econ. Behav.* 8: 213–63.

Selten, R., and R. Stoecker. 1986. End behavior in sequences of finite prisoner's dilemma supergames. *J. Econ. Behav. Org.* 7: 47–70.

Shahshahani, S. 1979. A new mathematical framework for the study of linkage and selection. *Memoirs of the American Mathematical Society,* vol. 211. Providence RI: American Mathematical Society.

Sigmund, K. 1993. *Games of Life.* Oxford: Oxford University Press.

Swinkels, J. M. 1992. Evolutionary stability with equilibrium entrants. *J. Econ. Theory* 57: 306–32.

Taylor, P. D. 1979. Evolutionarily stable strategies with two types of players. *J. Appl. Prob.* 16: 76–83.

Taylor, P. D., and L. Jonker. 1978. Evolutionarily stable strategies and game dynamics. *Math. Biosci.* 40: 145–56.

Thomas, B. 1985. On evolutionarily stable sets. *J. Math. Biol.* 22: 105–15.

Thompson, F. B. 1952. Equivalence of games in extensive form. *Research Memorandum 759.* Los Angeles: Rand Corporation.

van Damme, E. 1991. *Stability and Perfection of Nash Equilibria,* 2nd ed. Berlin: Springer-Verlag.

Vega-Redondo, F. 1996. *Evolution, Games, and Economic Behavior.* Oxford: Oxford University Press.

von Neumann, J., and O. Morgenstern. 1944. *Theory of Games and Economic Behavior.* Princeton: Princeton University Press.

Weibull, J. 1995. *Evolutionary Game Theory.* Cambridge: MIT Press.

Weissing, F. 1991. Evolutionary stability and dynamic stability in a class of evolutionary normal form games. In R. Selten, ed., *Game Equilibrium Models I.* Berlin: Springer-Verlag, pp. 29–97.

Wiggins, S. 1990. *Introduction to Applied Nonlinear Dynamics and Chaos.* Berlin: Springer-Verlag.

Zahavi, A., and A. Zahavi. 1997. *The Handicap Principle: A Missing Piece of Darwin's Puzzle.* Oxford: Oxford University Press.

Zermelo, E. 1913. Über eine Anwendung der Mengenlehre auf die Theorie des Schachspiels. In *Proceedings Fifth International Congress of Mathematicians,* vol. 2. Cambridge: Cambridge University Press, pp. 501–4.

Index